Grea

Cler...son Tigers
Football

From the beginning of Football all the way to the 2017 National Championship

This book is written for those of us who love Clemson University and especially the CU Fighting Tigers Football Team. You'll like all the stories from the University's founding in 1889, just about 130 years ago, to the beginning of the football program, through the great coaches to CU as an annual National Champion contender. .

You will learn that Clemson Tigers are fierce and passionate competitors. From the stadium to the classroom to the research lab, the Clemson Tigers always play to win.

You will learn that CUs first official football game was in 1896 even before American football had been completely defined. You'll also learn why the immortal Walter Riggs is known as the father of Clemson Football and it is not just because he hired the famed John Heisman as the fourth Tiger coach shortly after the official beginning of football on campus.

From here, the book moves you one coach at time through the John Heisman years and to Frank Howard, the longest tenured Clemson Coach. Then, on the way to today, we stop for coaches Jess Neely and Danny Ford who brought in CUs first National Championship in 1981 and of course we take you to Coach Tommy Bowden and on to the great Dabo Swinney and the reigning 2017 National Champion Clemson Tigers. Go Tigers!

The history of Clemson Tiger Football as told here is just fascinating. This book captures the many great moments and the contributions of each of the 25 coaches and standout players such as Tajh Boyd, Refrigerator Perry, C.J Spiller, and of course DeShaun Watson. We look at every game in every season and we take the reader through great chapters about all of the Clemson teams with great stories and accounts of 121 seasons worth of great games (1222 games) with great moments.

This book is your finest source for a great read on your favorite college football team. It is the closest thing to an all-encompassing, full-blown encyclopedia of Clemson Football—a blow by blow history—with tales of the great moments. We capture all the action and all the memorable moments of Tigers football. This book is for your reading pleasure but also as a great reference for when you want to see how a particular Clemson game in any year happened to turn out.

If you are a Clemson Tigers fan. you will not want to put this book down.

Brian Kelly

LETS
GO
PUBLISH

Copyright © July 2017, Brian W. Kelly   Editor: Brian P. Kelly
Title: Great Moments in Clemson Tigers Football   Author Brian W. Kelly

All rights reserved: No part of this book may be reproduced or transmitted in any form, or by any means, electronic or mechanical, including photocopying, recording, scanning, faxing, or by any information storage and retrieval system, without permission from the publisher, LETS GO PUBLISH, in writing.

Disclaimer: Though judicious care was taken throughout the writing and the publication of this work that the information contained herein is accurate, there is no expressed or implied warranty that all information in this book is 100% correct. Therefore, neither LETS GO PUBLISH, nor the author accepts liability for any use of this work.

Trademarks: A number of products and names referenced in this book are trade names and trademarks of their respective companies.

Referenced Material: *Standard Disclaimer: The information in this book has been obtained through personal and third-party observations, interviews, and copious research. Where unique information has been provided, or extracted from other sources, those sources are acknowledged within the text of the book itself or in the References area in the front matter. Thus, there are no formal footnotes nor is there a bibliography section. Any picture that does not have a source was taken from various sites on the Internet with no credit attached. If resource owners would like credit in the next printing, please email publisher.*

Published by: ....LETS GO PUBLISH!
Editor in Chief ....Brian P. Kelly
Email: ....info@letsgopublish.com
Web site .... www.letsgopublish.com
Library of Congress Copyright Information Pending
Book Cover Design by **Michele Thomas**
Editor—Brian P. Kelly

ISBN Information: The International Standard Book Number (ISBN) is a unique machine-readable identification number, which marks any book unmistakably. The ISBN is the clear standard in the book industry. 159 countries and territories are officially ISBN members. The Official ISBN for this book is

978-1-947402-01-0

The price for this work is:..........   **$ 19.95 USD**

10   9   8   7   6   5   4   3   2   1

Clemson University Seasons by Year/Coach

Head coach	Year	Wins/	Losses/Ties		Conf.
Walter Riggs	1896	2	1	0	Indep
Wm. M. Williams	1897	2	2	0	Indep
John Penton	1898	3	1	0	Indep
Walter Riggs	1899	4	2	0	SIAA
John Heisman	1900	6	0	0	SIAA
	1901	3	1	1	SIAA
	1902	6	1	0	SIAA
	1903	4	1	1	SIAA
Shack Shealy	1904	3	3	1	SIAA
Eddie Cochems	1905	3	2	1	SIAA
Bob Williams	1906	4	0	3	SIAA
Frank Shaughnessy	1907	4	4	0	SIAA
John N. Stone	1908	1	6	0	SIAA
Bob Williams	1909	6	3	0	SIAA
Frank Dobson	1910	4	3	1	SIAA
	1911	3	5	0	SIAA
	1912	4	4	0	SIAA
Bob Williams	1913	4	4	0	SIAA
	1914	5	3	1	SIAA
	1915	2	4	2	SIAA
Wayne Hart	1916	3	6	0	SIAA
Edward Donahue	1917	6	2	0	SIAA
	1918	5	2	0	SIAA
	1919	6	2	2	SIAA
	1920	4	6	1	SIAA
E. J. Stewart	1921	1	6	2	SIAA
	1922	5	4	0	SoCon
Bud Saunders	1923	5	2	1	SoCon
	1924	2	6	0	SoCon
	1925	1	7	0	SoCon
Bud Saunders (4 games)	1926	2	7	0	SoCon

Bob Williams (5 games)					SoCon
Josh Cody	1927	5	3	1	SoCon
	1928	8	3	0	SoCon
	1929	8	3	0	SoCon
	1930	8	2	0	SoCon
Jess Neely	1931	1	6	2	SoCon
	1932	3	5	1	SoCon
	1933	3	6	2	SoCon
	1934	5	4	0	SoCon
	1935	6	3	0	SoCon
	1936	5	5	0	SoCon
	1937	4	4	1	SoCon
	1938	7	1	1	SoCon
	1939	9	1	0	SoCon
Frank Howard	1940	6	2	1	SoCon
	1941	7	2	0	SoCon
	1942	3	6	1	SoCon
	1943	2	6	0	SoCon
	1944	4	5	0	SoCon
	1945	6	3	1	SoCon
	1946	4	5	0	SoCon
	1947	4	5	0	SoCon
	1948	11	0	0	SoCon
	1949	4	4	2	SoCon
	1950	9	0	1	SoCon
	1951	7	3	0	SoCon
	1952	2	6	1	SoCon
	1953	3	5	1	ACC
	1954	5	5	0	ACC
	1955	7	3	0	ACC
	1956	7	2	2	ACC
	1957	7	3	0	ACC
	1958	8	3	0	ACC
	1959	9	2	0	ACC

Coach	Year	W	L	T	Conf
	1960	6	4	0	ACC
	1961	5	5	0	ACC
	1962	6	4	0	ACC
	1963	5	4	1	ACC
	1964	3	7	0	ACC
	1965	5	5	0	ACC
	1966	6	4	0	ACC
	1967	6	4	0	ACC
	1968	4	5	1	ACC
	1969	4	6	0	ACC
	1970	3	8	0	ACC
Hootie Ingram	1971	5	6	0	ACC
	1972	4	7	0	ACC
	1973	5	6	0	ACC
	1974	7	4	0	ACC
Red Parker	1975	2	9	0	ACC
	1976	3	6	2	ACC
Charley Pell	1977	8	3	1	ACC
Charley Pell (11 games)	1978 *	11	1	0	ACC
Danny Ford (1 game)					ACC
	1979	8	4	0	ACC
	1980	6	5	0	ACC
	1981	12	0	0	ACC
	1982	9	1	1	ACC
	1983	9	1	1	ACC
Danny Ford	1984	7	4	0	ACC
	1985	6	6	0	ACC
	1986	8	2	2	ACC
	1987	10	2	0	ACC
	1988	10	2	0	ACC
	1989	10	2	0	ACC
	1990	10	2	0	ACC
Ken Hatfield	1991	9	2	1	ACC

	1992	5	6	0	ACC
Ken Hatfield (11 games)	1993				ACC
		9	3	0	
Tommy West (1 game)					ACC
Tommy West	1994	5	6	0	ACC
	1995	8	4	0	ACC
	1996	7	5	—	ACC
	1997	7	5	—	ACC
	1998	3	8	—	ACC
Tommy Bowden	1999	6	6	—	ACC
	2000	9	3	—	ACC
	2001	7	5	—	ACC
	2002	7	6	—	ACC
	2003	9	4	—	ACC
	2004	6	5	—	ACC
	2005	8	4	—	ACC
	2006	8	5	—	ACC
	2007	9	4	—	ACC
Tommy Bowden (6 games)	2008				ACC
		7	6	—	
Dabo Swinney (7 games)					ACC
Dabo Swinney	2009	9	5	—	ACC
	2010	6	7	—	ACC
	2011	10	4	—	ACC
	2012	11	2	—	ACC
	2013	11	2	—	ACC
	2014	10	3	—	ACC
	2015	14	1	—	ACC
	2016	14	1	—	ACC

Total Games 1,222
Seasons   121
Total Wins 721
Total Losses 456
Total Ties 45   * Prior to Overtime Rules
Stats from   1896 Through August 2017

Acknowledgments:

I appreciate all the help that I received in putting this book together, along with the 114 other books from the past.

My printed acknowledgments were once so large that book readers needed to navigate too many pages to get to page one of the text. To permit me more flexibility, I put my acknowledgment list online at www.letsgopublish.com. The list of acknowledgments continues to grow. Believe it or not, it once cost about a dollar more to print each book.

Thank you all on the big list in the sky and God bless you all for your help.

Please check out www.letsgopublish.com to read the latest version of my heartfelt acknowledgments updated for this book. Thank you all!

In this book, I received some extra special help from many avid football friends including Dennis Grimes, Gerry Rodski, Wily Ky Eyely, Angel Irene McKeown Kelly, Angel Edward Joseph Kelly Sr., Angel Edward Joseph Kelly Jr., Ann Flannery, Angel James Flannery Sr., Mary Daniels, Bill Daniels, Robert Garry Daniels, Angel Sarah Janice Daniels, Angel Punkie Daniels, Joe Kelly and Diane Kelly.

References

I learned how to write creatively in Grade School at St. Boniface. I even enjoyed reading some of my own stuff as a toddler.

At Meyers High School and King's College and Wilkes-University, I learned how to research, write bibliographies and footnote every non-original thought I might have had. I learned to hate ibid, and op. cit., and I hated assuring that I had all citations written down in the proper sequence. Having to pay attention to details took my desire to write creatively and diminished it with busy work.

I know it is necessary for the world to stop plagiarism so authors and publishers can get paid properly, but for an honest writer, it sure is annoying. I wrote many proposals while with IBM and whenever I needed to cite something, I cited it in place, because my readers, IT Managers, could care less about tracing the vagaries of citations and their varied formats.

I always hated to use stilted footnotes, or produce a lengthy, perfectly formatted bibliography. I bet most bibliographies are flawed because even the experts on such drivel do not like the tedium.

I wrote 118 books before this book and several hundred articles published by many magazines and newspapers and I only cite when an idea is not mine or when I am quoting, and again, I choose to cite in place, and the reader does not have to trace strange numbers through strange footnotes and back to bibliography elements that may not be readily accessible or available. Academicians knowing all the rules of citation are not my audience. In this book, if you are a lover of Clemson Tigers football, you are my intended group of readers

Yet, I would be kidding you, if in a book about the great moments in Clemson University Football, I tried to bluff my way into trying to make you think that I knew everything before I began to write anything in this book. I spent as much time researching as writing. I might even call myself an expert of sorts now about the Tigers, a team that I have recently begun to watch and enjoy, especially when a great coach such as Dabo Swinney is on the sidelines.

Without any pain on your part you can read this book from cover to cover to enjoy the stories about the many great moments in the Clemson University of Football Program.

It took me about two months to write this book. If I were to have made sure that a thought of mine was not a thought somebody else ever had, this book never would have been completed or the citations pages would more than likely exceed the prose. Everybody takes credit for everything in sports writing—at least that's what I have found.

I used CU Season summaries and recaps from whatever source I could to get the scores of all the games. I verified facts when possible. There are many web sites that have great information and facts. Ironically most internet stories are the same exact stories. Who's got the original? While I was writing the book, I wrote down a bunch of Internet references and at one time, I listed them right here en masse in this article. They were the least read pages. No more. Unless I am citing a reference in a section of the book, you will not see the URL.

Since I am not a South Carolinian, but I love vacationing at Myrtle Beach, I want to visit SC and below often as winters in PA are very harsh and grey.

I have no favorite source for information to put in my books. However, I continually hunt for articles written by students to amplify the text I present.

While I was writing this book, because I was not sure that my citations within the text would be enough, and I was not producing a bibliography, I copied URLs into some of the book text in those cases in which I had read articles or had downloaded material and had brought articles or pieces of articles into this book. Hopefully, this will satisfy any request for additional citations. If there is anything which needs a specific citation, I would be pleased to change the text. Just contact me. Your stuff is your stuff.

Most of the facts in this book are also put forth in the Clemson Media Guide. Our thanks for the use of this material for the accurate production of this book. Additionally, when I was looking for some special games to highlight, I used a piece by Bob Bradley, Sports Information Director as a source for my facts.

http://www.clemsontigers.com/ViewArticle.dbml?ATCLID=205510943.

Preface:

This book is all about the great moments in Clemson Tigers football over the years. Along the way to today, we study the founding of Clemson University; then the preliminaries before CU football officially began, and then we delve right into the storied Clemson University Football Program--its struggles; its greatness; and its long-lasting impact on American life.

As a Pennsylvanian, I admit I wrote a similar book about Penn State Football but only after I had fulfilled the family Irish wish and had written about Notre Dame Football. Then, before Clemson whooped Alabama in the beginning of this year, I had figured Nick Saban could not be beaten—though I was not necessarily rooting for him—and so I selected Alabama as the third football team about which I would write about substantially. You've got to admit, they are a competent team. Now, I find myself writing about the National Champions, the Clemson Tigers, and I am honored to take up this challenge. As I am reviewing the preface right before publication, I have concluded that I think you are going to like this book.

Since none of the three, ND, PSU, or UA, invited me on campus to sign books, and none of them have appealing locations anyway, especially those in the North, I figured why not pick a state where I vacation such as Florida. But, I am not a fan of the Seminoles. I have friends in the Gainesville area so I picked the Gators and that book came out a few months ago.

Before I decided to write this book about Clemson Football, I was thinking about writing about Army as they have two National Championships and they played some great football when American football was first being defined—plus like many, I served some time in the Army. But then, I remembered how rivetted I was to my seat watching DeShaun Watson and the Dabo Swinney squad on January 9, 2017 put a stinging defeat on Alabama.

I also got to thinking that I like South Carolina as a state. It is so nice that I choose to go there on vacations. Though Myrtle Beach is on the other side of the state from Clemson, the weather is fine in both sections of the state and the Tiger country is beautiful.

This is not the first book I wrote about South Carolina. I am the proud author of a book with a catchy title called Take the Train to Myrtle Beach, which I wrote several years ago and updated last summer. I look forward to my first trip to Clemson to sign some books in the Fall. Don't forget to invite me.

When you are ready to invite me to "Death Valley," aka Frank Howard Field at Clemson Memorial Stadium, I will be pleased to arrive in Clemson, SC with bells on. Perhaps somebody could get me fifty-yard line seats in a game in which CU is playing against one of my old-time favorites, ND or PSU, or quite frankly, any team. I'd be happy to do some signing before and after the game, and at the bookstore the day before and after. I'll wait 'til the signing is finished to move on to the whistle wetting period. I'll sign until you tell me "No more!"

I respect Clemson an awful, especially now that I have completed all the research necessary to print this book. I am sure long-term Clemson fans will admit that as a Pennsylvanian, for me it was easy to grow up a Penn State Fan. ND of course has always been as close to me as a family religion.

I began to pay attention to Clemson a few years ago when DeShaun beat Deshone in one of the toughest games of my life. Clemson beat both Notre Dame and the torrential rain. It was tough for me because ND lost and because I was in the first couple days of a herniated disc recovery that sidelined me for two months. Thank God for laptops. I noted that those Clemson players sure know how to play great football.

I watched the end of season games and would not miss the January Championship game in which Clemson was barely beaten by less than a touchdown. I was in awe of the Clemson Team and I was again amazed by the outstanding play of QB Deshaun Watson. What a football player. What a team

Of course, in 2017, I was attached to the TV for the Alabama rematch nail-biter game and saw the best player in the country, Deshaun Watson win the game for Dabo Swinney and for Clemson.

Well deserved. It's time for another. I have enjoyed writing this book immensely. Go Tigers!

Supporters who love Clemson University will read this book and get an immediate burst of emotions such as warmth and love for their favorite team. You will love this book because it has it all – every great season and every great game. Go Clemson Tigers!

This book walks you through the whole CU football journey. Then, we look at the players on the early teams who succeeded despite Clemson not yet having a big-time program. This period began in 1896. Like all new teams, you can imagine the struggle of playing on a college football team when getting the right equipment was one of the biggest issues.

The 25 great CU coaches are listed within the football seasons in which they coached--from season 1 in 1896 to season 122 in 2017. In other words, the seasons are examined chronologically and the coaches and certain games and certain players are highlighted within the seasons in which the games were played. I sure hope you enjoy this unique approach.

Before Frank Howard put in a thirty-year stint starting in 1940, few of CU's 16 coaches to that point took the team for more than a couple years. Yet, they still produced some powerful teams with powerful players. Of the 25 coaches in the Fighting Tigers history, just six had losing seasons. That's a lot of winning for any football program.

Clemson Tigers are a long-time football power

One hundred twenty-one years is a long time to be playing football. The Clemson Tigers are recognized today as one of the finest teams in the nation, ready to win a national championship at the drop of the next hat. In fact, it was less than a year ago that the hat dropped for the second time.

In 1953, Clemson joined the ACC and have been playing many of the best football teams in the nation ever since by competing in the NCAA Division I Football Bowl Subdivision. Some say the SEC was better in 2016 than the ACC but then again, Clemson, a mainstay of the ACC is the reigning national champion. You can read about Clemson success before and after it joined the ACC right here in this book and decide for yourself how great the Fighting Tigers play the game of Football.

Your author would like you to know that when football season closes in the second week of January each year, there is now a great football item—this book—that is available all 52 weeks of the year and in fact all 365 days each year. It does not rely on the stadium gates being open for you to get a great dose of Clemson Tigers Football. Just begin reading right here.

It is now available for you to add to your Clemson Football experience. and your book collection. Once you get this book, it is yours forever unless, of course you give it away to one of the many who will be in awe, and who will accept it gladly. For those who love to use gadgets to read, this book is also available on Kindle.

We open the book the first story set shortly after the beginning of college football as a sport in America. It then moves on to the first official game with the first official coach and all the way to Coach Swinney's National Championship game. It tells a story about all the football seasons and the great coaches and great players and great moments from the first coached game in 1896 to today.

You are going to love this book because it is the perfect read for anybody who loves the Clemson Tigers and wants to know more about the most revered athletes to have competed in one of the finest football programs of all time.

Few sports books are a must-read but Brian Kelly's <u>Great Moments in Clemson Tigers Football</u> will quickly appear at the top of Americas most enjoyable must-read books about sports. Enjoy!

Who is Brian W. Kelly?

Brian W. Kelly is one of the leading authors in America with this, his 119th published book. Brian is an outspoken and eloquent expert on a variety of topics and he has also written several hundred articles on topics of interest to Americans.

Most of his early works involved high technology. Later, Brian wrote a number of patriotic books and most recently he has been writing human interest books such as <u>The Wine Diet</u> and <u>Thank you, IBM</u>. His books are always well received.

Brian's books are highlighted at <u>www.letsgopublish.com</u>. Quantities from 20 to 1000 can be made available from <u>www.bookhawkers.com.</u> You may see most of Brian's works by taking the following link <u>www.amazon.com/author/brianwkelly</u>.

The Best!

Sincerely,

Brian W. Kelly, Author
Brian P. Kelly, Editor in Chief
I am Brian Kelly's eldest son.

Table of Contents

About the Author

Brian Kelly retired as an Assistant Professor in the Business Information Technology (BIT) Program at Marywood University, where he also served as the IBM i and Midrange Systems Technical Advisor to the IT Faculty. Kelly designed, developed, and taught many college and professional courses. He continues as a contributing technical editor to a number of technical industry magazines, including "The Four Hundred" and "Four Hundred Guru," published by IT Jungle.

Kelly is a former IBM Senior Systems Engineer. His specialty was problem solving for customers as well as implementing advanced operating systems and software on his client's machines. Brian is the author of 119 books and hundreds of magazine articles. He has been a frequent speaker at technical conferences throughout the United States.

Brian was a candidate for the US Congress from Pennsylvania in 2010 and he ran for Mayor in his home town in 2015. He loves Clemson Tigers Football and can't wait to get back down to South Carolina in the fall. When he comes he'll be glad to sign your books. God bless the Tigers!

Chapter 1 Introduction to Clemson University (CU) Football

Clemson's 120th Year in 2015!

Coach Swinney leading the Tigers onto the field

The Clemson Tigers have fielded a team every season since the inaugural 1896 season. That's a lot of football games. To be exact, it's 1,222 games in its 121 seasons, and the Tigers have a fine all-time record of 721 wins, 445 losses, and 45 ties. That's a lot of great Clemson football folks.

Officially the Clemson recognizes a long football history that dates back to 1896. If you are from South Carolina, or some other rival school, you might not be so kind. Such rivals might ask if Clemson even had a football team before 1981 with Danny Ford and the Clemson University First National Championship. Of course, they don't know how to read as the immortal Frank Howard had an extremely successful thirty-year tenure from 1940 through 1969.

After Howard, Hootie Ingram and Red Parker had a tough time getting wins for the team. They combined for a seven-year losing record of 29-46-2 before even the great Charlie Pell, who stopped by Clemson for two years (1977 & 1978) could not put them back on the plus side of the win column even though he picked up 18 wins with just four losses and a tie.   Combining the trio's record post Frank Howard and pre-Danny Ford, we get come up with 47-50-3. Knowing what we know now, however, once Pell arrived the wins began to accumulate.

So, IMHO, it is an unfair shot to suggest the Tigers were no place as the program has produced well over 700 wins with a late start in 1896 when many of the legendary teams had already been legends for ten or twenty years or more. Like most startups, CU did have its share of medsa mediocre seasons but they more or less ended in the1940's with Frank Howard and those who followed.

From the time of Danny Ford in 1980, to today, the Clemson Tigers have been on a rip with 338 wins, 153 losses, and 5 ties. Sometimes I wish the NCAA would just go away. This is the fifth book that I have researched and written about big-time college football, and I am beginning to see a pattern. When a team that is trying to break into the big-time has a good or great year, the NCAA is likely to impose sanctions.

I could have predicted it from heuristic analysis. During the Danny Ford years, Clemson was not supposed to be such a winning team and so, the NCAA stepped in with its sanctions.

1. Clemson University shall be publicly reprimanded and censured, and placed on probation for a period of two years, effective November 21, 1982, it being understood that should any portion of the penalty in this case be set aside for any reason other than by appropriate action of the Association, the penalty shall be reconsidered by the NCAA; further, prior to the expiration of this period of probation, the NCAA shall review the athletic policies and practices of the university.

2. The university's intercollegiate football team shall end its 1982 and 1983 football seasons with the playing of its last regularly scheduled, in-season contest and the university shall not be eligible to participate in any postseason football competition.

3. During the 1983 and 1984 football seasons, the university's intercollegiate football team shall not be eligible to appear on any television series or program subject to the administration or control of this Association or any other television programs involving live coverage.

There are more.

My point is that it was only when Clemson began to make trouble for the expected winners did the NCAA clamp down. Maybe I am wrong but I have seen this pattern before.

Danny Ford was a great coach and brought home all the bacon one time during his tenure. The NCAA spots great programs and great coaches and the sanctions bomb comes down. Only mediocre coaches want to win because another

Dabo Swinney is a great coach and he takes a back seat to no other coach in college football. He brought in a National Championship and a ton of great seasons even before that. Check out his Clemson record below. His football legacy is from hard work. He came to Clemson in 2008 and there was not even a hint of losing season upon his arrival. By 2012, Clemson was a major contender for national laurels. In the 2015 Championship game. Just five points separated Clemson from dethroning Alabama but five points made the difference.

With an even more determined team, in 2016, Swinney's offense and defense would not be picked apart even in the big games. They won the ACC and then went on the beat the vaunted SEC Champion Alabama in a great game to cap their season. Dabo Swinney is being compared to Danny Ford, and that sure is a compliment but the comparisons have to do with the NCAA sniffing around and finding violations. I hope none of this is true. Like I said. We might be better off as a country without the current NCAA.

Year	School	G	W	L	T	Pct
2008	Clemson	7	4	3	0	.571
2009	Clemson	14	9	5	0	.643
2010	Clemson	13	6	7	0	.462
2011	Clemson	14	10	4	0	.714
2012	Clemson	13	11	2	0	.846
2013	Clemson	13	11	2	0	.846
2014	Clemson	13	10	3	0	.769
2015	Clemson	15	14	1	0	.933
2016	Clemson	15	14	1	0	.933

This book that you are reading celebrates Clemson University of South Carolina; its founding; its struggles; its greatness; and its long-lasting impact on American life. People like me, who love the Tigers, will love this book. Clemson Haters will want their own copy just for additional ammo. Yet, it won't help them! Hah!

We begin the rest of the Clemson Fighting Tigers football story in Chapter 2 with the founding of Clemson University institution almost 139 years ago and we continue in subsequent chapters, right into the founding of the full Clemson football program in 1896 after the students had been begging the argument by playing American football on the campus in intramural fashion. The Clemson athletes even played other colleges to help sharpen their game and add some zip to their unofficial seasons.

In defining the format of the book, we chose to use a timetable that is based on a historical chronology. Within this framework, we discuss the great moments in Clemson University football history, and there are many great moments. No book can claim to be able to capture them all, as it would be a never-ending story, but we sure do try.

No Heisman's for Clemson???

Though there still are no Heisman Trophy's yet for Clemson but a few close calls, nobody can deny that the founder of the Heisman award, John Heisman, shown below, was the third head coach at Clemson. Heisman was as good as it gets as a coach and his record was 19-3 in four seasons. of coaching the Tigers.

© Oberlin College Archives

John Heisman with famous Heisman Pose at Oberlin Before Clemson

The Coolest Pre-Game Tradition in College Football

The Clemson Tigers have the coolest pre-game tradition in College Football. When you go to a Clemson Home game, make sure you do not miss it. It culminates in the most exciting 25 seconds in college football.

Clemson Players "Running Down the Hill"

The following is courtesy of Clemson University

When Don Munson ran down the hill for the first time, he didn't know what he was in for. This was in 2010, the year he began working full-time for the Clemson athletic department. Before the Tigers' home opener that September, Munson turned to coach Dabo Swinney, shook his hand, and told him how much he appreciated being part of the team's pregame ritual. Swinney responded by slapping Munson on the back and saying, "You have no idea." "It was absolutely true," said Munson, who's in his first year as the Tigers' radio play-by-play announcer. He was about to participate in what Brett Musburger (and many others) have called "the most exciting 25 seconds in football."

Every Clemson entrance is an event. Ten minutes before the start of each home game, the Tigers leave their locker room (located underneath the west end zone stands) and board buses [yes busses for a home game—with the bus route lined with fans. that take them on a short ride to the north side of Memorial Stadium. At that point, the players file out and assemble on top of a hill above the east end zone. Then, after rubbing Howard's Rock (more on that later), a cannon fires, sending the team down the hill and onto the field.

"You're up on that hill looking over the sea of people and I'm telling you it gets your blood flowing, man," Munson said. "It's crazy. I've had players describe it as [feeling like] gladiators. They look upon themselves as kind of walking into that Roman Coliseum.

"The guy that's in the booth with me, Rodney Williams, he was a great player at Clemson in the '80s. I can tell the effect that it has on him. It still is an emotional thing. I've seen ex-players cry at this thing. Literally, just weep. They know what it's all about."

According to the university, the tradition was borne out of necessity: The first 20,000 seats in Clemson Memorial Stadium were built and ready for use before the 1942 season. The shortest entry into the stadium was a walk down Williamson Road from Fike Field House's dressing rooms to a gate at the top of the hill behind the east end zone.

There were no dressing facilities in the west end zone-only a big clock where the hands turned, and a scoreboard, which was operated by hand. The team would dress at Fike, walk down Williamson Road, come in the gate underneath where the big scoreboard now stands and jog down the hill for its warm-up exercises.

Things changed in the 1960s, when S.C. Jones, a Clemson alum, gifted then-coach Frank Howard a hunk of white flint from Death Valley, California. (By then, Memorial Stadium had been nicknamed Death Valley.) Howard hated the present at first, but eventually came around. In 1966, the rock was positioned on top of a pedestal located on top of the hill. The players didn't begin rubbing what became known as Howard's Rock until September 23, 1967. Before the Tigers beat Wake Forest that day, Howard allegedly told his team: "If you're going to give me 110 percent, you can rub that rock. If you're not, keep your filthy hands off it."

Members of the Clemson University ROTC guard Howard's Rock. Photo by Joshua S. Kelly-USA TODAY Sports

Since then—except for a stretch from 1970 to early 1972 when coach Hootie Ingram was at the helm—the Tigers have rubbed Howard's Rock and run down the hill before every game at Memorial Stadium.

"What other entrance in America is like that?" Munson said. "There isn't one."

This is Munson's first season in the booth. For four years, he ran down the hill with Swinney and the Tigers.
"I'll be really honest with you," he said. "I actually miss it."

Clemson Football: The All-Time Dream Team

http://bleacherreport.com/articles/1296550-clemson-football-the-all-time-dream-team

ON AUGUST 15, 2012, BLEACHER REPORT'S COLBY LANHAM wrote a great piece about the all-time Clemson Dream Team. It covers bases we have not seen over the past few years of great Dabo Swinney led Clemson football so we include it here as another perspective of the great football players to have one-time played for Clemson University. When you have an opportunity, take the link below and read this recent perspective. It is worth your time.

Here is Colby Lanham's beginning in italics below:

Clemson football is a celebrated, major NCAA Division I college football program. That's a dictionary definition of it.

But to its devoted fanbase, it is tradition and a way of life in college football.

Clemson has seen plenty of greatness within Death Valley stadium, from back in its high days in the '80s, claiming its only national championship, all the way to today, where fans are more excited than ever after winning its first ACC Championship since 1991.

But what would the Clemson Football All-Time Dream Team look like? If you could put together the greatest Tigers on one team and watch them all touch Howard's Rock as they run down The Hill, who would be a part of that unit on offense and defense?

Here's a possible roster of what that All-Time Dream Team would look like.

Here is the link for those who want to read the whole piece:

http://bleacherreport.com/articles/1296550-clemson-football-the-all-time-dream-team

How would anybody construct a dream team covering 121 years of Clemson football if given the mission. Many have tried and I read their works to help me find the consensus great players in Clemson history. My thanks to them all.

There have been many surveys that included fans, former Clemson players, coaches, and administrators to select their top Clemson football players of the Century. In most cases, the participants in the surveys and interviews have followed Clemson football for at least 20 years and some for over 50 years. Some of the players that we highlight in the proper chronological order in this book are from some of those surveys. In all cases, the player is clearly a great Clemson gridiron stalwart. Whenever you see the term Player Highlights, you can expect a well-researched snap biography of a great Clemson Player. When possible, I include a picture. Enjoy!

Chapter 2 The Founding of Clemson University

One of the Beautiful Sites on CU Campus

The Clemson short story: Courtesy of Clemson University

Clemson was founded in 1889 through a bequest from Thomas Green Clemson, a Philadelphia-born, European-educated engineer, musician and artist who married John C. Calhoun's daughter, Anna Maria, and eventually settled at her family plantation in South Carolina. A longtime advocate for an agricultural college in the Upstate, Clemson left his home and fortune to the state of South Carolina to create the institution that bears his name.

In November 1889, Gov. John Peter Richardson signed a bill accepting Clemson's gift, which established the Clemson Agricultural College and made its trustees custodians of Morrill Act and Hatch Act funds, federally provided for agricultural education and research purposes by federal legislative acts.

Initially an all-male, all-white military school, Clemson Agricultural College opened in July 1893 with 446 students. Clemson became a coeducational, civilian institution in 1955 and was the first traditionally white institution in South Carolina to desegregate since Reconstruction. With academic offerings and research pursuits, the institution became Clemson University in 1964.

-- End of Clemson short story

Fort Hill Plantation

Historic Home of VP John C, Calhoun

This is the historic home of South Carolina's only Vice President of the United States, John C. Calhoun. It is operated by Clemson University for the public good. You can take tours of this beautiful area courtesy of Clemson University. This massive property sits on 814 acres that were bequeathed in 1888 to the State of South Carolina by the son-in-law of John C. Calhoun, with the stipulation that it never be changed. It is known as Fort Hill and as noted, it is run by Clemson as a Museum House. You'll enjoy the tour for

$5/adults, $4/seniors, $2/children. FYI, Tours are offered every day, except university holidays.

Fort Hill History

Fort Hill was the home of John C. Calhoun, South Carolina's pre-eminent 19th century statesman, from 1825 until his death in 1850. The antebellum plantation home, office and kitchen are furnished mostly with family artifacts.

It was through a succession of Calhoun-Clemson women that Fort Hill came into Thomas Green Clemson's possession. In 1888, Clemson bequeathed the Fort Hill plantation and cash to the state of South Carolina for the establishment of a scientific and agricultural college. He willed that Fort Hill "shall always be open for the inspection of visitors."

The land that would become home to Clemson University started with John C. Calhoun and his wife, Floride Bonneau Calhoun, who owned the land. Floride's family had come into much Upcountry land in 1802. Fort Hill, then known as Clergy Hall, was built in 1803 as the manse for Old Stone Church just a few miles away. When Fort Hill came up for

sale, Floride's mother purchased the property.
She and husband, John C., were living in Fort Hill when Floride inherited the title upon her mother's death in 1836. When John C. died in 1850, Floride became the sole owner of the Fort Hill home and 1,341 acres of land. When she died in 1866, portions of the property then went to their daughter and sole surviving child, Anna Maria Calhoun, who had married Thomas Green Clemson. The Clemson's' daughter, Floride Elizabeth, also inherited a portion.

Anna Maria Calhoun Clemson willed her share of Fort Hill to her husband, Thomas Clemson, who inherited it when she died in 1875. Today, Fort Hill is just as Thomas Clemson envisioned — preserved, restored and open to the public for tours.

People of Fort Hill

Thomas Green Clemson

Thomas Green Clemson was a scientist, mining engineer, diplomat to Belgium under four U.S. presidents and considered the first secretary of agriculture. He was as unique as he was highly educated, skilled, pragmatic, visionary and complex. Upon his death in 1888, he left his estate and his fortune for the betterment of education in South Carolina.

Anna Maria Calhoun Clemson

Graceful and interested in politics, Anna Maria Calhoun Clemson
was the daughter of John C. Calhoun. She married Thomas Green
Clemson in November 1838 and willed her share of Fort Hill to
Clemson, who inherited it when she died in 1875.

The African-American Experience at Fort Hill

African-Americans were a vital force in the operation and economy
of Fort Hill, the home of John C. and Floride Calhoun from 1825 to
1850, Andrew Pickens and Margaret Green Calhoun from 1851 to
1871, and Thomas Green and Anna Clemson from 1872 to 1888.

Like many Southern planters of the time, Calhoun raised cotton as a
cash crop using enslaved African-American labor to run his

household and plantation. The Calhouns owned skilled workers such as gardeners, seamstresses, and carpenters in addition to agricultural workers and field hands. Since the slaves who occupied Fort Hill left no written record, their perspective is virtually voiceless in history.

Read more about African Americans at Fort Hill.

https://www.clemson.edu/about/history/properties/fort-hill/african-americans.html

Chapter 3 Mission of Clemson University

Anderson Hall (1913) West University Avenue NATIONAL REGISTER 1979

This building was originally called Language Hall, Anderson Hall was designed as a multiple purpose building. Later renamed to honor James N. Anderson, first Dean of the Graduate School, it housed the classrooms and offices for the Departments of English, Language, His-tory and Mathematics. In addition, the offices of the President, the Registrar and the Graduate School were in this building.

Mission Description, Vision, & Statement

Clemson will be one of the nation's top-20 public universities.

Mission Statement

Clemson University was established to fulfill our founder's vision of "a high seminary of learning" to develop "the material resources of the State" for the people of South Carolina. Nurtured by an abiding land grant commitment, Clemson has emerged as a research university with a global vision. Our primary purpose is educating undergraduate and graduate students to think deeply about and engage in the social, scientific, economic, and professional challenges of our times. The foundation of this mission is the generation, preservation, communication, and application of knowledge. The University also is committed to the personal growth of the individual and promotes an environment of good decision making, healthy and ethical lifestyles, and tolerance and respect for others. Our distinctive character is shaped by a legacy of service, collaboration, and fellowship forged from and renewed by the spirit of Thomas Green Clemson's covenant.

University Description

Clemson University is a selective, public, research university in a college-town setting. Clemson's desire is to attract a capable, dedicated and diverse student body of approximately 20,000 undergraduate and graduate students, with priority to students from South Carolina.

The University offers a wide array of high quality baccalaureate programs built around a distinctive core curriculum. Graduate, continuing education, doctoral and research programs contribute to the state of knowledge and to the economic future of the state, nation and world.

The university provides bachelor's, master's and doctoral degrees in more than 100 majors through five academic colleges: The College of Agriculture, Forestry and Life Sciences; the College of Architecture, Arts and Humanities; the College of Business and Behavioral Science; the College of Engineering and Science; and the College of Health, Education and

Human Development.

Clemson combines the benefits of a major research university with a strong commitment to undergraduate teaching and individual student success. Students, both undergraduate and graduate, have opportunities for unique educational experiences throughout South Carolina, as well as in other countries.

Experiential learning is a valued component of the Clemson experience, and students are encouraged through Creative Inquiry, internships, and study abroad, to apply their learning beyond the classroom. Electronic delivery of courses and degree programs also provide a variety of learning opportunities. Clemson's extended campus includes teaching sites in Greenville and Charleston, five research campuses and five public service centers throughout the state of South Carolina, as well as four international sites.

The University is committed to exemplary teaching, research and public service in the context of general education, student engagement and development, and continuing education. In all areas, the goal is to develop students' communication and critical-thinking skills, ethical judgment, global awareness, and scientific and technological knowledge.

The distinctive character of Clemson is reflected in the culture of collegiality and collaboration among faculty, students, staff, the administration, and the university board.

This tribute has been approved by the Clemson University Board of Trustees, October 19, 2012 & approved by the SC Commission on Higher Education, March 22, 2013

Chapter 4 CU "Un-Official" Football Teams

Early Clemson Football Team

1890's: Nearly 50 years from the founding

You could not find a football game on South Carolina campuses at any college through most of the 1890's but by the end football was on its way. There was lots of baseball, which was the main sport on South Carolina college campuses during this early period.

Recreational levels (intramural) of football began at some institutions by the 1880s. Founded in 1889, it was not too long afterwards that spot games of football were being played wherever students could find a field to play the game. South Carolina College (later became the University of South Carolina) played football before all other schools. It became a very popular sport between groups of students who just seemed interested in its recreational value.

In October 1888 a student wrote, in a half joking manner, that football was good for health, because after playing a game players bloodied themselves to the point that they "never need to be bled by a physician." Though we do not see it much today, for thousands of years, physicians relied heavily on a single treatment for hysteria, heart disease and just about every other malady. They called it *bloodletting*. The theory behind the practice changed often over time, but the practice itself remained much the same -- with doctors often bleeding patients until they were weak, pale and, sometimes, unconscious. The student was joking but he may have been right.

Two other South Carolina Schools, Wofford and Furman seemed to have gained knowledge of football prior to their first game in December 1889 through recreational contests held on their campuses. Unlike pure intramural sports, however, they played each other. And even after the first game between the two schools, intramural contests between classes at various campuses became an annual contest in the late fall.

In 1911, long after varsity football came to South Carolina campuses, and after the intercollegiate season, the University of South Carolina conducted a competition between the four classes for the Football Trophy. Similarly, class competitions were held on campuses from Greenville to Newberry even when intercollegiate competition was suspended by most upstate schools during the first decade of the 20th century. South Carolina loved its football as did one of its sons, Clemson University.

John Heisman is one of the great immortal notables who coached at Clemson. He was respected nationwide as a football guru. Heisman first coached in 1892 at Oberlin College in Ohio. The College was founded way back in 1833. The Oberlin Review wrote about Heisman in 1892: "Mr. Heisman has entirely remade our football. He has taught us scientific football." They did not name the trophy after him because he was a slouch.

The Akron (Ohio) Beacon noted: "Trainer Heisman has shown what can be done with a new man, even in one short month of training. The advancement of the men has been remarkable."

Soon to be a head football coach at Clemson, even before Clemson began its program, Walter Riggs, the father of Clemson football, tracked down John Heisman. He was growing tomatoes and strawberries in Texas for supplemental income in 1894. Riggs offered Heisman $500 to coach football at Auburn. Heisman agreed. In 1890, John Heisman would be coaching at Clemson College (not yet a University).

There is very little written to almost nothing written about Clemson intramural football other than that we know it did exist. Unlike other schools, there appeared to be no unofficial intercollegiate games between pickup teams from Clemson and other colleges or universities or even athletic clubs before Clemson began its varsity football program. But, this history more than likely is inexact.

In my research, I was fortunate to find a wonderful article that appears to have been produced by the SC state government that puts the beginning of football at Clemson in perspective. Since it is public domain, and it provides great insights about South Carolina Football, with copious insights into Clemson Football, I have included it here. There is a huge bibliography following the article and for your edification, I have included it also. The States of both North and South Carolina primed their colleges and universities to be the best in college football. Clemson was one of the SC colleges that definitely got that message.

Origins and Development of College football in South Carolina, 1889-1930

Another source of early football is a book that I wrote in early 2017 titled, *American College Football: The Beginning* – available on Amazon and Kindle. ALs, Chapter 6 of this book has some great insights. Clemson began its football program in 1896. Here is the article from the State of South Carolina:

"The colors of the two institutions were conspicuous. Furman's banner of purple and white floated in the air and the students wore badges of the same color . . . the players were dressed in canvas cloth uniforms and wore caps of

purple and white. The old gold and black of Wofford was everywhere to be seen . . ."[1]

Such was the splendor surrounding the second year of intercollegiate competition between the two upstate college rivals in January 1891 as the teams formed on the field of Wofford's home ground in Spartanburg. Although the new game of "football" had only begun to take root in the Palmetto State less than a decade before, it was gaining a significant following on these two upstate campuses. At this early stage, though, the rules were different from what they have become. In fact, it probably resembled a rugby match more than what we see in college stadiums today. Scrimmage lines were unbalanced, the forward pass was illegal, and scoring a touchdown only earned four points, while the extra point, or goal, as it was called then, earned two.

On the sidelines there were few, if any bleachers, but the fan support, with perhaps one- hundred, was enthusiastic and partisan in cheering for their respective team. But as the fans of this third intercollegiate football game in South Carolina cheered they could hardly have foreseen how the game would steadily grow from a contest between amateurs into tightly organized teams with well-paid coaches and very demanding alumni, all with a passionate desire to win. By 1930 college football was established on virtually every college campus in the state. [2]

In the early years of collegiate football teams in the Palmetto state used faculty advisors with personal interest in football who aided fledgling teams in the upstate to the low country. Such people had usually played the game at a northern school before coming south. Paid coaches came later once the game was more established. Yet even though unpaid such coaches were not supposed to coach during games.

Only the team captain could give instruction during the matches. Even so the games of this early period could become violent and injuries followed. But this was only one of the reasons most college presidents and their faculties discouraged football. As football took root on South [2] Carolina campuses professors and administrators feared that too much student attention to the game and its players distracted them from their academic pursuits- concerns that had already affected colleges in the northeast where football began more than three decades before.[3]

Neither administrations at Wofford or Furman seemed concerned about their students playing the new game as they would a decade later. Instead the president and his trustees appeared indifferent since they did not support it financially or attend the first games. The early years of college football in the Palmetto state were organized and supported by the players with moral support from the rest of their student bodies. As already indicated a faculty member often helped to train players but everything else, from uniforms, transportation to games, to arranging games were the responsibility of the players and their student managers. A faculty member served as a liaison for their institution to monitor college interests and be sure that integrity was maintained.

In South Carolina's early years of intercollegiate football were truly amateur contests little more than a step above class football competitions staged on most campuses.[4] Baseball was the main sport on South Carolina college campuses through the 1890s yet recreational levels of football began at some institutions by the 1880s.

At what was then South Carolina College (later became the University of South Carolina) football was already a popular sport between groups of students who just seemed interested in its recreational value.

In October 1888 a student wrote, in a half joking manner, that football was good for health, because after playing a game players bloodied themselves to the point that they "never need to be bled by a physician."[5] Wofford and Furman seemed to have gained knowledge of football prior to their first game in December 1889 through recreational contests held on their campuses. And even after the first game between the two schools, intramural contests between classes at many campuses became an annual contest in the late fall. In 1911, after the intercollegiate season, University of South Carolina had a competition between the four classes for the Football Trophy.

Similarly, class competitions were held on campuses from Greenville to Newberry even when intercollegiate competition was suspended by most upstate schools during the first decade of the 20th century.[6][3]

But without its introduction from northern transplants neither class or varsity football would have advanced much in the state.

The most noted of these early northern pioneers to come to South Carolina was the future innovator and coaching legend, John Heisman. An 1892 graduate of the University of Pennsylvania and football star, in 1899 Clemson College lured him from Auburn in Alabama to lead the upstate school to its earliest football success in a brief four-year tenure. The second paid coach in the state, Heisman is the most famous coach of the early years of college football in South Carolina.

Less heralded northern transplants brought the game to other state campuses including Yale graduate Elwin Kerrison who trained the Wofford team for the first Furman contest in 1889. It was unclear if Kerrison played at Yale but he certainly must have known about the game since the Connecticut school was one of college football's top teams in the country with a tradition of winning championships.

When University of South Carolina began a varsity program in 1894 it also enlisted a faculty advisor with northern roots and continued to do so until the school hired its first paid coach two years later.[7] But while these northerners introduced the game they could not coach in the modern sense of the word, at least not until Heisman took over at Clemson.

No coach or trainer is mentioned in the reports for the 1891 Wofford-Furman game. And except for Clemson and South Carolina, the games between other South Carolina schools seemed genteel affairs where the both sides respected the competitive spirit of the other.

The Furman writer who accompanied the 1891 team to Spartanburg for the third contest described a friendly and spirited cheering between the rival fans as the teams prepared for the muddy match in rain and cold wind. Although a low scoring affair in which the visitors prevailed 10-0, the sides had a hotly contested game in which Wofford's tackling and blocking for their running backs was their best feature. It was mainly Furman's better teamwork that seemed to overcome the home side in the end.

The Wofford writer concurred although he attributed the loss to insufficient practice time along with injuries to key players before the contest.[8] During the 1890s South Carolina and Clemson began varsity programs in 1894 and 1896, respectively, but none of the state's other colleges began intercollegiate programs until the new century.

North of South Carolina, the University of North Carolina had begun playing a small schedule of intercollegiate games in the late 1880s and to the west, [4] the University of Georgia began playing other colleges in 1891 followed by Georgia Tech. During this first decade of intercollegiate football the state's colleges occasionally scheduled these out-of-state schools.[9]

But there were a few schools within the Palmetto State that began to play football that by law could not compete with South Carolina, Clemson, or the small upstate schools. These were the black schools in Orangeburg and Columbia. Sadly, the early records for these programs are meager leaving the historian with just a few facts.

Privately supported Claflin College of Orangeburg, SC had a team by 1899 but none of its early records are extant. Eight years later its neighbor, South Carolina State College, began an intercollegiate team, defeating Morehouse College in that year's first and only match. The following year, the Orangeburg school tied Allen University of Columbia and lost the other four games that season.

Within three years of its first varsity season State College became part of a segregated college league called the Georgia- South Carolina Intercollegiate Association (later renamed the South Atlantic Conference), winning that conference's title for the first time in 1919. Allen University was part of this league during the same period.[10]

On the South Carolina coast the College of Charleston began its first intercollegiate squad in 1899, defeating the more experienced Furman, 22-0 but losing to South Carolina, 18-0.

After the first year, the College did not play another team outside of Charleston for the next three years. The low country school, like other programs in the state, focused its competition on local rivals, particularly the city YMCA, teams of former college players living in the city, and even high schools.

Its future town rival, the Citadel, would not have a varsity squad until 1905. With a small student body of barely 100 and a very small budget, the college's local competitive schedule seemed linked to cost factors.[11] But as the game was introduced to Charleston colleges the upstate institutions that introduced varsity football to the state banned it. Both Wofford and Furman had intermittent years when football at the varsity level was absent.

The Spartanburg school did not play intercollegiate football for a three-year period from 1897 to 1899. Furman had no schedule in 1894 and then, like Wofford, had a three-year hiatus in the late 1890s. As the new century began both schools returned to varsity play for two years with [5] Wofford playing its fullest schedule in 1901 with six games.

And then intercollegiate play ended for more than a decade.[12] By this time the game, while growing in popularity on most South Carolina college campuses, had become a major distraction among student bodies according to the faculty and administrators at Wofford and Furman.

Concern that football marginalized the academic purpose of their institutions was coupled with what Wofford President Henry Snyder described as "the unadulterated spirit of battle appealing primarily to the primitive instincts of man . . ." Furthermore, the two schools' presidents claimed that permitting football in the fall, when baseball already took up the spring term, meant that academics would be compromised in both the fall and spring terms to the severe detriment of their small student bodies.[13]

Another factor that influenced their decision could be linked to the strong religious affiliation of both colleges. With strong ties to the Method denomination at Wofford and the Southern Baptists at Furman, and, condoning violent, unsportsmanlike conduct that football generated led to criticism from lay and clergy alike. By the end of 1896 the Board of Education of the South Carolina Methodist Conference denounced football not only as brutal and wasteful of "time and money" but destructive of intellect and morals at Wofford.

Eventually the trustees accepted the Conference recommendation, but only in part. Intercollegiate games continued until 1903 when the Methodist school ended varsity play for the next decade but class football still continued. In 1896 Furman's board seemed less critical, at first, for they continued to allow some football off campus but strictly at the expense of the students who participated. Then, seven years later, the board banned inter-collegiate play because it was "too rough and expensive" but, curiously, encouraged class football on campus.

As off-campus football disappeared on these and other upstate colleges the ban may have also been connected to the growing national press' criticism of the game that was carried in at least one state newspaper.[15] Columbia's State newspaper followed the intense criticism of football in the Northeast, especially as the season ended in December 1905.

It quoted a Boston paper that claimed that football rules, as then permitted, "encouraged brutality and roughness, and put a premium on deceit." That same month the Columbia paper reported that one of the biggest northern colleges, Columbia University, had banned football outright.[16][6] Despite these bans, the game at public supported state colleges continued with opponents from other states.

But for the two biggest schools in South Carolina the growing rivalry between Clemson and University of South Carolina became the biggest clash in the state as the new century began. By 1908 one former player recalled years later that football was displacing baseball as the premier game on South Carolina's campus and most of the other colleges. The bitter rivalry between the two biggest schools in the state had already become legendary.

The first full manifestation of the Carolina vs. Clemson face-off came in the aftermath of Carolina's 1902 victory, 12-6. It began shortly after the game's conclusion when South Carolina students produced a "transparency" of a gamecock crowing over a crouching tiger. When they marched down Columbia's Main Street with it in their midst Clemson students confronted them resulting for a brief time in "a scrimmage in which it is said knives and swords and knucks (sic) were used."

No one was seriously hurt but the transparency was badly damaged. Following the melee, the Carolina faithful returned to campus to produce another copy to use in the following day's Elks' parade. Clemson cadets were livid once more.

Efforts by authorities on both sides failed to find a compromise. The cadets marched to the brick wall of the Horseshoe on Sumter Street ready to storm the Carolina campus and destroy the new copy. At the last moment, cooler heads prevailed when a three-man committee of each side met and agreed to allow each side to get one half of the image and burn it before the other. [17] While little blood was shed, in the wake of this incident Carolina's board chose to ban the Clemson game for the next seven years.

Then three years later Carolina ended intercollegiate competition for the 1906 season. Apparently, the game's brutal nature and the student body's fanatical interest made the trustees decide that banning football was the best option for the school. However, USC's decision did not influence either Clemson or the two Charleston institutions to follow the same course.

As far as the College of Charleston and the Citadel were concerned their budding rivalry was the biggest for either in the first decade of the twentieth century. Although the college began playing regular inter-collegiate football two years before the military college, the cadets did not take long to catch up to their city neighbors.

After fierce opposition to student petitions that requested football, the commandant and his board reluctantly granted permission in late1904. Fears by the Citadel leaders that the game interfered with cadets' academic and 7 military training had finally been overcome.

The new Citadel team played mostly local teams both colleges and high schools. In this first decade of play one opponent included the "Medicos," a team of medical students from the Medical College of South Carolina.

But rival for the new Citadel varsity was the College of Charleston. And the biggest game in these early years probably was the 1910 contest between the two schools. [18] In October the Citadel seemed poised for another win over their city rival, having a larger, more physical side compared to the smaller college squad.

Furthermore, the cadets had not allowed their city rivals to score on them since 1907. Nevertheless. the bigger side was stymied all day, while the quicker, smaller "Maroons," found ways through and around the cadet defense.

The culminating play of the game, sealing the upset, was devised in a huddle by Alex "Frau" Pregnall, the College's speedy quarterback. After the ball was centered, Pregnall hid behind his backfield, stuffed the ball under his jersey (a legal move at this time), and took off. While the rest of his backfield headed around one end of the line the quarterback took off around the opposite end toward the Citadel goal line. Perplexed at first, the cadet defense only realized the ruse after Pregnall was well down the field. Although tackled just a few yards from a score after a sixty-yard gallop, it took just one more play for him to take it over sealing the victory, 11-0.[19]

Such a triumph, the only one over the Citadel in the College of Charleston's brief football history, was followed after the game by one of the college's biggest celebrations in the early sporting history of Charleston.

In the evening, a large parade of student fans marched through several streets in the center of the city, dressed in robes of white and banging two big drums while others made more noise with mouth organs and sundry other instruments.

Along the way they stopped to serenade businesses and undisclosed residences, including the Charleston News and Courier offices.20 College of Charleston fan support, coupled with the near riot in Columbia eight years before, is indicative of how college football had evolved into more than a game on most campuses across the state. Winning, especially against bitter rivals, was more important than having just a sporting competition.

The almost friendly atmosphere in the early contests between Furman and Wofford had changed. As the new century began nasty encounters between rival fans and players on the field began to resemble some of the games in the Northeast. An alum of the South

Carolina team of 1908 recalled a half[8] century later that in his playing days a bonfire and loud cheering began on campus the night before the Carolina- Clemson contest.

If the Gamecocks were victorious the student body had a "shirt tail parade" into downtown Columbia. At the game, itself the sidelines were jammed with over-zealous fans milling about, following the progress of the ball during each play. Shouts of all kinds, including advice to their teams and game officials, were punctuated by "waving streamers, sticks and derby hats." A similar atmosphere surrounded Citadel games.

Grandstands in these early years were few and often temporary; one paid thirty-five cents to sit, while the fans that stood on the sidelines paid ten cents less. These supporters often stepped onto the field of play forcing the game to be held up while officials shooed them off. And fights between rival fans made disruption of play even more frequent.[21] The teams on the field gave no quarter to their opponent either.

At Citadel games a former Bulldog, James Hammond, Class of 1907, recalled that "Anything went and there were plenty of injuries." Smaller players carrying the ball were nearly torn apart when their linemen pushed the ball carrier forward to gain yardage while the defensive team "dragged" him by the neck to hold him back. And verbal abuse between rival players could be just as abusive. This was especially the case when a player transferred from one school to another. One former Charleston native, who had played a season at the Citadel, recalled that when he changed sides the following season to join the rival Charleston Athletics, he was cursed at regularly during the game, but in Gullah.[22]

Based on such rough, abusive behavior, it would seem, as one historian has argued, that in the early decades of college football women were excluded from the sidelines or kept segregated from boisterous male fans. Granted few South Carolina colleges in the early twentieth century allowed women students. Those that did, South Carolina was one, had just a small cohort of co-eds, usually little more than ten per cent. Some all-male campuses, such as Furman, had a separate female campus.

Young ladies who attended Furman games usually had a male escort. Usually unescorted women who attended came in carriages and watched the game from them, somewhat protected from potentially rowdy fans, but not always. In Greenville at the November 1893, Furman game, Wofford had a contingent of female fans that came from Converse, Spartanburg's college for women. Here they seemed not to be segregated from the rest of the fans.

With nearly one [9] thousand in the temporary stands, the crowd included "an array of feminine beauty that could only be produced in the genial clime of the fair South-land."[23] At other Wofford games it seemed that female fans were more protected. The young women stood in the "neighboring piazzas" waving Wofford's black and gold covers.

At the most male-oriented college in the state, the Citadel, several "female sponsors" attended the home games to encourage the team and its cadets before and during each game. Young women from the all-female Chicora College in Columbia came to Carolina games escorted by male students. After one of the big victories over a rival in 1910 Carolina students made a procession to Chicora to proclaim their triumph to the girls on campus.[24]

Whether the growing excitement generated by the games at Carolina, Clemson, and Charleston had an impact or not, by 1913 the decade-long moratorium imposed by presidents at Furman and Wofford was wavering. Students of both schools had never liked the prohibition and each year had attempted, but failed, to have football reinstated.

Then, at the end of 1912, Furman's student body overwhelmingly voted that a three-student delegation plead their case to the Furman board meeting in Abbeville that December. Although what the argument was that persuaded the board to suspend their ban is unrecorded, the campus had a huge celebration when their representatives telegraphed the student body back in Greenville afterwards announcing the games' reinstatement. But perhaps the board had not needed too much persuasion.

Seven years later, on the eve of another football season, one Furman student proclaimed that the football team had a new and significant "drawing card" with a new stadium which would help encourage increase Furman's student body to five hundred. The team with the new stadium was now more than just a way to increase school spirit but it promoted the school beyond the confines of Greenville and helped with new student recruitment. It is difficult to know if the latter rational helped change the minds of other college administrations about allowing football but all had students' bodies that wanted the game allowed on their campuses.

Wofford reintroduced the game a year after its Greenville rival. Newberry College officially introduced inter-collegiate football the same year that Furman had reinstated it. Erskine College, a Presbyterian institution in Abbeville County, began its first team in 1915.

In each case the student body had lobbied for several years to either reinstate the game or allow it on campus for the first time. Presbyterian College in 10 Clinton, SC began play in 1913 after the faculty committee accepted a student petition with ninety signatures that football be permitted.

Perhaps because of student lobbying, college administrations began to realize that football at their campuses would help bring new students that everyone eagerly wanted.[25] Just as football began its renaissance on upstate campuses the nation found itself slowly getting entangled in an international crisis, World War I.

Until the United States declared war on Imperial Germany and its allies in April 1917, college football remained unaffected. Even in the fall season of 1917 college teams in the state seemed to carry on as they had in peace time. The only difference was that on most schedules one or two military teams were included. Along with Guildford (in North Carolina) and Presbyterian, Wofford also played the First New York Ambulance football team.

The military team was part of the 27th Division that came to train at the newly established Camp Wadsworth located on the western outskirts of Spartanburg. The army team was defeated by the college boys, 21-0. In Columbia, where Camp Jackson was established about the same time, the University of South Carolina used former players, then training at the camp, to serve as officials for their first game of the season versus Newberry.[26]

The new army installations that were forming in South Carolina (and across the nation) in the summer and fall of 1917 provided much more than just football officials and new opposition on the field. Because the new army recruits included former college players most units formed teams that had intra-squad games on base. Most military camps also formed all-star teams that competed against other military bases.

While their schedules were usually just a few games in the fall they provided great interest both on and off base. When Camp Jackson's team prepared to play Camp Gordon of Atlanta, Georgia in November, the local coverage of the game was extensive.

The State noted that both squads consisted of many stars from South Atlanta colleges, including Clemson and USC. The game was played at Melton field, the home field for the University of South Carolina, ending in a 10-0 victory for Camp Jackson.[27] A year later Army authorities initially discouraged football on those campuses that had Student Army Training Corps units.

Since most colleges in South Carolina had their male students enrolled it appeared that little, if any, football would be played for the 1918 season. But the Army's stand on football changed within a month. In early October, it was 11 announced in a Columbia newspaper that football would be permitted although travel and schedules would be curtailed. But more than the war situation seemed to curtail football, at least during the month of October.

In this period, the influenza pandemic had its greatest impact throughout the state and the nation, closing most public activities from church services to cinemas. It also had impact on football games. The University of South Carolina played just four games that year while Wofford and the Citadel had only three, all in November or December.

Military teams such as Camp Jackson and the Charleston Navy Yards Training Service teams continued play but with longer schedules.[28] Once the Armistice was signed in November 1918, ending the Great War, the reduced football on South Carolina's college campuses expanded with longer seasons and improved facilities. The only exception was the College of Charleston. With its student body of barely 100 and a miniscule budget, 1913 was its last season on the gridiron.

During the college's final two seasons its teams earned just one victory in ten games, ending its last season with embarrassing defeats to its Citadel rivals, 72 to 0, and Newberry, 39 to 0.[29] The rest of the state's schools continued, with improved student and financial support, under the umbrella of a formal league association. By 1914 the South Carolina Intercollegiate Athletic Association had most state schools under its umbrella with a written code of ethics and sportsmanship agreed upon by all members.

Although not all schools obeyed the code it was apparent intercollegiate athletics, especially football, had become more than just an occasional sport for nearly all the state's campuses. By the early 1920s the state's two largest schools left the state conference to join a new Southern Intercollegiate Conference. In 1921 Clemson became one of the first members with several other Southern schools, including Alabama, Georgia, and North Carolina, forming a fourteen-team conference known today as the Southern Conference.

The following year South Carolina joined with four other institutions. This association with formal rules regulated team behavior on and off the field with regard to recruiting and conference championships. Although the decade's perennial power, Furman, did not join the Southern Conference until the 1930s, it seemed satisfied with its dominance within the state football ranks until then.[30] [12]

By 1919 Furman began a run of titles that surpassed all the other state colleges through the twenties. Any qualms by the Furman administration about football had disappeared. In 1919 a new 10,000 seat Manly Stadium was inaugurated for the new season. This facility, with better players and a young, successful coach, Billy Laval, led to the Baptist-affiliated school's dominance of the state college ranks with six state titles through 1927.

By the 1922 season Furman Professor W.H. Coleman proudly wrote that students and faculty were united in their support of the football team in its mounting success, "The strong, clean teams that have represented Furman on diamond and gridiron . . . have added new brilliance to the name and fame of Furman." The Greenville college's strong football team gave the institution greater name recognition which many students and faculty thought attracted not only better athletes but more new students in general. [31]

None of the other state schools could claim such a record but all tried to build winning programs through hiring better coaches and recruiting top players. Clemson and Carolina built on their rivalry that had been cemented before 1917. Neither consistently challenged Furman in the decade after World War I but they never stopped trying. After the 1927 season Carolina went to the extreme of luring Furman's successful coach, Billy Laval, to Columbia. Although after his second season the new coach accused Carolina's student body of lacking sufficient spirit and commitment to the football team, there was still enough campus support that included the "Cheerios," student cheering section numbering 275.

Even with a loss to Clemson in 1929, the annual rivalry between the two state schools drew 14,000 fans. Indifferent records on the field could not dampen significant interest in the Gamecocks despite Laval's criticism.[32] Within the segregated college varsity programs of the state the competition to win had become just as strong even if it did not get the same coverage as its white college counter parts.

By the mid to late 1920s African American journalists began to scrutinize several black college athletic programs, including Claflin and South Carolina State. Noted civil rights leader, scholar and editor of the NACCP magazine, the Crisis, W.E.B. DuBois, severely criticized several black college athletic programs for recruiting abuses in which players had regular roster spots even though their academic records were poor to nonexistent.[33]

A DuBois assistant, George Streator, wrote in 1932 that for several years [13] South Carolina State, Claflin, and Allen had admitted athletes without reviewing their transcripts.

In particular he claimed that State had placed athletes on its football team who had played for the "last eight years" on teams in the region, he did not enumerate at what level but he seemed to suggest that they had played on other college teams.[34] Problems with illegal recruiting had become big issues in white schools across the nation by the 1920s. The University of South Carolina had already become embroiled in illegal recruiting prior to World War I.

After the 1914 season, with only two victories over its arch rival Clemson since their first game in 1896, Carolina alumni and local Columbia supporters decided to bring in players with better football credentials. By the middle of the 1915 season its surprising wins over state and out-of-state competition drew the suspicion of Clemson officials and investigators from around the state. Even Carolina faculty expressed suspicions. As one professor wrote to USC President Currell, "We're importing 'ringers' from Massachusetts, Pennsylvania, Illinois, and heaven only knows where else."[35]

Before the Clemson game in latc October several Carolina players were barred from playing because of eligibility questions. The rival match ended in a 0-0 tie. But the issue continued to affect the rest of the season with Davidson cancelling its game with Carolina outright after further evidence proved the original suspicions to be accurate.

With Carolina's student honor system severely compromised the president had to act. Currell dismissed two players for falsifying their records and two others left on their own accord to avoid further publicity.

In addition, the Gamecocks had to forfeit three of their early wins of the 1915 season. While the school regained some of its respect in the academic community the next year it suffered another dismal season.[36] In any event by the end of the First World War colleges across the state had decided that competitive football teams were important for their campuses.

So even as Clemson and South Carolina had 5-5 records against each other during the decade and only moderate success against other competition within and beyond the Palmetto State any reservations about varsity football were forgotten. Similarly, other schools in the Palmetto State, from Erskine and Wofford to the Citadel in Charleston, had modest football records but it did not discourage varsity play.

Erskine had only two winning seasons after 1921. Likewise, Wofford had few wins to boast about during the decade, losing all six games against its Furman rival during the decade. While there is still more research 14 15 required to delineate the social and economic impact of football on South Carolina college campuses, this paper has tried to demonstrate that college football had become a main stay by the twenties for the Palmetto State. Although the money and influence it has on today's campuses is considerably greater football's social and economic value was already accepted and promoted by students and most of South Carolina's college faculties and administrations by 1930.[37]

Notes

[1] Undated news clipping, Furman football folder, (probably the January 1891 based on Furman Football Media Guide, 2008, 199), Special Collections and Archives, Furman University Library, Greenville, SC. The author has not found a rule book or clear description of how these first games were played in South Carolina. The best idea of how football was played in the early years see, Wofford College Journal, January 1891, 20- 22, Wofford College Archives, Spartanburg, SC.

[2] Ibid.

[3] For analysis of the origins of football in the US and its early history and controversy in the 1880s through the 1900s see John S. Watterson, College Football: History, Spectacle, Controversy, (London: John Hopkins University Press, 2000), 23-24, 28, 78, 171-172; John H. Moore, "Football's Ugly Decades, 1893- 1913," in Steven A. Reiss, The American Sporting Experience, (West Point, NY: Leisure Press, 1994), 168, 171-172. For some early rules of football and their evolution see David M. Nelson, The Anatomy of the Game, (Newark, De: University of Delaware, 1991), 436- 438.

[4] Undated news clipping [1891], Furman football folder. Wofford College Journal, January 1891.

[5] Carolyn B. Matalene and Katherine C. Reynolds, (ed.) Carolina Voices: Two Hundred Years of Student Experiences, (University of South Carolina Press: Columbia, 2001), 97.

[6] For early inter-mural football at Carolina, Garnet and Black, 1912; for Newberry College see Gordon C. Henry, (ed.) God Bless Newberry College: Memories of Newberry College's Yesterday and Today, (Newberry College, Newberry, SC, 2006), 170; for Wofford College see junior class team photo, 1904, Wofford College Archives, Spartanburg, SC.

7 John Heisman published resume, Clemson, 1900, Football folder, Special Collections, Clemson University Libraries, Clemson, S.C. John Heisman: Principles of Football, (University of Georgia Press, Athens, 2000), originally published 1922. For Wofford see Wofford College Journal, (December 1889), 21 and South Carolina see Garnet and Black, 1901, University of South Carolina Library, Columbia, SC.

[8] Undated newspaper clipping, [1891], Furman football file," Furman. The Wofford Journal, (January 1891), 19, Wofford College Archives.

[9] For Georgia and North Carolina see Stegeman, The Ghost of Herty Field, 2-3, 10, 27. 16

[10] Claflin team photo, dated 1899, is in possession of John Daye, Irmo, SC, but nothing further has been found to date about the team. For early SC State College football records, A Century of Football SC State University, 2007 Bulldog Media Guide, 70; South Carolina State College Athletic Reunion, April 5-8, 1990, this pamphlet provides more details about its early football history, including conflicting information on the college's first opponent in 1907, according to this they defeated Georgia State, South Carolina State University Library Archives, Orangeburg, SC, the author thanks his colleague, Elaine Nichols, for locating this.

[11] Schedule for College of Charleston, 1903-1912, compiled by John Daye, Irmo, SC, copy provided the author.

[12] The schedules for both schools are based on Furman 2008 (Football) Media Guide, 166-167.

[13] Edited versions of the letters from Wofford and Furman, as well as Presbyterian and Erskine, were solicited by Newberry College Board

Chair, George Cromer, in 1911 when that school began contemplating the introduction of varsity football, see Henry "God Bless Newberry College, 169

[14] David D. Wallace, History of Wofford College, 1854- 1949, (Nashville, TN: Vanderbilt University Press, 1951), 109.

[15] Alfred S. Reid, Furman University: Toward a New Identity, 1925-1975, (Durham: Duke University Press, 1976), 22; Robert N. Daniel, Furman: A History, (Greenville: Furman University, 1951), 107, 110.

[16] For the State articles from the Northeast see December 6, 20, 1905, I wish to thank Ann Watts, Columbia, SC for locating these two articles.

[17] For growing importance of football on campus see James H. Hammond narrative on early football at Citadel and Carolina, Class of 1907, in a letter dated August 4, 1961, Hammond Papers, Manuscripts Room, South Caroliniana Library, USC, Columbia, SC, the author thanks Ann Watts of Columbia, SC for locating this fascinating account. For account of the 1902 near riot see, Matalene and Reynolds, Carolina Voices, 100-102.

[18] For the beginning of Citadel football see Hammond narrative, 1961, SCL; for the College of Charleston see Katherine Chaddock and Carolyn Matalene (ed.) College of Charleston Voices: Campus and Community through the Centuries, (The History Press: Charleston, 2006), 95-96.

[19] Chaddock and Matalene, College of Charleston Voices, 95-96. The author is indebted to William Pregnall, Irvington, Va. for sharing his memories of his father's athletic career and a copy of his unpublished manuscript about his father that included several copies of news articles, including a description of the 1910 game dated October 23, 1910.

[20] Chaddock and Matalene, College of Charleston Voices, 96.

[21] James Hammond narrative, Class of 1907, SCL; this account seems to have confused the dates since Carolina did not play Clemson during the years 1903 to 1908 although he refers to the

game as taking place in 1908. Since Hammond was recalling events more than a half a century later he probably meant to say 1909 when the rivalry resumed.

[22] Ibid.

[23] Wofford College Journal, December 1893, 118.

[24] Wofford College Journal, April 1893; James Hammond narrative, Class of 1907, SCL. 17

[25] Bonhomie (Furman annual) 1913, Special Collections, Furman; Henry, God Bless Newberry College, 176; Lowry Ware, A Place called Due West, n.d., thanks to Richard Haldeman of Due West for providing this information and notes to the author. For Presbyterian College student petition and faculty agreement to allow football see Faculty Committee Minutes, (May 29, 1913, 72), Special Collections, Presbyterian College Library, Clinton, SC.

[26] State, 1, 5, 14 Oct 1917

[27] State, 1, 10 Nov. 1917; thanks to John Daye, Irmo, SC, for providing further details about military teams during World War I. He will detail this and more in a forthcoming book scheduled for release in summer, 2010, "Armed Services Football: A History of Service Teams in Wartime and Peace."

[28] For Army's changes in football for colleges in 1918 see The State, 13 Sept., 4 October 1918, thanks to Kate Jernigan, USC student volunteer intern, for locating this information. On the impact of the influenza on the state and nation see Fritz Hamer, ed. Forward Together: South Carolinians in the Great War, (Charleston: The History Press), 44-48. For reduced schedules for these teams see John C. Griffin, The First Hundred Years: A History of South Carolina Football, (Atlanta: Longstreet Press, 1992), 157; www.ahtletics.wofford.edu/sports then click on Football archives; Citadel Bulldogs [Football] Media Guide, 2009, 131.

[29] Chaddock and Matalene, College of Charleston Voices, 95; College of Charleston football record came from South Carolina colleges football records file (compiled by Rich Topp, Chicago, Ill.) shown at

the SC State Museum exhibition, "Mud, Sweat, and Cheers: A History of Palmetto State football," 1 August 2008- 8 February 2009; on funding problems at this time see Walter Fraser, Jr., Charleston! Charleston! (University of South Carolina Press: Columbia, 1991), 350. Note that although published sources claim all football ended at the College after 1913, it appeared that at least one more game was played after the war against Erskine, see The State, October 14, 1921. The author is indebted to John Daye, Irmo, SC, for providing this source.

[30] For an early reference to the state association see "Presbyterian College Faculty Minutes," (1913), (1914), Special Collection, PC Library; for the 1920s see Furman Football Program, 1928, Special Collections, Furman Library. For the history of the Southern Conference see its web site, http://www.soconsports.com/ViewArticle.dbml?DB_OEM_ID=400 0&KEY=&ATCLID =... Other members of the original conference were Auburn, Georgia Tech, Kentucky, Maryland, Mississippi State, North Carolina State, Tennessee, Virginia, Virginia Tech and Washington & Lee

[31] Official Furman Football Program, 1922, Special Collection, Furman.

[32] Garnet and Black, 1929. During the twenties Carolina lost seven and won just three over Furman from 1919 to 1930. Clemson's record during the same period was little better at six losses, three wins and one tie, Furman 2008 Football Media Guide, 199. For fan attendance see New York Times, October 25, 1929, the author thanks Debra Bloom, Librarian, Richland County Library, Columbia, SC, for locating this article.

[33] Patrick B. Miller (ed.), The Sporting World of the Modern South, (Chicago: University of Illinois Press, 2002), 137-138.

[34] Ibid., 138-139. 18

[35] Miller, Sporting World in South, 139. Daniel Hollis, University of South Carolina: College to University, (University of South Carolina Press: Columbia, 1956), 282-284.

[36] Ibid., 284

[37] The records of the schools in the 1920s are based on data compiled in, Furman 2008 Media Guide, 167-168 ; Ware, A Place called Due West, n.d., "Erskine College football results, 1915-1951," thanks Richard Haldeman, Due West, SC, for supplying a copy of this to the author.

Chapter 5 CU Launches First "Official" Football Team

Riggs,	Coach #1
Williams	Coach #2
Penton	Coach #3
Riggs	Coach #1 repeat

Year	Coach	Record	Conf	Record
1896	Walter M. Riggs	2-1-0	SIAA	0-0-0
1897	Wm. M. Williams	2-2-0	SIAA	0-1-0
1898	John Penton	3-1-0	SIAA	1-1-0
1899	Walter M. Riggs	4-2-0	SIAA	1-2-0

Finally, after the college had been operating as an academic institution for seven years, just in time for the fall season in 1906, Clemson threw its hat in the football ring. Actually, CU had its hat gently placed there by a great man and a great coach, Walter Riggs.

1896 Team Picture below: Clemson's First Varsity Football Team

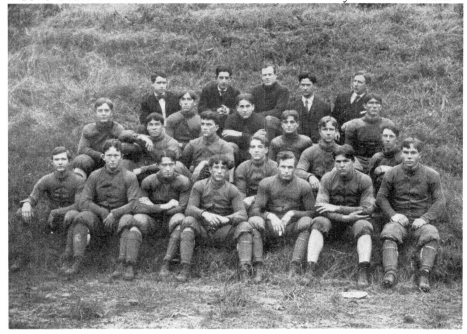

Clemson's football program is a long and storied one. Some say that the Clemson program does not necessarily command the prestige of

programs like Oklahoma, Notre Dame, or Michigan. However, the coaches over the past thirty years have really made the nation notice Clemson, especially with its second National Championship in the 2016 season.

Walter Riggs--Clemson's 1st Head Football Coach

Quite Frankly, Clemson has always been a great team from its first season in 1896 to its last season 120 years later in 2016. After all, John Heisman was brought to Clemson by Walter Riggs as he was preparing to be the Clemson president. Only a few teams in the nation have a John Heisman on their immortal coaches list.

So, with two National Championships, a winning tradition, having beaten state rival South Carolina often, and having celebrated many influential head coaches and players, Clemson surely needs to make no apologies for its record.

The man who made it all happen was named Walter M. Riggs. He was responsible for the creation of an official Clemson University football program as well as its continuation and livelihood throughout the beginning of the twentieth century.

Riggs was quite a guy. He graduated from what is now Auburn University in 1892 where he played on their newly formed football team, back when American football rules were just being created by another Walter. Walter Camp worked hard to perfect the game of American football so as to differentiate it from Rugby and Soccer.

Riggs was a versatile young man and his interests were many. He was a natural leader. For example, he was the head of the Auburn Glee club and was a member of Phi Delta Theta. He was pretty good with the books also as he earned a Bachelor of Science degree in both mechanical and electrical engineering.

Riggs loved football at a time when many schools were just toying around with the notion of Walter Camp style American football. He soon became the head coach of the Auburn Tigers (1893), but he chose to move to Clemson after the 1895 season. At Auburn, Riggs had recruited John Heisman for the coaching staff and when Riggs came to Clemson, he was so respected that he was able to hand over control of Auburn's program to this same John Heisman. Yes, this is the Heisman that the trophy is named after.

And, so, as the Administration was ready to give in to pressure to form a team, they were able to snag Walter Riggs to be their first Clemson football head coach in 1996. Like everybody in football back then, when temporary bleachers were often unaffordable by colleges, Riggs had to improvise.

He ignored the property of Auburn on the older, very worn Auburn jerseys and because he and his new team were low on money, Riggs stole a few of the Auburn practice jerseys for the newly minted

Clemson players. The navy color was mostly faded out. Only a discerning eye could detect a blue. Auburn was orange and blue and so Clemson's official colors became orange, and later on, a faded navy-purple color called Regalia.

Riggs did not bother innovating on silly things like names because after all everybody has one. So, while he was stealing the jerseys, he stole the mascot name – Tigers. The Auburn Tigers never missed it as they still have it. So, Clemson also owes its mascot, the Fighting Tiger to Riggs's Auburn affections for the Tiger. Like I said, Riggs was quite a guy. In a time when nobody had anything, Riggs made due and he got the Clemson football program off the ground.

Not only did hc bring the notion of football to Clemson, but he received the honor of being the head coach to start the program and then again in 1899 when there were no finds for the athletic department. Ironically, this year, 1899, was the first year that Clemson ever played Auburn.

Riggs was not the finesse and mathematical strategy coach that John Heisman was and so Auburn, under Heisman took advantage of Riggs years away from the game in 1900. Under the guidance of John Heisman, Auburn won that first meeting of "cousin by coaches' teams" 34-0. In 1900, Riggs had had his fill as he was destined for other tasks at Clemson. He officially stepped down as head coach.

John Heisman really liked Walter Riggs and that says something nice about both of the men. So, Riggs hired Heisman to coach from 1900 to 1903. Clemson's first home game under Heisman was against Davidson College on Bowman Field in 1900.

Riggs continued to work for the university as a professor in engineering, but his real passion was for athletics. He created the position of athletic director, which is currently held today by Dan Radakovich. Riggs became the president of the Southern Intercollegiate Athletics Association (SIAA) in 1912. The SIAA had 72 members when it was dissolved and comprised almost all of the members of the current Southeastern Conference (SEC), six from the Atlantic Coast Conference (ACC) and the University of Texas at Austin in the Big 12, as well as other schools that are not in Division I football.

In order to alleviate the usage of Bowman Field, a rag tag field that had served its time, a new field was to be built on the north side of campus. In 1915, it was finished and it was aptly named Riggs Field. Riggs Field was the first of many solely athletic facilities to be built on Clemson's campus. It was where the Clemson football team played until they moved to Memorial Stadium in 1942. Now it is currently being used by the men's and women's soccer teams and has been since 1980.

Walter Riggs died in 1924, two days before his 51st birthday. Some say that he worked himself too hard. In the end, his dedication and sacrifice has led Clemson to be a home for one of the top athletic programs in the nation.

In a fitting turn of events, the Clemson football team played Auburn to kick off its 2016 football season on September 3. Knowing that Clemson became National Champions, we all know it would have been quite difficult if the C Tigers lost to the A Tigers. It did not happen that way. On its way to the Championship, the Clemson Tigers survived a tough battle against an always tough Auburn Tigers squad, and won the game W (19-13). The stadium crew spent the next day cleaning up all the bitten nails. Go Fighting Tigers!

OK, so now that we have introduced the first official encounter with an oval shaped ball (football), made possible by the perspicacity of Walter M. Riggs, the first coach of the Clemson Fighting Tigers, let's look at the game as played on 1896 in the Clemson football inaugural season, known forever to the common folk such as you and me as Clemson's first football game.

1896: Clemson Tigers Coach Walter M. Riggs

The 1896 Clemson Tigers football team represented the Clemson Agricultural College during the 1896 college football season. Professor / Coach Walter Riggs brought the game to Clemson from his alma mater, Auburn, where he was a member of Auburn's first football team. The Tigers completed their first season with a record of 2–1. They became members of the Southern Intercollegiate

Athletic Association (SIAA) from day one and continued from 1896–1921, at which time, they joined the Southern Conference (SoCon).

They got their wins over upstate neighboring SC colleges Furman and Wofford, and they got their only loss of the season in the first installment of what immediately became a rivalry with South Carolina.

All Clemson games were played in the opposing school's home city as the Clemson Tigers were not yet prepared to play at home. The rivalry matchup with South Carolina was held on a Thursday morning at the South Carolina state fair, a tradition that would endure until 1960. In this encounter, Riggs served as the team's coach while R. G. Hamilton was the first team captain. Rules at the time prohibited the coach from offering direction from the sidelines.

The games of the season

The season opened up on October 31 at Furman, a team that had been playing for several years. The game was played in Greenville, SC. The Clemson Tigers emerged victorious with a nice but close win W (14–6).

Not many Clemson fans know R.G. Hamilton, but you should. Hamilton was the captain of Clemson's first football team in 1896. Below is some information on Clemson's first football team from an article on Clemson's web site:

After grueling practices, the first-ever Clemson football game day finally arrived. On October 31, 1896, Clemson traveled to Furman (probably by train). George Swygert, center on the first Clemson football team, recalls the Furman game and the first season as follows:

"With Professor Riggs as our coach we got in shape fairly well. Our first game was with Furman, the biggest men I have ever seen, and believe it or not we won that game. We had a few trick plays. One was when the play ended near the side lines, our lightest end would hide the ball under his sweater and as the two teams moved toward the center of the field for the next play, he appeared to be injured, and then when things were clear, he made a bee-line for the goal.

This worked maybe once a game, it worked against Furman our first game."

Very few details of the Clemson-Furman game are known, but it is known that Charlie Gentry scored Clemson's first touchdown in history. The Tigers defeated Furman 14-6 at Greenville, SC. Below is a rare photo of Clemson's first football team.

Clemson's First Football Team 1896 Another Picture

On November 12, the Tigers traveled to South Carolina to play in Columbia against the Gamecocks. It was called Big Thursday. SC had much more experience with American Football and were able to defeat Riggs' Tigers by a close score of L (6-12. On November 21, the Saturday before Thanksgiving, another more experienced team, Wofford played the Clemson Tigers at their home field in Spartanburg, SC. The Clemson Tigers were a tough team and took no prisoners as they beat Wofford, W (16–0)

And so, the inaugural season with professor / coach Riggs was very successful at 2 wins and just one loss. The Tiger had become unleashed and many great games and a great winning tradition would come from this, Clemson's first football season.

There was a contagion of great coaches spawned by the greatness of one coach to a protégé at the time. For example, Jack "Pee Wee" Forsythe, was the first Head Coach for the Florida Gators. He was a former Clemson Tigers lineman who played for coach THE John Heisman from 1901 to 1903. Isn't football great?

<< The 1st Gator Coach. Jack Forsythe was a real coach but he also played on the team as an end, just like Knute Rockne was an end. Forsythe used a technique known as the Minnesota shift to get the advantage over opponents.

Since 1906, when Clemson's own Jack Forsythe enabled the Gators' debut, Florida has had a football season every year until 1943 when the war demands were such that even if a university could field a team, they would have a tough time finding another team to play.

Another pic of the 1896 Team is shown above:

1897: Clemson Tigers Coach William M. Williams

The rules of football were in flux at this time. One rule was changed in 1897. A team scoring a touchdown received five points, and the goal after touchdown added another point. This scoring value would remain until 1912.

<<< Coach William Williams

The 1897 Clemson Tigers football team represented the Clemson Agricultural College during the 1897 college football season as a member of the SIAA. William M. Williams served as the team's coach for his first season while W. T. Brock was the captain. The Tigers completed their second season with a record of 2–2-0 and an 0-1 record in the SIAA. They had nice wins over South Carolina and a Charlotte YMCA team, and they lost to Georgia and North Carolina. Since there was no home field yet, all games were played in the opposing school's home city. Despite this disadvantage, and the small number of games played, the team was state champion.

Games of 1897 the season.

The Fighting Tigers kicked off the season at Georgia at Herty Field in Athens, GA. This matchup would blossom into a rivalry over the years. The Tigers lost the game. Next, on Oct 23, Clemson traveled to Charlotte to play their YMCA team. The Tigers won the game W (10-0). The next trip was to play North Carolina at Chapel Hill and the Tigers suffered their second loss L (0-28). In a game that gave the Tigers their first state championship, they beat South Carolina at Columbia on what has been dubbed Big Thursday W (18-6).

1898: Clemson Tigers Coach John Penton

The 1898 Clemson Tigers football team represented the Clemson Agricultural College during the 1898 college football season as a member of the SIAA.

<<< Coach John Penton— Penton served as the team's coach for his first season while Shack Shealy was the captain. The Tigers completed their second season with a record of 3–1-0 and a 1-1 record in the SIAA. They had nice wins over Bingham Military School, South Carolina and Georgia Tech and they lost to Georgia again. For the first time, Clemson played a home game in Calhoun SC on October 20 against Bingham Military School, and a neutral site game at Augusta, Georgia against Georgia Tech.

The season opener was Oct 8 at Georgia in an SIAA game. The Tigers got their one loss out of the way in the first game played in Herty Field in Athens GA. L (8-20). The next game was Oct 20 at an undisclosed location on campus against the Bingham Military School W (55-0) The Tigers were on the rod on Nov 17 after a month off up to Columbia SC on Big Thursday and they claimed a fine win v SC's Gamecocks W (24-0). Finishing up the season, on Nov 24, Clemson shut out Georgia Tech W (23-0) for their first SIAA victory. Nice season

1899: Clemson Tigers Coach William M. Riggs

The 1899 Clemson Tigers football team represented the Clemson Agricultural College during the 1899 college football season as a member of the SIAA. William Riggs, who was a professor at Clemson, and who had coached its first team, came back for an encore. So, he served as the team's coach for his second season while J. N. Walker was the captain. The Tigers completed their fourth season with a record of 4-2-0 and a 1-2 record in the SIAA. As you can see, the team was able to secure more games each season.

They had nice wins over Davidson, South Carolina and SIAA Georgia Tech and they lost to SIAA Georgia again. They also lost to SIAA Auburn. Clemson again did not host any games, but played a mix of away and neutral site games. Walter Riggs picked up a labor of love again as coach, having also led the team in its inaugural 1896 season.

The season opened on Oct 7 at Georgia. Again, the SIAA Conference Georgia Bulldogs beat the Clemson Tigers but each time the score is closer. This game was played in Herty Field in Athens, GA L (0-11). On Oct 14, the Tigers beat Davidson at Rock Hill, SC W (10-0). Another tough SIAA team, Auburn beat Clemson two weeks later on Oct 28 at their stadium in Auburn, AL L (0-34). On Nov 9, the Tigers beat the Gamecocks of SC on Big Thursday W (24-0).

On Nov 18, the Fighting Tigers traveled to play North Carolina. A&M at Rock Hill, SC in the first Textile Bowl W (24-0) Later historians think the series began in 1981 but it has been played 85 times including 1899. The Textile Bowl is an American college football rivalry game played annually by the Clemson Tigers football team of Clemson University and the NC State Wolfpack football team of North Carolina State University. The rivalry game has been formally known as the Textile Bowl for some time. The south is big on textiles. On Nov. 30, Clemson played at Greenville SC against Georgia Tech and the Tigers beat the Yellow Jackets in a blowout W 41–5. The next season, John Heisman came to town.

Before John Heisman came to Clemson for the 1890 season, Clemson's record was 9-6-0 overall and 2-4-0 in the SIAA. 9-6-0 is not a bad start for a brand- new football program. Winning in a tough conference always take some time. John Heisman's time had come.

Chapter 6 Historic Clemson Fields & Stadiums

First there was Bowman Field

From its initial land donation, the Clemson Campus began huge. Its setting is suburban, and the campus size is 17,000 acres. With such a huge land mass, there would be no excuse for the University to not have terrific athletic fields with plenty of space for both varsity play and pure fun for students.

Though Clemson opted to play all away games for many of its early football years while the campus was being prepared for sports, eventually, one of their academic instructors worked hard enough to make sure Clemson was able to play home games. Cut from some of the 17,000 acres, Bowman Field is an extremely large, open grassy area located in front of Sikes Hall, Tillman Hall, Godfrey Hall, Holtzendorff Hall, and Mell Hall. It is the front lawn of the campus.

The field is named for Randolph T. V. Bowman, an instructor in forge and foundry, at Clemson Agricultural College of South Carolina from February 1895 to April 1899, just after the college opened in 1889. who also served as an assistant football coach.

Bowman met with an early death at 23 years of age on April 14, 1899. The field became the parade ground for Clemson cadets and the home of Clemson University's first football, baseball, basketball teams, track and even soccer teams.

Randolph Bowman had apparently suffered from ill-health from his early years, yet he persevered as if he had no handicaps. He received a great tribute from Clemson President Henry Simms Hartzog who noted that "Though physically unable to take any considerable part in athletics, he helped [...] by his counsel and presence."

Just before his death, Bowman finished carving the commemorative plaques for Professor Henry Aubrey Strode, Clemson College's first president, and Professor W. L. McGee, now displayed in Tillman Auditorium. Bowman Field, Clemson's "front lawn", of course is named in his honor: Bowman is said to have personally cleared the former sedge field of rocks and other detritus so that it could be used as an athletics ground.

Yes, while serving as an assistant coach, Bowman took responsibility for much of the hard work required in clearing of the field area for use as an athletics field.

The two 19th-century cannons located on the field were nicknamed Tom and Jerry by the class of 1952. Bowman Field sure has a lot of history.

It is a great testimony to the spirit of Randolph Bowman that he received the honor of the first Clemson field being named after him. He was quite a young man. Like many other greats in life, Bowman was not blessed with all the physical gifts that assure a successful life, yet, he not only persevered, he conquered all the Bogeymen he faced in life but one.

Despite his powerful spirit, even he could not chase away the Grim Reaper and so he died a young man, with many accomplishments and many accomplishments that would have come. The Randolf Bowman story is inspiring. In many ways, it resembles two of my favorite perseverance fables-- The Little Engine That Could and The King and The Spider.

Randolph Bowman was in many ways like Vikram, the brave king who learned to believe in himself as noted in his own words: "If a small spider can face failure so bravely, why should I give up? He was also like the little Blue Train, The Little Engine That Could, who would not give up when bigger trains said no, and he carried the toys to the other side of the mountain so as not to disappoint the children.

But, even more special than the heroes in these fables, Randolph Bowman was just like the real Randolph Bowman. He was true to himself and all those he met. He never said no to a worthwhile challenge and he would succeed when others would give up without even picking up the cup. Clemson University is honored to have Randolph Bowman in its proud institutional and football legacy. I was very moved by his personal story.

Clemson continued over the years to improve Bowman Field even after Riggs Field and Memorial Stadium were built. I am sure Randolph Bowman would humbly approve. Today Bowman Field is regarded as "sacred soil," having played such a large part in Clemson's history and being the central location for leisure activity for students. On most any day with nice weather you are likely to see students laying out, tanning, studying, throwing frisbee, playing football, volleyball, soccer, or even playing with their dogs.

Bowman Field is used by many organizations throughout the year for a whole variety of different activities. Clemson AFROTC can be seen using the field for practice marches on most Thursday afternoons. Clemson fraternities and sororities also use Bowman Field for their many activities like Powderpuff Football. First Friday activities are usually held here and once a year, Homecoming floats are built on Bowman Field, in full view of all passing pedestrians and motorists. Habitat for Humanity builds a house for charity right on Bowman Field every year at Homecoming. Its use for parking vehicles for football games was discontinued in the 1990s over concerns of the damage done to the lawn.

Riggs Field

Bowman Field served all of Clemson's needs from 1889 to 1915. Riggs Field became Clemson's second football field, with a tour of duty from the football program lasting from 1915to 1941. Just like Bowman Field is still in high use today, so also is Riggs Field. It has now been remodeled into the university's soccer stadium.

The Original Riggs Field Circa 1915

As you recall, the founder of Clemson Football was Walter Merit Riggs who was Clemson's President and the first (and fourth) head football coach. Riggs is given credit for being the "Father of Clemson Football" insofar as his bringing the game from Auburn to the new Clemson campus is concerned.

When Clemson played its first football game against Furman on October 31, 1896, only two people on the Clemson campus had ever seen a football game - Riggs, and Tiger backfielder Frank Thompkins, a Tiger team plank-holder.

Riggs Field was designed in 1915 to replace Bowman Field. It was located right behind the Rudolph E. Lee-designed YMCA building, and it was finished the following year. Players would dress inside the Y and then come down the staircase from the rear portico of the structure to field level. Having the Y so close meant no locker room facilities were required at Riggs.

Riggs Field was dedicated October 2, 1915, prior to the football game with Davidson College. A parade to the field formed in front of the main building at 3 p.m. led, in this order, by the Cadet Band, speakers, Athletic Council, Alumni, faculty, and the Corps of Cadets.

"Upon entering Riggs Field, the body took a 'C' formation and poured forth a thrilling volume of patriotic Tiger yells and songs." (The Tiger, 5 October 1915, Volume XI, Number 3, page 1.)

Presentation of the field to the Corps of Cadets by Dr. Walter Merritt Riggs followed. Prof. J. W. Gantt, President of the Athletic Association, introduced Dr. Riggs as "the man who has done more for the athletics at Clemson and probably more for Southern athletics than any other man." "In presenting the field to the corps of cadets, Dr. Riggs said in part; 'This magnificent field is a token of recognition by the Trustees of Clemson College of the importance of military and athletic training for the cadets. It is to be a place for the teaching of the principles of team work and fair play.

On the crest of the hill stands the main Building which represents the intellectual side of life. In the immediate fore-ground you can see the Textile Building. Here the brain and hand are trained to work together. Just to our left is the magnificent new Y. M. C. A. Building, standing for the development of spirit, mind, and body. In the immediate vicinity in the back are the churches, which are agents in the influencing of our spiritual natures.

This large and beautiful athletic field was built to stand for the development of the physical man, and, whether in real work or in play the hope was for the field to be used as an agency in the developing of high and honorable men. (Mostly from The Tiger, 5 October 1915, page 1.)

Prof. Gantt then introduced Mr. H. C. Tillman, Class of 1903 and President of the Clemson Alumni Association, who christened the new playing field. Tillman offered these words: "Students who have been and are to be, no matter how much we love other things, we love our athletic ficld bcst. Therefore, this field should be named for him who has done most for our athletics. Dr. Riggs is not only the father of athletics at Clemson but has coached our teams. It is not alone for gratitude, but for a sense of love and esteem that we name this field. May it bring victory to the Tigers' lair, and may it be represented by the honor and spirit Dr. Riggs has always shown. In the name of all students and lovers of Clemson, I christen this Field Riggs Field."

A few minutes later, Dr. Riggs made the initial kick-off in the first football game to be played on the new field. Clemson and Davidson play to a 6-6 tie.

Riggs Field was the place for football for many years. Construction got underway for the new Memorial Stadium in October, 1941. The last game played on Riggs Field was against Wake Forest, on November 15, 1941. It was a fitting sendoff to the old Riggs football venue as the Tigers shut out the Demon Deacons, 29-0. Three weeks later, the Japanese Navy attacked Pearl Harbor, Hawaii, setting America's involvement in World War II into motion.

As football games were played in Memorial Stadium, Riggs Field, just like Bowman Field began to be used for other worthwhile athletic and recreational purposes. For example, in 1973, Riggs Field was the location for a closing scene of the Burt Lancaster film The Midnight Man.

Riggs Field, with its large half-mile oval cinder track, remained an intramural space through the 1970s, providing a site for Greek Week, Dixie Day, and the Special Olympics. In late March 1980, without informing anyone, the athletic department began grading of the historic Riggs Field site for transformation into the new soccer stadium. Dixie Day was moved to the soccer field located north of Death Valley on short notice.

The remodeled facility, seating 6,500, opened its new era on September 1, 1987 with a Men's soccer team win over UNC-Asheville, 8-0.

In early September 2011, the stadium which surrounds Riggs Field was named Ibrahim Stadium after the late Dr. I.M Ibrahim, who is credited with starting Clemson's men's soccer program in 1967 and who led the team to national titles in 1984 and 1987.

Riggs Kept Improving

In 2013, Riggs Field completed another round of renovations. As part of the renovation, stands were constructed to replace bleachers on the north side of the stadium. Additionally, a new entrance was constructed on the side of the stadium and pedestrian improvements were installed along the north side between the stadium and highway SC 93. A memorial to Walter Riggs was constructed at the new entrance on the north side. Renovations were completed in time for the 2013 soccer season.

Celebrating 100 Years of Riggs

On October 2, 2015, Clemson University celebrated Riggs Field's 100th anniversary. The Clemson University men's and women's soccer teams both played vs Virginia Tech and Wake Forest, respectively. Special promotions included a museum in the nearby indoor track to display artifacts and photos from Riggs Field's history, 2000 commemorative scarves to celebrate the occasion, and one uniform was given away during the women's game.

Riggs Field 2015 Construction

Historic Riggs Field Now Built for Soccer

Memorial Stadium – AKA Death Valley

Courtesy of Clemson tigers.com

Clemson Memorial Stadium is the third venue in which the Clemson Tigers played the game of football. With this latest iteration, many more fans could enjoy the game. Everybody has an opinion of "Death Valley." Opposing players from the 1970s and 1980s, professional players from the 1990s, and just about everybody else enjoy the ambiance of this special setting and most understand that this is what college football is all about.

The storied edifice added to its legend when the first meeting of father and son head coaches (Bowden Bowl I) took place before a sellout crowd of more than 86,000 fans in 1999. Clemson has ranked in the top 20 in the nation in average attendance 22 consecutive seasons. That includes 2001 when Clemson set an ACC record for total attendance. Last season, the streak continued when Clemson averaged nearly 79,000 fans per game.

The facility's mystique is derived from its many traditions, which date to its opening in 1942, the legendary games and players, and Clemson's corresponding rate of success. Clemson has won 227 games in 63 years there and has won over 71 percent of the contests (227-88-7). Thirty-nine times since 1983, a crowd has exceeded 80,000.

The stadium has definitely been good to the Tigers, but the stadium was constructed against the advice of at least one Clemson coach. Just before Head Coach Jess Neely left for Rice after the 1939 season, he gave Clemson a message. "Don't ever let them talk you into building a big stadium," he said. "Put about 10,000 seats behind the YMCA. That's all you'll ever need."

Instead of following Coach Neely's advice, however, Clemson officials decided to build the new stadium in a valley on the western part of campus. The place would take some clearing-there were many trees, but luckily there were no hedges. The crews went to work, clearing, cutting, pouring, and forming. Finally, on September 19, 1942, Memorial Stadium opened with Clemson thrashing Presbyterian by a score of 32-13. Those 20,000 seats installed for Opening Day would soon grow; and grow and grow.

When the original part of the stadium was built in the early 40's, much of the work was done by scholarship athletes, including many football players. The first staking out of the stadium was done by two members of the football team, A.N. Cameron and Hugh Webb. Webb returned to Clemson years later to be an architecture professor, and Cameron went on to become a civil engineer in Louisiana.

The building of the stadium did not proceed without problems. One day during the clearing of the land, one young player proudly announced that he was not allergic to poison oak. He then commenced to attack the poison oak with a swing blade, throwing the plants to and fro. The next day, the boy was swollen twice his size and was hospitalized.

There are many other stories about the stadium, including one that Frank Howard put a chew of tobacco in each corner as the concrete poured. Howard said that the seeding of the grass caused a few problems. "About 40 people and I laid sod on the field," he said. "After three weeks, on July 15, we had only gotten halfway through." "I told them that it had taken us three weeks to get that far, and I would give them three more week's pay for however long it took. I also told them we would have 50 gallons of ice cream when we got through. After that it took them three days to do the rest of the field.

Then we sat down in the middle of the field and ate up that whole 50 gallons."

Howard said that on the day of the first game in the stadium, "the gates were hung at 1:00 and we played at 2:00." But that would be all of the construction for a while. Then in 1958, 18,000 sideline seats were added and in 1960, 5,658 west endzone seats were added in response to increasing attendance.

With the large endzone, "Green Grass" section, this expansion increased capacity to 53,000. Later, upper decks were added to each side of as crowds swelled - the first in 1978 and the second in '83. This increased capacity to over 80,000, which makes it one of the largest on-campus stadiums.

The effect of spiraling inflation has had in this century can be dramatically seen in the differences in stadium construction. The original part of the stadium was built at a cost of $125,000 or at $6.25 a seat. The newest upper deck was finished in 1983 at a cost of $13.5 million, or $866 a seat.

The capacity for Clemson Memorial Stadium in 2005 was listed as 77,381 during construction of the WestZone area. The new capacity with the completion of the WestZone in 2006 is 80,301. Previously, capacity was listed as 81,473. When we listed that number in previous years, we counted 6,000 people on the hill. Our new capacities (2005 and 2006) count just 4,000 people on the hill and that accounts for the fact that our new capacity in 2006 is lower than what it had been previously.

Phase II of the WestZone project includes coaches' offices, administrative offices, a new strength and conditioning area, a large team room/auditorium, an expanded equipment room and athletic training facilities. Life improves as time passes and people work hard.

Through the years, Memorial Stadium has become known as "Death Valley." It was tagged this by the late Presbyterian coach, Lonnie McMillan. After bringing his P.C. teams to Clemson for years and getting whipped, McMillan said the place was like Death Valley. A few years later the name stuck.

In 1974, the playing surface was named Frank Howard Field for the legendary coach because of his long service and dedication to the University.

Luckily, the stadium wasn't built behind the YMCA.

Clemson's Top Single Season Attendance Figures

Rank	Year	Home Games	Total	Average	Head Coach
1.	1988	6	490,502	81,750	Danny Ford
2.	2006	7	570,542	81,506	Tommy Bowden
3.	2001	6	480,911	80,152	Tommy Bowden
4.	1990	6	475,174	79,196	Ken Hatfield
5.	1989	6	473,566	78,927	Danny Ford
6.	2004	6	472,939	78,823	Tommy Bowden
7.	1986	5	393,500	78,700	Danny Ford
8.	2000	7	548,647	78,378	Tommy Bowden
9.	1999	5	391,510	78,302	Tommy Bowden
10.	2005	6	469,391	78,232	Tommy Bowden

Pre-Game Festivities

Howard's Rock

Chapter 7 The Evolution of Modern American Football

Yale vs. Columbia

Lots of playing before playing became official

The official agreed upon date for the first American-style college football game is November 6, 1869. If you can find a replay of this game someplace in the heavens, however, you would find it would not look much like football as we know it. But, it was not completely soccer or rugby either.

Before this game, teams were playing a rugby style similar to that played in Britain in the mid-19th century. At the time in the US, a derivative known as association football was also played. In both games, a football is kicked at a goal or run over a line. These styles were based on the varieties of English public school football games. Over time, as noted, the style of "football" play in America continued to evolve.

On November 6, 1869, the first football game in America featured Rutgers and Princeton. Before the teams were even on the field it was being plugged as the first college football game of all time. Penn State did not get a Rugby team until the early 1960's. Nobody at Penn State in 1869, from what I could find, was even thinking about the game of football.

The first game of intercollegiate football was a sporting battle between two neighboring schools on a plot of ground where the present-day Rutgers gymnasium now stands in New Brunswick, N.J. Rutgers won that first game, 6-4.

There were two teams of 25 men each and the rules were rugby-like, but different enough to make it very interesting and enjoyable.

Like today's football, there were many surprises; strategies needed to be employed; determination exhibited, and of course the players required physical prowess.

1st Game Rutgers 6 Princeton 4 College Field, New Brunswick, NJ

At 3 p.m. the 50 combatants as well as 100 spectators gathered on the field. Most sat on a low wooden fence and watched the athletes discard their hats, coats and vests. The players used their suspenders as belts. To give a unique look, Rutgers wore scarlet-colored scarfs, which they converted into turbans. This contrasted them with the bareheaded boys from Princeton.

Two members of each team remained more or less stationary near the opponent's goal in the hopes of being able to slip over and score from unguarded positions. Thus, the present day "sleeper" was conceived. The remaining 23 players were divided into groups of 11 and 12. While the 11 "fielders" lined up in their own territory as defenders, the 12 "bulldogs" carried the battle.

Each score counted as a "game" and 10 games completed the contest. Following each score, the teams changed direction. The ball could be advanced only by kicking or batting it with the feet, hands, heads or sides.

Rutgers put a challenge forward that three games were to be played that year. The first was played at New Brunswick and won by Rutgers. Princeton won the second game, but cries of "over-emphasis" prevented the third game in football's first year when faculties of both institutions protested on the grounds that the games were interfering with student studies.

This is an excerpt of the Rutgers account of the game on its web site. A person named Herbert gave this detailed account of the play in the first game:

"Though smaller on the average, the Rutgers players, as it developed, had ample speed and fine football sense. Receiving the ball, our men formed a perfect interference around it and with short, skillful kicks and dribbles drove it down the field. Taken by surprise, the Princeton men fought valiantly, but in five minutes we had gotten the ball through to our captains on the enemy's goal and S.G. Gano, '71 and G.R. Dixon, '73, neatly kicked it over. None thought of it, so far as I know, but we had without previous plan or thought evolved the play that became famous a few years later as 'the flying wedge'."

"Next period Rutgers bucked, or received the ball, hoping to repeat the flying wedge," Herbert's account continues. "But the first time we formed it Big Mike came charging full upon us. It was our turn for surprise. The Princeton battering ram made no attempt to reach the ball but, forerunner of the interference-breaking ends of today, threw himself into our mass play, bursting us apart, and bowing us over. Time and again Rutgers formed the wedge and charged; as often Big Mike broke it up. And finally, on one of these incredible break-ups a

Princeton bulldog with a long accurate, perhaps lucky kick, sent the ball between the posts for the second score.

It was at this point that a Rutgers professor could stand it no longer. Waving his umbrella at the participants, he shrieked, "You will come to no Christian end!"

Herbert's account of the game continues: "The fifth and sixth goals went to Rutgers. The stars of the latter period of play, in the memory of the players after the lapse of many years, were "Big

Mike" and Large (former State Senator George H. Large of Flemington, another Princeton player) ...

The University of Notre Dame did not get into the football act until the late 1880's. At this time, the rules of rugby kept changing to accommodate the infatuation for the Americanized style of "football" play that would ultimately become the American game of football.

Walter Camp: the father of American football?

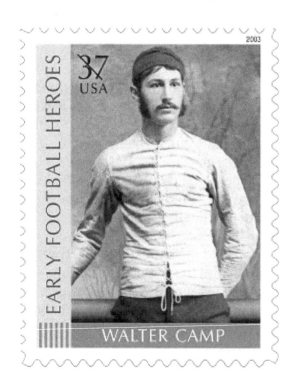

Walter Camp was a very well-known rugby player from Yale. In today's world, he would have been characterized as a rugby hero. It was his love of the game, his knowledge of the game as it was played, and his innovative mind that caused him to take the evolution of football even further. He pioneered the changes to the rules of rugby that slowly transformed the sport into the new game of American Football.

The rule changes that were introduced to the rugby and

association style (like soccer) of play were mostly those authored by Camp, who was also a Hopkins School graduate. For his original efforts, Walter Camp today is considered to be the "Father of American Football". Among the important changes brought to the game were the introduction of a line of scrimmage; down-and-distance rules; and the legalization of interference (blocking).

There was no such thing in those days as a forward pass and so the legalization of interference in 1880 football permitted blocking for runners. The forward pass would add another dimension to the game that made it much different than rugby or association football.

Soon after the early football changes, in the late nineteenth and into the early twentieth centuries, more game-play type developments were introduced by college coaches. The list is like a who's who of early American College Football. Coaches, such as Eddie Cochems, Amos Alonzo Stagg, Parke H. Davis, Knute Rockne, John Heisman, and Glenn "Pop" Warner helped introduce and then take advantage of the newly introduced forward pass. College football as well as professional football, were introduced prior to the 20th century. Fans were lured into watching again and again once they saw the game played.

College football especially grew in popularity despite the existence of pro-football. It became the dominant version of the sport of football in the United States. It was this way for the entire first half of the 20th century. Bowl games made the idea of football even more exciting in the college ranks. Rivalries grew and continued and the fans loved it! This great football tradition brought a national audience to college football games that still dominates the sports world today.

This book has little to do with pro-football or any other sport. However, there is no denying that the greatest college football players more often than not eventually found their fortunes in professional football. Pro football can be traced back to the season that Notre Dame brought forth a real football team after a two-year lapse from its last half-Rugby season in 1889. It was 1892 when William "Pudge" Heffelfinger signed a $500 contract to play for the Allegheny Athletic Association against the Pittsburgh Athletic Club.

Twenty-eight years later, the American Professional Football Association was formed. This league changed its name to the National Football League (NFL) just two years later. Eventually, the NFL became the major league of American football. Originally, just a sport played in Midwestern industrial towns in the United States, professional football eventually became a national phenomenon. We all know this because from August to February, in America, many of us are glued to our TV sets or chained to our seats in some of the most intriguing pro-football stadiums in America.

Rules and Penalties

The big problem players from different teams and different geographies had when playing early American-style football in college was that the style of play was not standardized. The rulebooks were not yet written or were at best incomplete and disputable.

A rule over here, for example, would be a penalty over there. And, so in the 1870's there was a lot of work to try to make all games to be played by the same rules. There were minor rule changes such as team size was reduced from 25 to 20 but of course over the years, this and all other rules continued to evolve. For years, there was no such thing as a running touchdown. The only means of scoring was to bat or kick the ball through the opposing team's goal.

Early rugby rules were the default. The field size was rugby style at 140 yards by 70 yards v 120 X 53 1/3 (including end zones) in today's football game. There was plenty of room to huff and puff and almost get lost. There were no breaks per se for long periods. Instead of fifteen minute quarters, the game was more like Rugby and Soccer with 45 minute halves played continuously.

In 1873 to put some order to the game, Columbia, Princeton. Rutgers, and Yale got together in a hotel in New York City and wrote down the first set of intercollegiate football rules. They changed a few things along the way but the end-product was a much more standard way of playing football games. Rather than use the home team's rules, all teams then were able to play by the same rules

Harvard did not to comply with American rules

For its own reasons, Harvard chose not to attend the rules conference. Instead, it played all of its games using the Harvard code of rules. Harvard therefore had a difficult time scheduling games. In 1874, to get a game, Harvard agreed to play McGill University from Montreal Canada. They had rules that even Harvard had never seen. For example, any player could pick up the ball and run with it, anytime he wished.

Another McGill rule was that they would count tries (the act of grounding the football past the opponent's goal line. Since there was no end zone, which technically makes a football field of today 120 yards long, a touchdown gave no points. Instead, it provided the chance to kick a free goal from the field. If the kick were missed, the touchdown did not count.

In 1874 McGill and Harvard played a two-game series. Each team could play 11 men per side. This was in deep contrast to the even earlier days of college football before standard rules when games were played with 25, 20, 15, or 11 men on a side.

The first game was played with a round ball using what were known as the "Boston" rules (Harvard). The next day, the teams played using the McGill rules, which included McGill's oval ball which was much like an American football, and it featured the ability to pick up the ball and run with it. Harvard enjoyed this experience especially the idea of "the try" which had not been used in American football. Eventually, the try evolved into the American idea of a touchdown and points were given when a try was successful.

Not all the rules lasted the duration and some were very strange by today's standards. One of the most perplexing rules was that a man could run with the ball only while an opponent chose to pursue him. When a tackler abandoned the ball-carrier, the latter had to stop, and was forced to kick, pass or even throw away what was called "his burden."

McGill has a great account of this match on their web site. Type *McGill web site football against Harvard* into your search engine.

Their players wore no protective pads. Woolen jerseys covered the torso, while white trousers encased the players' legs. Some trousers were short and some were long. It did not seem to matter for the game. A number of the men wore what they called black "football turbans" which were the ancestors of the modern helmet; others chose to wear white canvas hats.

The Harvard players wore undershirts made of gauze. Think about that for a while. They also wore what were called *full length gymnasium costumes*. They also wore light baseball shoes. Most of the team wore handkerchiefs, which were knotted about their heads.

The gauze undershirts were a trick. There was strategy in this choice of top uniform. When a player was first tackled, the gauze would be demolished and the next opponent would have nothing to grab other than "slippery human flesh." Harvard won this game by a score of 3-0

The next go at playing by the rules was when Harvard took on Tufts University on June 4, 1875. This was the first American college football game played using rules similar to the McGill/Harvard contest. Tufts won this game. Despite the loss, Harvard continued pushing McGill style football and challenged Yale.

The Bulldog team accepted under a compromise rule set that included some Yale soccer rules and Harvard rugby rules. They used 15 players per team. It was November 13, 1875 for this first meeting of Harvard v Yale. Harvard won 4-0. Walter Camp attended the game and the following year he played in the game as a Yale Bulldog.

Camp was determined to avenge Yale's defeat. Onlookers from Princeton, who saw this Harvard / Yale game loved it so much, they brought it back to Princeton where it was quickly adopted as the preferred version of football.

Once Walter Camp caught onto the rugby-style rules, history says he became a fixture at the Massasoit House conventions. Here the rules of the game were debated and changed appropriately. From these meetings, Camp's rule changes as well as others were adopted.

Having eleven players instead of fifteen aided in opening the game and it emphasized speed over strength. When Camp attended in 1878, this motion was rejected but it passed in the 1880 meeting. The line of scrimmage and the snap from center to the quarterback also passed in 1880. Originally the snap occurred by a kick from the center, but this was later modified so the ball would be snapped with the hands either as a pass back (long snap) or a direct snap from the center.

It was Camp's new scrimmage rules, however, which according to many, revolutionized the game, though it was not always to increase speed. In fact, Princeton was known to use line of scrimmage plays to slow the game, making incremental progress towards the end zone much like today during each down.

Camp's original idea was to increase scoring, but in fact the rule was often misused to maintain control of the ball for the entire game. The negative effect was that there were many slow and unexciting contests. This too would be fixed with the idea of the first down coming into play.

In 1982, at the rules meeting, Camp proposed that a team be given three downs to advance the ball five yards. These rules were called the down and distance rules. Along with the notion of the line of scrimmage, these rules transformed the game of rugby into the distinct sport of American football.

Among other significant rule changes, in 1881, the field size was reduced to its modern dimensions of 120 by 53 1/3 yards (109.7 by 48.8 meters). Camp was central to these significant rule changes that ultimately defined American football. Camp's next quest was to address scoring anomalies. His first cut was to give four points for a touchdown and two points for kicks after touchdowns; two points for safeties, and five points for field goals. The notion of the foot in football /rugby explains Camp's rationale.

In 1887, game time was fixed at two halves of 45 minutes each. Additionally, college games would have two paid officials known as a referee and an umpire, for each game. In 1888, the rules permitted tackling below the waist and then in 1889, the officials were given whistles and stopwatches to better control the game.

An innovation that many list as most significant to making American football uniquely American was the legalization of blocking opponents, which back then was called "interference." This tactic had been highly illegal under the rugby-style rules and in rugby today, it continues to be illegal.

The more those who know soccer and football find rugby to be more like soccer.

Though *offsides* is a penalty infraction today, *offsides* in the 1880's in rugby was very much the same as *offsides* in soccer. The prohibition of blocking in a rugby game is in fact because of the game's strict enforcement of its *offsides* rule. Similar to soccer, this rule prohibits any player on the team with possession of the ball to loiter between the ball and the goal. Blocking continues as a basic element of modern American football, with many complex schemes having been developed and implemented over the years, including zone blocking and pass blocking.

Camp stayed active in rule making for most of his life. He had the honor of personally selecting an annual All-American team every year from 1889 through 1924. Camp passed away in 1925. The Walter Camp Football Foundation continues to select All-American teams in his honor.

With many rule changes as noted, as American style rugby became more defined as American football, more and more colleges adopted football as part of their sports programs. Most of the schools were from the Eastern US. It was not until 1879 that the University of Michigan became the first school west of Pennsylvania to establish a bona-fide American-style college football team.

Back then, football teams played whenever they could in the fall or the spring. For example, Michigan's first game was in late spring, near the end of what we would call the academic year. On May 30, 1879 Michigan beat Racine College 1–0 in a game played in Chicago. In 1887, Michigan and Notre Dame played their first football game, which did not benefit from Camp's rules.

The first night time game

It was not until September 28, 1892 that the first nighttime football game was played. Mansfield State Normal played Wyoming Seminary in Mansfield, Pennsylvania. These schools are close to where I live. The game ended at a "declared" half-time in a 0–0 tie. It had become too dark to play.

Wyoming Seminary was not a college and to this day it is not a college. I live about five miles from the school. It is a private college preparatory school located in the Wyoming Valley of Northeastern Pennsylvania. During the time period in which the game was played, it was common for a college and high school to play each other in football—a practice that of course has long since been discontinued.

The reason that it got too dark to play, ironically was not because the game began at dusk. Mansfield had brought in a lighting system that was far too inadequate for game play. This historical game lasted only 20 minutes and there were only 10 plays. Both sides agreed to end at half-time with the score at 0-0. Though it may seem humorous today, for safety reasons, the game was declared ended in a 0-0 tie after several players had an unfortunate run-in with a light pole.

Mansfield and Wyoming Seminary are thus enshrined in football history as having played in the first night game ever in "college football." History and football buffs get together once a year to celebrate the game in what they call "Fabulous 1890's Weekend." This historic game is reenacted exactly as it occurred play by play just as the actual game is recorded in history. Fans who watch the game are sometimes known to correct players (actually actors) when they deviate from the original scripted plays. Now, that shows both a love of the game and a love of history.

Mansfield and Wyoming Seminary's game added additional fame to both schools when the 100th anniversary of the game just happened to occur on Monday, September 28, 1992. Monday Night Football celebrated "100 years of night football" with its regularly scheduled game between the Los Angeles Raiders and the Kansas City Chiefs at Arrowhead Stadium. The Chiefs won 27–7 in front of 77,486 fans. How about that?

More football history was recorded when Army played Navy in 1893. In this game, we have the first documented use of a football helmet by a player in a game. Joseph M. Reeves had been kicked in the head in a prior football game. He was warned by his doctor that he risked death if he continued to play football. We all know how tough the Midshipmen and Black Nights (Cadets) are regardless of who they may be playing. Rather than end his football playing days prematurely. Reeves discussed his need with a shoemaker in Annapolis who crafted a leather helmet for the player to wear for the rest of the season.

Football conferences

Things were happening very quickly in the new sport of football. Organization and rules became the mantra for this fledgling sport. It was being defined while it was being played. Formal college football conferences were just around the corner. In fact, the Southeastern Conference and the Atlantic Coast Conference both got started in1894.

The forward pass

None of Camp's rules for American Football included the most innovative notion of them all – the forward pass. Many believe that the first forward pass in football occurred on October 26, 1895 in a game between Georgia and North Carolina. Out of desperation, the ball was thrown by the North Carolina back Joel Whitaker instead of having been punted. George Stephens, a teammate caught the ball.

Despite what most may think or surmise, it was Camp again when he was a player at Yale, who executed the first game-time forward pass for a touchdown. During the Yale-Princeton game, while Camp was being tackled, he threw a football forward to Yale's Oliver Thompson, who sprinted to a touchdown. The Princeton Tigers naturally protested and there appeared to be no precedent for a referee decision. Like many things in football including a game-beginning coin-toss, the referee in this instance tossed a coin, and then he made his decision to allow the touchdown.

Hidden ball trick

Dome one-time tricks have not survived football. For example, on November 9, 1895 Auburn Coach John Heisman executed a hidden ball trick. Quarterback Reynolds Tichenor was able to gain Auburn's only touchdown in a 6 to 9 loss to Vanderbilt. This also was the first game in the south that was decided by a field goal.

The trick was simple but would be illegal today. When the ball was snapped, it went to a halfback. The play was closely masked and well screened. The halfback then thrust the ball under the back of the quarterback's (Tichenor) jersey. Then the halfback would crash into the line. After the play, Tichenor "simply trotted away to a touchdown."

The end of college football?

Football was never a game for the light of heart. You had to be tough physically and tough mentally to compete. Way back in 1906, for example complaints were many about the violence in American Football. It got so bad that universities on the West Coast, led by California and Stanford, replaced the sport with rugby union. At the time, the future of American college football, a very popular sport enjoyed by fans nationwide was in doubt. The schools that eliminated football and replaced it with rugby union believed football would be gone and rugby union would eventually be adopted nationwide.

Soon other schools followed this travesty and made the switch. Eventually, due to the perception that West Coast football was an inferior game played by inferior men when compared to the rough and tumble East Coast, manhood prevailed in the West over the inclination to make the game mild. The many tough East Coast and Midwest teams had shrugged off the loss of the few teams out West and they had continued to play American style football.

And, so the available pool of rugby union "football" teams to play remained small. The Western colleges therefore had to schedule games against local club teams and they reached out to rugby union powers in Australia, New Zealand, and especially, due to its proximity, Canada.

The famous Stanford and California game continued as rugby. To make it seem important. The winner was invited by the British Columbia Rugby Union to a tournament in Vancouver over the Christmas holidays. The winner of that tournament was rewarded with the Cooper Keith Trophy. Nobody in America cared. Eventually the West Coast came back to football.

Nonetheless the situation of injury and death in football persisted and though there was a lot of pushback, it came to a head in 1905 when there were 19 fatalities nationwide. President Theodore Roosevelt, a tough guy himself, is reported as having threatened to shut down the game nationwide if drastic changes were not made. Sports historians however, dispute that Roosevelt ever intervened.

What is certified, however, is that on October 9, 1905, the President held a meeting of football representatives from Harvard, Yale, and Princeton. The topic was eliminating and reducing injuries and the President according to the record, never threatened to ban football. The fact is that Roosevelt lacked the authority to abolish football but more importantly, he was a big fan and wanted the game to continue. The little Roosevelts also loved the sport and were playing football at the college and secondary levels at the time.

Meanwhile, there were more rule changes such as the notion of reducing the number of scrimmage plays to earn a first down from four to three in an attempt to reduce injuries. The LA Times reported an increase in punts in an experimental game and thus considered the game much safer than regular play. Football lovers did not accept the new rule because it was not "conducive to the sport."

Because nobody wanted players injured or killed in a game, on December 28, 1905, 62 schools met in New York City to discuss major rule changes to make the game safer. From this meeting, the Intercollegiate Athletic Association of the United States, later named the National Collegiate Athletic Association (NCAA), was formed.

The forward pass is legalized

One rule change that was introduced in 1906 was devised to open up the game and thus reduce injury. This new rule introduced the legal forward pass. Though it was underutilized for years, this proved to be one of the most important rule changes in the establishment of the modern game.

Because of these 1905-1906 reforms, mass formation plays in which many players joined together became illegal when forward passes became legal. Bradbury Robinson, playing for visionary coach Eddie Cochems at St. Louis University, is recorded as throwing the first legal pass in a September 5, 1906, game against Carroll College at Waukesha.

Later changes were in the minutia category but they added discipline and safety to the game without destroying its rugged character. For example, in 1910, came the new requirement that at least seven offensive players be on the line of scrimmage at the time of the snap, that there be no pushing or pulling, and that interlocking interference (arms linked or hands on belts and uniforms) was not allowed. These changes accomplished their intended purpose of greatly reducing the potential for collision injuries.

As noted previously, great coaches emerged in the ranks who took advantage of these sweeping changes. Amos Alonzo Stagg, for example, introduced such innovations as the huddle, the tackling dummy, and the pre-snap shift. Other coaches, such as Pop Warner and Notre Dame's Knute Rockne, introduced new strategies that still remain part of the game.

Many other rules changes and coaching innovations came about before 1940. They all had a profound impact on the game, mostly in opening up the passing game, but also in making the game safer to play without diminishing its quality.

For example, in 1914, the first roughing-the-passer penalty was implemented. In 1918, the rules on eligible receivers were loosened to allow eligible players to catch the ball anywhere on the field. The previously more restrictive rules allowed passes only in certain areas of the field.

Scoring rules also changed which brought the scoring into the modern era. For example, field goals were lowered from five to three points in 1909 and touchdowns were raised from four to six points in 1912.

Jim Thorpe, Circa 1915

Star Players:

Star players emerged in both the collegiate and professional ranks including Jim Thorpe, Red Grange, and Bronko Nagurski were other stars. These three in particular, were able to move from college to the fledgling NFL and they helped turn it into a successful league.

Notable sportswriter Grantland Rice helped popularize the sport of football with his poetic descriptions of games and colorful nicknames for the game's biggest players, including Notre Dame's "Four Horsemen" backfield and Fordham University's linemen, known as the "Seven Blocks of Granite".

Legends existed all during the formation of football. There was Stagg, Halas, Warner, Thorpe, Heisman, Grange, Rockne and The Four Horsemen.

The Heisman

In 1935, New York City's Downtown Athletic Club awarded its first Heisman Trophy to University of Chicago halfback Jay Berwanger. He was also the first ever NFL Draft pick in 1936. The trophy continues to this day to recognize the nation's "most outstanding" college football player. It has become one of the most coveted awards in all of American sports.

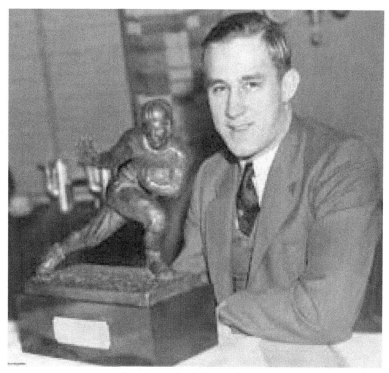

Jay Berwanger, 1ˢᵗ Heisman Winner

New formations and play sets continued to be developed by innovative coaches and their staffs. Emory Bellard from the University of Texas, developed a three-back option style offense known as the wishbone. Bear Bryant of Alabama became a preacher of the wishbone.

The strategic opposite of the wishbone is called the spread offense. Some teams have managed to adapt with the times to keep winning consistently. In the rankings of the most victorious programs, Michigan, Texas, and Notre Dame are ranked first, second, and third in total wins.

And so that is as far as we will take it in this chapter about the early evolution of football. With so many conferences and sports associations as well as pro, college, high school, and mini sports, something tells me we have not yet seen our last rule change.

Chapter 8 John Heisman Era 1900-1903

Heisman   Coach #4

Year	Coach	Record	Conf	Record
1900	John Heisman	6-0-0	SIAA	3-0-0
1901	John Heisman	3–1–1	SIAA	1-0-1
1902	John Heisman	5–2–1	SIAA	5-0-0
1903	John Heisman	6–1–1	SIAA	2-0-1

1900 Clemson Football Team Picture Coach John Heisman

John Heisman is one of the most well-known football figures of all
time. There would be no reason for me to research his life in full in
order to provide you what is already written about this great man and
great coach.

The following account of John Heisman and his impact on the Clemson Football program is presented below in an article written on October 18, 2000, by Sam Blackman, the Associate Sports Information Director at Clemson, University. Our thanks to Clemson University for making this available.

John Heisman
Head Coach Years: 1900-1903
Record at Clemson: 19-3-2
Winning Percentage: .833

A name synonymous with not only the early years of Clemson football but the collegiate game is John Heisman.

A stern disciplinarian, he expected his players to be of high character and performance both on the football field and in the classroom. Heisman coached the Tigers in 1900 to 1903 and was responsible for putting the Clemson name among the annals of the great early collegiate teams.

JOHN HEISMAN COACHED AT CLEMSON FROM 1900-03 AND WAS LATER INDUCTED INTO THE COLLEGE FOOTBALL HALL OF FAME.

Heisman was brought to Clemson by a professor and later University President, Walter Riggs. In the spring of 1894, Riggs was a graduate manager for the Auburn football team, and he was responsible for finding a coach for the 1895 season. Riggs wrote to Carl Williams of Pennsylvania, captain of the 1894 team asking him to suggest a suitable coach. He replied recommending J.W. Heisman, an ex-Penn player, and his coach at Oberlin a few years earlier.

After several weeks, Riggs finally found Heisman in Texas, where he was engaged in raising tomatoes. Having sunk about all of his capital into the tomato venture, he was glad to go back to his old love of football and he readily went to coach at Auburn for $500.OO a year. Riggs later was hired as a professor at Clemson and he hired Heisman at Clemson in 1900. (Riggs started the Clemson football program in 1896 and was head coach in 1896 and 1899).

Heisman began his coaching career at Oberlin in 1892 and lasted 36 years in the profession. His career included positions at Akron, Auburn, Clemson, Georgia Tech, Penn, Washington and Jefferson, and Rice University. He had an overall career record of 185 wins, 70 losses, and 17 ties.

He invented the hidden ball trick, the handoff, the double lateral, and the "Flea flicker." He pioneered the forward pass, and originated the center snap and the word "hike" (previously the center used to roll the ball on the ground to the quarterback).

Heisman took Clemson to a 19-3-2 record in his four seasons. His .833 winning percentage. is still the best in Clemson history. He was also the Clemson baseball coach between 1901-1904.

Clemson was a powerhouse during his tenure and was a most feared opponent. His secret was that he depended on smart, quick players rather than large size and brawn.

William Heisman, a nephew of John Heisman often told a story on how his famous uncle stressed academics.

"I remember a story Coach Heisman used to tell me about this famous football player he confronted in the locker room before a big game. My uncle came busting through the door and went over to this guy and said, 'You can't play today because you haven't got your grades up to par. 'The player looked up at my uncle and said, 'Coach, don't you know that the sportswriters call this toe on my right foot the million-dollar toe?' My uncle snapped back right quick and said, `What good is it if you only have a fifteen-cent head?

Another favorite Heisman story was the speech he used to make before a season began. Heisman would face his recruits holding a football. "What is it?" he would sharply ask. Then he would tell his players, "a football was a prolate spheroid, an elongated sphere-in which the outer leather casing is drawn up tightly over a somewhat smaller rubber tubing." Then after a long pause he would say, "better to have died as a small boy than to fumble this football."

Heisman broke down football into these percentages: talent 25%; mentality 20%; aggressiveness 20%; speed 20%; and weight 15%. He considered coaching as being a master-commanding, even dictatorial. He has no time to say 'please' or `mister', and he must be occasionally severe, arbitrary, and something of a czar."

On November 29,1900, Clemson defeated Alabama 35-0, which allowed Heisman's team to finish the season undefeated with a 6-0 record. This was Clemson's first undefeated team and was the only team to win all of its games in a season until the 1948 squad went 11-0. The Tigers only allowed two touchdowns the entire 1900 season.

Clemson opened the 1901 season with a 122-0 win over Guilford. The Tigers averaged 30 yards per play and a touchdown every minute and 26 seconds. The first half lasted 20 minutes while the second half lasted only 10 minutes. Legend has it that every man on the Clemson team scored a touchdown in this game.

In his third season, on November 27, 1902, Clemson played in the snow for the first time in a game against Tennessee. The Tigers won the game, 11-0, and claimed the Southern Intercollegiate Athletic Association crown. (An early conference that had several southern colleges and universities as members).

In his final season in 1903, Clemson defeated Georgia Tech 73-0 on October 17, 1903. Clemson rushed the ball 55 times for 615 yards, while Tech ran the ball 35 times and collected 28 yards. The second half was shortened to 15 minutes.

On November 24, 1903 Clemson participated in its "First Bowl Game" as Clemson and Cumberland met on this date for the Championship of the South. The contract for the game was drawn up just two weeks before the game was to be played. Cumberland, who had earlier defeated Auburn, Alabama, and Vanderbilt was considered to be champion of the southern states of Louisiana, Mississippi, Alabama, Tennessee, and Kentucky. While Clemson was considered to be the best team in Virginia, North Carolina, South Carolina and Georgia. The game was played on a neutral site, Montgomery, AL. Cumberland and Clemson fought to a 11-11 tie. In this game, John Maxwell scored as a result of a 100-yard kickoff return. After the news came back to Clemson that the game ended in a tie, the students and the local towns people built a bonfire and paraded around the campus.

John Heisman's 19-3-2 record Is still the best in Clemson history on a percentage basis. The man named after the famous trophy that each year honors the best player in college football holds the distinction of building the early foundation of Clemson's football tradition.

1900: Clemson Tigers Coach John Heisman

In 1900, another rule affected how when a touchdown was to count as a touchdown. This year's change was of the definition of touchdown, which was changed to include situations where the ball becomes dead on or above the goal line.

Walter Riggs continued to help the football program. In fact, he led the effort to raise the $415.11 to hire Auburn's football coach John Heisman, the first Clemson coach who had experience coaching at another school. Heisman was already a coaching legend when he came to Clemson.

As Riggs recalled, "By 1899 the Clemson football team had risen steadily until its material was equal to that of any southern college, and the time had come to put on the long-planned finishing touch." Heisman once described his style of play at Clemson as "radically different from anything on earth".

When the team took the field in 1900, they wore jerseys and stockings bearing distinctive orange and purple stripes.

The 1900 Clemson Tigers football team represented the Clemson Agricultural College during the 1900 college football season as a member of the SIAA. John Heisman was the fourth head football coach at Clemson, having been recruited for the Job by William Riggs, well known professor and football coach. This was the first of four years for John Heisman at the helm of the Fighting Tigers. Norman Walker was the team captain. The Tigers completed their fifth season with a record of 6-0-0 and a 3-0 record in the SIAA.

They had a nice win over Davidson on opening day. It was then the largest score ever made in the South and the season's only home game for the Tigers. For the first time this year, the Tigers beat Georgia. They were simply outstanding. In the fifth year of the program, the Tigers outscored their opponents 222–10. As noted, the 64–0 win over Davidson on opening day was then the largest score ever made in the South. That was worth repeating. Also, worth repeating is that the Clemson Tigers were undefeated and untied in 1900 under John Huntsman

Games of the 1900 Season

The season opened on Oct 19 at home in Calhoun SC against Davidson W (64-0). Three days later, on Oct 22, the Tigers were in Spartanburg, SC for a W (21-0) win against Wofford. The real score was not kept as Clemson agreed that every point scored after the first four touchdowns would not count.

Going into the South Carolina game, Clemson had been strong on offense, but weak on defense. Kinsler and Douthit were both injured.

And, so, on Nov 1, on Big Thursday, despite what might have been, Clemson ripped SC W (51-0). The Tigers rolled up a 51–0 score on in-state rival South Carolina. Then, for the first time in five meetings, on Nov 10, Clemson did the impossible. The Tigers beat the well-experienced Georgia Bulldogs at Herty Field in Athens, GA W (39-5). It wasn't even close.

Before the game with Georgia at Georgia, students in the dorms barraged Clemson players with bits of coal. Clemson went on to beat the Bulldogs for the first time, pulling away in the second half to overwhelm the Bulldogs 39–5, and achieve the season's first great victory. The starting lineup on the team was Bellows (left end), Dickerson (left tackle), George (left guard) Kinsley (center), Woodward (right guard), Walker (right tackle), Lynah (right end), Lewis (quarterback), Forsythe (left halfback), Hunt (right halfback), Douthit (fullback).

On Nov 24, Clemson faced its toughest opponent of the year VPI aka Virginia Tech, but the Fighting Tigers prevailed against the Hokies W (12-5). On November 29, Clemson got its rivalry with Alabama started right when it whooped the Crimson White W (35-0). Yes, the history of the two teams battling for dominance goes back to 1900

The season closer was played on Thanksgiving against the Alabama Crimson White, as noted, it was Clemson's first meeting with Alabama, at Birmingham's North Birmingham Park. The Tigers won 35–0. Clemson back Claude Douthit scored four touchdowns. After the Tigers forced an Alabama punt to open the game, Douthit scored three consecutive touchdowns for Clemson en route to an 18–0 lead. Douthit scored first on a 5-yard run, next on a short reception and finally on a second short touchdown run.

M. N. Hunter then scored for Clemson on a long run just before the break and made the halftime score 23–0. In the second half, the Tigers extended their lead to 35–0, behind a long Jim Lynah touchdown run and Douthit's fourth score of the day on a short run. With approximately four minutes left in the game, both team captains agreed to end the game early due to an unruly crowd and impending darkness.

Tigers take all the 1900 SIAA marbles

The Tigers ended the season with the outright SIAA title. It was both Clemson and Heisman's first conference championship and undefeated, untied season. The season saw "the rise of Clemson from a little school whose football teams had never been heard of before, to become a football machine of the very first power." Judging from the 2017 results, things have not changed much.

1901: Clemson Tigers Coach John Heisman

The 1901 Clemson Tigers football team represented the Clemson Agricultural College during the 1901 college football season as a member of the SIAA. John Heisman was the head football coach in his second of four seasons at Clemson. The Tigers completed their sixth season overall and sixth in the SIAA with a record of 3-1-1 and a 1-0-1 record in the SIAA.

They had a record-breaking-win over Guilford on opening day W (122-0). On October 5, home at Bowman Field. Rumor was that everybody on the team scored that game. On Oct 19, they tied the Volunteers at Waite Field in Knoxville Tennessee T (6-6). On Oct 26 v Georgia, at Herty Field in Athens, GA, the Tigers beat the Bulldogs for the second year in a row, W (29–5). The next week, Oct 31, it was off to Columbia SC to play a tough VPI team for the second year in a row. The Tigers lost this close one L (17-11). Idle for a month, Clemson picked it up again on Nov 28 and beat North Carolina in Charlotte W (22-10).

1902: Clemson Tigers Coach John Heisman

The 1902 Clemson Tigers football team represented the Clemson Agricultural College during the 1902 college football season as a member of the SIAA. John Heisman was the head football coach in his third of four seasons at Clemson. The Tigers completed their sixth season overall and sixth in the SIAA with a record of 6-1-0 and a 5-0 undefeated record in the SIAA, winning the conference championship. The lone loss was their first to rival South Carolina since 1896. It was a controversial game that ended in riots and banning further play between the teams until 1909.

1902 Clemson Football Team, John Heisman Coach

This year, John Heisman got a raise and was paid $815.11 to coach the football team. The team's captain was Hope Sadler. This was the first season with both Sadler and Carl Sitton at ends. One writer recalls, "Sitton and Hope Sadler were the finest ends that Clemson ever had perhaps."

The season opened on Oct 4 with a home W (11–5) victory over North Carolina A&M in the Textile Bowl. On October 18, at Georgia Tech, Clemson walloped the Yellow Jackets W (44–5). The day before the game, Clemson sent in scrubs to Atlanta, checked into a hotel, and partied until dawn. The varsity sat well rested in Lula, Georgia as Tech betters were fooled. All tricks were permitted without the NCAA's ever watchful eye.

Clemson scored first on an 80-yard end run from Carl Sitton. The starting lineup was Sitton (left end), Barnwell (left tackle), Kaigler (left guard), Green (center), Forsyth (right guard), DeCosta (right tackle), Sadler (right end), Maxwell (quarterback), Gantt (left halfback), Lawrence (right halfback), Hanvey (fullback). Week 3: at Furman On Oct 24, Clemson prevailed at Furman W (28-0). The Tigers made their first touchdown after three minutes of play. On one play, Heisman used a tree to his advantage.

On Oct 20, Clemson lost L (12–6) to rival South Carolina in Columbia, for the first time since 1896, the first year of the rivalry. There were a lot of shenanigans. The Carolina fans that week were carrying around a poster with the image of a tiger with a gamecock standing on top of it, holding the tiger's tail as if he was steering the tiger by the tail," Jay McCormick said. "Naturally, the Clemson guys didn't take too kindly to that, and on Wednesday and again on Thursday, there were sporadic fistfights involving brass knuckles and other objects and so forth, some of which resulted, according to the newspapers, in blood being spilled and persons having to seek medical assistance.

After the game on Thursday, the Clemson guys frankly told the Carolina students that if you bring this poster, which is insulting to us, to the big parade on Friday, you're going to be in trouble. And naturally, of course, the Carolina students brought the poster to the parade. If you give someone an ultimatum and they're your rival, they're going to do exactly what you told them not to do."

As expected, another brawl broke out before both sides agreed to mutually burn the poster in an effort to defuse tensions. The immediate aftermath resulted in the stoppage of the rivalry until 1909.

Clemson gained only 2 and a half yards in the first half. On a triple pass around end, Sitton made a 30-yard touchdown in the second half. More than 5,000 were in attendance.

On Nov 8, Clemson defeated the Georgia Bulldogs at Georgia by a score of W (36–0). One writer called it "the hardest fought football game ever seen here."

On Nov 15, Clemson beat Auburn W (15-0). The Tigers scored three touchdowns on Auburn, using double passes at times.

On Nov 27 Week 7 at Tennessee, Clemson closed the season. Tennessee had already won a then-school record six games, and the beat Clemson W (11–0). Tennessee's Tootsie Douglas still holds the record for the longest punt in school history, when he punted a ball 109 yards (the field length was 110 yards in those days). It was in a blizzard."

1903: Clemson Tigers Coach John Heisman

The 1903 Clemson Tigers football team represented the Clemson Agricultural College during the 1903 college football season as a member of the SIAA. John Heisman was the head football coach in his last of four seasons at Clemson. The Tigers completed their eighth season overall and also their eighth in the SIAA with a record of 4-1-1 and a 2-0-1-- undefeated record in the SIAA. Clemson won the conference co-championship. Their lone loss was to North Carolina at Chapel Hill in a real nail-biter.

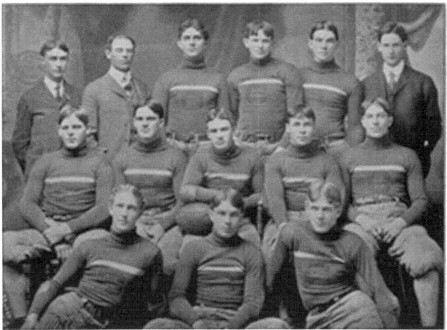

1903 Clemson Football Team John Heisman Coach

During the season, the team competed in an early conference championship game, tying Cumberland 11–11 in the contest. This was John Heisman's last season coaching Clemson. The Tigers had some great moments such as thrashing Georgia Tech's Yellow Jackets 73–0, leading to Heisman's later job-offer at Georgia Tech Even great coaches need to eventually go where other colleges can pay well for their services.

Before the season, teams had to acclimate themselves to the new point system. For the 1903 season, the point values were different from those used in contemporary games. In 1903, for example, a touchdown was worth five points, a field goal was worth five points and a conversion (PAT) was worth one point.

Hope Sadler was again the Tigers'' team captain. This was the last season with both Sadler and Carl Sitton at ends. As noted several times previously, one writer recalls, "Sitton and Hope Sadler were the finest ends that Clemson ever had perhaps."

Games of the 1903 season.

On Oct 10, Clemson shut out Georgia W (29-0) at Herty Field in Athens Georgia. The Bulldogs offered Clemson a bushel of apples for every point over 29 it scored against rival Georgia Tech. Clemson would win W (73-0) v Georgia Tech in Atlanta a week later on Oct 17 on a mud-soaked field, leading to Heisman's later job at Tech. Sitton had to sit out the game.

On Oct 28, it was North Carolina A & M in the Textile Bowl played in Columbia SC W (24-0). While the Aggies gained much using conventional football, Clemson had to use many trick plays Oliver Gardner played for A&M. John Heisman got married soon after the game. North Carolina was next at Chapel Hill. The North Carolina Tar Heels then squeaked out a win over Clemson in a nail biter L (6-11). The Tar Heels handed Clemson its only loss of the season. Carolina's Newton scored first, with a bloody nose. He also scored the second touchdown. Clemson had one touchdown by Johnny Maxwell called back due to an offside penalty.

The Tigers came back on November 21 against Davidson at Latta Park, Charlotte NC for a nice win W (24-0). Charlotte, NC Clemson won easily over Davidson 24–0. One writer noted "Clemson playing against eleven wooden men, would attract more attention. "Then in the SIAA Championship game on November 26, the Clemson Tigers were tied by the Cumberland Phoenix T 11-11) in Montgomery Alabama to become co-champions of the conference.

In this game billed as the "SIAA Championship Game." Cumberland rushed out to an early 11–0 lead. Wiley Lee Umphlett in Creating the Big Game: John W. Heisman and the Invention of American Football writes, "During the first half, Clemson was never really in the game due mainly to formidable line play of the Bridges brothers– giants in their day at 6 feet 4 inches–and a big center named "Red" Smith, was all over the field backing up the Cumberland line on defense. Clemson had been outweighed before, but certainly not like this."

Quarterback John Maxwell, 1903

Quarterback John Maxwell returned a kickoff for a touchdown. A contemporary account reads "The Clemson players seemed mere dwarfs as they lined up for the kickoff. To the crowd on the sidelines it didn't seem that Heisman's charges could possibly do more than give a gallant account of themselves in a losing battle."

A touchdown was scored by fullback E. L. Minton (touchdowns were worth 5 points). Guard M. O. Bridges kicked the extra point. Halfback J. A. Head made another touchdown, but Bridges missed the try. After halftime, Clemson quarterback John Maxwell raced 100 yards for a touchdown. Clemson missed the try. Cumberland fumbled a punt and Clemson recovered. Cumberland expected a trick play when Fritz Furtick simply ran up the middle and scored.

One account of the play reads "Heisman saw his chance to exploit a weakness in the Cumberland defense: run the ball where the ubiquitous Red Smith wasn't. So, the next time Sitton started out on one of his slashing end runs, at the last second he tossed the ball back to the fullback who charged straight over center (whcre Smith would have been except that he was zeroing in on the elusive Sitton) and went all the way for the tying touchdown." Jock Hanvey kicked the extra point and the game ended in an 11–11 tie.

<<< Captain Hope Sadler 1903 The winning team was to be awarded the ball. Captain W. W. Suddarth of Cumberland wanted captain Hope Sadler of Clemson to get the ball, and Sadler insisted Suddarth should have it. Some ten minutes of bickering was resolved when the ball was given to patrolman Patrick J. Sweeney, for warning the media and fans to stay down in front and allow spectators to see the game.

The school claims a share of the title. Heisman pushed for Cumberland to be named SIAA champions at year's end. It was Heisman's last game as Clemson head coach, who was hired at Georgia Tech for $450 more per year. After getting married and being offered a 25% pay increase, Heisman could not say no. Too bad Clemson was not able to pay Heisman what he was worth.

Chapter 9 Shack Shealy and Eddie Cochems Era 1904-1905

Coach # 5 Shack Shealy
Coach # 6 Eddie Cochems

Year	Coach	Record	Conference	Record
1904	Shack Shealy	3-3-1	SIAA	3-2-1
1905	Eddie Cochems	3-2-1	SIAA	3-2-1

1904 Coach Shack Shealy

1904 Clemson Tigers Football Coach Shack Shealy

The 1904 Clemson Tigers football team represented the Clemson Agricultural College during the 1904 college football season as a member of the SIAA. Shack Shealy, formerly a team captain, was the head football coach in his first and only season at Clemson. The Tigers completed their ninth season overall and also their ninth in the SIAA with a record of 3-3-1 overall and 3-2-1 in the SIAA. They gained ninth place of 19 teams in the SIAA. Joe Holland was the captain

On Oct 8, the season began against Alabama in West End Park, Birmingham. The Fighting Tigers played well and beat the Crimson White W (18-0). On Oct 15, the Tigers lost to SIAA co-champion Auburn at home (Bowman Field) L (0-5). Then, in another home match, on Oct 22, the Tigers defeated Georgia W (10-0) co-champion. Sewanee was always a tough team and this year Clemson got to find out how tough this SIAA competitor really was on Oct 27. The Tigers lost their second of two SIAA games in Colombia SC to the Sewanee "Iron Men" L (5-11).

Georgia Tech came back the following week in Piedmont Park Atlanta GA on Nov 5 to avenge the prior year's 73-0 trouncing by tying the Tigers T (11-11). The Tigers traveled to Waite Field in Knoxville Tennessee to beat the Volunteers on Nov 12 and prevailed in a close match W (6-0). On Nov 24, in what had once been the Textile Bowl, Clemson lost its final game of the season to North Carolina A &M in Raleigh NC, on Nov 24 L (0-18)

1905 Clemson Tigers Football Coach Eddie Cochems

The 1905 Clemson Tigers football team represented the Clemson Agricultural College during the 1905 college football season as a member of the SIAA. Eddie Cochems, one of the immortals and early tradesmen in football strategies was the head football coach in his first and only season at Clemson. Eddie Cochems was just getting started but he would become well known in College football. He was a future innovator of the forward pass. Clemson was not his first choice. He had just lost out to Phil King for the Wisconsin job, when he accepted to coach Clemson's 1905 team. A fine coach, Cochems left after just one year.

The Tigers completed their tenth season overall and also their tenth in the SIAA with a record of 3-2-1 overall and 3-2-1 in the SIAA. They gained fifth place of 169 teams in the SIAA. Puss Derrick was the captain. Though the team finished fifth in the SIAA, they did not play all teams. Sports pundit John de Saulles rated Clemson as the third best team in the SIAA.

1905 Clemson Coach Eddie Cochems

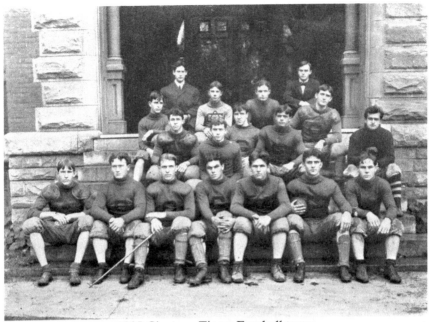

1905 Clemson Tigers Football team

<<< Puss Derrick, Clemson Captain
On Oct 14, in the season home opener,
Tennessee marched into Bowman Field to
play Eddie Cochems' Tigers and the tough
Volunteers came away with a tie T (5-5).
On the road the next week, Oct 21 at
Georgia, the Tigers laid a wallop to the
Georgia Bulldogs W (35-0). On Oct 25 at
the State Fairgrounds in Columbia SC,
The Fighting Tigers got the best of
Alabama W (25-0).

On November 11, at Auburn, an inspired Clemson team triumphed v
these Tiger rivals W (26-0). So far, there were no losses but that
would not last more than one week. On November 11, the Clemson
Tigers traveled to Dudley Field in Nashville Tennessee and they were
shut out badly by a tough Vanderbilt team L (0-41). By November
30, the next game, the Tigers had regained composure and they
played a tough game in Grant Field Atlanta GA but it was not tough
enough to defeat Georgia Tech's Yellow Jackets who stung the
Tigers L (10-17)

Chapter 10 Bob Williams & Frank Shaughnessy Era 1906-1907

Coach # 7 Bob Williams
Coach # 8 Frank Shaughnessy

Year	Coach	Record	Conf	Record
1906	Bob Williams	3-3-1	SIAA	4-0-1
1907	Frank Shaughnessy	4-4-0	SIAA	1-3-0

1906 Clemson Tigers Football Coach Bob Williams

<<< Coach Bob Williams

The 1906 Clemson Tigers football team represented the Clemson Agricultural College during the 1906 college football season as a member of the SIAA. Bob Williams, a coach who would be at the Clemson helm for six years at various times, but none longer than two years, was the head football coach in his first of six seasons at Clemson and his only year in a row this time. The Tigers completed their eleventh season overall and also their eleventh in the SIAA with a record of 4-0-3 overall and 4-0-1 in the SIAA. Fritz Furtick was the captain. The team finished tied for first place in the SIAA.

Heralding one of the best defenses in the South for the season, the Tigers allowed no touchdowns scored by their opponents in seven games, and only 4 points scored overall. The team tied with Vanderbilt for the SIAA title, but few writers chose them over the vaunted Commodores.

On Oct 13, the Tigers tied VPI T (0-0) at home. On Oct 20, Clemson beat Georgia at home W (6-0). The it was North Carolina A &M at Columbia SC in the second scoreless tie of the season T (0-0). This was followed by a repeat no-score tie v Davidson at Davidson, NC T 0-0).

Fritz Furtick Captain 1906 Clemson Tigers

In a nail biter v Auburn on Nov 10 at home in Bowman Field, The Clemson Tigers beat the Auburn Tigers W (6-4). Next was Tennessee at Bowman Field on Nov 19 W (10-0). In the season finale, Bob Williams' Tigers put it all together and beat Georgia Tech on November 29 at Grant Field in Atlanta, GA W (10–0)

The GA Tech game was sweeter than usual because John Heisman was the Tech Coach. In this 10–0 victory over John Heisman's Georgia Tech team, Captain Fritz Furtick scored Clemson's first touchdown. An onside kick set up the second TD.

Clemson's first forward pass ever took place during the game. Left end Powell Lykes, dropped back to kick, but lobbed a 30-yard pass to George Warren instead. Baseball star Ty Cobb was in attendance at this game.

The starting lineup was Coagman (left end), Lykes (left tackle), Gaston (left guard), Clark (center), Carter (right guard), McLaurin (right tackle), Coles (right end), Warren (quarterback), Allen (left halfback), Furtick (right halfback).

Bob Williams coached just one year in this stint, his first of four separate times being named the Clemson head football coach. He would be back in 1909 for another one-year stint.

1907 Clemson Tigers Football Coach Frank Shaughnessy

<<< Coach Shaughnessy

The 1907 Clemson Tigers football team represented the Clemson Agricultural College during the 1907 college football season as a member of the SIAA. Frank Shaughnessy was the head football coach. The Tigers completed their twelfth season overall and also their twelfth in the SIAA with a record of 4-4 overall and 1-3-0 in the SIAA. They gained tenth place of 13 teams in the SIAA. Mac McLaurin was the captain.

The Clemson Fighting Tigers began the 1907 with a new coach, Frank Shaughnessy and they played their first three games at home at Bowman Field. They opened the season with Gordon State, a small Institute that had some tough players. They won the game on Sept 28 by a touchdown, with five points at the time W (5-0). On Oct 9, the Tigers beat Maryville W (35-0) and then Tennessee gave Clemson its first loss in a tight match L (0-4). On Oct 31, the Tigers came back ten days later against North Carolina in Columbia SC for the win W (15-6).

On Nov 4, the Tigers traveled to Auburn and were bcaten by the Auburn Tigers L (0-12). Next it was Georgia on Nov 9 in Augusta L (0-8). On Nov 9, Davidson beat the Tigers at Bowman Field L (6-10). The Tigers won the last game of the season v Georgia Tech at Grant Field in Atlanta GA 6-5) with John Heisman as the GA Tech coach.

Chapter 11 Stein Stone, Frank Dobson & Bob Williams Era 1908-1915

Coach #7 Bob Williams
Coach #9 Stein Stone
Coach #10 Frank Dobson

Year	Coach	Record	Conference	Record
1908	Stein Stone	1-6-0	SIAA	0-4-0
1909	Bob Williams	6–3-0	SIAA	1-2-0
1910	Frank Dobson	4-3-1	SIAA	2-3-1
1911	Frank Dobson	3-5-0	SIAA	3-5-0
1912	Frank Dobson	4-4-0	SIAA	3-3-0
1913	Bob Williams	4-4-0	SIAA	2-4-0
1914	Bob Williams	5-3-1	SIAA	2-2-0
1915	Bob Williams	2-4-2	SIAA	2-2-0

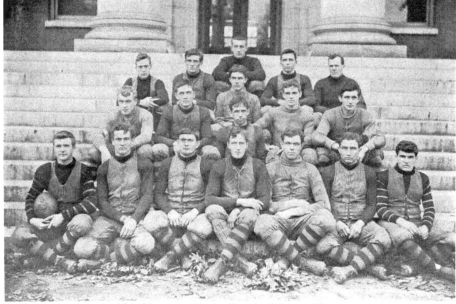

1908 Clemson Tigers Football Team Picture

1908 Clemson Tigers Football Coach Stein Stone

<<< Coach Stein Stone

The 1908 Clemson Tigers football team represented the Clemson Agricultural College during the 1908 college football season as a member of the SIAA. Stein Stone was the head football coach in his first and only year. The Tigers completed their thirteenth season overall and also their thirteenth in the SIAA with a record of 1-6 overall and 0-4-0 in the SIAA. They finished in last place out of twelve active SIAA teams. Sticker Coles was the captain.

The Tigers opened the season at home in Bowman Field on Sept 26 at home with a win against Gordon W (15-0). It would be the only win of the season. The losses for the season were as follows:

Oct 10, Home, VPI, L (0-6)
Oct 17, Dudley Field Nashville, Vanderbilt, L (0-41)
Oct 28, Columbia SC, Davidson, L (0-31)
Nov 5, Augusta Ga., Georgia, L (0-6)
Nov 14, 15th & Cumberland Field Knoxville, Tennessee L (5-6)
Nov 26, Grant Field Atlanta GA, L (6-30)

It was the Fighting Tigers worse season ever and something had to be done. 1906 Coach Bob Williams was asked to come back and give it a try.

1909 Clemson Tigers Football Coach Bob Williams

The 1909 Clemson Tigers football team represented the Clemson Agricultural College during the 1909 college football season as a member of the SIAA. Bob Williams was the head football coach for the second time for another one year stint. The Tigers completed their fourteenth season overall and also their fourteenth in the SIAA with a record of 6-3 overall and 1-2 in the SIAA. They finished in ninth place out of fourteen active SIAA teams. C. M. Robbs was the captain.

Clemson 1909 Football Team Coach Bob Williams

The Tigers opened the season at home with Gordon at Bowman Field in a nice win. W (26-0) The next week, the team traveled to Miles Field in Blackburg VA to play VPI in a tough game. VPI barely defeated the Tigers L (0-6). On Oct 9, at Charlotte, NC, Clemson defeated Davidson W (17-5). Then, on Oct 16 in a really tight game, at the Birmingham Fairgrounds in Alabama, the Tigers were beaten by the Crimson White L (0-3).

On Oct 23, Port Royal played the Tigers at home and were beaten W (19-0) in a shutout game. On Nov 4, the Clemson squad traveled to Columbia, South Carolina to beat the Gamecocks W (6-0). Then, on Nov 10, at Augusta, GA, in the rivalry game, the Tigers beat the Bulldogs in a close match W (5-0).

In a first-time matchup, the Tigers traveled to College Park Stadium in Charleston, SC to play the Citadel. The Fighting Tigers won the game W (17-0). In the season ending game with Georgia Tech, at Grant Field in Atlanta, GA, the John Heisman coached team Georgia Tech team overpowered the Tigers L (3-29).

1910 Clemson Tigers Football Coach Frank Dobson

The 1910 Clemson Tigers football team represented the Clemson Agricultural College during the 1910 college football season as a member of the SIAA. Frank Dobson was the head football coach for year one of a three-year stint. The Tigers completed their fifteenth season overall and also their fifteenth in the SIAA with a record of 4-3-1 overall and 2-3-1 in the SIAA. They again finished in ninth place out of fourteen active SIAA teams. W. H. Hanke was the captain. In 2016, Clemson placed its membership in the SIAA during this season in dispute.

Opening the season on Sept 24, the Tigers crushed Gordon W (26-0) at home at Bowman Field, On Oct1, the Tigers played their first game against Mercer at home and were beaten in a very close match L (0-3). Howard was another first. They invited the Tigers to play in Homewood AL, and the Clemson obliged with a nice win W (24-0). Clemson then traveled to College Park Stadium on Oct 15 to beat the Citadel W (32-0).

In the Auburn rivalry, played in Auburn AL this particular year, the Tigers lost L (0-17). On Nov 3, at Columbia SC on Big Thursday, the Clemson Fighting Tigers defeated the Gamecocks W (24-0). Then came the first tie of the season on Nov 10 against Georgia in Augusta, T (0-0). Meanwhile John Heisman was fine tuning his Yellow Jacket Team to be contenders. Georgia Tech shut out the Tigers on Nov 24 at Grant Field in Atlanta L (0-34).

Clemson's 10th Football Coach 1910 -1912 Frank Dobson

1911 Clemson Tigers Football Coach Frank Dobson

The 1911 Clemson Tigers football team represented the Clemson
Agricultural College during the 1911 college football season as a

member of the SIAA. Frank Dobson was the head football coach for the second year of a three-year stint. The Tigers completed their sixteenth season overall and also their sixteenth in the SIAA with a record of 3-5 overall and 3-5 in the SIAA. They again finished in eleventh place out of eighteen active SIAA teams. Paul Bissell was the captain.

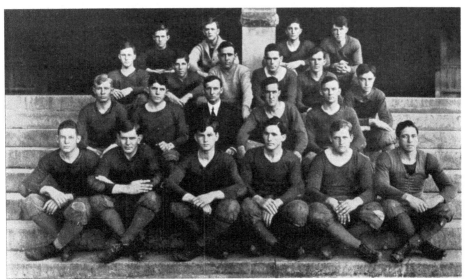

1911 Clemson Football Team Frank Dobson Coach

Auburn came to Bowman Field for the season opener on Oct 14 and they handily beat the Tigers L (0-29). Next on Oct 21, came Howard to Bowman Field and the Tigers prevailed W (15-0). On Big Thursday, Oct 25, at home, v Florida Gators, the Tigers suffered their second home loss of the season L (5-6). Next came the Big Thursday game on Nov 2 after traveling to Columbia SC, the Tigers beat the Gamecocks W (27-0). Then, on Nov 4, CU traveled to the home of the Citadel at College Park Stadium, Charleston SC and prevailed W (18-0).

November 9 brought on the Georgia Bulldogs at Augusta GA. This time, the Dogs got all the bites. L (0-23). Mercer was next in Columbus GA and they beat the Tigers good, L (6-30). It was another bad finish to a so-so-year as John Heisman's Georgia Tech Yellow Jackets shut down the Clemson offense completely L (0-31).

1912 Clemson Tigers Football Coach Frank Dobson

For the 1912 season, the value of a touchdown was increased to six points. The end-zone area was also added. Before the addition of the end zone, forward passes caught beyond the goal line resulted in a loss of possession and a touchback. The increase from five points to six did not come until much later in Canada, and the touchdown remained only five points there until 1956.

The 1912 Clemson Tigers football team represented the Clemson Agricultural College during the 1912 college football season as a member of the SIAA. Frank Dobson was the head football coach for the third year of a three-year stint. The Tigers completed their seventeenth season overall and also their seventeenth in the SIAA with a record of 4-4-0 overall and 3-3-0 in the SIAA. They finished in twelfth out of twenty active SIAA teams. W. B. Britt was the captain.

The season opener was on Oct 5 at Howard in Homewood AL. The Tigers were a well-oiled machine in their first start under third-year coach Frank Dobson and they walloped Howard W (59-0). On Oct 12, in the Tigers home opener at Bowman Field, they shut out Riverside Military Academy W (26–0). Next was a loss to Auburn on Oct 19 at Drake Field in Alabama L (6-27). Clemson then crushed the Citadel at home on Oct 26, W (52-14). On Big Thursday in Columbia SC, the Gamecocks of South Carolina defeated the Clemson Fighting Tigers L (7-22)

The Tigers traveled to Augusta GA on Nov 7 to and were defeated by the Bulldogs L (5-27). On Nov16, the Clemson squad survived against Mercer in Macon GA W (21-13). Then again, after traveling to Grant Field in Atlanta GA, on Nov 28, the CU was shut out by John Heisman's Georgia Tech Yellow Jackets L (0-23)

1912 Clemson Football Team

A pattern seemed to be developing in the past few seasons which were captured in this chapter. Clemson was not beating the better teams; was walloping the smaller teams; and sometimes was having trouble with the teams in the mid-size group. This was not the recipe of success for a team that would one day win the National Championship. Change was coming as Bob Williams was about to come back the following year for his third stint of four as a Clemson Head Coach.

1913 Clemson Tigers Football Coach Bob Williams

The 1913 Clemson Tigers football team represented the Clemson Agricultural College during the 1913 college football season as a member of the SIAA. Bob Williams was the head football coach for the first year of his third stint as Clemson head coach. The Tigers completed their eighteenth season overall and also their eighteenth in the SIAA with a record of 4-4-0 overall and 2-4-0 in the SIAA. They finished in tenth out of eighteen active SIAA teams. The SIAA membership was in flux at the time. A. P. Gandy was the captain.

The Clemson Fighting Tigers began the season at home on Oct 4 with a close nailbiter of a win over Davidson W (6-3). On Oct 11 at Alabama playing in the UA Quad field in Tuscaloosa, AL, the Tigers were shut-out L (0–20). Alabama and Auburn were big rivals at the time and it is ironic that the following week on Oct 18 at home v Auburn, the Tigers lost by the same exact score L (0-20). By the time Big Thursday came around Bob Williams' Tigers were ready on Oct 30 to shut-out South Carolina at Columbia SC W (32-0).

Though the Tigers were still taking their lumps v the better teams, they seemed to be doing better with Coach Williams. On Nov 6, the squad lost a tough close on against Georgia in Augusta L (15-18). Then, they beat the Citadel on Nov 8 in Charleston W (7-3) in another close match. On November 17, the Tigers let it all out in a rout over Mercer at Macon GA W (52-0). Though they were playing much better, John Heisman's Georgia Teach team was a well-poled machine when they met on Nov 27. Heisman's boys easily beat the Clemson Fighting Tigers L (0-34).

1914 Clemson Tigers Football Coach Bob Williams

In 1914, the founder of Clemson football, Walter Riggs, as College President was working behind the scenes to give the football team a big boost. His plan was to build a nice stadium on campus for Clemson to host its football games. This would not come in 2014, however.

The 1914 Clemson Tigers football team represented the Clemson Agricultural College during the 1914 college football season as a member of the SIAA. Bob Williams was the head football coach for the second year of a four-year stint. The Tigers completed their nineteenth season overall and also their nineteenth in the SIAA with a record of 5-3-1 overall and 2-2-0 in the SIAA. They finished in eighth out of nineteen active SIAA teams. William Schilletter was the captain.

Clemson 1914 Football Team Bob Williams Coach

On Oct 3 at t Davidson in Davidson, NC, the Tigers played the Wildcats to a scoreless tie T (0–0). On Oct 10, the Tigers traveled to Waite Field in Knoxville Tennessee to play Tennessee and the squad was shut out by the Volunteers L (0-27) Something was wrong in Denmark as the Tigers were held scoreless in their first two games. Things did not improve on Oct 17 at Drake Field in Auburn AL as for the third week in a row the Fighting Tigers showed little fight and were shutout again L (0-28). Finally, on Oct 22, in Greenville SC, the Tigers got some points on the board in a thumping shutout of Furman W (57-0).

CU looked good again, knowing they could score, on Big Thursday, Oct 29 at Columbia SC, they whooped South Carolina W (29-6). The Citadel played tough against CU at College Park Stadium in Charleston, SC, but were defeated W (14-0). The next game against Georgia was a big one because Georgia had been beating the Tigers regularly for a number of years. Not this year, as Clemson defeated Georgia at Sanford Field on Nov 7 in Athens GA W (35-13). The next week the Tigers showed they were back by beating a tough VMI team in a nail-biter W (27-23). Could they beat John Heisman's Georgia Tech Yellow Jackets? That answer came on November 26 as the margin of victory for the Yellow Jackets triumph over the Tigers was smaller but Heisman's team won another one L (6-26).

1915 Clemson Tigers Football Coach Bob Williams

In 1915, Walter Riggs, College President was able to pull it off and the Clemson Tigers began to play games on the newly constructed Riggs Field. It was Clemson's new home stadium. Riggs Field would host the football team until Memorial Stadium was built in 1942.

The 1915 Clemson Tigers football team represented the Clemson Agricultural College during the 1915 college football season as a member of the SIAA. Bob Williams was the head football coach for the third year of a four-year stint. The Tigers completed their twentieth season overall and also their twentieth in the SIAA with a record of 2-4-2 overall and 2-2-0 in the SIAA. They finished in twelfth out of twenty-three active SIAA teams. W. K. McGill was the captain.

Looking at just the record, one would conclude that Bob Williams' Tigers did not play as well as in 1914. However, when you look closely at the scores you find a story of a fine defense without a corresponding offense to match. The tough games lost in this season, and there were twice as many as those won, were by margins of two touchdowns or less. Many games were decided by two or three points.

Coach Bob Williams left Clemson and quit coaching after the 1915 season. However, Clemson brought him back one mere time in 1929 for five games to finish the season so there was a deep fondness for coach Williams. He was a great coach. Between 1915 and 1926, Williams practiced law in Roanoke, Virginia, and was the city's mayor.

He returned to coach Clemson for the final 5 games of 1926. He died after a stroke in Deland, Florida in 1957. He goes down in history as one of the great pioneer coaches of the early football era. It helps to recall that in the 1902 season when Williams was coaching South Carolina, his Gamecocks beat John Heisman's Clemson Tigers ruining Heisman's undefeated season. That alone gives Williams some great credentials.

Games of the Season

On Oct 2, CU began the 2015 season at home in Riggs Field, the first game ever played there, with a tie against Davidson T (6-6). The Tigers then traveled to Tennessee on Oct 9 and beat a tough Volunteers team in a very close match W (3-0). The Oct 16 Auburn game was played in Anderson SC and Auburn won in a close game W (14-0). On Big Thursday in Columbia SC, Oct 28, The Gamecocks and Tigers played to a scoreless tie T (0-0)

Riggs Field – The First Game Oct 2, 1915 v Davidson

On Nov 6, CU traveled to Greeneville, SC to play North Carolina in a losing effort that was very close L (7-9). Next came a tough VMI team in a game played at Richmond VA. It was another close call but the Tigers were on the underside of the score L (3-6). It had to be getting frustrating for the team to be losing such close ones. Georgia was another loss on Nov 25 at Sanford Field in Athens GA, L (0-13). This year, there was no Georgia Tech game scheduled. The Tigers were glad to get this strange season behind them.

Tell me more about **Riggs Field**

April 3, 2002
✿Welcome to Historic Riggs Field
by Sam Blackman

Author's Note. This well-written tribute piece by *Sam Blackman* of the Tigers staff puts the importance of Walter Riggs and Riggs Field in perspective. Both were major building blocks to the ultimate success of Clemson University and its College Championship Football Team.

t

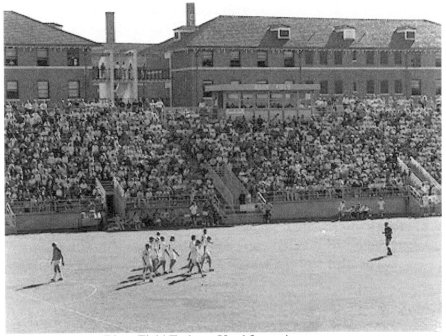

Riggs Field Today – Used for various purposes

Welcome to Historic Riggs Field!

Saturday will be a special occasion as a Clemson varsity football team will return to Riggs Field for a football game for the first time since 1941. The varsity's last game here was on November 15, 1941, a 29-0 victory over Wake Forest.

This facility was the home of Clemson football from 1915-41 and it saw many landmark accomplishments for the Clemson program. It is being used today because Frank Howard field and surrounding facilities are undergoing renovations.

Perhaps one of the first big "stepping stones" in helping make Clemson successful in football and other areas of athletics even today was the construction of Riggs Field. Named after one of the most beloved leaders of the early years, Riggs Field is in its 88th year of service to Clemson University.

What made Riggs Field so significant to the school at the time it was first built in 1915? It was the first major facility on the Clemson University campus dedicated to intercollegiate athletics. Prior to Riggs Field, Clemson's teams played on Bowman Field in front of Tillman Hall. This field was used as the parade grounds for the corps of cadets, and served as the home of the football, track, baseball and yes, even the basketball team-one could imagine the overuse of Bowman field.

Riggs Field gave the football team a place to play and practice on its adjunct fields. The baseball field was constructed where the tennis courts are now and the track encircled the football field.

Construction of Riggs Field started in the early summer of 1914. Approximately $10,000 was appropriated for the construction of the facility that covered almost nine acres. Before its completion the Clemson Board of Trustees unanimously agreed to name the new athletic complex, Riggs Field in honor of Clemson's first football coach and originator of the Clemson Athletic Association, Dr. Walter M. Riggs.

Riggs was the first football coach at Clemson in 1896. He stepped down as head coach in 1897 to devote full time to academics, as he was also an engineering professor. He also coached the team in 1899 because the athletic association was low on funds. However, in 1900, the search for a new coach must have become serious, as Riggs hired John Heisman to coach the Tigers.

Although no longer the head coach, Clemson athletics and Riggs could not be split. Riggs also was the equivalent of an athletic director, managing the money and making contracts with other teams. The well-respected Riggs was also president of the Southern Intercollegiate Athletic Association (SIAA) an early conference presiding the Southern Conference. Riggs later became president of Clemson on March 7, 1911. He served in this capacity until his death in 1924.

Riggs Field was dedicated in grand fashion on October 6, 1915. The band, corps of cadets, along with faculty and alumni marched from Tillman Hall to the new field. According to The Tiger, the group formed a "C" formation on the field and poured forth a thrilling volume of patriotic Tiger yells and songs. Professor J.W. Gantt, President of the Athletic Association, introduced Dr. Riggs as, "the man who has done more for the athletics at Clemson and probably more for southern athletics than any other man."

In presenting the field to the corps of cadets, Dr. Riggs said, "This magnificent field is a token of recognition by the Trustees of Clemson College of the importance of military and athletic training for the cadets. It is to be a place for the teaching of the principles of teamwork and fair play. This large and beautiful athletic field is to stand for the development of the physical man and whether in real work or in play, it is hoped that this field will be used as an agency in the development of high and honorable men. "Whether victorious or defeated, may the men of this field always be gentlemen of the highest type. A few minutes later, Dr. Riggs made the initial kickoff in the first football game played on the new field. While on the field, he wore a new orange and blue sweater he had just received from Auburn, his alma mater, as they too wanted to congratulate Clemson and Dr. Riggs for their accomplishments. Clemson and Davidson played to a 6-6 tie that day.

While looking at the well-manicured surface today, many other facets about this historic place come to mind.

This ground is where Clemson's first All-American played, O.K. Pressley in the late 20s. He was a center and a linebacker for the Tigers in 1926-28. Another incredible feat that is still a Clemson record occurred when Maxcey Welch scored five touchdowns in Clemson's 75-0 win over Newberry on October 17, 1930.

It was also home to Clemson's most versatile athlete, Banks McFadden (see front cover of this program). McFadden was an All-American in both football and basketball in the same calendar year in 1939. He was named the nation's most versatile athlete for 1939-40. He was a record setter on the field as a runner, passer and punter. He led the Tigers to state championships in track twice in his three years on the team. He was also the star player who led Clemson to a surprise 6-3 win over Boston College in the 1940 Cotton Bowl, the Tigers first ever bowl appearance.

Head Football Coach Frank Howard coached his first game, a 38-0 win over Presbyterian on September 21, 1940. In Howard's first game as head coach, Clemson scored on the first offensive play as George Floyd reversed around left end and raced 18 yards untouched for a Clemson touchdown.

In1940, Clemson won the Southern Conference football title while calling Riggs Field Home. It was the first of eight conference championships for the Tigers under Frank Howard.

Clemson' football teams compiled a 57-16-6 record during their 27 years at Riggs field and that .759 winning percentage is actually better than the winning percentage the Tigers have earned in Death Valley (72 percent). The baseball team won over 70 percent of its games there when the diamond was part of the complex.

Riggs Field today is considered to be one of the top if not top soccer facilities in the nation. It has been the home of Clemson's soccer program since 1980 and the men's team has compiled a 283-53-20 record there. The1987 NCAA Men's Soccer Final Four was contested here and Clemson won the National Championship before a crowd of 8,332, then an all-time record crowd for a NCAA Championship soccer match. Since 1996, the Clemson Lady Tiger soccer team has an impressive 82-12-4 record at Riggs Field.

As one looks from Riggs Field and sees the grand clock tower of Tillman Hall guarding campus, it is only appropriate that these two symbols of the university are so close in proximately as both have played such a significant role in Clemson history.

Chapter 12 Wayne Hart & Edward Donahue Era 1916-1918

Coach # 11 Wayne Hart
Coach # 12 Edward Donahue

Year	Coach	Record	Conference	Record
1916	Wayne Hart	3-6-0	SIAA	2-4-0
1917	Edward Donahue	6-2-0	SIAA	4-1-0
1918	Edward Donahue	5-2-0	SIAA	3-1-0
1919	Edward Donahue	6-2-2	SIAA	2-2-2
1920	Edward Donahue	4-6-1	SIAA	2-6-0

1916 Clemson Tigers Football Coach Wayne Hart

<<< Coach Wayne Hart 1916

The 1916 Clemson Tigers football team represented the Clemson Agricultural College during the 1916 college football season as a member of the SIAA. Wayne Hart was the head football coach for his first and only year The Tigers completed their twenty-first season overall and also their twenty-first in the SIAA with a record of 3-6-0 overall and 2-4-0 in the SIAA. They finished in fifteenth out of twenty-five active SIAA teams. S. S. Major was the captain. Stumpy Banks caught two touchdowns against rival South Carolina.

On Sept 30, the Gators kicked off the season at home against Furman with a close win W (7-6). On Oct 7 v. Georgia in Anderson, SC, the Tigers were shut out L (0-26). Then on Oct 14, at Riggs Field, Tennessee beat the Tigers in another shutout L (0-26). On Oct 20, CU traveled to Drake Field at Auburn AL and were shut out again 0-

28. So far, with just one TD scored for the whole year with the season half gone, things were not promising.

On Big Thursday in Columbia SC, on Oct 26 CU defeated the Tar Heels W (27-0). Then on Nov 11 at Broad Street Park in Richmond VA, the Tigers were thumped by VMI L (7-37). Citadel was ready to win on Nov 16 and they beat the Tigers in a close match at the County in Orangeburg, SC L (0–3). Back at the home field on Nov 22, CU beat Presbyterian in a shutout W (40-0). As a season closer in Charlotte, NC, Davidson shut out the Tigers in a big loss L (0-33).

1917 Clemson Tigers Football Coach Edward Donahue

<<< Edward Jiggs Donahue

The 1917 Clemson Tigers football team represented the Clemson Agricultural College during the 1917 college football season as a member of the SIAA. Edward Donahue was the head football coach for his first of four seasons.

The Tigers completed their twenty-second season overall and also their twenty-second in the SIAA with a record of 6-2-0 overall and 4-1-0 in the SIAA. They finished in third out of sixteen active SIAA teams. F. L. Witsel was the captain. Stumpy Banks scored five touchdowns against Furman for a school record. caught two touchdowns against rival South Carolina. John Heisman ranked Clemson fourth in the south, or third in the Southern Intercollegiate Athletic Association.

The season opened at home in Riggs Field, Calhoun, SC, on Oct 6 with a nice win v Presbyterian W (13-0). Furman was next at Greenville SC on Oct 13 in a big shutout W (38-0). Auburn came to play at Riggs Field on Oct 19 and gave the Tigers their first defeat of the season L (0-7). The following Big Thursday, Oct 25, at Columbia SC, the Tigers beat the Gamecocks W 21-13).

On Nov 1 at Wofford in Spartanburg, SC, CU won W (27–16). Then on Nov 16 at the County Fairgrounds in Orangeburg SC, the Tigers shut out the Citadel W (20-0). Clemson then beat the Florida Gators at Jacksonville Florida in a blowout W (55-7). With just one close loss on the record and a fine season going, the last game was against Davidson at Charlotte NC. The Wildcats out it together and beat the Tigers L (9-21)

1918 Clemson Tigers Football Coach Edward Donahue

World War I caused many colleges to skip the 1917 football season. In 1918 about thirty major colleges across the country dropped the sport either temporarily or permanently as getting players had become a major difficulty. Each of the major services has football teams during the war as a source of recreation and camaraderie. Some were very, very good because the Army, Navy, etc. had a lot of former college players in the camps with which to form teams. Colleges were very agreeable in playing the service camps.

The 1918 Clemson Tigers football team represented the Clemson Agricultural College during the 1918 college football season as a member of the SIAA. Edward Donahue was the head football coach for his second of four seasons. The Tigers completed their twenty-third season overall and also their twenty-third in the SIAA with a record of 5-2-0 overall and 3-1-0 in the SIAA. They finished in fourth out of ten active SIAA teams. Stumpy Banks was the captain.

Coach Donahue was a busy guy as WWI came to an end in 1918. He was a great athlete and a great coach. In the Academic Year 1918-1919, he not only coached football, but also basketball, baseball, and track teams to enable their seasons.

On Sept 27, Camp Sevier came to Riggs Field for the Tigers Home opener and were defeated W (65-0). On Oct 5, the Tigers played

Heisman's Georgia Tech Yellow Jackets again and were shut out L (0-28). Then, a month later, Nov 2 at South Carolina in the Big Thursday Game at Columbia, SC, the Clemson Fighting Tigers were strong and defeated the Gamecocks in a big shutout W (39-0). On Nov. 9, Camp Hancock came to Riggs Field to play the Tigers and this well-staffed service team shellacked the Tigers L (13-66).

On Nov 16, CU defeated the Citadel in Columbia SC W (7-0). On November 23, the Tigers walloped Furman at home W (67-7). To close the 1918 season at home, CU defeated Davidson W (7-0).

1919 Clemson Tigers Football Coach Edward Donahue

The 1919 Clemson Tigers football team represented the Clemson Agricultural College during the 1919 college football season as a member of the SIAA. Edward Donahue was the head football coach for his third of four seasons. The Tigers completed their twenty-fourth season overall and also their twenty-fourth in the SIAA with a record of 6-2-2 overall and 2-2-2 in the SIAA. They finished in tenth out of twenty-three active SIAA teams. Stumpy Banks was the captain.

The Clemson Fighting Tigers got the season rolling on Sept 27 at home against Erskine at home, Riggs Field in Calhoun SC with a big walloping shutout W (53-0). The following week on Oct 3, CU shut out Davidson W (7-0) at home. Then, Ed Donahue took the CU team to Grant Field in Atlanta GA to play John Heisman's Georgia Tech squad. The Yellow Jackets shut out the Tigers L (0-28). The next loss was at Drake Field in Auburn AL, v the Tigers on Oct 17. Clemson went down in another shutout L (0-7) but the game was very close.

On Oct 25, Tennessee lost to the Tigers at home (14–0). Then on Big Thursday in Columbia SC, South Carolina was defeated by Clemson, W (19-6). The next game was against Presbyterian at home and the Tigers chalked up another win W (19-7).

On Nov 13, at the County Fairgrounds in Orangeburg, SC, the Tigers shut out the Citadel W (33-0). On Nov 21 at Riggs Field, Furman tied the Tigers T (7-7). At Sanford Field in Georgia, the Tigers tied the Bulldogs in a scoreless match T (0-0).

1920 Clemson Tigers Football Coach Edward Donahue

The 1920 Clemson Tigers football team represented the Clemson Agricultural College during the 1920 college football season as a member of the SIAA. Edward Donahue was the head football coach for his fourth (last) of four seasons. It was Donahue's worst record. The Tigers completed their twenty-fifth season overall and also their twenty-fifth in the SIAA with a record of 4-6-1 overall and 2-6-0 in the SIAA. They finished fifteenth out of twenty-four active SIAA teams. Boo Armstrong was the captain.

The season opened on Sept 24 with the first of five home games at home in Riggs Field, Calhoun SC. The Clemson Fighting Tigers shut out Erskine W (26-0). On Oct 1, Presbyterian tied the Tigers T (7-7). On Oct 2, the day after the tie, the Tigers defeated Newberry W (26-6). On Oct 10, CU defeated Wofford W (13-7). It was not until Oct 15 that the Tigers suffered their first defeat in a shutout at the hands of Auburn L (0-21).

On October 23 at Tennessee's 15th and Cumberland Field in Knoxville, TN, the Wildcats beat the Tigers L (0–26). On Oct 28, in the Big Thursday annual rivalry in Columbia, SC, South Carolina beat Clemson by a field goal L (0-3). In the closest game since Heisman went to Georgia Tech, the Tigers almost prevailed against the Yellow Jackets but came up short L (0-7). Recovering quickly from the Tech loss, on Nov 11, the Tigers shut out the Citadel at the County Fairgrounds at Orangeburg, SC W (26-0). For the first time, on Nov 20, in Greenville SC, Furman beat the Tigers L (0-14). In the season finale, Georgia shellacked Clemson at Sanford Field in Athens Ga, L (0-55).

Chapter 13 E J Stewart & Bud Saunders Era 1921-1926

Coach # 13 E J Stewart
Coach # 14 Bud Saunders

Year	Coach	Record	Conference	Record
1921	E J Stewart	1-6-2	SIAA	0-4-2
1922	E J Stewart	5-4-0	SIAA/SoCon	2–2-1
1923	Bud Saunders	5-2-1	SoCon	1–1-1
1924	Bud Saunders	2-6-0	SoCon	0-3-0
1925	Bud Saunders	1-7-0	SoCon	0-4-0
1926	Bud Saunders	2-2-0	SoCon	1-1-0
1926	Bob Williams	0-5	SoCon	0-2-0

1921 Clemson Tigers Football Coach E J Stewart

1921 Clemson Coach EJ Stewart

The 1921 Clemson Tigers football team represented the Clemson Agricultural College during the 1921 college football season as a member of the SIAA. E. J. Stewart was the head football coach for his first of two seasons. So far, no coach for Clemson has stayed more than four years. It is surprising that the team has done so well without such consistency in coaching.

The Tigers completed their twenty-sixth season overall and also their twenty-sixth in the SIAA with a record of 1-6-2 overall and 0-4-2 in the SIAA. They finished twenty fifth out of twenty-six active SIAA teams. J. H. Spearman was the captain.

The Season opened in Danville Kentucky on Oct 1 v Centre, who beat new coach Stewart's Tigers L (0-14). The Tigers first win came on Oct 7 against a weak Presbyterian team in the home opener at Riggs Field, Calhoun, SC, W (34-0). The big opponents began to fire at Clemson first on Oct 14 when Auburn walloped the Tigers at Drake Field in Alabama L (0-56). Furman then gained a tie from CU on Oct 21 at Greenville SC T (0-0).

On Big Thursday, there was no celebrating as the Gamecocks of SC soundly defeated Clemson L (0-21) in Columbia SC. An always tough Georgia tech team put a hit on the Tigers on Nov 5 at Grant Field in GA L (7-48). The Citadel then tied the Tigers in a scoreless match T (7-7) on Nov 10 at the County Fairgrounds in Orangeburg, SC. On Nov 18, Erskine beat the Tigers at home L (0-13) and then on Nov 24 at Sanford Field in Athens GA, the Bulldogs shut out the Tigers L (0-28) The best one could say about it was that it was a miserable season. Everybody was glad it was in the past and looking forward to rebuilding the team.

1922 Clemson Tigers Football Coach E J Stewart

The 1922 Clemson Tigers football team represented the Clemson Agricultural College during the 1922 college football season as a member of the SoCon. E. J. Stewart was the head football coach for his second of two seasons. The Tigers completed their twenty-seventh season overall and their first in the Southern Conference with a record of 5-4-0 overall, 2-4 in SIAA, and 1-2 in the SoCon. They finished twelfth out of twenty active SoCon teams. E. H. Emanuel was the captain.

This year, after 26 years as part of the SIAA, Clemson made a big switch to the Southern Conference. The SIAA was more or less going away and most of the bigger teams were moving to the Southern Conference. In this transition year, Clemson played as members of both the Southern Intercollegiate Athletic Association and newly formed Southern Conference. SIAA only games were matchups with Centre, The Citadel, and Furman.

Clemson began this season with three home games in Riggs Field, Calhoun SC, on the Clemson Campus. The first on Sept 30 was a loss to Centre L (0-21). The second on Oct 7 was a blowout against Newberry W (57-0) and the third was a low scoring shutout against Presbyterian W (13-0). On Oct 26, Big Thursday, Clemson kicked a field goal to beat South Carolina at Columbia SC. On November 4, at Grant Field in Atlanta GA, the Yellow Jackets of Georgia Tech stung the Tigers again L (7-21).

On Nov 11, in College Park Stadium, Charleston, SC, the Tigers shut out the Citadel W (18–0). On Nov 18, CU womped Erskine at home W (52-0). On Nov 25, Clemson could not get by a tough Furman team from Greenville SC, and were defeated L (6-20). On Dec 2, Clemson played the up and coming Florida Gators and were beaten up L (14-47).

1923 Clemson Tigers Football Coach Bud Saunders

The 1923 Clemson Tigers football team represented Clemson College during the 1923 college football season as a member of the SoCon. Bud Saunders was the head football coach for his first of four seasons. The Tigers completed their twenty-eighth season overall and their second in the Southern Conference with a record of 5-2-1 overall, 1-1-1 in the SoCon. They finished twelfth out of twenty active SoCon teams. Butch Holohan was the captain.

Clemson began the season with two home games. The first was against Auburn on Sept 29. It was a scoreless tie T (0-0). It was one of just a few good tough showings against Auburn. It was a good sign for the future. The second home game was Oct 6 v Newberry in which the Tigers gained a nice shutout W (32-0). At tough Centre squad at Danville Kentucky was next on the schedule and they overwhelmed the Tigers L (7-28). The next game was a nail biter in the state rivalry on Big Thursday between the Gamecocks and the Tigers at Columbia SC. The Tigers were pleased to take a win from the birds for such a tough game played on Big Thursday, Oct 25 W (7-6).

VPI, one of the Tigers toughest opponents over the years was next on the schedule for November 3. The game played at Miles Field in Blacksburg VA was not too close but it was not a blowout either. Nonetheless, VPI won the match L (6–25). Davidson, always a taught opponent in Clemson's early seasons was tough again but the Tigers prevailed on Nov 9 at home W (12-0). New teams always get better, and this year's Presbyterian game at home was no given. Nonetheless the Tigers won (20-0) On Nov 29, one time pushover Furman were giving nothing up playing Clemson at Greenville SC. Despite the opposition's best efforts, however, Clemson won W (7-6)

1924 Clemson Tigers Football Coach Bud Saunders

<<< Coach Bud Saunders

The 1924 Clemson Tigers football team represented Clemson College during the 1924 college football season as a member of the SoCon. Bud Saunders was the head football coach for his second of four seasons. The Tigers completed their twenty-ninth season overall and their third in the Southern Conference with a record of 2-6-0 overall, 0-3-0 in the SoCon. They finished twenty-first of twenty-three active SoCon teams. Charlie Robinson was the captain.

Every now and then, there is a winter so bad, if you were asked in the beginning by God if you would give up those three or so months of your life so that you could be in the springtime the next day, there are times, when you are young you might say yes. There are probably sometimes when if you really knew how bad it would be, you would definitely say yes. Every now and then a football year comes by in which we wish we could skip it, and move on to the next year. If we never had to face such a year, and we could change history, we might even X it from the record. Maybe???

The 1924 Clemson Tigers football team, which represented Clemson College during the 1924 college football season was a very poor team record wise and there is little happiness for any of us in recounting all of the foibles. So, let's talk about the two positives first.

On September 12 in the home opener at Riggs Field in Calhoun GA, Clemson whipped Elon, a new team on the schedule, into complete oblivion, with a 60-0 trouncing. It was a game just a step above playing against the practice tackling dummies. My apologies to the Elon fans. But, this Clemson group was not tough—even against Presbyterian who they would typically take to the woodshed and clean their clocks. Presbyterian had a chance of winning this year in a home game shutout with a low score of W (14-0) There were no more W's this year. Believe me, I regret to report that.

So, rather than lament any more, I will simply report the rest of this season which consisted of all losses as follows:

Oct 4 at Auburn	Drake Field, Auburn, AL	L (0–13)
Oct 23 at SC	(Big Thursday)	L (0–3)
Nov 1 VPI	Riggs Field, Calhoun, SC	L (6–50)
Nov 8 at Davidson	Charlotte, NC	L (0–7)
Nov 11 at Citadel	Anderson, SC	L (0–20)
Nov 27 Furman	Riggs Field, Calhoun, SC	L (0–3)

1925 Clemson Tigers Football Coach Bud Saunders

The 1925 Clemson Tigers football team represented the Clemson College during the 1925 college football season as a member of the

SoCon. Bud Saunders was the head football coach for his third of four seasons. The Tigers completed their thirtieth season overall and their fourth in the Southern Conference with a record of 1-7-0 overall, 0-4-0 in the SoCon. They were tied for twenty-first with Maryland which was also last of 22 active SoCon teams. G. I. Finklea was the captain.

On September 26 Presbyterian had gotten powerful enough to beat Clemson at home on opening day at Riggs Field in Calhoun, SC L (9–14). It was as if no effort was expended to win games. It was one season worse than the prior. From the football history books, I see no other reason than the coach. On Oct 3, in a close match v a great team Auburn, CU lost L (6-13). Then on the road on Oct 10 at Kentucky's McLean Stadium in Lexington, KY, the Tigers endured another close loss L (6–19). In a type of game that had rarely occurred ever in Clemson History, on Oct 22 on Big Thursday, Clemson got thumped by a typical pushover team South Carolina in a game played at Columbia, SC L 0–33. Everybody was wondering what happened to Clemson.

On Oct 29, at Wofford in Spartanburg, SC, another loss L (0–13). Then, on Nov 7 Florida whooped the Tigers at Riggs L (0–42). Hoping for a win but not expecting one, Clemson finally won a game on Nov 14 at The Citadel in College Park Stadium, Charleston, SC-- W (6–0). Finishing the season off with no fanfare at all, Clemson dropped another on Nov 26 v Furman in Greenville, SC L (0–26). Fans and the administration did not think it could get worse than 1924 but it had.

1926 Clemson Tigers Football Coach Bud Saunders

The 1926 Clemson Tigers football team represented the Clemson College during the 1926 college football season as a member of the SoCon. Bud Saunders was the head football coach for his fourth of four seasons. Saunders resigned after the first four games of the 1926 season. Bob Williams, who had previously served as Clemson's head coach in 1906, 1909, and from 1913 to 1915, led the team for the final five games of the season. The Tigers completed their thirty-first season overall and their fifth in the Southern Conference with a record of 2-7-0 overall, 1-3-0 in the SoCon. They were ranked 18th out of 22 active SoCon teams. B. C. Harvey was the captain.

On Sept 18, Clemson defeated Erskine in the home opener W (7-0). The Tigers then lost to Presbyterian on Sept 25, L (0-14). Auburn shellacked the Tigers in week 3 of the season on Oct 2 at Drake Field in Auburn, AL, L (0-47). In his last win as a Clemson coach, on Oct 9, Bud Saunders' Tigers beat NC State in the Textile Bowl at home in Riggs Field, Calhoun, SC, W (7-3). Bud Saunders resigned and the team was then coached by Bob Williams' for the remainder of the season.

On Oct 21 at South Carolina played in Columbia, SC on the rival Big Thursday matchup, the Gamecocks prevailed over the Tigers L (0-24). On Oct 28, Wofford beat Clemson in Spartanburg, SC L (0-3). On Nov 6, the Tigers played at Fleming Field in Gainesville, FL and were shut out by the Gators L (0–33). On Nov 13, the Citadel beat the Tigers at home L (6-15). Then, in the final game of the year, on Nov 30, Furman controlled the game and beat Clemson L (0-30).

Chapter 14 Josh Cody Era 1927-1930

Coach #15 Josh Cody

Year	Coach	Record	Conference	Record
1927	Josh Cody	5-3-1	SoCon	2-2-0
1928	Josh Cody	8-3-0	SoCon	4-2-0
1929	Josh Cody	8-3-0	SoCon	3-3-0
1930	Josh Cody	8-2-0	SoCon	3-2-0

1927 Clemson Tigers Football Coach Josh Cody

The 1927 Clemson Tigers football team represented Clemson College during the 1927 college football season as a member of the SoCon.

Josh Cody was the head football coach for his first of four seasons. The Tigers completed their thirty-second season overall and their sixth in the Southern Conference with a record of 5-3-1 overall, 2-2-0 in the SoCon. They were ranked 9th out of 22 active SoCon teams. Bud Eskew was the captain.

The 1926 season was strange to say the least. Though Bob Williams was a fine coach, he had not coached anywhere in over ten years and was not familiar with the team, nor the team with him. It was a relief for Clemson to have such a year behind them. Josh Cody was a fine coach wherever he coached and so the Tigers were pleased to begin a season with him as their head coach.

On Sept 24, after losing two in a row to Presbyterian, the Cody's Tigers managed a scoreless tie at home T (0-0) at Riggs Field on the Clemson Campus in Calhoun, SC. Clemson fans and Alumni knew the team was back when they beat a strong Auburn team on Oct 1 at home W (3-0). After two games, the fans were hoping they'd see some touchdowns soon. They came on Oct 8 when Clemson traveled to Riddick Stadium in Raleigh NC to play NC State in the Textile Bowl. The Tigers lost the game but scored their first touchdown under Josh Cody L (6-18). There was more scoring against Erskine at home on Oct 14 as the Tigers offense began to click-- W (25-6).

On Oct 20, the Tigers beat South Carolina in Columbia on Big Thursday W (20–0). On Oct 29, at home, Clemson lost to Wofford L (0-6). The next week on Nov 5, the Tigers came back to beat the Citadel at Johnson Hagood Stadium in Charleston SC W (13-0). Next was a tough loss as Georgia overwhelmed the Tigers at Sanford Field in Athens L (0-32) on Nov 12. On Nov 24, Furman beat the Tigers at Greenville SC L (0-28)

1928 Clemson Tigers Football Coach Josh Cody

The 1928 Clemson Tigers football team represented Clemson College during the 1928 college football season as a member of the Southern Conference (SoCon.) Josh Cody was the head football coach for his second of four seasons. The Tigers completed their thirty-third season overall and their seventh in the Southern Conference with a record of 8-3-0 overall, 4-2-0 in the SoCon. They were ranked 7th out of 22 active SoCon teams. O.K. Pressley was the captain.

The season began well at home in Riggs Field, on the Clemson campus at Calhoun SC with a nice win over Newberry on Sept 22 W (30-0). The next win came against Davidson the following week on Sept 29. W (6-0). Auburn was next at Drake Field in Auburn Al in another W (6-0) victory. On Oct 12, the winning score was about the same W (7-0) as the Textile Bowl was played game in Florence SC. The extra point was the only scoring difference.

The Clemson offensive drought was about to change on Oct 19 when Erskine was shellacked by the Tigers W (52-0). On Oct 25, on Big Thursday, the Tigers whooped the Gamecocks W (32-0) in Columbia SC.

Captain O.K. Pressley starred in this rivalry game with South Carolina, recording four tackles for a loss in a row despite a hand injury. He was the first Clemson Tiger to make any All-America team when he was selected third-team All-America at season's end.

On Nov 3, Ole Miss defeated the Tigers in the first game ever played between the two L (7-26) The game was played at Hemingway Stadium in Oxford, MS. On Nov 10, Clemson traveled to Lynchburg. The Gators played the Tigers on Nov 17 at Jacksonville FL and prevailed against CU L (6-27). On Nov 29, the Tigers beat Furman at Greenville, SC   W 27–12. In the season finale on Dec 8, the Citadel got the best of Clemson at Johnson Hagood Stadium in Charleston, SC L (7–12).

Player Highlights O.K. Pressley C 1926-28

In 1928, Pressley was voted Third-team All-American by Newspaper Enterprise of America, John Heisman, and Walter Trumbull. He was the first Tiger named to any All-America team. Pressley was the starting center from 1926-28. He was honored by being captain as a senior in 1928.

Center / Captain O. K. Pressley Ready to snap the ball

Pressley was rugged and durable. He started 25 games at center in his three years out of a possible 29 games Clemson had a school-record eight wins his senior year...O.K. Pressley was All-Southern in 1928.

1929 Clemson Tigers Football Coach Josh Cody

The 1929 Clemson Tigers football team represented Clemson College during the 1929 college football season as a member of the Southern Conference (SoCon). Josh Cody was the head football coach for his third of four seasons. The Tigers completed their thirty-fourth season overall and their eighth in the Southern Conference with a record of 8-3-0 overall, 3-3 in the SoCon. They were ranked twelfth out of 23 active SoCon teams. O.D. Padgett was the captain.

The season home opener resulted in a huge win on Sept 21 v Newberry at home in Riggs Field on the Clemson campus in Calhoun, SC W (68–0). On Sept 28, at Davidson in Charlotte, SC, the Tigers prevailed against the Wildcats W (32-14). On Oct 5, Clemson beat Auburn W (26-7). On Oct 11, the Tigers won the Textile Bowl by shutting out NC State at Florence SC W (26-0).

The Tigers then traveled to Spartanburg SC and collected a nice shutout victory from Wofford on Oct 18 W (30-0). On Oct 24, in the Big Thursday rivalry played in Columbia SC, the Tigers beat the Gamecocks W (21-14). On Nov 2 at McLean Stadium in Kentucky, the Tigers were shellacked by the Wildcats L (6-44).
On Nov 9, the Tigers lost to a stubborn and tough VMI team at Norfolk VA L (0-12). Always having a tough time with the Gators, this year was no different as the Tigers were beaten on the Gators home turf (Fleming Field) in a close match L (7-13). The Clemson Fighting Tigers finished the season with two home wins. The first was against the Citadel W (13-0), and the second was against an always tough Furman team W (7-6)

1930 Clemson Tigers Football Coach Josh Cody

The 1930 Clemson Tigers football team represented Clemson College during the 1930 college football season as a member of the Southern Conference (SoCon). Josh Cody was the head football coach for his fourth and last of four seasons. This would be Cody's best season. The Tigers completed their thirty-fifth season overall and their ninth in the Southern Conference with a record of 8-2-0 overall, 3-2 in the SoCon. They were ranked ninth out of 23 active SoCon teams. Johnnie Justus was the captain.

The Tigers began the season at home for two games at Riggs Field on the Clemson campus in Clemson, SC. In the first game on Sept 20, the Tigers beat Presbyterian W (28-7) and on Sept 27, the team shut out Wofford W (32-0). After traveling to Florence SC on Oct 3, the Tigers then beat The Citadel in a close match W (13-7). The Textile Bowl came next at Charlotte NC on Oct 11 v NC State and the Tigers shut out the Wolfpack. Back at home against a weak Newberry Team on Oct 17, the Tigers got in a lot of touchdowns on the way to a W (75-0) blowout / shutout.

On Oct at South Carolina in Columbia, SC for the Big Thursday matchup, the Tigers won W 20–7. The Tigers were undefeated when on Nov 1, the squad traveled to Tennessee's Shields-Watkins Field in • Knoxville, TN, and they were shut out by the Volunteers, L (0–27). Next on Nov 8 at VMI's Bain Field in Norfolk, the Tigers gained a shutout W (32–0). Then, on Nov 15 at Florida in Jacksonville, the Tigers were shut out L (0-27). The Tigers rebounded in the season finale in a close game v Furman W (12-7).

Unidentified Clemson Game at Riggs Field from Depression Era

Chapter 15 Jess Neely Era 1931-1939

Coach # 16 Jess Neely

Year	Coach	Record	Conference	Record
1931	Jess Neely	1-6-2	SoCon	
1932	Jess Neely	3-5-1	SoCon	
1933	Jess Neely	3-6-2	SoCon	
1934	Jess Neely	5-4-0	SoCon	
1935	Jess Neely	6-3-0	SoCon	
1936	Jess Neely	5-5-0	SoCon	
1937	Jess Neely	4-4-1	SoCon	
1938	Jess Neely	7-1-1	SoCon	
1939	Jess Neely	9-1-0	SoCon	

Coach Jess Neely

Jess Neely

Jess Neely was the first Clemson head coach to stay more than four consecutive years at Clemson. He added needed stability to a program that was just waiting to break out. Nothing worth having is easy. Jess Neely knew that his team needed to be financed properly in order to survive and be able to win in the Southern Conference. After his 1-6-2 season his first year, at other institutions that were well endowed and had a lot of rich alums, they would be calling for his head.

In the two articles, I selected with which to introduce this great coach and great man, Jess Neely, you will learn that he was more about goodness and reality than anything else. Sure, winning mattered, but the college could not expect the students to pay for their uniforms during the great depression and it was tough to get anybody to give up a dime even if the cause was worthwhile.

Neely kept at it and succeeded and he eventually had a great four-year record, capped by one of the finest bowl game victories over a coach who would soon have four national championships to his credit. Who knows if Clemson would have made it through the war years without the boost that the programs created by Jess Neely gave to the Clemson Tigers. We'll never have to answer that because Jess Neely was there at the right time and Clemson continues as the beneficiary.

The first piece is from the Clemson Media Guide and the second is from an author who wrote a nice book about Clemson's great coaches.

Jess Neely
Head Coach Years: 1931-1939
Record at Clemson: 43-35-7
Winning Percentage: .547

Perhaps one of Clemson's most beloved coaches was Jess Neely. Neely influence and inspiration is still present today as the IPTAY Scholarship Club was founded during his coaching Tenure. IPTAY is the lifeblood of the Clemson Athletic Department. It provides funds for athletic scholarships and capital improvements.

Thousands of athletes have benefited through the IPTAY Scholarship fund since its inception in 1934. That first year of IPTAY, Neely and his staff convinced 160 people to pay $10.00 a year to Clemson, for a grand total of $1,600 the first year, (not bad during the middle of the great depression.)

Neely was head coach at Clemson from 1931 through 1939 and spent the next 26 years at Rice University in Houston.

Neely coached Clemson to its first bowl game, the 1940 Cotton Bowl, where the Tigers capped a 9-1-0 season by beating Boston College 6-3. Clemson ended the season ranked 12th in the final Associated Press poll, its first top 20 season in history. Boston College was ranked 11th going into the game and it was Clemson's first win over a top 20 team in its history. The team featured the play of Banks McFadden Clemson's first Associated Press All American. Clemson had a 43-35-7 record during Neely's tenure.

Neely coached Rice to four Southwest Conference Championships and six bowl appearances, the last being a trip to the Bluebonnet Bowl in 1961.

During 40 years of college coaching he compiled a record of 207-99-14. Neely is eighth in college football history in victories by a Division I-A coach heading into the 1995 season. For his accomplishments, he was inducted into the College Football Hall of Fame in 1971.

Neely graduated from Vanderbilt in 1924, after lettering three years in football and serving as captain of the 1922 team. He coached a year of high school football before returning to his alma mater to obtain a law degree. But he never practiced.

He coached four years at Southwestern college in Clarksville, Tenn. and then went to the University of Alabama in 1928. It was there that he met Frank Howard. Neely brought Howard to Clemson as line coach in 1931. Howard replaced him in 1940 and remained as head coach for 30 years. In 1967, Neely returned to his alma mater as athletic director. He officially retired in 1971, but continued to coach golf until 1981, when he moved back to

Texas.

"If I didn't look in the mirror every day, I wouldn't know how old I am, "Neely once said. "Working with the boys makes you feel young, I feel that in athletics the boys learn a sense of loyalty and sacrifice and values they don't learn anywhere else.

"They learn to compete," he said, "and that is what life is all about-its competition.

"If they make good in football, chances are they'll be successful elsewhere. I like to see that those boys make something of themselves. That is my reward.

"The boys go to college to study and get that degree. Playing football is a side activity. When fellows go to a school first to play football they get an entirely wrong sense of values.

"And when you start them off with the wrong sense, it isn't difficult for them to go astray."

"He was a cool, southern gentlemen, but he worked us like dogs. The work- outs were always twice as hard as the games, "said Dick Maegle. "There were no superstars, no victory that was better than all the other victories. To him football was a team game and we were all team players." Maegle was the player tackled in a famous episode in the 1954 Cotton Bowl, when frustrated Tommy Lewis came off the bench to stop a certain touchdown. Rice won that game, 28-6.

Neely died at the age of 85 in 1983, but his landmark accomplishments in the 1930s at Clemson contributed significantly to Clemson's outstanding football tradition.

The numbers and the names have changed since 1995 but the idea has not. Jess Neely, whose first Clemson season at 1-6-2 season will be explored after the below book excerpt is presented chapter next article shortly, is on the 1995 list below:

All-Time I-A Coaching Victories (Not Including Wins Since 1995)		
Paul 'Bear' Bryant	Maryland, Kentucky, Texas A&M, Alabama	323
Amos Alonzo Stagg	Springfield, Chicago, Pacific	314
Glenn 'Pop' Warner	Georgia, Cornell, Carlisle, Pittsburgh, Stanford, Temple	313
Joe Paterno	Penn State	268
Bobby Bowden	Samford, West Virginia, Florida State	250
Woody Hayes	Denison, Miami (OH), Ohio State	238
Bo Schembechler	Miami (OH), Michigan	234
Jess Neely	Rhodes, Clemson, Rice	207

Source: 1996 Clemson Football Media Guide

Clemson's best coaches: Neely, birth of IPTAY

By Robert MacRae June 30, 2014 4:38 am ET

As they sat in a parked car outside old Florence Memorial Stadium in Florence, S.C., following a 6-0 loss to the Citadel on October 16, 1931, Jess Neely, assistant coach Joe Davis, Captain Frank Jervey and Captain Pete Heffner talked quietly about the future of its Clemson football program.

Jervey, who the Jervey Athletic Center is named for today, was working in Washington, D.C. at the time as a liaison between the military and the college, while Heffner was a member of the military staff at Clemson and had a strong interest in athletics. He also assisted with coaching in his spare time.

"What we ought to do is get the alumni to give Jess some backing by helping him finance the football team," said Heffner in the book The Clemson Tigers from 1896 to Glory.

The Tigers were in the midst of a 1-6-2 season with the only win coming a few weeks earlier against NC State. This was the first year of what is commonly known in Clemson lore as the "Seven

Lean Years." Neely, who went go on to become one of the nation's most successful coaches at Rice, knew he was going to need something more if Clemson was going to stay competitive on the gridiron.

In hearing Heffner's suggestion, Jervey asked Neely how much the school should ask its alumni for. The Clemson coach responded by suggesting the idea of a $50 Club.

"If I could get $10,000 a year to build the football program, I could give Clemson fans a winning team," Neely said.

And thus, the concept of the first booster club organization in college athletics was born.

Through the help of Rupert H. Fike, the idea of $50 a year was scaled down to $10 under the slogan "I Pay Ten A Year." Aka "IPTAY"

On August 21, 1934, Fike informed Neely that the IPTAY Club had been organized and that a constitution was formulated. The constitution stated the purpose of the Clemson Order of IPTAY "shall be to provide annual financial support to the athletic department at Clemson and to assist in every other way possible to regain for Clemson the high athletic standing which rightfully belongs to her."

After three consecutive losing seasons from 1931-'33, the 1934 season slowly started a trend which saw Clemson's fortunes on the football field turn around. That year, the Tigers beat archrival South Carolina for the first time in four years, 19-0, on their way to a 5-4 record. In 1935, Clemson improved to 6-3 under Neely and again beat the hated Gamecocks, this time 44-0.

The Tigers beat USC in 1936 and 1937, and though they did not have great years as a whole, they also did not have a losing record, setting the stage for one of the best four-year runs in Clemson history.

In 1938, Clemson produced a 7-1-1 team, which included a 34-12 win over the Gamecocks. In 1939, the Tigers pounded South Carolina, 27-0, on their way to an 8-1 record. At season's end,

Clemson was extended an invitation to its first bowl game—the Cotton Bowl, and of course accepted.

The Tigers were scheduled to play the Eagles of Boston College on January 1, 1940 in Dallas, TX. It was dubbed the "farmer boys" against "the city slickers" and the farmer boys won, 6-3.

"If I didn't look in the mirror every day, I wouldn't know how old I am," Neely once said. "Working with the boys makes you feel young. I feel that in athletics the boys learn a sense of loyalty and sacrifice and values they don't learn anywhere else.

"They learn to compete and that is what life is all about – it's competition. If they make good in football, chances are they'll be successful elsewhere. I like to see that those boys make something of themselves. That is my reward. The boys go to college to study and get that degree. Playing football is a side activity. When fellows go to a school first to play football they get an entirely wrong sense of values.

"And when you start them off with the wrong sense, it isn't difficult for them to go astray."

Neely died at the age of 85 in 1983, but his landmark accomplishments in the 1930s at Clemson contributed significantly to Clemson's outstanding football tradition.

His 1939 Clemson team was perhaps one of the most significant in Clemson football history because so much of the history and heritage of Clemson football documents 1939 as a cornerstone year. Not only was it Clemson's first bowl team, it was Clemson's first team to be ranked and the first to end a season in the top 20. The Tigers finished 12th in the final Associated Press Poll.

Clemson opened the year with its annual victory over Presbyterian, then suffered its only loss, a 7-6 squeaker, to Tulane in New Orleans. The Tigers then went on to win their last seven regular season games.

Oddly enough, the loss to the GreenWave, saw Banks McFadden, also known as "Bonnie Banks," first rise to national prominence.

Many observers say that is where McFadden made the All-America team on his punting exhibition, especially on his quick-kicks from the single-wing tailback position.

McFadden averaged over 43 yards a kick on 12 punts that afternoon and had six punts of at least 50 yards, still a single-game record at Clemson.

End of piece

Player Highlights Banks McFadden CB 1936-40

No book about Clemson greats could be written without discussing Banks McFadden.

<< Banks McFadden

To repeat, in any book such as this that honors great Clemson players, we could not leave off an athletic legend like Banks McFadden, who is without a doubt one of the greatest Clemson athletes of all time. Pulling full-time duty with football, basketball, and baseball, McFadden excelled as a defensive back thanks to his great athleticism that few could match. He is one of just three Football Tigers to have his jersey and number retired.

Check out the years in which McFadden played and then please remember we already declared that McFadden is widely considered to be the greatest athlete in Clemson University history, after lettering in three sports (football, basketball and track).

McFadden was All-American in both football and basketball in the same calendar year (1939), He is the only Clemson athlete to do that. In 1939-40, he was named the nation's most versatile athlete. He was also Clemson's first wire-service AP All-American.

Banks was a record setter on the field as a runner, passer, and punter. A born athlete, he kept busy in all sports seasons. For example, he led the Tigers to state championship in track twice in his three years...

He was elected to National Football Hall of Fame in 1959 and he received the Distinguished Alumni Award from Clemson in 1966. He is a charter member of the Clemson Athletic Hall of Fame and the state of South Carolina Athletic Hall of Fame.

As noted above but worthy of mention again, McFadden is the only Tiger to have his jersey retired in two sports.

He was a great football player and had options after college. He was the #4 pick of the Brooklyn Dodgers (football) after the 1939 season, that is still the highest draft pick ever by a Clemson player. It took eleven passes to get to DeShaun Watson this year.

As noted, Banks played one year in the NFL and led the league in yards per rush...coached the defensive backs at Clemson for 26 years, he was also the head basketball coach from 1947-56...Clemson's McFadden Building, dedicated in 1995, is in his honor...named to Clemson's Centennial team in April, 1996...ranked as Clemson's #1 football player of all-time by a panel of Clemson historians in 1999. That is how good he was.

In 1939, McFadden was voted the Associated Press' "Athlete of the Year". McFadden was also a two-time All-American in basketball (1938 and 1939) and lead the Tigers basketball team to a Southern Conference championship in 1939.

McFadden also played halfback and punter on the football team and was named Clemson's first Associated Press All-American in football

in 1939, which saw the Tigers play and win their 1st bowl game
(1940 Cotton Bowl Classic).

Upon graduating, McFadden played football for the National
Football League's Brooklyn Dodgers. He was the #4 overall NFL
draft pick in 1940. In his first, and only, year as a professional he
played in 11 games. He had the longest rush in the NFL that year -
75 yards. He was tied for second for most yards per attempt with a
4.8 yards per carry average.

He was also fifth in the league for most rushing yards per game.
Defensively he had two interceptions. Despite his success, McFadden
preferred the small-town life and the family atmosphere of Clemson.
He returned to the state of South Carolina to coach at his alma
mater. A great Clemson Tiger for sure.

Neely always fought adversity at Clemson with slow and well
thought out solutions. How many coaches today could win 36 games
in six seasons with only 14 of those 56 games played at home?

Only once did Clemson play as many as four games at home in a
year during Neely's stay, and only twice were there three home
games in a year. Thirteen of the 56 games were played on neutral
sites. Even his 1939 team—his best at Clemson—only played two
games at home, opening the season with an 18-0 win over
Presbyterian and then in the seventh game, a 20-7 victory over Wake
Forest.

The 1939 team was called "Road Clemson" because of this.
But despite the tough road schedule, the Tigers stayed strong. With
the exception of the Tulane loss, they were only behind twice in their
nine wins. And though players went both ways in those days,
Clemson only gave up 45 points in 10 games.

The Tigers suddenly found themselves—a group of players from
small town environments—playing big-time football. Neely rewarded
the team for its efforts by taking all 51 players to Dallas for the
Cotton Bowl game.

While in Dallas for the bowl game, talk was rampant that Neely
might leave Clemson for the head coaching job at Rice. Bill Sullivan

was the publicity man for Frank Leahy and Boston College, and he said he was in the hotel room in Dallas when Neely told a small group that he would definitely take the Rice offer.

Frank Howard, who was Neely's line coach, spoke up and said: "Well, I'm not going with you." And according to Sullivan, Neely said: "I hadn't planned to ask you."

When Howard was confronted with this, he denied it and said that J.C. Littlejohn, Clemson's business manager, had promised him the Clemson head coaching job if Neely left.

Neely is still known today as one Clemson's most beloved coaches. His influence and inspiration is still present thanks to the IPTAY Scholarship Club as it is the lifeblood of the Clemson Athletic Department.

From 1931-'39, Clemson had a 43-35-7 record during Neely's tenure. After the Tigers' Cotton Bowl win over Boston College, Neely spent the next 26 years at Rice University in Houston.

During 40 years of college coaching he compiled a record of 207-99-14. For his accomplishments, he was inducted into the College Football Hall of Fame.

Article Editor's note: This story was an insert from the book I co-authored last summer called Clemson: Where the Tigers Play, *which you can buy on amazon.com. This is the third story in a series of stories that chronicles how these coaches turned Clemson into the football power it has come to be over the years*

1931 Clemson Tigers Football Coach Jess Neely

The 1931 Clemson Tigers football team represented Clemson College during the 1931 college football season as a member of the Southern Conference (SoCon). Jess Neely was the head football coach for his first of nine seasons. The Tigers completed their thirty-sixth season overall and their tenth in the Southern Conference with a record of 1-6-2 overall, 1-4-0 in the SoCon. They were ranked ninth out of 23 active SoCon teams. A. D. Fordham was the captain.

On Sept 25. In the Clemson home opener, Presbyterian tied the Tigers at Riggs Field on the Clemson Campus in Clemson, SC. T (0-0). On Oct 3 at Tennessee's Shields-Watkins Field in Knoxville, TN, the Vols overwhelmed the Tigers L (0–44). On Oct 10, at NC State in Charlotte, NC. The Tigers engaged the Wolfpack in the Textile Bowl and gained their only win of the season. W (6-0). On Oct 6, at the Citadel in a game played at Florence NC, the Citadel beat Clemson L (0-6). On Oct 22, at Columbia SC, the Tigers lost to South Carolina L (0-21) in the Big Thursday game.

On Oct 31 Oglethorpe beat the Tigers at Riggs Field L (0-12). The next week on Nov 7, v VMI, at Bain Field in Norfolk VA, the Tigers lost a close one L (6-7)

Alabama was beginning to flex its muscles in the Southern Conference and on Nov 14, the Crimson Tide flattened Clemson L (7-74). Clemson was having a very bad season. On Nov 26, The Tigers managed a pride saving scoreless tie v Furman in Greenville SC T (0-0).

1932 Clemson Tigers Football Coach Jess Neely

The 1932 Clemson Tigers football team represented Clemson College during the 1932 college football season as a member of the Southern Conference (SoCon). Jess Neely was the head football coach for his second of nine seasons. The Tigers completed their thirty-seventh season overall and their eleventh in the Southern Conference with a record of 3-5-1; 0-4-0 in the SoCon. They were ranked twenty-first, tied with Mississippi State out of 23 active SoCon teams. Bob Miller was the captain.

The season opener was on Sept 23 when Presbyterian came to play the Tigers at home at Riggs Field on the Clemson campus in Clemson, SC. CU won the game W (13–0) On Oct 1, Clemson traveled to Grant Field in Atlanta GA expecting the best but they succumbed to a tough Georgia Tech L (14-32). On Oct 8, at Riddick Stadium in Raleigh NC, in the Textile Bowl, the Tigers managed to give the game to NC State L (0-13). Finally, a team showed up at Riggs Field willing to lose but not wanting to lose, who lost anyway.

The Tigers beat Erskine W (19-0) Moving through the schedule, we come across the Big Thursday extravaganza on Oct 20, played at Columbia, SC v the South Carolina Gamecocks. In years other than the seven lean years, this was a given win. But, this year, SC shut out the poorly financed Clemson Tigers on Big Thursday L (0-14).

Moving right along through a bad season, ties such as the one on Oct 29 at Davidson in Richardson Stadium •in Davidson, NC start to look good because they count positively in a perverse sort of way T (7–7). On Nov 5, at the Citadel, the Tigers finally stole a win W (18–6). Then, on Nov 11 at home, v Georgia, the Bulldogs were unrelenting and they pulled off a win v the Tigers L (18–32). Then, as a season finale, on Nov 24, the Tigers lost to a team that loves to beat them, Furman at the opponent's home field in Greenville, SC, L (0-7).

1933 Clemson Tigers Football Coach Jess Neely

The 1933 Clemson Tigers football team represented Clemson College during the 1933 college football season as a member of the Southern Conference (SoCon). Jess Neely was the head football coach for his third of nine seasons. The Tigers completed their thirty-eighth season overall and their twelfth in the Southern Conference with a record of 3-6-2; 0-3-0 in the SoCon. They were ranked twenty-first, tied with Mississippi State out of 10 active SoCon teams. John Heinemann was the captain.

You may have noticed that instead of twenty-three teams as in 1932, the 1933 Southern Conference (SoCon) consisted of just ten teams. Saturday Down South (saturdaydownsouth.com) describes what happened in 1933 as follows:

"The unwieldy Southern Conference has split along geographical lines and out of the break today emerged a new group of thirteen schools, mostly of the deep South, to be known as the Southeastern Conference." This group included the core of today's SEC —Alabama, Auburn, Georgia, Florida, LSU, Ole Miss, Mississippi State, Kentucky, Tennessee and Vanderbilt —along with Georgia Tech, Tulane, and Sewanee (also known as the University of the South). The remaining Southern Conference schools were all located in Maryland, Virginia or the Carolinas: Virginia, Virginia Tech, Virginia Military Institute, Washington & Lee, Maryland, North Carolina, North Carolina State, Duke, South Carolina and Clemson; seven of those schools —along with Wake Forest, which joined the Southern Conference in 1936 — left in 1953 to form the Atlantic Coast Conference.

Games of the 1933 Season

On opening day Sept 23 at Riggs Field on the Clemson Campus in Clemson SC, Presbyterian tied the Orange and Purple T (6-6). Then, on Sept 30, a tough Georgia Tech team took no prisoners at Grant Field in Atlanta GA defeating Clemson L (2-39). The Tigers then beat NC State at home in the Textile Bowl W (9-0). On Oct 13, a newly scheduled team George Washington invited the Tigers to Griffith Stadium in DC and played Clemson to a scoreless tie T (0-0). This was the first night game in Clemson's history, as played on October 13 against George Washington at Griffith Stadium in Washington, D. C.

Big Thursday was next on Oct 19 at Columbia SC as the Gamecocks beat the Tigers L (0-7). The next loss was Ole Miss in a game played at Meridian MS L (0-13). On Nov 4, in Charlotte NC, the Clemson shut out Wake Forest W (13-0). Clemson then played Wofford on Nov 11 in Spartanburg, SC for a very close loss L (13-14). Mercer was next at Savannah GA for another tough Clemson loss L (0-13). Clemson recovered briefly and bet the Citadel the following week Nov 25 W (7-0). The Tigers closed out the season on Nov 30, losing to Furman in Greenville, SC L (0-6).

This was the third losing season of the period of years known as the seven lean years. The biblical connotation is clear but most Clemson fans were looking for seven or more years of plenty. The next season would mark the midpoint of the seven lean years.

1934 Clemson Tigers Football Coach Jess Neely

The 1934 Clemson Tigers football team represented Clemson College during the 1934 college football season as a member of the Southern Conference (SoCon). Jess Neely was the head football coach for his fourth of nine seasons. The Tigers completed their thirty-ninth season overall and their thirteenth in the Southern Conference with a record of 5-4-0; 2-2-0 in the SoCon. They were ranked fifth out of 10 active SoCon teams. Henry Woodward was the captain.

The season began with Presbyterian at home at Riggs Field on the Clemson Campus in Clemson, SC. (Clemson SC was formerly known as Calhoun SC) with a well-earned win W (6-0). In the Georgia Tech rivalry on Sept 29, the Tigers played the Yellow Jackets very close for the first time in a while. A victory soon would not be too much to imagine. This time, the Tigers lost L (7-12). The Tigers next played at Duke Stadium on Oct 6 in Durham NC and they lost to the Blue Devils L 6-20). This was followed on Oct 13 at McLean Stadium in Lexington KY as the Tigers came close but no cigar to the Wildcats L (0-7). Clemson was playing good football but in many cases, were outmanned by the financial resources of their opponents.

On Oct 25, on Big Thursday at Columbia Municipal Stadium in Columbia SC, SC, on a Big Thursday, the Tigers beat the Gamecocks solidly W (19-0). On Nov 3, at Riddick Stadium in Raleigh NC in the Textile Bowl, the Tigers beat the NC State Wolfpack W (12-0). Alabama had switched to the SEC Conference in 1933 and both teams played a non-conference game on Nov 10, at Denny Stadium in Tuscaloosa, AL. The SEC conference Alabama squad shellacked the SoCon Clemson team L (40-0). On Nov 17 at Savannah GA, the Tigers beat Merced W (32-0) and on Nov 29, Clemson played Furman at home and got the W, W (7-0).

1935 Clemson Tigers Football Coach Jess Neely

The 1935 Clemson Tigers football team represented Clemson College during the 1935 college football season as a member of the Southern Conference (SoCon). Jess Neely was the head football coach for his fifth of nine seasons. The Tigers completed their fortieth season overall and their fourteenth in the Southern Conference with a record of 6-3-0; 2-1-0 in the SoCon. They were ranked fourth out of 10 active SoCon teams. Henry Shore was the captain.

Presbyterian was first on the schedule for 1935 again at home in Riggs Field on the Clemson Campus in Clemson SC. Clemson won the game on Sept 21, W (25–6). Next was VPI at Miles Stadium in Blacksburg, VA for a nice Clemson win W (28-7) September 28 at VPI's Miles Stadium, Blacksburg, VA. On Oct 5, Wake Forest came to Clemson and were defeated W (13-7). Sitting undefeated after three games, things were going good for Neely's Tigers before they traveled to Duke on Oct 12, and were beaten convincingly by the Blue Devils L (12-38)

On Oct 24 at Columbia Municipal Stadium in Columbia, SC, on Big Thursday, the Tigers overwhelmed the Gamecocks in a big shutout win W (44-0). On Nov 2, Clemson traveled to Mercer in Augusta GA and triumphed W (13-0). Then it was off to Denny Stadium in Tuscaloosa AL to play the crimson Tide. Alabama was at its best and they shut out the visiting Tigers L (0-33) at Johnson Hagood Stadium on Nov 16, the Tigers beat The Citadel W 6-0). In the season finale-- in a two-point nail-biter, at Greenville, SC, Furman beat the Tigers L (6-8) on Nov 28.

1936 Clemson Tigers Football Coach Jess Neely

The 1936 Clemson Tigers football team represented Clemson College during the 1936 college football season as a member of the Southern Conference (SoCon). Jess Neely was the head football coach for his sixth of nine seasons. The Tigers completed their forty-first season overall and their fifteenth in the Southern Conference with a record of 5-5-0; 3-2-0 in the SoCon. They were ranked fourth out of 15 active SoCon teams. Net Barry was the captain.

On Sept 19, the season startup game was a nice win against Presbyterian at Riggs Field on the Clemson Campus in Clemson SC W (19-0). On Sept 26 at home, Clemson beat VPI W (20-0). On Oct 3, Alabama's Crimson Tide shut out the Tigers in a one-way game at Denny Stadium in Tuscaloosa AL. L (0-32). On Oct 10, at Duke Stadium in Durham NC, the Tigers were shut out by Duke L (0-25). Duke would have a perfect SoCon record 7-0-0 in 1936 and would be crowned the Conference Champions.

On Oct 16,   at Wake Forest in Wake Forest, NC, the Tigers were defeated L (0–6). The squad recovered on Oct 22, Big Thursday on the game against South Carolina at Columbia W (19-0). On Oct 31, after having lost the prior fifteen encounters with Georgia Tech, the Clemson Fighting Tigers finally won against this major rival. At Grant Field in Athens GA in a nail-biter, W (14-13). On Nov 7at Johnson Hagood Stadium on Charleston SC one week later, on Nov 7, Clemson beat the Citadel W (20-0). On Nov 14, at Kentucky, the Tigers lost a close match to the Wildcats, L (6-7). Finishing the season up at home, the Tigers were shut out by the Furman Paladins L (0-12).

1937 Clemson Tigers Football Coach Jess Neely

The 1937 Clemson Tigers football team represented Clemson College during the 1937 college football season as a member of the Southern Conference (SoCon). Jess Neely was the head football coach for his seventh of nine seasons. The Tigers completed their forty-second season overall and their sixteenth in the Southern Conference with a record of 4-4-1; 2-0-1 in the SoCon. They were ranked third out of 15 active SoCon teams. H. D. Lewis was the captain.

On Sept 18 in the home opener, the Tigers beat Presbyterian in a blowout at Riggs Field on the Clemson Campus in Clemson SC, 46-0 On Sept 25, the Tigers traveled to Tulane Stadium in New Orleans, and were beaten by the Green Waves L (0–7). Army beat Clemson on Oct 2 at Chichie Stadium in West Point, NY   L (6–21). Next on Oct 9 at Georgia's Sanford Stadium in Athens GA, the Tigers lost their third in arrow L (0-14). The Big Thursday game came on Oct 21 as the Tigers beat the Gamecocks of SC at Columbia Municipal Stadium in Columbia, SC W (34–6).

On Oct 30, The Tigers shut out Wake Forest at home W (32–0). Then, at Grant Field in Atlanta GA, the Yellow Jackets of Georgia Tech defeated the Tigers in a close match L (0-7). On Nov 13, the Tigers took on the Gators at Florida Field in Gainesville FL and won a nail-biter W (10-9). An always tough Furman team invited the Tigers to play in Sirrine Stadium in Greenville SC and tied Clemson in a scoreless match T (0-0).

Jess Neely's work in getting donations and financing for the team was finally beginning to pay off and the next two years would show a marked improvement before Frank Howard came in to guide the Tigers for the next thirty years. You may recall Jess Neely was the coach who suggested not to build the Death Valley Stadium because about 10,000 seats by the old YMCA was all the Tigers needed. During the next two tears from this, Neely had his opportunity to shine a lot better than his stadium prediction.

1938 Clemson Tigers Football Coach Jess Neely

The 1938 Clemson Tigers football team represented Clemson College during the 1938 college football season as a member of the Southern Conference (SoCon). Jess Neely was the head football coach for his eighth of nine seasons. The Tigers completed their forty third season overall and their seventeenth in the Southern Conference with a record of 7-1-1; 3-0-1 in the SoCon. They were ranked second out of 15 active SoCon teams. Charlie Woods was the captain.

Presbyterian was at Riggs Field again on the Clemson campus in Clemson NC to kick off the football season against the Tigers. They were shut out w (26-0) on Sept 17. A week later, on Sept 24 at Tulane Stadium in New Orleans, Clemson beat Tulane W (13-10). On Oct 1, #2 ranked Tennessee beat the Tigers for their only loss of the season at Shields Watkins Field in Knoxville L (7-20). On Oct 8. VMI tied the Tigers at Memorial Stadium in Charlotte NC T (7-7). Then, for Big Thursday on Oct 20, in Columbia Municipal Stadium, Columbia SC, the Tigers beat the SC Gamecocks w (34-12)

On Oct28, at Wake Forest, Clemson won W (7-0) The following week on Nov 5, Clemson traveled to George Washington at Greenville NC and won the game via shutout W (27-0). The Tigers grabbed another shutout the following week Nov 12 at Kentucky's McLean Stadium in Lexington KY, W (14-0). Wrapping up the season again v a tough Furman team, the Tigers prevailed W (10-7).

1939 Clemson Tigers Football Coach Jess Neely

The 1939 Clemson Tigers football team represented Clemson College during the 1939 college football season as a member of the Southern

Conference (SoCon). Jess Neely was the head football coach for his ninth (last) of nine seasons. The Tigers completed their forty fourth season overall and their eighteenth in the Southern Conference with a record of 9-1-0; 4-0 in the SoCon.

They were listed along with Duke at the top of the SoCon standings for 1939 out of 15 active SoCon teams. Joe Payne was the captain. Clemson participated in its first bowl game, beating a tough Boston College coached by the immortal Frank Leahy in the 1940 Cotton Bowl Classic. It was a great season changer for the Tigers. The seven lean years were officially over.

On Sept 23, the season began again with Presbyterian at home at Riggs Field on the campus of Clemson University in Clemson SC. Clemson shut out the Blue Hose W (18-0. Just a week later on Sept 30 at Tulane, the Tigers lost a tight one in Tulane Stadium, New Orleans, LA   L (6–7). Then, on Oct 7 v NC State in the Textile Bowl in Charlotte, NC, W (25–6). On Big Thursday at Columbia Municipal Stadium in Columbia, SC, the Tigers shut out the Gamecocks of SC W (27–0)

Navy played the Tigers for the first time on Oct 28 at Thompson Stadium in Annapolis, MD. Clemson had a tough time but won W (15–7). Then in Washington DC at on Nov 3 at George Washington, the tigers won another close one W (13–6). Coming back home on Nov 11, the Tigers beat Wake Forest at Riggs Field W (20–7). Getting close to the season finale, on Nov 18, at Southwestern Presbyterian, the #16 ranked Tigers won at Memphis, TN W (21–6). As the season closed on Nov 25, Furman always was there for the last game at Sirrine Stadium in Greenville, SC, The Tigers triumphed W 10–7.

Not typically being a bowl contender, the Clemson Fighting Tigers were unaccustomed to the great accolades as brought forth during the 1939 season. The year was so good the team was invited to the Cotton Bowl Classic. The participants in the January 1, 1940 Cotton Bowl game were the #11 Boston College Eagles vs the #12 Clemson Tigers. The great Cotton Bowl classic game was played at Dallas Texas and though the well-known Frank Leahy coached the Eagles and Jess Neely, known for his great work at Clemson coached the Tigers. In this highly publicized game. Neely beat Leahy but not much more than a nudge W (6-3) What a win for Clemson and what a loss for Boston College.

Chapter 16 Frank Howard Era 1940-1964

Coach # 17 Frank Howard

Year	Coach	Record	Conference	Record
1940*	Frank Howard	6-2-1	SoCon	4-0-0
1941	Frank Howard	7-2-0	SoCon	5-1-0
1942	Frank Howard	3-6-1	SoCon	2-3-1
1943	Frank Howard	2-6-0	SoCon	2-3-0
1944	Frank Howard	4-5-0	SoCon	3-1-0
1945	Frank Howard	6-3-1	SoCon	2-1-1
1946	Frank Howard	4-5-0	SoCon	2-3-0
1947	Frank Howard	4-5-0	SoCon	1-3-0
1948*	Frank Howard	11-0-0	SoCon	5-0-0
1949	Frank Howard	4-4-2	SoCon	2-2-0
1950	Frank Howard	9-0-1	SoCon	3-0-1
1951	Frank Howard	7-3-0	SoCon	0-1-0
1953	Frank Howard	3-5-1	ACC	1-2-0
1954	Frank Howard	5-5-0	ACC	1-2-0

Frank Howard 1940-1969 Longest Seving Clemson Coach

1940 Clemson Tigers Football Coach Frank Howard

The 1940 Clemson Tigers football team represented Clemson College during the 1940 college football season as a member of the Southern Conference (SoCon). Frank Howard was the head football coach for his first of thirty seasons. The Tigers completed their forty-fifth season overall and their nineteenth in the Southern Conference with a record of 6-2-1; 4-0-0 in the SoCon. The Tigers came in first in the SoCon out of 15 active SoCon teams. Red Sharpe was the captain. Coach Frank Howard got the Tigers off to a great start in his first year at the helm

On Sept 21, the home opener was again against Presbyterian at Riggs Field on the campus of Clemson University in Clemson, SC. The Tigers shut out the Blue Hose W (38-0). On Sept 28, the Tigers played Wofford at home and beat the Terriers W (26-0). The next game was at American Legion Memorial Stadium in Charlotte NC. It was the annual Textile Bowl on Oct 5 with NC State. The Tigers beat the Tar Heels W (26-0). Wake forest gave the Tigers their fourth win in a row in a home game on Oct 12 W (39-0) and so far, the Tigers were competing in an undefeated season. On Big Thursday Oct 24 at Columbia SC, the Tigers beat the Gamecocks W 21-13).

On Nov 2, the Tigers traveled to Tulane Stadium in New Orleans Tulane at and were beaten in s shutout by the Green Wave for the first loss of the season. Then the Auburn Tigers beat the beat the Clemson Tigers on Nov 9 at Auburn Stadium in AL, L (7-21). The Tigers came back for a tie at Southwestern Presbyterian at Crump Stadium in Memphis TN on Nov 16 T (12-12). Then, on Nov 23the Tigers played Furman at Sirrine Stadium in Greenville, SC on the way to a nice victory W 13–7.

1941 Clemson Tigers Football Coach Frank Howard

The 1941 Clemson Tigers football team represented Clemson College during the 1941 college football season as a member of the Southern Conference (SoCon). Frank Howard was the head football coach for his second of thirty seasons. The Tigers completed their forty sixth season overall and their twentieth in the Southern Conference with a record of 7-2-0; 5-1-0 in the SoCon. The Tigers came in third in the

SoCon out of 15 active SoCon teams. Duke was again # 1. Wade Padgett was the captain.

Player Highlights Joe Blalock WR 1938-41

Clemson®

JOE BLALOCK

In these early days of football, there were lots of opportunities for firsts. For example, Joe Blalock was Clemson's first two-time All-American. He was a starter as a sophomore when real Freshman were prohibited from playing in the 1940's. He started on the 1940 Cotton Bowl team. He led the Tiger receiver squad for three straight years. For many years, he was tied for seventh in Tiger history in career touchdown catches (11). He averaged 20.3 yards per catch in his career, still the school record on a yards per catch basis...

When he graduated, he was a fifth-round pick of the Lions after the 1941 season. To keep in shape and because he loved Sports, Blalock also played Clemson basketball in 1940-41. He is a charter member of the Clemson Athletic Hall of Fame being inducted in 1973. He has many accolades and awards such as being inducted into the state of South Carolina Hall of Fame and being named to Clemson's Centennial team in 1996. Blalock died August 21, 1974. In 1999, an esteemed panel of historians slotted Joe Blalock as Clemson's #16 gridder of all-time.

The season began at home on Sept 20 v Presbyterian at Riggs Field on the campus of Clemson University in Clemson SC. The Tigers beat the Blue Hose W (41-12) On Sept 27, Clemson traveled to Lynchburg, VA and played VIMI at City Stadium for the win W (36-7). On Oct 4, in the Textile Bowl at American Legion Stadium in

Charlotte NC, the Tigers beat the Wolfpack W (27-6). On Oct 11, the Tigers got the rare treat of traveling to Boston to play in Fenway Park against Boston College. They had beaten BC, coached at the time by the immortal Frank Leahy in their first outing in the Cotton Bowl in 1939; They beat the Eagles again W (26-13). Denny Myers had taken over for Leahy at BC.

On Oct 23 at South Carolina, on Big Thursday, the Tigers suffered a rare loss while nationally ranked at #14 to the unranked Gamecocks in a close match L (14-18). Then next venue was Griffith Stadium in Washington DC v George Washington. The Tigers picked up a nice 1in W (19-0). On Nov 15, at home, the Tigers shut out Wake Forest W (29-0). The next week Nov 22 at Sirrine Stadium in Greenville SC, the #18 rankcd Tigers beat Furman W (34-6). In the season finale on Nov 29 at Auburn, the Tigers were ranked #16 going in but were nonetheless beaten by the Auburn Tigers L (7-28).

1942 Clemson Tigers Football Coach Frank Howard

The 1942 Clemson Tigers football team represented Clemson College during the 1942 college football season as a member of the Southern Conference (SoCon). Frank Howard was the head football coach for his third of thirty seasons. The Tigers completed their forty seventh season overall and their twenty-first in the Southern Conference with a record of 3-6-1; 2-3-1 in the SoCon. It was a poor season for sure. The Tigers came in ninth in the SoCon out of 16 active SoCon teams. WM & Mary were #1 in the Conference. Charlie Wright was the captain. The new Memorial Stadium was inaugurated September 19 with a win against Presbyterian. Clemson's 200th win came on Big Thursday against South Carolina. From that point on Riggs Stadium was for special events and other sports than football.

On Sept. 19, another season began with Presbyterian feeling the first Clemson hit. This was not Frank Howard's best team nor perhaps his best effort. The typical pushover Blue Hose almost snuck through the net but Clemson held them back in a tougher than should-have-been game W (6-4). The game was played at Clemson's new Memorial Stadium as Riggs field had gone into a football retirement of sorts. Memorial Stadium was built on the Campus of Clemson University and its nickname over the years was Death Valley because so many teams went in full of life and came out clinging to their survival instincts. Presbyterian, in this first game almost ruined the inauguration parade, they played so hard. But the Tigers would have none of it and won the game even without their best team of the ages on the field.

The Offense was taking a long time to make it to the goal line in the early games even the second game v VMI on Sept 26, at City Stadium at Lynchburg. The scoring disease was apparently contagious. Nobody in this game could score a point and the game ended in a scoreless tie T (0-0). The Tigers would have loved a tie in their next game but somebody on the opposing team at American Legion Memorial Stadium in the Textile Bowl played in Charlotte NC v the Wolfpack knew how to get an extra point and that was the difference in the game.

The Tigers lost by one point against NC State L (6-7). It seemed that other than an always tough Auburn Tigers, all the teams including Clemson who once knew how to score points had forgotten how it was done. Boston College on Oct 10 had gotten a shot to minimize the effects of the scoring disease and so for the first time. The Eagles defeated Clemson L (7-14) at Fenway Park.

On Oct 22, Clemson got a reprieve and scored 18 points against the Gamecocks of South Carolina at Carolina Stadium on Big Thursday to emerge victorious W (18-6). Wake Forest got a similar reprieve and were able to score 19 v Clemson en-route to victory on Oct 31 L (6-19).

The disease came back v George Washington at home as the Tigers could not find the goal line L (0-7). On Nov 14, it took one of the Service groups to pass the twenty-point threshold as Clemson lost to the Jacksonville Naval Air Station in Jacksonville, FL   L (6–24). With two games left in a terrible season, the Tigers went on to play hard against Furman on Nov 21 but had a tough time scoring again and lost the home game L (7-12).

Auburn's Tigers were known to take no prisoners and their Tigers routed the Clemson Tigers, who ironically scored their second highest point title of the season while the Clemson defense went on vacation at Auburn Stadium in Alabama, capping off a lousy season with a L (13-41) big loss.

1943 Clemson Tigers Football Coach Frank Howard

The 1943 Clemson Tigers football team represented Clemson College during the 1943 college football season as a member of the Southern Conference (SoCon). Frank Howard was the head football coach for his fourth of thirty seasons. The Tigers completed their forty eighth season overall and their twenty-second in the Southern Conference with a record of 2-6-0; 2-3-0 in the SoCon. It was an even poorer season than the poor Clemson season before. Frank Howard of course did not get his many Clemson accolades and his many uniform Chevrons for seasons such as this.

The Tigers came in seventh in the SoCon out of 10 active SoCon teams. Duke was again at the top of the Southern Conference. The conference itself was being depleted and was down to ten members. Ralph Jenkins was the Clemson Captain for 1943. The new Memorial Stadium had been inaugurated September 19 of the prior year with a close win against Presbyterian. This year, Clemson would not be so fortunate.

On Sept 25, Presbyterian noticed that Clemson for its own reasons was not playing its best football. Frank Howard had yet to set his eternal pattern to become an immortal coach in motion and the Clemson teams under his tutelage were not improving. Or if they were improving it was not noticeable to the discerning eyes of the general public—especially those who rooted exclusively for Clemson.

And, so just like every other year for many years, Clemson chose to kick off its home season at the home Ball Park, Memorial Stadium in Clemson, SC against a team that was willing to play an away game every year at Clemson, Presbyterian. Now the Blue Hose were never push-overs and they were always hoping to place a lick on Clemson but had yet to be able to do so. Well, until this year. Clemson seemed to have a problem getting that extra point after a touchdown when it was one point no matter how ya got it. This was another one of those years. Both teams scored two touchdowns but only one team was able to squeeze an extra point into the score and that team unfortunately for Tigers Fans was not Clemson.

And, so, Presbyterian licked Clemson at home in the season opener for the first time ever L (12–13). I already told you all this was a bad year so we won't spend a lot of words talking about the exact hurts of the season, while we give the scores and the mini-skinny of the games. Every game has coverage in this book but not ad-nauseum.

On Oct 2 at NC State in the American Legion Memorial Stadium in Charlotte, NC, Clemson and NC engaged in the Textile Bowl. Clemson won W (19–7). On Oct 9, Clemson lost against VMI at Victory Stadium in Roanoke, VA   L (7–12). On Oct 21, at South Carolina in Carolina Stadium, Columbia, SC in the Big Thursday encounter, Clemson lost a big game to the Gamecocks L (6–33) Then on October 30, Clemson kept the losing slide operative as it succumbed to Wake Forest at home L (12–41).

After a number of years, Clemson was on Nov 6 again playing at Davidson in Richardson Stadium, Davidson, NC. It was a good choice for the schedule as Clemson won this game W (26–6). It was a great victory in a poor year otherwise. Giving the military its opportunity to be the best that it could be, on Nov 13, Clemson played against Georgia Pre-Flight in Greenville, SC, and were whipped by the stronger military team L (6–32). During the war years, many teams would fall to teams run by the service academies giving our war heroes a chance to play college football.

On Nov 20, Clemson took another crack at the almost impregnable Georgia Tech Bulldogs ranked #15 nationally at the time. The game was played in Grant Field, Atlanta, GA, and Clemson had a tough time keeping its head above water in this major loss L (6–41). That concluded the 1943 season for the Tigers.

1944 Clemson Tigers Football Coach Frank Howard

The 1944 Clemson Tigers football team represented Clemson College during the 1944 college football season as a member of the Southern Conference (SoCon). Frank Howard was the head football coach for his fifth of thirty seasons. The Tigers completed their forty ninth season overall and their twenty-third in the Southern Conference with a record of 4-5; 3-1 in the SoCon. It was a much better season than the two poor Clemson seasons before. But, it was not a Cigar Season. The Tigers came in third in the SoCon out of 10 active SoCon teams. Duke was again at the top of the Southern Conference. The conference itself was not depleted this year as it held steady at ten members. Ralph Jenkins was again the Clemson Captain for 1944

On Sept 23, the Tigers got off to a good start v Presbyterian at Memorial Stadium on the campus of Clemson University in Clemson, SC W (34–0). On Sept 30, the Tigers were walloped and shutout by Georgia Tech's Yellow Jackets at Grant Field in Atlanta, GA L (0–51). On Oct 7 in the Textile Bowl played at American Legion Memorial Stadium in Charlotte, NC, Clemson prevailed W (13–7). On Oct 19 at South Carolina in Carolina Stadium, Columbia, SC on Big Thursday, the Tigers beat the Gamecocks W (20–13). Then on Oct 28 at nationally ranked #20 Tennessee at Shields-Watkins Field in Knoxville, TN, the Volunteers beat the Tigers L (7–26)

On Nov 4 at Wake Forest's Groves Stadium in Wake Forest, NC, the Tigers were beaten in a close match. On November 11, the Frank Howard's Fighting Clemson Tigers came back against the Virginia Military Institute (VMI) in Victory Stadium in Roanoke VA and soundly defeated the Keydets W (45-12). The next game was a loss at Tulane on Nov 18 at Tulane Stadium in New Orleans L (20-36). The season then ended on a loss on Nov 24 at Sanford Stadium in Athens GA as the Tiger s were taken down by the Bulldogs L (7-21)

1945 Clemson Tigers Football Coach Frank Howard

The 1945 Clemson Tigers football team represented Clemson College during the 1945 college football season as a member of the Southern Conference (SoCon). Frank Howard was the head football coach for his sixth of thirty seasons. The Tigers completed their fiftieth season overall and their twenty-fourth in the Southern Conference with a record of 6-3-1; 2-1-1 in the SoCon. The Tigers came in fourth in the SoCon out of 11 active SoCon teams. Duke was again at the top of the Southern Conference. Ralph Jenkins was captain for the third year in a row in 1945

Frank Howard's Clemson Players Taking a Water Break

On Sept 22, Presbyterian brought a very weak team to Memorial Stadium on the campus of Clemson University in Clemson, SC and the team gave the Tigers a nice practice game. W (76-0). On Sept 29, Clemson realized it was not enough practice as the Tigers were shut out by the Bulldogs of Georgia L (0-20) at Sanford Stadium in Athens GA. In the Textile Bowl v NC State at Riddick Stadium in Raleigh NC, the Tigers got back on the winning side in a close match W (13-0). Still engaged in WWII, the Pensacola Naval Air Station came to play the Tigers on Oct 13, and almost got the win, losing by just one point W (7-6). On Big Thursday, Oct 19 in Carolina

Stadium, the Gamecocks and the Tigers played to a scoreless tie T (0-0).

The Tigers traveled to Burdine Stadium in Miami FL for their next encounter on Nov 2, and the squad was barely beaten by the Hurricanes L (6-7). On Nov 10 at home, the Tigers shut out VPI W (35-0). The following week on Nov 17, at Tulane, Clemson overpowered the Green Wave W (47-20) On Nov 24, the Tigers beat Georgia Tech W (21-7) at Grant Field in Atlanta GA. The GA Tech win was not expected and so on Dec 1, when the Tigers played at Wake Forest, the team was ranked #16 nationally. The ranking did not help as unranked Wake Forest beat the Clemson squad--L (6-13)

Player Highlights Ralph Jenkins C 1943-45

<< Ralph Jenkins.

Jenkins made second-team All-American in 1945. He also played in the 1946 Blue-Gray Classic game which was always a big-deal. Ralph was one of the first Tigers chosen to an All-Star game and he made All-American as a junior. He started only four games as a senior due to injury.

Jenkins was a three-time captain. He was that smart and that dedicated to the game. He is the first three-time captain in Tiger history and as of course we all can assume by being highlighted in this book, he was one of the top centers in Tiger history.

Ralph Jenkins started about as many games a as a healthy man could from 1943-45. In fact, he started all 27 games at center his freshman, sophomore, and junior seasons. He was just the second Clemson offensive lineman to earn All-America honors. When it was time to graduate, despite his injury as a senior, he was a 14th-round pick of the Steelers after the 1946 season. He played one year of pro ball in 1947. He was such a standout Clemson Player that he was inducted into the Clemson Hall of Fame in 1995.

1946 Clemson Tigers Football Coach Frank Howard

The 1946 Clemson Tigers football team represented Clemson College during the 1946 college football season as a member of the Southern Conference (SoCon). Frank Howard was the head football coach for his seventh of thirty seasons. The Tigers completed their fifty-first season overall and their twenty-fifth in the Southern Conference with a record of 4-5-; 2-3 in the SoCon. The Tigers came in tenth in the SoCon out of 16 active SoCon teams. Duke was again at the top of the Southern Conference. Chip Clark was the captain.

On Sept 21 in the season opener at Clemson Memorial Stadium on the Campus of Clemson University in Clemson, SC, the Tigers shut out Presbyterian W (39-0). On Sept 27 at Georgia in Sanford Stadium Athens GA, the Tigers lost their first game of the season to the Bulldogs L (12-35). In the annual Textile Bowl, the Wolfpack of NC State beat the Tigers L (L (7-14). Wake Forest then beat the Tigers at Groves Stadium, Wake Forest NC on Oct 12 L (7-19).

On Big Thursday Oct 24, South Carolina beat Clemson at Carolina Stadium L (14-26). Then there was a close game at VPI at Miles Stadium in Blacksburg, VA won by the Tigers over the Keydets W (14-7). The next encounter was a big loss on Nov 9 to a tough Tulane Team in New Orleans L (13-54). Then it was a nice win against Furman on Nov 16 at home W (20-6). To make the season a big success, in the finale, the Clemson Tigers beat the always-tough Auburn Tigers at the Cramton Bowl Stadium in Montgomery Alabama W (21-13).

1947 Clemson Tigers Football Coach Frank Howard

The 1947 Clemson Tigers football team represented Clemson College during the 1947 college football season as a member of the Southern Conference (SoCon). Frank Howard was the head football coach for his eighth of thirty seasons. The Tigers completed their fifty-second season overall and their twenty-sixth in the Southern Conference with a record of 4-5-; 1-3 in the SoCon. The Tigers came in twelfth in the SoCon out of 16 active SoCon teams. WM & Mary won the Southern Conference in 1947. Cary Cox was the Clemson team captain.

On September 20, Clemson kicked off its home season at Memorial Stadium, aka Death Valley on the college campus in Clemson, SC v an always-willing Presbyterian. The Tigers shut out the Blue Hose W (42-0) for a nice season beginning. It just took one more game for the Tigers to register their first loss v Boston College at the Baseball Braves Field in Boston MA L (22-32). On Oct 4, my wedding Anniversary but one year before I was born. Wake Forest beat the Tigers in a close match at home L (14-16). NC State then prepared for the Textile Bowl at Riddick Stadium in Raleigh Stadium, Raleigh NC and the Wolfpack took no prisoners in their defeat of the Clemson Tigers L (0-18).

There was a time or so it seemed that Clemson never lost to South Carolina. Those days were in the past. On Oct 23 at South Carolina in Carolina Stadium, Columbia, on Big Thursday, the Gamecocks had their fill and beat the Tigers L (19–21). On Oct 31, it was another loss – this time at Georgia in Sanford Stadium, Athens, GA. L (6-21). Furman never gives up but this year, they were beaten by Clemson at Surrine Stadium in Greenville, SC   W (35–7). For the first time ever, the Tigers played the Dukes of Duquesne at Forbes Field pro baseball park in Pittsburgh, PA and triumphed W (34–13). On Nov 22, Auburn played the Tigers at home and were defeated by the other Tigers W (34–18)

1948 Clemson Tigers Football Coach Frank Howard

The 1948 Clemson Tigers football team represented Clemson College during the 1948 college football season as a member of the Southern Conference (SoCon). Frank Howard was the head football coach for his ninth of thirty seasons. The Tigers completed their fifty-third season overall and their twenty-seventh in the Southern Conference with a record of 11-0; 5-0 in the SoCon. The Tigers came in a clean first in the SoCon out of 16 active SoCon teams in 1947. Bob Martin & Phil Prince were co-captains for the 1948 Clemson team.

Player Highlights Bobby Gage (1945-48)

BOBBY GAGE

Nobody contests that Bobby Gage was one of the finest all-around football players in Clemson history. He played in the two-platoon era and he really had an effect on three platoons because he changed the course of games with his punt and kickoff returns. Gage played everywhere and he was great.

Looking closely ag his stats in 1948 shows a season in which he had a 100-yard rushing game (12-104 vs. Furman), a 172-yard passing game (against Mississippi State), a two-interception game on defense (also against Mississippi State) and a 100-yard punt return game (101 on three returns against NC State). His 90-yard punt return in that game proved to be the game winner and is still the longest punt return by a Clemson player in the history of Death Valley.

Bobby Gage was the true triple threat football player of the 1940s. He ended his career with 35 touchdowns, eight on rushes, 24 touchdown passes, one via punt return, one via kickoff return and even one on a reception. He still ranks in the top 10 in Clemson history in total offense and interceptions defensively. That is success on both sides of the ball, something you don't see today.

For his accomplishments in 1948, Gage was named a first-team All-American. He was a first-round draft choice of the Pittsburgh Steelers after the season. There were many great young men on Clemson's 1948 team that posted a perfect 11-0 record, the first perfect season at Clemson in 48 seasons. But, Gage might have been the top all-around player and senior leader. He had the stats to back it up.

It was not easy to become an All-American yet in his senior-year, he crossed the All-American threshold as a QB after leading Clemson to an 11-0 season and a 24-23 Gator Bowl win over Missouri. He was a unanimous choice as MVP in the 1949 Gator Bowl...

Gage was in the top 10 in career total offense at Clemson with 3,757 yards. When the greats were reported, he was tied for seventh in Tiger history in career interceptions (10). He also had perhaps the best all-around passing game in Tiger history when he completed 9-11 for 245 yards and two scores versus Furman in 1947. Gage knew the game and played it very well.

Bobby had four touchdown passes against Auburn in 1947, He was the first Tiger to do that. He was even better. He was called on the first-round of the NFL draft pick as the sixth selection of the Steelers. He played with the Steelers for two years.

He was inducted into the 1976 Clemson Athletic Hall of Fame. He was an inductee also to the state of South Carolina Hall of Fame in 1978. Gage was also named to the Gator Bowl Hall of Fame in 1990. After leaving the pros, he worked in the south in a big industry -- textiles at Chemurgy Products, Inc.

He was ranked as Clemson's #5 gridder of all-time by a panel of historians in 1999...At the time, he resided in Greenville, SC. The South Carolina gridders love South Carolina as their home. What is there not to love?

Player Highlights #6 Fred Cone (1948-50)

Every coach has a great recruiting story but there is no question that Coach Frank Howard has one of the best. The most unusual recruiting story that you can find at Clemson was the case of Fred Cone. In the summer of 1947, Coach Frank Howard was informed by his sister, who lived in Mississippi, that there was a terrific athlete related to her next-door neighbor. When Howard turned in the names of his scholarship players for the fall of 1947, he had one spot left, so he added Fred Cone to the list, sight unseen. How's that for a guided light?

Had he wanted to watch Cone play high school football he could not have done it. Cone did not play football in high school. Howard's sister was simply impressed with is athletic ability diving into the neighbor's pool.

By his sophomore year, 1948, Cone was leading the Tigers to an undefeated season, Clemson's first perfect year since 1900. Cone had 635 yards rushing and seven TDs, leading Clemson to the Gator Bowl, where Clemson downed Missouri 24-23. His second-effort run on fourth-and-three for a first down in the final minutes allowed Clemson to run out the clock and claim the landmark victory.

Two years later, Cone was leading Clemson to another undefeated season and he garnered first-team All-Southern honors. He scored 15 touchdowns and gained 845 yards in 1950 and concluded his career with 31 touchdowns, a record. After his Hall of Fame career at Clemson, Cone went on to a Hall of Fame career with the Green Bay Packers. He led the NFL in field goals in 1955.

In 1997 he was inducted into the Clemson Ring of Honor—a distinction he richly deserves. Not a bad record for someone who never played high school football.

I was born in January 1948 and so when I write one of these special Great Moments books, it is always a great moment when I hit the events in the football season of 1948. I do not read ahead so I am always surprised to see how it goes. Clemson was as good as any other team in the country in the year of my birth but, nonethless, the Southern Conference had been the Conference from which the better teams were leaving for many years.

The SEC was grabbing the really tough teams at the time. When we look around the country at college football in 1948, if Clemson, undefeated at 11-0, was not close enough in the AP or Coach's polls to win the National Championship, then we all are asking, then who?

Well, it ins't as easy as it looks to figure out the sentimetality from the reality. Clemson and its opponents were reasonably unknown to the rest of the voting country especially the Associated Press. Hey, who trusts the press about anything today. Anywy these polls were all we had to go by back in 1948.

So, I dug into the many archives, many of which are slanted to see what was going on that would preclude Clemson from being National Champions with an 11-0 record. After an undefeated season and being a unanimous # 1 team in the Southern Conference, why not?

Here is what they say in a nutshell: Lots has been written. Michigan won it all in 1948. Unlike Clemson which went 11-0, the Wolverines went 9-0 and they had enough "press and pundit" clout to claim the #1 spot in the final AP poll over 9-0 Notre Dame. Michigan felt this season made up for the 1947 season when Notre Dame got the crown. It made up up for 1947, when Michigan had also gone 9-0, but finished #2 to Frank Leahy's 9-0 Notre Dame.

They used this as an excuse: Michigan had capped the 1947 season with a huge 49-0 rout of Southern Cal in the Rose Bowl, and the AP conducted a post-bowl poll that went with Michigan at #1 over Notre Dame, but the AP had declared that the post-bowl poll was not "official." This season, it was Notre Dame that played a game against

Southern Cal after the final AP poll. That's because the AP poll ended before their December 4th trip to Southern Cal, where Notre Dame was tripped up by a 14-14 tie to 6-3-1 USC, finishing the Irish at 9-0-1.

Because of that upset, there were no apparent contenders to Michigan's crown this season, since they did not even look at the Southern Conference. Thus, all the reporters who live around the big colleges declared Michigan as the unanimous choice for 1948 mythical national champion (MNC) amongst organizations listed in the NCAA Records Book, even math-based ratings.

Michigan would be the only team in contention. This meant 2 MNCs in a row for Michigan. Pundits across the country did mention Clemson but pooh poohed the great Southern Team's existence in the standings. They suggested that Clemson went 11-0, but their schedule was weak and they performed rather poorly, so they were not a contender at all.

The skinny was that Clemson had played just one team that was ranked by the original AP poll, #20 Wake Forest, and Clemson finished ranked just #11 themselves. They did better in the other poll for 1948 finishing #8, and their Gator Bowl opponent, 8-3 Missouri, was ranked #10.

Clemson won the Gator Bowl 24-23. But that's the only ranked opponent they played according to the pollsters, and they struggled to win 6-0 over 3-6-1 North Carolina State, 13-7 at 3-5 South Carolina, 26-19 at 5-2-2 Boston College, 21-14 over 6-4 Wake Forest, and 7-6 at 1-8-1 Auburn.

Meanwhile, according to the experts, Michigan played 5 ranked teams and only one of their wins was close (touchdown or less), 13-7 at 6-2-2 Michigan State (#17) in their opener. They beat 8-2 Northwestern (#3) 28-0. All commentaries are biased but in this book at least, we show you why the big shots chose not to give Clemson its proper roll of the dice for the Natonal Championship. Regardless, the Tigers were undefeated and that is pretty darn good when you play eleven games and win them all.

California went 10-0 in the regular season, but they lost 20-14 to 8-2 Northwestern in the Rose Bowl to blow a shot at a share of the MNC. This became a habit for Cal: they would go unbeaten during the regular season in 1949 and 1950, and then lose the Rose Bowl following each of those seasons as well.

An always powerful Army team, especially during the WWII years, started this season 8-0, but they were tied by 0-8-1 Navy in their finale to finish 8-0-1, probably the biggest upset in college football history.

10-1 Oklahoma took their upset early, losing 20-17 at 7-2-1 Santa Clara in their opener. 9-1 Tulane lost 13-7 at 7-3 Georgia Tech in their 2nd game, and 8-1 Mississippi lost 20-7 at Tulane. 8-1 Cornell lost 27-6 to 8-0-1 Army at home. Again, 11-0 is not too shabb in anybody's league.

In the season opener against Presbyterian, Clemson chose to make it a memorable night game. It was the first time Memorial Stadium hosted a night game -- ever. It was in this season opening shutout W (53-0) victory over Presbyterian. As we have learned Memorial Stadium is where Clemson plays its home games. It is convenient as it sits right on the Clemson Campus in Clemson, SC.

On Oct 2, Clemson beat NC State at home in the Textile Bowl W 6–0. On Oct 9, the Tigers traveled to Scott Field in Starkville MS to play Mississippi State with a nice win W (21-7) Next on Oct 21, South Carolina had designs on an upset over the Tigers but the Gamecocks were brushed back at Carolina Stadium in Columbia, SC on Big Thursday for a Clemson win W (13-7). Traveling again to the site where the Bost on Barves played for years, on Oct 29, the Tigers beat the Eagles of Boston Collegeat Braves Field in Boston, MA W (26–19). On Nov 6, the Tigers beat Furman at home in a big shutout W (41–0).

Finally, Clemson was able to beat Wake Forest at home W (21-14)) on Nov 13. The next week, it was Duquesne at home in a big win W (42-0).Next was Auburn at Ladd Stadium in Mobile AL for a nice win W (7–6). In the final game of the season, on December 4 at The Citadel's Johnson Hagood Stadium in Charleston, SC   the Tigers won W (20-0)

The Tigers had such a great season, they were warded a national bowl bid – the Gator Bowl v Missouri at Gator Bowl Stadium in Jacksonville FL. The Tigers put it all together on January 1, 1949 and beat Missouri W (24-23) for a great Gator Bowl victory W (24-23) in a nail-biter.

Highlight Game Clemson 24, Missouri 23

Jan. 1, 1949 at Jacksonville, FL (Gator Bowl)

Clemson's 1948 team was undefeated, but the team was wearing a lucky horseshoe all year long. Clemson had so many close games that year, but the Tigers won them all. College Football Coach Darrell Royal's comment might apply here "Luck is what happens when preparation meets opportunity." Of course, Clemson's own John Heisman would take the luck but he preached discipline: "Gentlemen, it is better to have died as a small boy than to fumble this football." Coach Howard took the luck this season and ran with it.

This season had some wins that only fate can explain. Of example, Clemson beat NC State 7-0 on a 90-yard punt return by Bobby Gage. Phil Prince blocked a punt at South Carolina that Rabbit Thompson returned for a touchdown, giving the Tigers the 13-7 win over South Carolina. And in the last game of the season, Clemson simply humiliated Auburn 7-6 in a driving rainstorm.

The Tigers kept the lucky horseshoe for their Gator Bowl appearance against Missouri. This game was voted the best Gator Bowl game of the first 25 that were played. Clemson had them 24-16 when they scored a touchdown to cut the margin to one point with about four minutes left.

Clemson got the ball back and Howard was hoping and trying to run out the clock to come home with a one-point win. It was fourth-and-three near midfield. Coach Frank Howard decided to go for it because he felt the team had not effectively stopped Missouri's offense all day. He called a play that gave the ball to Fred Cone on a running play. Cone hit a stone wall, but he kept his legs churning, and he bounced outside a little so that overall, he gained six yards for the first down. Clemson ran the clock out for the victory. As you may be able to determine, Fred Cone was as strong as an ox.

Coach Howard had a problem giving up even little secrets. For example, there is nobody who can relate to anybody else what the coach saw as his most memorable game. However, Frank Howard had no problem telling the world that the run by Fred Cone was his most memorable play.

During the previous season a group of students had come over to see Coach Howard to try to get him to resign. The team was not doing well at 1-5 at the time. Coach Howard stood his ground and he told those boys we were going to win the final three games of the 1947 season, thcn have a very good season the next year. Some have concluded that Howard did not know what he was talking about, but nonetheless he proved to be correct. Clemson won 14 straight games after he met with those students, including this undefeated season. Aren't true football stories the best?

1949 Clemson Tigers Football Coach Frank Howard

The 1949 Clemson Tigers football team represented Clemson College during the 1949 college football season as a member of the Southern Conference (SoCon). Frank Howard was the head football coach for his tenth of thirty seasons. The Tigers completed their fifty-fourth season overall and their twenty-eighth in the Southern Conference with a record of 4-4-2; 2-2-0. in the SoCon. The Tigers came in eighth in the SoCon out of 16 active SoCon teams. Gene Moore was the team captain for the 1949 Clemson team.

From writing these season summaries, I have learned that one thing you can count on until 1949 is that Presbyterian will show up for the season home opener at whichever stadium Clemson assigns, and they will do their best to defeat the Tigers. You can count on that like a gold standard.

In 1949, Presbyterian came in as usual to play at Clemson Memorial Stadium on the campus of Clemson Univesity in Clemson, SC, even before Clesmosn was a university, and as usual they were overwhelmed by the top-light play of the Tigers. This year the toll was CU 69, PU 7. It was a big win W (69-7) over Presbyterian and it helped the Clemson squad get accustomed to playing in their new really big stadium.

On Sept 24, Rice tried its luck with the Tigers at Rice Field in Houston, TX and the Owls dominated to win L (7–33). Then came some of the usual southern suspects including NC State on Oct 1 at Riddick Stadium in Raleigh, NC—the almost annual Textile Bowl. The Tigers picked up a tough win W (7–6). On Oct 8, at home, the Tigers tied Mississippi State T (7-7). Then, at Carolina Stadium in Columbia SC, on Big Thursday, Oct 20, the Tigers lost to SC L (13-27.

The Tigers, home for the next three games, were met with mixed results, negative for the first two games. Wake Forest beat the Tigers Oct 29 L (21-36; then Boston College had its way L (27-40) before the Tigers recovered and beat Duquesne at home W (33-20. Clemson then beat Furman on Nov 19 at Sirrine Stadium in Greenville, SC W (28–21). Wrapping up the season, the Tigers took on Auburn at Ladd Stadium in Mobile, AL and the match result in a tie T (20–20). And so went the season. Could have been better but it wasn't

1950 Clemson Tigers Football Coach Frank Howard

The 1950 Clemson Tigers football team represented Clemson College during the 1950 college football season as a member of the Southern Conference (SoCon). Frank Howard was the head football coach for his eleventh of thirty seasons. The Tigers completed their fifty-fifth season overall and their twenty-ninth in the Southern Conference with a record of 9-0-1; 3-0-1. in the SoCon. The Tigers came in second in the SoCon out of 17 active SoCon teams. Fred Cone was the team captain for the 1950 Clemson team.

Player Highlights Jackie Calvert S, QB 1948-1950

Calvert was an NEA first-team All-America safety. He was a great one for sure. He still holds the career record for rushing yards per attempt (5.92). He was designated the honor of team co-captain for

the 1951 Orange Bowl team. He was always a top all-purpose
yardage gainer that season with 1,220 yards,

<< Jackie Calvert

He could easily be described as
a fine all-around back but he
was more than that.

When this record was retrieved,
Calvert was still second in Tiger
history in career yards per pass
attempt (8.76)...also seventh in
career passing efficiency.

Calvert was a 25th-round draft
pick of the Los Angeles Rams
after the 1950 season...one of
the stalwarts on two undefeated
Clemson teams...nicknamed
"The Kid".

For years, he resided in
Murrells Inlet, SC.

Continuing with the season's games on Sept 23, Presbyterian came to
Memorial Stadium on the college campus at Clemson, SC to be shut
out W (54–0). On Sept 30, #17 ranked Missouri came to play the
Tigers at home and lost W (34-0). Next home game was on Oct 7 as
NC State in the Textile Bowl in which the Tigers prevailed W (27-0).
Then, on Oct 19 at Carolina Stadium in Columbia SC on Big
Thursday, the Gamecocks tied the Tigers T (14-14)) With a little
extra rest after the Thursday game, the Tigers beat Wake Forest in a
close match at Groves Stadium in Wake Forest NC W (13-12).

On Nov 4, the Tigers beat Duquesne Dukes at home W (53020).
Following this, it was a game at Braves Field in Boston v Boston
College in which the Tigers prevailed upon the Eagles for the win, W
(35-14). Following this it was Furman on Nov 18 at home W (57-2).

Auburn was next in a great shutout game for the Tigers at Auburn W (40-0)

Clemson was invited to Miami Burdine Stadium on Jan 1, 1951 for the Orange Bowl and the Tigers beat the Hurricanes in a great victory W (15-14)

1951 Clemson Tigers Football Coach Frank Howard

The 1951 Clemson Tigers football team represented Clemson College during the 1951 college football season as a member of the Southern Conference (SoCon). Frank Howard was the head football coach for his twelfth of thirty seasons. The Tigers completed their fifty-sixth season overall and their thirtieth in the Southern Conference with a record of 7-3-0-; 3-1-0. in the SoCon. The Tigers came in sixth in the SoCon out of 17 active SoCon teams. Bob Patton was the team captain for the 1951 Clemson team.

On Sept 22, the Tigers shellacked Presbyterian in the home opener W (53-6) in Memorial Stadium on the Clemson Campus in Clemson, SC. On Sept 29, Clemson traveled to Rice Stadium in Houston TX, and beat the Owls W (20-14). On Oct 6 at NC State's Riddick Stadium in Raleigh, NC the #18 ranked Tigers beat the Wolfpack in the Textile Bowl W (6–0). On Oct 13, at Pacific Memorial Stadium in Stockton CA, the #16 Clemson Tigers lost a close match to the #20 ranked Pacific Tigers L (7-13). On Oct 25, at South Carolina in Carolina Stadium, Columbia, SC on Big Thursday, the Tigers were shut out by the Gamecocks L (0–20).

The Tigers then played Wake Forest at home on Nov 3 and beat the Demon Deacons W (21-6). Still home for the second week in a row, on Nov 10, the Clemson Fighting Tigers beat the Boston College Eagles W (21-2). The next game was at Sirrine Stadium on Nov 17 in Greenville, SC. The Tigers beat the Paladins W (34–14). On Nov. 24 at home, the Clemson Tigers shut out the Auburn Tigers W (34-0).

The Tigers were invited to play the Gator Bowl at Gator Bowl Stadium in Jacksonville on January 1, 1952 and they lost to the Miami Hurricanes L (0-14)

1952 Clemson Tigers Football Coach Frank Howard

The 1952 Clemson Tigers football team represented Clemson College during the 1952 college football season as a member of the Southern Conference (SoCon). Frank Howard was the head football coach for his thirteenth of thirty seasons. The Tigers completed their fifty-seventh season overall and their thirty-first in the Southern Conference with a record of 2-6-1; 0-1-0 in the SoCon. The Tigers came in fifteenth in the SoCon out of 17 active SoCon teams. George Rodgers was the team captain for the 1952 Clemson team.

After playing in the 1950 Orange Bowl and the 1952 Gator Bowl, in spite of the Southern Conference's ban on postseason play, Clemson was declared ineligible for the conference championship. In part, this was due to the ban. Unfortunately, Clemson and six other schools left the Southern Conference where it was tough to compete with the deck stacked. These teams formed the Atlantic Coast Conference (ACC) in 1953. It was a great move for them and a great move for Clemson. Too bad the somewhat corrupt NCAA still exists to punish teams that do not favor their college heritage.

On Sept 20, the home opener was again against Presbyterian in Memorial Stadium on the Clemson Campus in Clemson, SC, W (53-13). In another home match on Sept 27, Villanova beat Clemson L (7-14). It was already shaping up as "one of those seasons." Clemson would come up with few wins. The next three games were losses at Maryland on Oct 4, 0-29; at Florida on Oct 11, L (13-54), and at South Carolina on Oct 23 L (0-6).

The next win would be the last and it would come at Braves Field in Boston MA v the BC Eagles on Oct 31, W (13-0). Before ending the season with two more losses, the Tigers tied Fordham at Coffee Field in the Bronx T (12-12). The next loss was Nov 15 v Kentucky at McLean Stadium in Lexington, KY L (14-27). In the season finale, Clemson fought Auburn tough but it was not enough and the Auburn Tigers triumphed with one field goal L (0-3).

Player Highlights Tom Barton G 1950-1952

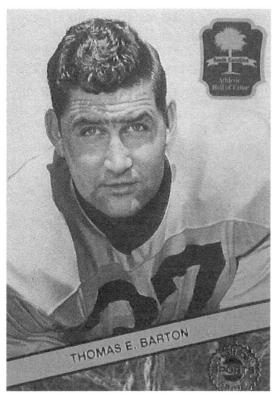

THOMAS E. BARTON

Playing football in the war years was difficult. Barton spent two years in the Navy prior to attending Clemson. Soldiers in all branches of the service around this time were the toughest athletes in any of the nation's schools. They had faced death and football, no matter how dangerous for others, seemed more like fun for the returning veterans than their prior diet of war related activities.

Barton was named to all-state, All-South and All-America teams during his senior year. He was well liked and respected by teammates and in fact was nicknamed "Black Cat."

He received the Blue Key Award as the Outstanding Athlete-of-the-Year in 1952. Barton also played in the 1953 All-Star College-Pro Game in Chicago. He was a sixth-round pick of the Pittsburgh Steelers after the 1952 season and was inducted into the Clemson Hall of Fame in 1987 and the state of South Carolina Hall of Fame in 1987.

After graduating from Clemson, he went on to earn Master's and Doctoral degrees in education. He then served as President of Greenville Technical College.

1953 Clemson Tigers Football Coach Frank Howard

The 1953 Clemson Tigers football team represented Clemson College during the 1953 college football season as a member of the newly formed Atlantic Coast Conference (ACC). Frank Howard was the head football coach for his fourteenth of thirty seasons. The Tigers completed their fifty-eighth season overall and their first in the Atlantic Coast Conference with a record of 3-5-1; 1-2 in the ACC. The Tigers came in sixth in the ACC out of 7 active ACC teams. Dreher Gaskin and Nathan Gressette were the team captains for the 1953 Clemson team.

On Sept 19, Clemson began the season at home against Presbyterian at Memorial Stadium on the campus of Clemson College in Clemson, SC W (33-7) On Sept 26, Clemson tied Boston College at Fenway Park T (26-26). On Oct 3, at home the Tigers were shut out by the Maryland Terrapins L (0-20). Miami then laid a big hurt on Clemson on Oct 9 at Burdine Stadium in Miami FL L (7-39).

The Tigers lost another game against South Carolina on Big Thursday at Carolina Stadium L (7-14). They had a one game rebound on Oct 31 at home, beating Wake Forest W (18-0). On Nov 7, at Grant Field in Atlanta GA, the Tigers loss to the GA Tech Yellow Jackets L (7-20) They then put together another one-game rebound against The Citadel in Johnson Hagood Stadium Charleston SC W (34-13). The season finale was against the Auburn Tigers who manhandled the Clemson Tigers L 19-45) at home. There were no bowl game offerings.

1954 Clemson Tigers Football Coach Frank Howard

The 1954 Clemson Tigers football team represented Clemson College during the 1954 college football season as a member of the newly formed Atlantic Coast Conference (ACC). Frank Howard was the head football coach for his fifteenth of thirty seasons. The Tigers completed their fifty-ninth season overall and their second in the Atlantic Coast Conference with a record of 5-5-0; 1-2-0 in the ACC. The Tigers came in fifth in the ACC out of 8 active ACC teams. Buck George, Scott Jackson, Mark Kane, Clyde White were the team captains for the 1954 Clemson team.

On Sept 18 in the season opener at Memorial Stadium on the campus of Clemson College in Clemson SC, the Tigers shut out the Blue Hose W (33-0). Clemson then lost to Georgia on Sept 25 at Sanford Stadium in Athens, GA L (7–14). The second loss of the season came

the following week on Oct 2 when VPI came to town and beat the
Tigers L (7-18). The next game was played in Gator Bowl Stadium v
14 Florida on Oct 9, W (14-7).

On the Big Thursday rivalry day, Oct 21 at Carolina Stadium in SC,
the Tigers were beaten in a close match by the Gamecocks L (8-13).
On October 30, the Tigers beat the Demon Deacons at American
Legion Memorial Stadium in Charlotte, NC W (32–20). Playing at
home on Nov 6, the Tigers beat Furman W (27-6). Then, on Nov 13,
at #17 Maryland in Byrd Stadium College Park MD, the Terrapins
shut-out the Tigers L (0-16). On Nov 20, the Clemson Tigers played
at #18 Auburn's Stadium in Auburn, AL. They were beaten by the
Auburn Tigers L 6–27. With no bowl offers, the Citadel was the last
game on the schedule. It was a home game and the Tigers finished
the year on a positive note with this shutout shellacking of the
Bulldogs W (59–0)

Chapter 17 Frank Howard Era 1955-1969

Coach # 17 Frank Howard

Year	Coach	Record	Conference	Record
1955	Frank Howard	7-3-0	ACC	3-1-0
1956*	Frank Howard	7-2-2	ACC	4-0-1
1957	Frank Howard	7-3-0	ACC	4-3-0
1958	Frank Howard	8-3-0	ACC	5-1-0
1959*	Frank Howard	9-2-0	ACC	6-1-0
1960	Frank Howard	6-4-0	ACC	4-2-0
1961	Frank Howard	5-5-0	ACC	3-3-0
1962	Frank Howard	6-4-0	ACC	5-1-0
1963	Frank Howard	5-4-1	ACC	5-2-0
1964	Frank Howard	3-7-0	ACC	2=4-0
1965*	Frank Howard	5-5-0	ACC	5-2-0
1966"	Frank Howard	6-4-0	ACC	6-1-0
1967*	Frank Howard	6-4-0	ACC	6-0-0
1968	Frank Howard	4-5-1	ACC	4-1-1
1969	Frank Howard	4-6-0	ACC	3-3-0

* Five conference championships from 1955 to 1969

1955 Clemson Tigers Football Coach Frank Howard

The 1955 Clemson Tigers football team represented Clemson College during the 1955 college football season as a member of the newly formed Atlantic Coast Conference (ACC). Frank Howard was the head football coach for his sixteenth of thirty seasons. The Tigers completed their sixtieth season overall and their third in the Atlantic Coast Conference with a record of 7-3-0; 3-1-0 in the ACC. The Tigers came in third in the ACC out of 8 active ACC teams. Don King was the team captain for the 1955 Clemson team.

On Sept 17, the season opener was against Presbyterian at home at Memorial Stadium on the Clemson Campus in Clemson SC. The Tigers shut-out the Blue Hose W (33-0). On Sept 24, the Tigers traveled to Virginia to Scott Stadium in Charlottesville, VA W (20–7). On Oct 1, at home, the Tigers defeated the Georgia Bulldogs W (7–26). On Oct 8, at Rice Stadium in Houston Texas, the Tigers lost to the Owls L (7-21). On Oct 20 on Big Thursday, the Tigers beat the SC Gamecocks W (28-14) at Carolina Stadium in Columbia SC.

On Oct 29, Clemson beat Wake Forest at home W (19-13). On Nov 5, at Victory Stadium in Roanoke VA, Clemson defeated VPI W (21-16). On Nov 12, the Tigers lost to # 2 ranked Maryland at home L (12-25). On Nov 19 at Ladd Memorial Stadium in Mobile AL, the Auburn Tigers defeated the Clemson Tigers L (0-21). On Nov 26, Clemson traveled to Sirrine Stadium in Greenville SC and beat Furman W (40-20.

1956 Clemson Tigers Football Coach Frank Howard

The 1956 Clemson Tigers football team represented Clemson College during the 1956 college football season as a member of the newly formed Atlantic Coast Conference (ACC). Frank Howard was the head football coach for his seventeenth of thirty seasons. The Tigers completed their sixty-first season overall and their fourth in the Atlantic Coast Conference with a record of 7-2-2; 4-0-1 in the ACC. The Tigers came in first in the ACC out of 8 active ACC teams. Charley Bussey was the team captain for the 1956 Clemson team. For such a great season, and winning the ACC, Clemson was invited to the Orange Bowl to play Colorado.

On Sept 22, Clemson beat Presbyterian at home to kick off the season at Memorial Stadium on the Clemson Campus in Clemson, SC W (27-7). Then on Sept 29 the Tigers played #the 19 ranked Florida Gators at Florida Field at Gainesville FL in a back and forth game that resulted in a tie T (20-20). On Oct 6, at Riddick Stadium in Raleigh NC, in the Textile Bowl, the Tigers defeated the Wolfpack W (13-7). On Oct 13, the Tigers won their next game against Wake Forest at Bowman Gray Stadium in Winston-Salem, NC W (17–0). On Oct 25 in the rivalry game v South Carolina at Carolina Stadium, the Tigers won on Big Thursday in a nail-biter W (7-0)

Still undefeated after five games, the Tigers won their fourth in a row against VPI on Nov 3 at home W (21-6). The second tie of the season came on Nov 10 at Maryland's Byrd Stadium in College Park MD T (6-6). Still undefeated and ranked #13, the Tigers suffered their first loss against Miami at Burdine Stadium in Miami L (0-21). Clemson won their next two home games. The first on Nov 24 was against Virginia W (7-0) and the second on Dec 1 against Furman W (28-7)

In the Orange Bowl played at Burdine Stadium in Miami FL, #20 Colorado defeated #19 Clemson in a tight match L (21-17)

Player Highlights Joel Wells, RB 1954-1956)

Joel Wells was a running back who wore number-70. In the defense minded 1950s, Wells broke the ACC rushing record his junior season with 782 yards, then bettered that total with 803 as a senior. That junior year he reached 782 yards in just 135 carries, a 5.8 average that still ranks among the top 10 single season averages in Clemson history.

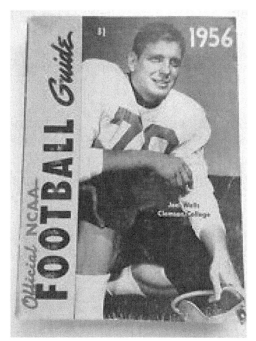

<< Joel Wells

How respected was Wells nationally? In 1956 his picture adorned the cover of the NCAA media guide. He was the first running back in Clemson history to rank among the top 20 in the nation in rushing in consecutive seasons. His number-seven ranking in yards per game in 1955 is still the highest ranking by a Clemson running back.

This two-time All-ACC running back is still in the top 15 in Clemson history in rushing and he led the Tigers in rushing three straight seasons. He might have saved his best game for last when he ran for 125 yards in 18 carries against Colorado in the 1957 Orange Bowl. He scored two touchdowns in that game, including a 58-yard jaunt that is still the Clemson record for a touchdown run in a bowl game by a running back.

He was the first Clemson running back to rank in the top 20 in the nation in rushing in consecutive seasons. He ranked seventh in rushing in 1955 and 18th in 1956.

Wells was truly an all-around player. Remember, in the 1950s, players went both ways. He was a strong tackler who also had five career interceptions. He had a 21-yard average on kickoff returns for his career and also had 11 punt returns for 85 yards. On top of that, he had a 20-yard average on 10 receptions for his career. Altogether, Wells had 2482 total performance yards.

Joel Wells was a third-team All- American in 1955...He had already broken the ACC rushing record as a junior.

He enjoyed being a two-time first-team All-ACC selection and as of this report, he was still ranked in the top 20 in career rushing at Clemson. He led Clemson in rushing three straight seasons (1954-56), he was the first Tiger to ever do that. Wells played in the 1957 Senior Bowl which was one of my favorite games when the College All Stars played the winning pro team from the year before. Bring this game back, please.

Wells was inducted into the Clemson Hall of Fame in 1974) and also the state of South Carolina Hall of Fame the same year, 1974. He is ranked as Clemson's #25 most important gridder of all-time by a panel of historians in 1999. When the report was made, he was living in Greenville, SC. Like I have said, SC players like living in SC.

He was a mainstay of the Clemson squads of his era. When he graduated, he was a second-round draft pick, which meant at the time with so few NFL Teams that he as an 18th selection overall, of the Green Bay Packers after the 1956 season.

He was a second-round selection of the Green Bay Packers in 1957. Instead of the Packers, Wells played four years with the Montreal

Alouettes of the CFL In 1961, for one year, he played with the Giants. Wells played four years in the Canadian Football League before finishing his career with the New York Giants of the NFL.

1957 Clemson Tigers Football Coach Frank Howard

The 1957 Clemson Tigers football team represented Clemson College during the 1957 college football season as a member of the newly formed Atlantic Coast Conference (ACC). Frank Howard was the head football coach for his eighteenth of thirty seasons. The Tigers completed their sixty-second season overall and their fifth in the Atlantic Coast Conference with a record of 7-3-0; 4-3-0 in the ACC. The Tigers came in third in the ACC out of 8 active ACC teams. John Grdijan and Leon Kaltenback were the team captains for the 1957 Clemson team. No bowl games this year.

On Sept 21, for the twenty-eighth time in a row, Clemson opened its home season against Presbyterian. This year, the game was played at Memorial Stadium on the campus of Clemson College in Clemson SC. Presbyterian once was competitive enough to beat Clemson but in recent years, the matches were not competitive and Clemson always won. This year was like the recent games as the Tigers shut out and shellacked a very game Blue Hose Team W (66-0). And so, in 1957, Clemson played its last game against Presbyterian College. Presbyterian as noted had been Clemson's season-opening game from 1930 until 1957.

Kenan Memorial Stadium in Chapel Hill, NC was the venue for the second game of Clemson's 1957 season. North Carolina's Tar Heels pummeled the Clemson Tigers this time on Sept 28 in a shutout L (0-26). NC State got the word that NC teams could win and they did just that in a Clemson home game celebrating the Textile Bowl L (7-13). On Oct 12, at Virginia's Scott Stadium in Charlottesville, VA, the Tigers picked up their second win W 20–6 v the Hokies.

Big Thursday again was celebrated on a Thursday at Carolina Stadium in Columbia SC as the Tigers managed a close shutout against the Gamecocks W (13-0). On Nov 2, the Tigers traveled to the tropical climate of Houston Texas to play Rice at Rice Stadium and the Tigers pulled out a nice win W (20-7). Maryland played the

Tigers at home on Nov 9 and were beaten in a competitive game W (26-7).

Clemson was ranked #14 nationally when they played the #11 ranked Duke Blue Devils on Nov 16 at Duke Stadium in Durham NC and the Tigers needed just a little more oomph as they lost the game L (6-7). On Nov 23, Wake Forest took on Clemson at home and gave a good match but lost the game W)13-6) on Nov 23. On Nov 30, the Tigers played at Furman's Sirrine Stadium • in Greenville, SC, and finished the season with a nice W (45–6) win over the Paladins.

1958 Clemson Tigers Football Coach Frank Howard

The 1958 Clemson Tigers football team represented Clemson College during the 1958 college football season as a member of the Atlantic Coast Conference (ACC). Frank Howard was the head football coach for his nineteenth of thirty seasons. The Tigers completed their sixty-third season overall and their sixth in the Atlantic Coast Conference with a record of 8-3-0; 5-1 in the ACC. The Tigers came in first in the ACC out of 8 active ACC teams. Bill Thomas was the team captain for the 1958 Clemson team. Coach Frank Howard's 100th win came September 27 against North Carolina. Clemson also played its first game against #1 ranked team when they played LSU in the January 1959 Sugar Bowl.

For the season opener, there was no longer a lock on a win so the Tigers had to prepare extra hard as they no longer got an extra week and a great practice game v Presbyterian before the season's tough games began. Most season openers from this year forward had indeterminate winners.

Clemson opened the season ranked as #18 after their fine showing in 1957. It was on Sept 20 that Virginia came into Memorial Stadium on the Clemson College Campus in Clemson NC for the 1958 season opener and were beaten W (20-15). North Carolina was next at home and the Tigers pulled out another win W (26-21) Three is the charm and the Tigers picked up win # 3 at Byrd Stadium in College park MD. W (8-0). Four is better than three and four came to the

Tigers v Vanderbilt on Oct 11 at Dudley Field in Nashville TN W (8-0).

Game Highlight Clemson 26, North Carolina 21

Sept. 27, 1958 at Clemson, SC

This was just the second game of the 1958 season. Clemson had begun the season just a week earlier with a come from behind twice effort the week before to beat Virginia. The Tigers had to come from behind three times to win this game against North Carolina. There is a lot of history with this game as it was Coach Howard's 100th win as Clemson head coach. It was also the only time that Howard beat Jim Tatum, who was also a Hall of Fame Coach. Coach Tatum died prior to the next season.

This victory was important for Coach Howard and for Clemson football. Up until this game North Carolina always seemed to beat the Fighting Tigers. In the series, NC held a solid lead. But, this win started a string of six straight wins for Clemson over North Carolina. The lead persists as Clemson is proud to still lead in the series today.

Game Highlight Clemson 12, Vanderbilt 7

Oct. 11, 1958 at Nashville, TN

Clemson scored two touchdowns in the fourth quarter, including the last one on a short run by Harvey White with just three seconds left. It is still the latest Clemson has ever scored a touchdown to win a game. This was a key victory in a season in which Clemson would qualify for a bowl game.

This was another year that Frank Howard's boys had the lucky horseshoe. Clemson won four games with touchdowns in the fourth quarter that year and it took the Tigers to a bowl game.

The rivalry of Big Thursday was next at Carolina Stadium on Oct 23 in Columbia, SC for the first loss of the season L (6–26). There were few blowouts this year and the next one was another nail-biter on Nov 1 v Wake Forest but the Tigers prevailed at home W (14-12).

Ranked # 17 when they pulled into Grant Field in Atlanta GA on Nov 8, the Tigers were shut out by Georgia tech L (0-13).

On Nov 15, the Textile Bowl was the next big target and it was up for grabs v NC State's Wolfpack at Riddick Stadium in Raleigh, NC; but the Tigers prevailed W (13–6). Duke came to Clemson to play football and the Tigers beat the Blue Devils W (34-12). Furman played hard don Nov 29 but were overwhelmed again by the Tigers W (36-29).

On January 1, 1959, in a great effort, the Clemson Tigers lost to LSU at Tulane Stadium, New Orleans in the Sugar Bowl, L (0-7. Overall, the Bowl game was a bit disappointing but the Howard squad almost beat #1 LSU in the Sugar Bowl that year, but Billy Cannon threw a game-deciding touchdown pass to beat the Clemson Tigers. Cannon's pass was no fluke. As a junior, Cannon was the driving force behind the Fighting Tigers as they carved out a perfect season and captured the 1958 national championship ... He passed for a touchdown and he even kicked the extra point in LSU's 7-0 win over Clemson in the Sugar Bowl, and earned MVP honors.

1959 Clemson Tigers Football Coach Frank Howard

The 1959 Clemson Tigers football team represented Clemson College during the 1959 college football season as a member of the Atlantic Coast Conference (ACC). Frank Howard was the head football coach for his twentieth of thirty seasons. The Tigers completed their sixty-fourth season overall and their seventh in the Atlantic Coast Conference with a record of 9-2-0; 6-1 in the ACC. The Tigers came in first in the ACC out of 8 active ACC teams. Paul Snyder and Harvey White were team captains in 1959. The annual game against South Carolina was played on Thursday at the State Fair for the final time. Clemson's 300th win came in the Bluebonnet Bowl against TCU.

Player Highlights Lou Cordileone T 1957-59

Cordileone was a great Clemson player. He was named first-team All-American, Academic All-American, and Academic All-ACC in 1959 as a senior. He played two fine years before his senior year. He started on two ACC Championship teams that were nationally ranked 12th and 11th in 1958 and 1959, respectively

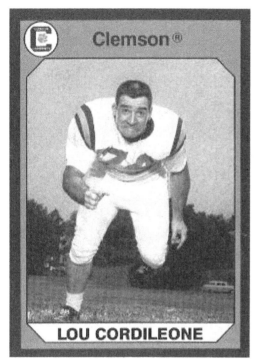

He played in two 1959 bowl games, the Sugar Bowl and the Bluebonnet Bowl. He was also adept at other sports such as playing right field in the College World Series for the Tigers in 1959. Not too shabby! He was a first-round draft pick in both the NFL and the AFL. The AFL breakaway was very successful in this era.

Cordileone was chosen by the Giants in the NFL and by the Buffalo Bills in the AFL. He was the 12th pick of the 1960 draft by the New York Giants.

Lou was the first Clemson player to play in the Hula Bowl, which we all know he enjoyed. He also played in the 1960 College All-Star Game in Chicago which once was called the Senior Bowl. Lou Cordileone, an All-American was named to Clemson's Centennial team in April 1996.

On Sept 19 at Kenan Memorial Stadium in Chapel Hill, NC the # 18 ranked Clemson Tigers barely beat the #12 North Carolina Tar Heels W 20–18. On Sept 26 at Virginia in a game played in Scott Stadium, Charlottesville, VA, the $ 5 ranked Tigers shut out the Wahoos W 47–0. On Oct 3 at #7 Georgia Tech in Grant Field, Atlanta, GA #6 Clemson lost the match L (6–16). On Oct 19 in the almost annual Textile Bowl, was also Clemson's home opener. It was played at Memorial Stadium on the campus of Clemson College in Clemson, SC. Clemson beat NC State W (23–0). On Oct 22 at South Carolina's Carolina Stadium in Columbia, SC on Big Thursday, the #17 Tigers beat the Gamecocks W (27–0)

Big Thursday Notes

Picture Clemson University Big Thursday Game by Will Vandervort

Coach Frank Howard is shown above blowing a good-by kiss to Big Thursday. Coach Howard felt the yearly matchup at South Carolina was not in Clemson's best interests. He did not like Big Thursday.

The following piece is from the Clemson Insider. It is titled *The death of Big Thursday*, by Robert MacRae. It ran November 16, 2012. It is a classic. Enjoy/

Today we continue our series of articles at theClemsonInisder.com that will take a look back at the best Clemson victories in the Clemson-South Carolina Rivalry. In the days leading up to the State's Big Game, we will count down, in our opinion, the Tigers 10 best victories over the hated Gamecocks.

No. 7: Clemson 27, South Carolina 0 (October 22, 1959)
Frank Howard had enough. Ever since Clemson first played South Carolina in 1896, Clemson's players, coaches, students and fans had to get on a train, hop on a bus or drive down to Columbia every October during State Fair Week to play the state's biggest game.

"We always had to sit in the sun, and we got tired of having to go down there every year," Howard said in the book The Clemson Tigers From 1996 to Glory. "We weren't getting half of the tickets, half of the program and concession sales, and it knocked one game out of our schedule because we could not play the Saturday before or the Saturday after the Thursday game."

In fact, Big Thursday, was a big pain in Clemson's side, despite the fact it was good for the state and the rivalry as a whole.

Big Thursday was played at mid-season and always during State Fair Week in Columbia. Originally a sideshow for the State Fair, it blossomed into the main attraction. The game was a state holiday as schools and state agencies closed their doors and took the day off on the fourth Thursday of every October.

"I came from Alabama, and I never saw anything there like the atmosphere before Big Thursday," said Clemson hero Gary Barnes to The (Columbia) State Newspaper in 2004. "Even the bus ride was special. People would be standing along the streets and roads cheering.

The rivalry is still there, but playing on Thursday like we did set the game apart and I don't know if that is true today."

Big Thursday was an event. Families made a holiday weekend out of the game.

"I came from the Tennessee mountains and I thought, 'Boy, this is peculiar.'" said Phil Prince, who blocked a punt that led directly to the Tigers' game-winning touchdown in 1948.

Though it was peculiar, it was an event Clemson was tired of participating in, even though the Tigers posted a 33-21-3 record against South Carolina during that time. By 1958, Clemson made additions to Memorial Stadium to increase its size, and more plans were on the way to make it the same size as Columbia's Carolina Stadium by 1960.

Plus as Howard said, "It was time to see some of those tourist dollars in Clemson, and give people the chance to see Clemson's beautiful campus."

Eventually, Clemson won out and it was decided the 1959 battle was going to be the last Big Thursday matchup in the history of the rivalry. Being the last Big Thursday Game was the only thing memorable about the 1959 game.

Well, that and Howard's famous goodbye kiss to Big Thursday above Carolina Stadium moments afterwards.

As for the game itself, the Tigers got two touchdown passes from Harvey White—one to Bill Mathis and one to Gary Barncs— a Mathis scoring run from four-yards out and a one-yard run by George Usry in the 27-0 victory. White finished the game with 162 passing yards.

It was a fitting end to what has become known as "The Death of Big Thursday."

The 1959 Season Continues

On Oct 31at Rice's Rice Stadium in Houston, TX, # 12 Clemson beat the Owls W 19–0. Clemson then played three home games in a row at Memorial Stadium. On Nov 7, the Clemson Fighting Tigers beat Duke in a close match W (6-0). On Nov 14, Maryland's Terrapins barley nipped the Tigers coming away with the win L (25-28).

On Nov 21, 1959 the Tigers nipped Wake Forest by a similar margin W (33-31).

Highlight Game Clemson 33, Wake Forest 31

Nov. 21, 1959 at Clemson, SC

This was a very exciting game in Death Valley. Some might say the score replicated that of a tennis match, up and down the field.

The Demon Deacons had the Tigers beaten in the fourth quarter, but in those days, maybe just that year, the NCAA had a crazy substitution rule stating that you could not reenter a game until the next quarter. Wake Forest substituted its quarterback late in the fourth quarter.

Clemson turned the ball over, so they had to put a substitute quarterback into the game. On a third-down play, Chuck O'Reilly, the substitute quarterback, threw the ball into the flat and the Tigers' George Usry intercepted.

Usry returned the interception about 75 yards. Two plays later, the same George Usry ran it in for the touchdown. So, Usry made the interception and then scored the winning touchdown. You wouldn't see that today because no one plays both ways anymore.

When Clemson scored that last touchdown to go ahead, 33-31, Furman Bisher of the Atlanta Constitution asked jokingly, "Does anyone remember how the first touchdown (of this game) was scored?" It was such a back and forth on the scores that it seemed like it had been a week ago. Of course, games weren't as high scoring in those days because offenses were much more conservative. Today, as we know, high scores are a lot more common.

On Nov 28, Furman seemed to be weakening as a team and provided minimal opposition in 1959 to the Tigers as they lost big W (56-3). #11 almost immediately Clemson signed up for the December 19 Bluebonnet Bowl v # 7 TCU at Rice Stadium • Houston, TX (Bluebonnet Bowl)   and Frank Howard's squad came away with a big win W (23–7).

1960 Clemson Tigers Football Coach Frank Howard

The 1960 Clemson Tigers football team represented Clemson College during the 1960 college football season as a member of the Atlantic Coast Conference (ACC). Frank Howard was the head football coach for his twenty-first of thirty seasons. The Tigers completed their sixty-fifth season overall and their eighth in the Atlantic Coast Conference with a record of 6-4; 4-2 in the ACC. The Tigers came in

fourth in the ACC out of 8 active ACC teams. Dave Lynn and
Lowndes Shingler were team captains in 1960.

On Sept 24, #9 ranked Clemson kicked off the season against Wake
Forest at Bowman Gray Stadium in Winston-Salem, NC with a nice
win (W 28–7). On Oct 1, in the home opener and the first of two
successive home games in Memorial Stadium on the campus of
Clemson College in Clemson SC, #7 ranked Clemson beat VPI W
(13-7) Now undefeated, the #8 ranked Tigers picked up their third
win without a defeat against Virginia W (21-7). Still ranked # 8 and
looking for four in a row, Duke put the kibosh to that line of thinking
as the Blue Devils beat the Tigers L (6-21) at Duke Stadium in
Durham, NC. Duke finished #10 nationally and won the ACC
Championship.

Now unranked, on Oct 29, Clemson traveled to Vanderbilt's Dudley
Field in Nashville, TN to lose to the Commodores in a real squeaker
L (20–22). On Nov 5, Clemson beat NC at home W (24-0). Then, in
the first meeting since Big Thursday went away, on Nov 12, Clemson
beat SC at home W (12-2). Instead of Big Thursday, the game was
labeled the Battle of the Palmetto State as the rivalry was still intense.

On Nov 19, Clemson traveled to Chestnut Hill MA, to play Boston
College and were defeated L (14-25). In the season finale, Furman
came to Memorial Stadium and were defeated by Clemson W (42-
14). For such a promising start, there would be no bowl games this
year for Clemson. For the next eight years of Frank Howard's time
with Clemson, the team would not win more than 6 games in a
season.

1961 Clemson Tigers Football Coach Frank Howard

The 1961 Clemson Tigers football team represented Clemson College
during the 1961 college football season as a member of the Atlantic
Coast Conference (ACC). Frank Howard was the head football
coach for his twenty-second of thirty seasons. The Tigers completed
their sixty-sixth season overall and their ninth in the Atlantic Coast
Conference with a record of 5-5; 3-3 in the ACC. The Tigers came in
fourth in the ACC out of 8 active ACC teams. Duke was again #1 in
the ACC. Ron Andreo, Calvin West were team captains in 1961.

After having won eighteen successive season openers in a row, on Sept 23, 1961, the Florida Gators, playing at Memorial Stadium on the campus of Clemson College in Clemson, SC would spoil the streak by beating the Tigers L (17-21) in a tough match. On Sept 30, Maryland would add to the misery at home by beating Clemson in another close one L (21-24). It was not until an away trip to Kenan Memorial Stadium in Chapel Hill, NC, on Oct 7 that the Tigers got their first win of the year with a shutout against North Carolina W (27-0). The losing continued the following week on Oct 14 as Wake Forest played Clemson at home and the home losing streak continued L (13-17). Looking for a win but playing at Cliff Hare Stadium in Auburn v the Auburn Tigers did not make it any easier as the Clemson Tigers lost their fourth out of five L (14-24).

Finally the home light was burning at the end of the tunnel as Tulane came to Clemson on Nov 4 and were beaten W (21-6). The South Carolina game (AKA the Battle of the Palmetto State) was played at Carolina Stadium again this year on Nov 11. The Tigers lost again L (14-21). Playing at home again on Nov 18, the Tigers beat the Furman Paladins W (35-6). On Nov 25, it was about time for the Textile Bowl v NC State W (20-0).

1962 Clemson Tigers Football Coach Frank Howard

The 1962 Clemson Tigers football team represented Clemson College during the 1962 college football season as a member of the Atlantic Coast Conference (ACC). Frank Howard was the head football coach for his twenty-third of thirty seasons. The Tigers completed their sixty-seventh season overall and their tenth in the Atlantic Coast Conference with a record of 6-4; 5-1 in the ACC. The Tigers came in second in the ACC out of 8 active ACC teams. Duke was again #1 in the ACC after being the only loss in Clemson's ACC season for 1962. Dave Hynes was the team captain.

Since Clemson stopped playing Presbyterian in every season opener, it was not assured of a victory and a nice warm-up game. This season began with a loss to Georgia Tech on Sept 22 in Grant Field, Atlanta GA L (9-26). The Tigers recovered the following week in the Textile Bowl on Sept 29 v NC State at Riddick Stadium in Raleigh, NC W

(7-0). Wake Forest invited Clemson to play the Deamon Deacons at Bowman Gray Stadium in Winston-Salem, NC. The Tigers won W (24–7). On Oct 13, Clemson hosted the Georgia Bulldogs who came came in tough and beat the Tigers L (16-14). Perennial ACC Champ Duke then beat Clemson at home on Oct 20 L (0-16).

On Oct 27 at Clemson, Auburn's Tigers beat Clemson's Tigers L (14-17). On Nov 3, North Carolina was next at the home field. This time, however, Clemson would win in a well-played game W (17-6) On Nov 10, the Tigers would travel to Sirrine Stadium in Greenville, SC to defeat Furman W (44-3). Traveling to Byrd Stadium in College Park, MD, the Tigers were able to defeat the Terrapins in a close match W (17-14). In the Battle of the Palmetto State at Clemson this time, the Tigers beat the Gamecocks W (20-17).

1963 Clemson Tigers Football Coach Frank Howard

The 1963 Clemson Tigers football team represented Clemson College during the 1963 college football season as a member of the Atlantic Coast Conference (ACC). Frank Howard was the head football coach for his twenty-fourth of thirty seasons. The Tigers completed their sixty-eighth season overall and their eleventh in the Atlantic Coast Conference with a record of 5-4-1; 5-2 in the ACC. The Tigers came in third in the ACC out of 8 active ACC teams. The once beaten NC & NC State teams shared the top spot in the ACC. Tracy Childers was the team captain.

Clemson began the 1963 season with a loss on Sept 21 to #4 Oklahoma in Oklahoma Memorial Stadium • Norman, OK, L 14–31. The Tigers lost again in week two on Sept 28 at #9 Georgia Tech's Grant Field in Atlanta, GA L)-27). This year, the Tigers lost the Textile Bowl to NC State's Wolfpack at home in Memorial Stadium on the campus of Clemson College, Clemson, SC, L (3-7) In the second home game in a row, the Tigers tied the Bulldogs of Georgia on Oct 12 T (7-7). An always tough Duke Squad played Clemson at Duke Stadium in Durham NC. Clemson lost the game after a slugfest of scoring L (30-35). Clemson traveled to Scott Stadium on Oct 26 to face Virginia and the Tigers beat the Wahoos W (35-0).

On Nov 2 at home, the Tigers beat the Wake Forest Blue Devils W 36-0). Then it was off to Chapel Hill NC for a close win against North Carolina W (11-7). Next on Nov 16 at home, Clemson beat Maryland W (21-6). Wrapping up the season on Nov 28, at Carolina Stadium • Columbia, SC (Battle of the Palmetto State), Clemson won in a nail-biter W (24-0). This game had originally been scheduled for Nov 23 but was moved to Nov 28 due to the Assassination of John F. Kennedy.

1964 Clemson Tigers Football Coach Frank Howard

The 1964 Clemson Tigers football team represented Clemson University during the 1964 college football season as a member of the Atlantic Coast Conference (ACC). Frank Howard was the head football coach for his twenty-fifth of thirty seasons. The Tigers completed their sixty-ninth season overall and their twelfth in the Atlantic Coast Conference with a record of 3-7-0; 2-4-0 in the ACC. The Tigers came in seventh in the ACC out of 8 active ACC teams. The twice-beaten NC State team garnered the top spot in the ACC. John Boyett, Ted Bunton were the team captains.

On Sept 19, at the hope opener of Memorial Stadium on the campus of Clemson University in Clemson, SC, the Tigers shut out the Furmin Paladins W 928-0). Then, on Sept 26, in the Textile Bowl at Riddick Stadium in Raleigh NC, Clemson was defeated by NC State L (0-9). The Tigers then traveled to Grant Field in Atlanta GA on Oct 3 and were defeated by Georgia Tech L (7-14). Traveling again to Georgia, this time on Oct 10 to play the Bulldogs at Sanford Stadium in Athens GA, Clemson was beaten again L (7-19). Still on the road on Oct 17, at Bowman Gray Stadium in Winston-Salem, NC, the Clemson Fighting Tigers put it together to beat Wake Forest W (21-2).

Still traveling on Oct 24 at TCU's Amon G. Carter Stadium in Fort Worth, TX, the Tigers were defeated L (10–14). Clemson then came back home for two games. In the first on Oct 31, against Virginia, Clemson prevailed W (29-7). The second was against North Carolina in which the Tigers were shut out by the Tar Heels L (0-29). On Nov 14, it was back north to Maryland at Byrd Stadium in College Park. The Tigers were shellacked in a shutout L (34-0). The season finale had become the annual SC game and so this year's Balttle of the Palmetto State was played at Clemson but the Tigers could not keep up with the Gamecocks in this low-scoring game and lost L (3-7).

1965 Clemson Tigers Football Coach Frank Howard

The 1965 Clemson Tigers football team represented Clemson University during the 1965 college football season as a member of the Atlantic Coast Conference (ACC). Frank Howard was the head football coach for his twenty-sixth of thirty seasons. The Tigers completed their seventieth season overall and their thirteenth in the Atlantic Coast Conference with a record of 5-5-0; 5-2-0 in the ACC. The Tigers came in first tied with co-champion NC State in the ACC out of 8 active ACC teams. Bill Hecht and Floyd Rogers were the team captains.

On Sept 18, Clemson kicked off the season with a home game v NC State in the Textile Bowl. Clemson's home games were played at the ever increasing in size Memorial field on the campus of Clemson University in Clemson, SC. Clemson gained the victory W (21-7).

Clemson was the co-ACC Champion in 1965, compiling a 5-5 record. Jimmy Addison was the QB for the Tigers in 1965 and he often handed the ball to Buddy Gore. Here is a picture of the game program from the game, depicting Little Red Riding Hood, aka the Tiger.

On Sept. 25 at Virginia's Scott Stadium in Charlottesville, VA   the Tigers beat the Wahoos W (20–14). On Oct 2, at Georgia Tech's Grant Field • Atlanta, GA, the Yellow Jackets prevailed L (6–38). Playing again in Georgia on Oct 9, #4 Georgia beat Clemson in Sanford Stadium in Athens, GA L (9–23). In a game so sparse of scoring, that it looks like a baseball score, Clemson beat Duke W (3-2) at Duke Stadium in Durham, NC.

On October 23 in the first of back-to-back home games at Memorial Stadium, Clemson beat TCU in another low-scoring game W (3-0).

The Tigers were able to put out a lot more offense at home on Oct 30 v Wake Forest's W (3–0). Kenan Memorial Stadium in Chapel Hill, NC was the sight of a tough loss on Nov 6 against North Carolina L (13–17). On Nov 13, the offense had little to deliver at home as Maryland defeated Clemson L (0-6) The Defense was doing quite well and in the season finale v South Carolina in the Battle of the Palmetto State. It continued to do well but the offense was again an inch short of success as SC defeated CU L (16-17).

1966 Clemson Tigers Football Coach Frank Howard

The 1966 Clemson Tigers football team represented Clemson University during the 1966 college football season as a member of the Atlantic Coast Conference (ACC). Frank Howard was the head football coach for his twenty-seventh of thirty seasons. The Tigers completed their seventy-first season overall and their fourteenth in the Atlantic Coast Conference with a record of 6-4-0; 6-1-0 in the ACC. The Tigers came in first place in the ACC out of 8 active ACC teams. Mike Facciolo was the team captains.

Looking at the list of scores at the beginning of the Frank Howard chapters and knowing that many teams fire coaches with just six wins, it took a few more Frank Howard wins to convince me of where his priorities were. Every time I looked, despite a so-so season, the Frank Howard led Clemson Fighting Tigers were in the hunt in the ACC, and many times like this year, they were the League Champions against some pretty good teams. Now I know and you know. It is a great honor to win the league championship in any league. As the ACC would become even more respected, the next step would be the national bowl games,

Games of the 1966 Season

Clemson was back to winning opening games. This one was at home in Memorial Stadium located on the campus of Clemson University in Clemson, SC. It was played on Sept 24 featuring Clemson's Tigers and Virginia's Wahoos. The Tigers were dominant on offense and won the flip-flop game by a close margin W (40-35). Clemson had gained its University status in 1964.

Clemson 40, Virginia 35

Sept. 24, 1966 at Clemson, SC

The Clemson Tigers were down 18 points with 17 minutes to play in this game. With a lot of guts and resolve, we came back on the passing of Jimmy Addison. Jimmy passed 65 yards to Jacky Jackson for a touchdown that put Clemson in front. Jackson took off down the sidelines and "Needle" hit him in stride.

That game was memorable because it was the first time that Howard's Rock was in Death Valley. Coach Howard went on his television show the next day and said he told his players prior to the game that if they rubbed that rock they would receive magical powers. But, if they weren't going to give 110 percent, to "keep your filthy hands off that rock." A legend was born on that day. Forever it is known as Howards' Rock!

Virginia had a quarterback named Bob Davis. He and Needle put on quite a passing show, even by the high standards of today. Both teams threw for over 300 yards, the only game that happened in Clemson history over the first 90 years of play. In fact, both QB's were named National Players of the Week by some services.

Clemson's Tigers went on to win the ACC Championship. The team could not have done it if they didn't pull off that comeback against Virginia.

On Oct 1, playing #9 Georgia Tech at Grant Field in Atlanta, GA, Clemson almost won but did not L (12-13). On Oct 8, Alabama played the Tigers at home at Denny Stadium in Tuscaloosa and beat the Clemson Tigers in a shutout L (0-26). The ever tough, often southern champion Duke Blue Devils played tough the following week on Oct 15, but the Tigers played a little tougher and beat them at home W (9–6).

Testing the waters on the national scene, on Oct 22, Clemson played the always championship contending #5 USC Trojans at Los Angeles Memorial Coliseum in Los Angeles, CA. Not bad for a whack at the big guns on the west coast, the Tigers lost   L (0–30).

Back in comfortable waters at Bowman Gray Stadium in Winston-Salem, NC, v Wake Forest, Clemson triumphed over the Demon Deacons W 23–21. On Nov 5, North Carolina played Clemson at home and were beaten solidly W (27-3). On Nov 12 at Maryland's Byrd Stadium in College Park, MD, Clemson won in a tough match W 14–10.

On Nov 19 in the annual Textile Bowl at NC State at Carter Stadium in Raleigh, NC, Clemson did not have enough to bring home the win L (14–23). Always ready for a great comeback, Clemson was ready for the Battle of the Palmetto State v South carolina on Nov 26 at home. Clemson enjoyed the nice victory W (35–10.

1967 Clemson Tigers Football Coach Frank Howard

The 1967 Clemson Tigers football team represented Clemson University during the 1967 college football season as a member of the Atlantic Coast Conference (ACC). Frank Howard was the head football coach for his twenty-eighth of thirty seasons. The Tigers completed their seventy-second season overall and their fifteenth in the Atlantic Coast Conference with a record of 6-4-0; 6-0 in the ACC. The Tigers came in first place again in the ACC out of 8 active ACC teams. Jimmy Addison and Frank Liberatore were the team captains.

Player Highlights Harry Olszewski OG 1965-1967

Harry Olszewski was a First-team consensus All-American, which means all his life his is a First-team consensus All-American. It is a big deal. He was the only unanimous choice to All-ACC team in 1967. But, Harry had been there before. It was his second straight year on the team...named to the Silver Anniversary All-ACC team in 1977

Olszewski had played in the East-West Shrine Bowl and the Senior Bowl. He nailed a 12-yard touchdown against South Carolina in his junior year while he was playing offensive guard. This was a real big deal as no Clemson offensive lineman has scored since.

In 1967, Harry won both the ACC and State Jacobs Blocking Trophy. How else could a guard become All-American but by great blocking. Olszewski was not shy about suiting up and getting on the gridiron to face opponents. He started 30-straight varsity games.

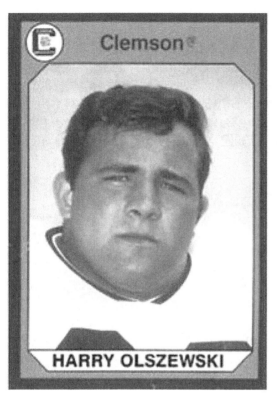

He was drafted in the third round by the Cleveland Browns, but he played for the Montreal Alouettes from 1969-1970. You can tell Harry Had fun but I'll bet his opponents did not like his shoving them around. He was inducted in 1980 to the Clemson Athletic Hall of Fame inductee, He also made it into the South Carolina Hall of Fame in 1990.

In the reflections of his work at Clemson, Harry also was named to Clemson's Centennial team in April, 1996. A great man and a great player,

Mr. Olszewski passed away in spring, 1998. He is ranked as Clemson's #17 gridder of all-time by a panel of historians who convened in 1999 and who had analyzed Harry's All-American History.

On Sept 23, Frank Howards' squad opened up the season with a win at home v Wake Forest W (23-6). This game and all home games this season was/ were played on the campus of Clemson University at Memorial Stadium, Clemson, SC. On Sept 30 #5 Georgia Bulldogs came to town and beat the Tigers L (17–24). On Oct 7, Clemson kept its state of Georgia bad-luck season streak going at Georgia Tech in Grant Field, Atlanta, GA L (0–10). Ever ready Auburn, taking no prisoners in the SEC for years, invited the Clemson Tigers to Cliff Hare Stadium in Auburn, AL for a tough loss L (21–43). Clemson got its composure back on Oct 21 at Duke's Duke Stadium in Durham, NC for a well needed victory W 13–7.

On Oct 28, and always-tough Alabama crimson Tide bought all of their regalia to Memorial Stadium at Clemson University to play a tough Tigers Team. The Crimson Tide squeezed out a nice win v the Tigers L (10-13). Frank Howard's teams did not fall easy. On Nov 4, at North Carolina's Kenan Memorial Stadium in Chapel Hill, NC, Clemson emerged victorious with a nice shutout W (17–0). Clemson won the next two home games. The first was v Maryland W (28-7) and the second was in the Textile Bowl v #10 NC State W (14-6). In the season finale in Nov 25, in the Battle of the Palmetto State, the Tigers beat the Gamecocks W (23-12) to finish the season on a high note.

Player Highlights Wayne Mass OT 1965-67

<< Rev. Wayne Mass

Wayne Mass was pleased to be a first-team All-American as a junior. He was that good. He was the recipient of the Jacobs Blocking Trophy for the ACC and South Carolina for the 1966 year. As he entered his time to be drafted, he went out as a fourth-rounder of the Chicago Bears in the 1968 draft,

He was the 99th player chosen in the draft He had been first-team All-ACC in 1966 and 1967, and he was inducted into the Clemson Hall of Fame in 1993. Wayne Mass loved football and he loved playing football. You can bet he enjoyed the trip to Hawaii in the 1968 Hula Bowl.

You would also slot him as a major player in the 1967 East-West game because he was ready to play for the East. As well expected for his great performances, Wayne Mass was named to Clemson's Centennial team in April, 1996...At the time of this report, he lived in Chicago, IL.

1968 Clemson Tigers Football Coach Frank Howard

The 1968 Clemson Tigers football team represented Clemson University during the 1968 college football season as a member of the Atlantic Coast Conference (ACC). Frank Howard was the head football coach for his twenty-ninth of thirty seasons. The Tigers completed their seventy-third season overall and their sixteenth in the Atlantic Coast Conference with a record of 4-5-1; 4-1-1 in the ACC. The Tigers came in second place in the ACC out of 8 active ACC teams. Billy Ammons, Ronnie Duckworth were the team captains.

On Sept 21, the Tigers visited the Demon Deacons of Wake Forest for the season opener for both teams. The tie game T (20-20) was played at Groves Stadium in Winston-Salem, NC. Then on Sept 28, at Georgia in a game played at Sanford Stadium in Athens, GA, the Bulldogs beat the Tigers L 13–31. On Oct 5 at Georgia Tech's Grant Field in Atlanta, GA, the Yellow jackets got the best of the Tigers but just barely L (21–24). In a year in which three tough teams will beat Clemson, this would be the third of the three. This game was at home and Auburn's Tigers were the predators v the Clemson Tigers. Auburn was able to pick up another win at Clemson's Memorial Stadium on the campus of CU in Clemson, SC by a respectable score of L 10–21.

Back at Memorial Stadium in Clemson, SC, Duke's Blue Devils took it on the chin from the Tigers on October 19 W (39–22). On Oct 26at Alabama's Denny Stadium in Tuscaloosa, AL, the Clemson Tigers were beaten L (14–21). On Nov 2, in the Textile Bowl at Carter Stadium in Raleigh, NC, the Tigers got the win against the Wolfpack W 24–19.

On Nov 9 at Maryland's Byrd Stadium in College Park, MD, the Tigers pinned a loss on the Terrapins W 16–0. Then, on Nov 16 at home, the Tigers beat the NC Tar Heels W 24–14. In another home match between Carolina teams, on Nov 23, South Carolina battled Clemson at home in the Battle of the Palmetto State, Clemson could not hold on and lost the battle L (3–7)

1969 Clemson Tigers Football Coach Frank Howard

The 1969 Clemson Tigers football team represented Clemson University during the 1969 college football season as a member of the Atlantic Coast Conference (ACC). Frank Howard was the head football coach for his thirtieth and last season of thirty seasons. The Tigers completed their seventy-fourth season overall and their seventeenth in the Atlantic Coast Conference with a record of 4-6-0; 3-3-0 in the ACC. The Tigers came in fourth place in the ACC out of 8 active ACC teams. Ivan Southerland & Charlie Tolley were the team captains.

Player Highlights Buddy Gore, RB 1966-68

Aubrey "Buddy" Gore was Clemson's greatest running back in the 1960s and perhaps during a 22-year period from 1956-78. Gore led the ACC in rushing in consecutive seasons, 1966-67, and was named the ACC Player of the Year as a junior, the first Tiger in history so honored.

<< Buddy Gore

Still an avid Clemson fan, who looks like he could still play today, Gore carried Clemson to the ACC Championship in 1966 and 1967.

His most celebrated performance came in his last game as a junior, at South Carolina. All Gore did was rush for 189 yards in 31 tough carries, leading Clemson to a 23-12 victory.

In addition to leading Clemson to the win over its arch rival, a win that gave Clemson the conference crown, he set the ACC single season rushing record and became Clemson's first 1000-yard rusher in the process. He ended the season with 1045 yards in just 10 games.

Gore also led the ACC in rushing in 1966 when he gained 750 yards. Twice he finished in the top 20 in the nation in rushing, including a number-eight ranking in 1967. That number-eight ranking is still the second highest ranking by a Clemson running back in history. His senior year he accumulated 776 yards, the third straight year he led Clemson in rushing.

While Gore ranks only fourth in Clemson history in career rushing, it must be remembered that he played just three years and 30 games. In his era, freshmen were ineligible and teams played just 10 games per year. Only Terry Allen has a higher rushing yards per game average over a career, and Gore still holds the school mark for all-purpose running yardage for a career with a 109.1 figure.

That last item speaks volumes about his consistency, all-around abilities and productivity.

Frank Howard loved Clemson and he chose to remain as Athletic Director for several more years. until 1971. In 1974, the playing field at Memorial Stadium, which he helped to build, was named in his honor. He was a great coach for a ton of teams that could play with the best of them. He was the first Clemson Coach to last for many years.

I would suspect that if Clemson were more interested in National Championships than Conference Championships among the great southern teams, Frank Howard would have been the guy to help tweak the recruiting and the game to assure that the institution got what it needed. No opponent ever pushed around a Frank Howard team, even without a zillion dollars in scholarships and endowments. Bravo Frank Howard! Bravo Clemson University!

Picture from Frank Howard's Last Home Game Nov 1 1969 v Maryland

This year's season opener was on Sept 20 at Virginia's Scott Stadium in Charlottesville, VA. Clemson was pleased to take away the win for its game efforts W (21–14). Georgia then came home to Clemson's home opener at Memorial Stadium on the campus of Clemson University in Clemson, SC, Sept 27, to win the game in shutout L (0-30). Clemson then traveled to Georgia Tech's Grant Field in • Atlanta, GA on Oct 4, my wedding anniversary pre-wedding to get a nice win W 21–10. On Oct 11, Clemson took on #20 Auburn at Cliff Hare Stadium in Auburn, AL, but could not keep up and lost in a shellacking shutout L (0–51). On Oct 18   Wake Forest came home to Clemson but lost W (28–14)

On Oct 25 Clemson was looking for a nice win over Alabama at home but it did not come in 1969 as the Crimson Tide dominated L (13-38) It would not always be like this game but Alabama, especially with the "Bear" coaching was always favored. On Nov1, at home, the Tigers whooped the Terrapins of Maryland W (40-0). Then, on Nov 8 at Duke's Duke Stadium in Durham, NC, Duke took the win L 27–34. Then, a week later on Nov 15 at North Carolina's Kenan Memorial Stadium in Chapel Hill, NC, the Tigers lost again L (15–32). In an early season finale on Nov 22, at Carolina Stadium • Columbia, SC in the Battle of the Palmetto State), the Gamecocks whooped the Tigers L (13-27).

Frank Howard was on his way out the door and it would have been great if he got a better sendoff but his thirty years at Clemson were absolutely great

If you die, somebody writes a nice Obit

Frank Howard was ready to go when he went but he did lament that the line to keep in at the head coaching job was not a lot longer... I think! He was a piece of work. He coached great teams and great players and nobody ever seemed to complain about his coaching work or the great players he produced. Howard did not even seem to care what they thought.

Clemson had been floundering between success and failure. It was not that they did not have great years and great coaches. It was that nobody until Jess Neely stayed long enough to give the Clemson program a fighting chance. Frank Howard liked to win but he was aware that a lot of coach's bur out by trying too hard to please a constituency that may already be OK with their performance. Frank Howard got thirty years out of simply being a great coach.

Like most observers of his era, it would be easy to suggest tome that Howard did not drive his team to ultimate excellence. Yeah! I get that but if you look at the scores of the games, Howard and company were always there but for very few runaways. Without having the opportunity to interview Frank Howard, I like him immensely and would love to have had or to have a few beers with him some time.

Bear Bryant died a quick death after a phenomenal career with Alabama. He did not get a lot of un after coaching. Frank Howard had it all but he did not have Bear Bryant's record. Howard, IMHO did what he needed to do to get his teams ready and ready to win and somehow when they played v ACC teams, his teams were ready to kill. Some might suggest that he did not do v SEC teams as well but I beg to differ. I say Howard's mission was to win the ACC Championship in which he was always a contender. In this he was extremely successful.

From my observations, Clemson did not fund a national championship caliber team during Thomas's tenure. Oh' don't get me wrong Clemson loved winning but the difference in funding from Conference Champion to National Champion is substantial. Frank Thomas brought a lot of fun to his team and to Clemson University by being the guy that could beat all the teams around him in the south. It meant more to everybody than coming in 32nd in the national championship race meant – or even a close #8. Meanwhile Frank Howard had about twenty great years after retirement. What old fart would not like that?

Here is the Obit which is a great recap of Mr. Frank Howard:

On January 27, 1996 Frank Howard went to his eternal rest at the age of 86 years old. He had quite a life after he retired as Clemson's head football coach in 1969 from Clemson's head coaching duties.

The NY Times Frank Lisky wrote this tribute upon his death on January 27, 1996. His tribute was titled:

Frank Howard, 86, the Coach of Top Clemson Football Teams

Frank Howard, the colorful coach who in 30 years took Clemson University from football obscurity to the ranks of the national elite, died yesterday at his home in Clemson, S.C. He was 86.

The sports information office at the university said the cause of death was congestive heart failure. Howard was hospitalized in November because of circulatory problems, last month after a fainting spell and this month after a minor heart attack.

After retiring from coaching in 1969, he was athletic director at Clemson until mandatory retirement in 1971. He then kept an office in the athletic department and, until three weeks ago, went there five days a week.

"I'm not sure what he did there," the sports information director, Tim Bourret, said. "Whatever a retired legend does."

Howard liked to say he retired for health reasons.

"The alumni got sick of me," he would say.

He had a quick sense of humor. In the late 1950's, after a loss to Duke, he was asked to define the turning point. "It was three years ago," he said, "when I didn't recruit any half backs."

Frank James Howard was born on March 25, 1909, on a cotton farm in Barlow Bend, Ala., a town that he said was "three wagon greasin's from Mobile." He called himself the Bashful Baron of Barlow Bend.

In high school he played football, baseball and basketball and was president of the junior and senior classes. At the University of Alabama, where he was an honor student on an academic scholarship, he was a 185-pound guard on the football team from 1928 to 1930

FOOTBALL AS AN AFTERHOUGHT?

When he could not find work as an accountant, he became an assistant football coach at Clemson under Jess Neely. "I also coached track, was ticket manager, recruited players and had charge of football equipment," Howard said. "In my spare time I cut grass, lined tennis courts and operated the canteen while the regular man was out to lunch."

In 1940, when Neely became coach at Rice, the Clemson athletic council interviewed Howard as a potential successor. As the council discussed what to do, Howard listened from the back of the room. Finally, a council member said, "I nominate Frank Howard."

Long pause.

"I second the nomination," Howard said.

He got the job, lost his copy of the one-year contract and never signed another. From 1940 to 1969 his teams compiled a 165-118-12 record. They won two championships in the Southern Conference and later six in the Atlantic Coast Conference. Between 1949 and 1959 Clemson played in six bowl games.

Shortly after he retired as coach, Clemson named its stadium Frank Howard Field. In 1989, he was inducted into the College Football Hall of Fame.

With all his success, his highest salary was $25,000 a year. The president of the university, Dr. R. F. Poole, feared that professors who carned less would be upset.

"He called me up and said that he didn't want me to tell anybody what I made," Howard once said. "I said: 'Doc, you don't have to worry. I'm as ashamed as you are of what you pay me.' "

Surviving are his wife of 62 years, the former Anna Tribble; a son, Jimmy, of Clemson; a daughter, Alice McClure of Gastonia, N.C., and three grandchildren.

Hootie Ingram Replaces Frank Howard as Clemson Head Football Coach

Hootie Ingram became the next Clemson Football Coach. We highlight his Clemson tenure and his Clemson teams in this book. There are great moments in every season for every football team though in some seasons there are more great moments than others. In the next chapter, we examine the coaching work of Hootie Ingram who took over for the immortal Frank Howard at Clemson in 1970 and left the University after the 1972 season. His record with the Tigers is not very good – 12-21 over the three years in which he was the head coach.

You know from having read this book about every season from the first Clemson Football Season that there have not been many unsuccessful coaches at Clemson, University. Perhaps if he had been given more time, he would have been ready and would have done well.

Ingram had never been a head coach before. He had been a high school football coach and he had worked as an assistant football coach at several colleges, including the University of Georgia and the University of Arkansas, both noteworthy programs, before receiving the head coaching assignment at Clemson University from 1970 to 1972

Some still contend that Ingram may be the victim of "wrong place at the wrong time." It is always easier to replace a coach that everybody hates and wants to get rid of than an immortal with a great overall record who everybody loves. All coaches, who come after a great one, encounter the issue. Then again others say, three years was enough time for him to leave the legend behind and make his own. It did not happen.

Ingram had the difficult task of replacing legend Frank Howard at Clemson. Nobody can deny that he was able only to muster 12 wins in three seasons before resigning.

Ingram was surely in the right business. He was an incredibly gifted athlete, playing his college ball at Alabama. He came to Tuscaloosa as a football and baseball player. He would earn three letters in each sport during his time there. He was first a defensive back and a darn good one. He intercepted 11 passes in the 1952 season but for team reasons at Alabama, he was nevertheless moved to quarterback in 1953. He played as QB for one season alongside Bart Starr. In 1954, he was moved to tailback, with the long-time Green Bay Packer, Starr starting at QB.

After leaving Clemson, Ingram stayed in college sports. He served as Florida State's athletic director from 1981-1989. He then took on the same role at his alma mater, Alabama. He was well respected. He installed Gene Stallings as head coach, who would go on to lead the Tide to a national championship in 1992. Ingram would eventually resign in 1995 amidst an NCAA investigation into rule violations.

There was an investigation that ran from late 1993 to August 1995, in which the NCAA "found" Alabama guilty of four major rules violations during the 1993 season. Stallings was implicated, along with athletic director Hootie Ingram.

Hootie Ingram was not fired but the NCAA reprimand had spoiled his effectiveness. He did what he felt he should do under the circumstances. He stepped down as Alabama's athletic director in August 1995 because the NCAA had placed the school on probation for three years. A stand-up guy, Ingram said he could no longer effectively serve as athletic director after the NCAA decision and he asked to be reassigned. He spent the final two years of his Alabama contract overseeing the expansion of the football stadium.

My opinion of NCAA sanctions is that they are often off the mark and have been unfair in cases that I have examined. Sometimes, looking at the backgrounds and the future accomplishments of some NCAA officials over the years, and sometimes the people in charge of investigations have a personal stake in the outcome. Nonetheless, the NCAA has ruined numerous promising careers of good people at all levels of college football programs.

Maybe one day I will write a book about it. This book is not about the NCAA so I will limit my comments. You can find many opinions of many football experts in many articles written over the years. Just one article from 2014 is titled: "Why Hasn't Congress Investigated Corruption in the NCAA?"

Despite his obvious failings on the gridiron as Clemson's head football coach. Ingram was overall a gift to the sport. In 1991, for example, he was inducted into the Alabama Sports Hall of Fame. In 1999, he was inducted into the Orange Bowl Hall of Fame. He was also honored in 1992 as a second-team defensive back on Alabama's "Team of the Century."

In 2007, the University of Alabama National Alumni Association presented Ingram with the Paul W. Bryant Alumni-Athlete Award. The award recognizes athletes whose accomplishments since leaving the University are "outstanding based on character, contributions to society, professional achievement and service."

Chapter 18 Hootie Ingram Era 1970-1972

Coach #18 Hootie Ingram I

Year	Coach	Record	Conference	Record
1970	Hootie Ingram	3-8-0	ACC	2-4-0
1971	Hootie Ingram	5-6-0	ACC	4-2-0
1972	Hootie Ingram	4-7-0	ACC	2-5-0

Hootie Ingram 1970-1972 Clemson Coach

1970 Clemson Tigers Football Coach Hootie Ingram

The 1970 Clemson Tigers football team represented Clemson
University during the 1970 college football season as a member of the
Atlantic Coast Conference (ACC). Hootie Ingram was the head
football coach for his first of three seasons. The Tigers completed
their seventy-fifth season overall and their eighteenth in the Atlantic
Coast Conference with a record of 3-8-0; 2-4-0 in the ACC. The
Tigers came in sixth place in the ACC out of 8 active ACC teams. B.
B. Elvington, Jim Sursavage, and Ray Yauger were the team
captains.

Player Highlights Dave Thompson OG 1968-1970

In 1970, Thompson was a First-team All-American guard. He was a
flexible player and did what the team needed. He played center in his
senior year. He was the recipient of the state of South Carolina
Jacobs Blocking Trophy in 1970. He was also pleased to accept
honors as First-Team All-ACC in 1970

Dave Thompson was a second-round pick of the Lions in 1971, he
was the 30th selection of the entire draft. He showed his stuff as a pro
by laying three years with the Detroit Lions and two years with the
New Orleans Saints

The season opener was earlier than normal this year as Clemson
began the year at Memorial Stadium located right on the campus of
Clemson University in Clemson, SC. The first two games of the
season were at home. And, so, on Sept 12, Clemson beat the Citadel
W (24-0) and one week later, on Sept 19, the Tigers beat the Virginia
Wahoos W 27-17). It was a fine start for new head coach Hootie
Ingram but it would not last. Three tough duck had lined up to play
the Tigers and after them, the season would continue to go south

Georgia, Georgia Tech, and Auburn, traditional tough rivals took the
smiles off Clemson fans. Then, Wake Forest and Duke kept the
smiles off until the Tigers were able to beat Maryland. Right after the
Maryland game, however, there were three more losses to complete
the season—Florida State, North Carolina and South Carolina. It
was not a good year.

Let me describe quickly the one win in October at Maryland's Byrd Stadium in College Park, MD. The Tigers were able to defeat the Terrapins W (24-11) despite the five losses preceding the game.

The bad news began on Sept 26 at Georgia's Sanford Stadium in Athens, GA L (0–38). The bad news continued with the exception of Maryland to the end of the season. On Oct 3, at #15 Georgia Tech's Grant Field • Atlanta, GA, L (7–28); On Oct 10 at home, Auburn Shut-out Clemson 0-44; On Oct 17, at Wake Forest's Groves Stadium in Winston-Salem, NC L (20–36).

Clemson lost its next home game on Oct 24 against Duke L (10–24). After the Maryland win, on Nov 7, the three final losses began at Florida State's Doak Campbell Stadium in Tallahassee, FL L (13–38). This was followed by a loss on Nov 14 at home against North Carolina L (7–42). In the season finale loss on Nov 21, a close home game against South Carolina in the big rivalry known as the Battle of the Palmetto State, Clemson lost the battle L (32–38) before 51,500.

1971 Clemson Tigers Football Coach Hootie Ingram

The 1971 Clemson Tigers football team represented Clemson University during the 1971 college football season as a member of the Atlantic Coast Conference (ACC). Hootie Ingram was the head football coach for his second of three seasons. The Tigers completed their seventy-sixth season overall and their nineteenth in the Atlantic Coast Conference with a record of 5-6-0; 4-2-0 in the ACC. The Tigers came in second in the ACC out of 7 active ACC teams. Larry Hefner and John McMakin were the team captains.

On Sept 11 in the home opener at Memorial Stadium on the campus of Clemson University in Clemson, SC, Kentucky beat Hootie Ingram's Tigers L (10-13). Clemson then lost to the two Georgia teams. On Sept 25, Georgia shut out Clemson at home L 0-28). On Oct 2 at Georgia Tech's Grant Field in Atlanta, GA, the Yellow Jackets beat the Tigers L (14–24). With a 0-3 record the season was not going well until the Tigers played the Duke Blue Devils on Oct 9 at Foreman Field in Norfolk, VA in the Oyster Bowl and took away a close but important win W (3-0) The Tigers got another win a week later on Oct 16 at City Stadium in Richmond against Virginia W (35-15)

Next, on Oct 23 at #5 Auburn's Cliff Hare Stadium in Auburn, AL, Clemson lost L (13–35). On Oct 30, Clemson picked up its third win of the season at home against Wake Forest in a nail-biter W (10-9) before 55,000. On Nov 6, at North Carolina's Kenan Memorial Stadium in Chapel Hill, NC, the Tigers were beaten by the Tar Heels. L 13–26. North Carolina would go on to win the ACC championship in 1971 with a 4-2 Clemson in second place. On Nov 13, the Tigers beat the Maryland Terrapins at home W (20-14).

In another home game, The Textile Bowl on Nov 20, Clemson was beaten by NC State L (23-31). On Nov 27 at South Carolina's Carolina Stadium in Columbia, SC, in the Battle of the Palmetto State, Clemson won the game W (17–7) before 57,242

1972 Clemson Tigers Football Coach Hootie Ingram

The 1972 Clemson Tigers football team represented Clemson University during the 1972 college football season as a member of the Atlantic Coast Conference (ACC). Hootie Ingram was the head football coach for his third and last of three seasons. The Tigers completed their seventy-seventh season overall and their twentieth in the Atlantic Coast Conference with a record of 4-7-0; 2-5-0 in the ACC. The Tigers came in fifth place in the ACC out of 7 active ACC teams. Wade Hughes, Buddy King, & Frank Wirth were the team captains.

On Sept 9. At Memorial Stadium on the campus of Clemson University in Clemson, SC, Clemson celebrated a victory over The Citadel W (13-0). On Sept 23, the Tigers traveled to Rice's Rice Stadium in Houston, TX and lost to the Owls L (10–29). On Sept 30, the Tigers faced off against #2 ranked Oklahoma and received a walloping at Oklahoma Memorial Stadium in Norman, OK L (3–52). On Oct 7 at Georgia Tech's Grant Field in Atlanta, GA, the Yellow Jackets beat Clemson L (9–31). On Oct 14, Duke shut out CU at home L (0–7).

On Oct 21 at home, Clemson beat Virginia W (37-21) before 31,000.
Clemson's next outing was on Oct 28 at Wake Forest in Groves
Stadium, Winston-Salem, NC. The Tigers shut out the Demon
Deacons W 31–0. On Nov 4 at home against North Carolina, CU
lost to the Tar Heels L (10–26). On Nov 11 at Maryland's Byrd
Stadium in College Park, MD, the Terrapins beat the Tigers L (6–31).
On Nov 18 in the Textile Bowl v NC State at Carter Stadium in
Raleigh, NC, the Tar Heels beat the Tigers L (17–42). On Nov 25,
the Battle of the Palmetto State was played at Clemson. The Tigers
squeaked out a one-point win against the Gamecocks W (7-6).

Just after competing this 4-7 season, the school put pressure on
Hootie Ingram to resign as head coach of the football team. Ingram
indeed did resign, which paved the way for Red Parker. In his three
years as head coach, Ingram's overall record was 12-21.

In the photo above, you can see Hootie Ingram (left), Clemson
President R.C. Edwards (center) and Hootie's replacement, Red
Parker (right) in a press conference announcing the coaching change.

.

Chapter 19 Red Parker Era 1973-1976

Coach # 19 Red Parker

Year	Coach	Record	Conference	Record
1973	Red Parker	5-6-0	ACC	4-2-0
1974	Red Parker	7-4-0	ACC	4-2-0
1975	Red Parker	2-9-0	ACC	2-3-0
1976	Red Parker	3-6-2	ACC	0-4-1

Red Parker Coaches the Tigers from the Sidelines

1973 Clemson Tigers Football Coach Red Parker

The 1973 Clemson Tigers football team represented Clemson University during the 1973 college football season as a member of the Atlantic Coast Conference (ACC). Red Parker was the head football coach for his first of three seasons. The Tigers completed their seventy-eighth season overall and their twenty-first in the Atlantic Coast Conference with a record of 5-6-0; 4-2-0 in the ACC. The

Tigers came in third place in the ACC out of 7 active ACC teams. Mike Buckner and Ken Pengitore were the team captains.

In the home opener on September 8 before 40,000 spectators, at Memorial Stadium on the campus of Clemson University in Clemson, SC, Clemson clung to a victory over the Citadel, W (14–12). On Sept 22, the Tigers traveled to Georgia's Sanford Stadium in Athens, GA, and lost their first game of the season L (14–31). On Sept 29 at Georgia Tech's Grant Field in Atlanta, GA (Rivalry), the Yellow Jackets got the win L (21–29). The next two games were played at home. The Tigers lost the first against Texas A & M on Oct 6 before 48,062. Then, on Oct 13, the Tigers beat the Wahoos of Virginia W (32-27).

On Oct 20 at Duke's Wallace Wade Stadium in Durham, NC, the Tigers picked up the win W (24–8). In the first of two successive home games, on Oct 27, NC State's Wolfpack beat the Tigers in the Textile Bowl L (6-29). On Nov 3, The Tigers beat Wake Forest W (35–8) before just 23,000. On Nov 10 at NC's Kenan Memorial Stadium in Chapel Hill, NC, Clemson triumphed over North Carolina W (37–29). On Nov 17 at home Maryland's Terrapins beat the Clemson Tigers L (13-28). Like clockwork in the Season Finale for SC and CU, in the Battle of the Palmetto State at Williams-Brice Stadium in Columbia, SC. Clemson lost a close battle L (20-32).

1974 Clemson Tigers Football Coach Red Parker

The 1974 Clemson Tigers football team represented Clemson University during the 1974 college football season as a member of the Atlantic Coast Conference (ACC). Red Parker was the head football coach for his second of three seasons. The Tigers completed their seventy-ninth season overall and their twenty-second in the Atlantic Coast Conference with a record of 7-4-0; 4-2-0 in the ACC. The Tigers came in third place in the ACC out of 7 active ACC teams. Willie Anderson, Mark Fellers, Jim Ness, and Ken Peeples were the team captains. This was the first season with more than six victories since 1959.

On Sept 14 in the season opener, the Tigers lost to #20 Texas A&M at Kyle Field, College Station, TX L (0–24). On Sept 21 at #15 NC State in the Textile Bowl at Carter Stadium in Raleigh, NC L (10–31). On Sept 28 at home the Tigers beat the Yellow Jackets W (21–17). Then, on Oct 5, Clemson beat the other Georgia team – first time in a while, at home W (28–24). On Oct 12, the Tigers traveled to Byrd Stadium in College Park, MD   and were pounded by the Terrapins L (0–41). In another home game, the Tigers beat Duke in a close match W (17-13).

On Oct 26 at Tennessee's Neyland Stadium in Knoxville, TN Clemson lost by just one point L (28–29). On Nov 2 at Wake Forest in Groves Stadium, Winston-Salem, NC, Clemson prevailed W (21–9). Then on Nov 9 at home, the Tigers defeated the Tar Heels of North Carolina in a shootout W (54-32). On Nov 16 at home, Clemson beat Virginia W (28-9). Then on Nov 23, at home against South Carolina in the Battle of the Palmetto State, the Tigers beat the Gamecocks W 39–21 before and attendance of 52,575.

1975 Clemson Tigers Football Coach Red Parker

<<< Coach Parker.

The 1975 Clemson Tigers football team represented Clemson University during the 1975 college football season as a member of the Atlantic Coast Conference (ACC). Red Parker was the head football coach for his third of four seasons. The Tigers completed their eightieth season overall and their twenty-third in the Atlantic Coast Conference with a record of 2-9; 2-3 in the ACC. The Tigers came in fifth place in the ACC out of 7 active ACC teams. Bennie Cunningham, Neal Jetton, Dennis Smith, Jimmy Williamson were the team captains. This was the first season with more than six victories since 1959.

On September 13, Clemson lost another home opener. This time, it was to Tulane L 13-17). As all home games, this one was played in Memorial Stadium right on the Clemson University Campus in Clemson, SC. On Sept 20, an always-ready SEC powerhouse, Alabama, coached by Paul "Bear" Bryant invited the Tigers to play at Bryant-Denny Stadium in Tuscaloosa, AL. It was not much of a game. The Crimson Tide shut-out and shellacked the Tigers in a big loss L (0-56). On Sept 27, Clemson then traveled to Georgia Tech's Grant Field in Atlanta, GA (Rivalry) and played well but lost L (28-33). The next big loss in an especially poor season was on Oct 4. This time, it was the Bulldogs at Georgia's Sanford Stadium in Athens, GA who beat the Tigers L (7–35)

On Oct 11 at home, the Tigers just about managed to beat the Demon Deacons of Wake Forest but in this season, it marked one of the high points W (16-14). On Oct 18, the Tigers lost to Duke at Wallace Wade Stadium in Durham, NC L (21–25). In the Textile Bowl on Oct 25, at home, NC State scored a lot of points in beating Clemson L (7-45). On Nov 1, Clemson kept the losing streak going to three games at home against Florida State L 7–43 before 33,000. On Nov 8, the Tigers managed to beat the Tar Heels of North Carolina at Kenan Memorial Stadium, Chapel Hill, NC   W (38–32). Then on Nov 15 at home, the Tigers lost a nail-biter to the Terrapins L (20-22) In the last game of the season between two South Carolina rivals, on Nov 22, the Tigers were thumped by the Gamecocks at Williams-Brice Stadium, Columbia, SC in the Battle of the Palmetto State. It was a shootout loss L (20–56) before 57,197 fans.

Player Highlights Bennie Cunningham (1972-75)

Bennie Cunningham continues to today as the most decorated tight end in Clemson history. He is A native of nearby Seneca, SC and gets to see Clemson play regularly. Cunningham was a two-time first-team All-American at Clemson in 1974 and 1975, one of just 12 multi-year All-Americans in school history.

Cunningham was a pro scouts dream. At 6-5 and 250 pounds, he could run like a deer, yet run over the opposition in heavy traffic. In addition to his great hands and quickness, he was a devastating blocker. Cunningham first came on the scene in 1973 when he started all 11 games and caught 22 passes for 341 yards. He also averaged 6.6 yards a rush on 11 carries as a runner. That is a bit more than coming on the scene!

BENNIE CUNNINGHAM

In 1974 Clemson's season long slogan was "Excitement Galore in '74". Cunningham did his part in the 7-4 season that included a perfect 6-0 home record, with seven touchdown receptions among his 24 catches, the most touchdown receptions ever by a Clemson tight end and one of the top five totals nationally that season for tight ends. Cunningham was named a first-team AP All-American that season.

The Tigers stumbled a bit in 1975 with an underclassman offense, but Cunningham still averaged 17-yards a catch, an incredible average for a tight end. After the season, he was named a first-team All-American by Sporting News for the second straight year.

Who would not want Bennie Cunnigham on their team? He was one of Super Bowl great Terry Bradshaw's favorite receiving targets. Any coach would love to have the type of player who would later become what everyone wants in today's world of college football.

Cunningham was tough, could block, and was actually an athletic freak with great hands. A historic tight end with both the Tigers and the Steelers—with whom he won two Super Bowl Rings. Cunningham would make any Clemson Dream Team, as he would be too big for both corners and safeties and too athletic for linebackers to handle

Cunningham lettered three straight years for the Tigers, leading the team in pass receptions in 1973 and 1974. He was named first-team All-ACC in 1974 and 1975. He was a two-time first-team All-America, who earned consensus All-America honors in 1974. He completed his Clemson career with 64 receptions for 1,044 yards and 17 TDs.

He was the 28th overall selection in the first round of the 1976 NFL, drafted by the Pittsburgh Steelers. Bennie played in the NFL for 10 seasons, all with the Steelers. He completed his professional career with 202 receptions for 2,879 yards and 20 touchdowns. In 1984 he was inducted into the Clemson Hall of Fame.

As a first-round draft choice of the Pittsburgh Steelers, still the only Clemson tight end in history be a first-round draft choice.

Cunningham might have had an even better NFL career. He caught over 200 passes for the Steelers in his 10-year NFL career and Bennie was a starter on two Super Bowl Championship teams.

In 2003, Cunningham was the only tight end chosen to the ACC's 50th Anniversary Team in 2003, as one of the Top 50 players in league history. He was also the recipient of Clemson's Frank Howard Award for 1974-75, as the top student-athlete who brought honor to Clemson.

1976 Clemson Tigers Football Coach Red Parker

The 1976 Clemson Tigers football team represented Clemson University during the 1976 college football season as a member of the Atlantic Coast Conference (ACC). Red Parker was the head football coach for his fourth of four seasons. The Tigers completed their eighty-first season overall and their twenty-fourth in the Atlantic Coast Conference with a record of 3-6-2; 0-4-1 in the ACC. For the first time, the Tigers came in seventh (last) place in the ACC out of 7 active ACC teams. Malcolm Marler, Mike O'Cain, Randy Scott, and

Joey Walters were the team captains. This was the first season that Clemson played so poorly in the ACC.

On Sept 11 at the home season opener on the campus of Clemson University at memorial Stadium in Clemson, SC, Clemson beat The Citadel in a close match W (10-7). On Sept 18 at home again, Clemson was beaten by Georgia L (0-41). The next time out was at Georgia Tech's Grant Field in Atlanta, GA. The game resulted in a tie T 24–24. Soon there would be no ties in NCAA Division I Football. The first division I overtime game and first double overtime game occurred in 1979 when Eastern Kentucky beat Nevada 33-30 in a Division I-AA playoff semi-final game.

On Oct 2*   at Tennessee's Neyland Stadium in Knoxville, TN, the Volunteers beat the Tigers L (19–21). On Oct 9 at Wake Forest's Groves Stadium in Winston-Salem, NC. The Demon Deacons defeated the Tigers L (14–20). On Oct 16, Clemson played another tie game. This time the opponent was Duke and it was a home game T (18-18. At NC State on Oct 23 in Carter Stadium in Raleigh, NC the Tigers lost the Textile Bowl to the Wolfpack L (21–38). On Oct 30 at Florida State's Doak Campbell Stadium in Tallahassee, FL, Clemson put it together for a win W (15–12). On Nov 6 at home, the Tigers were defeated by North Carolina L (23–27)

The next game on Nov 13 was at #6 Maryland. The Terrapins were having a good year. They shut-out Clemson L (0-2) at Byrd Stadium in College Park, MD L (0–20). On Nov 20 at home Clemson won the Battle of the Palmetto State v South Carolina (W (28-9).

Chapter 20 Charley Pell Era 1977 to 1978

Coach # 20 Charley Pell

Year	Coach	Record	Conference	Record
1977	Charley pell	8-3-1	ACC	4-1-1
1978	Charley Pell	11-1-0	ACC	6–0–0

Charley Pell and the Clemson Team

1977 Clemson Tigers Football Coach Charley Pell

The 1977 Clemson Tigers football team represented Clemson University during the 1977 college football season as a member of the Atlantic Coast Conference (ACC). Charley Pell was the head football coach for his first of two seasons. The Tigers completed their eighty-second season overall and their twenty-fifth in the Atlantic Coast Conference with a record of 8-3-1; 4-1-1 in the ACC. The Tigers came in second place in the ACC out of 7 active ACC teams. Steve Fuller, Steve Godfrey, and Randy Scott were the team captains.

On Sept 10, Maryland played Clemson in the home opener at Memorial Stadium on the campus of Clemson University in Clemson, SC. The Terrapins defeated the Tigers in a close match L (14-21). Clemson no longer was playing its opening days against weaker teams. Maryland had been tough during the 1970's and Charley Pell's Tigers, which did very well in this year, had a tough game. On Sept 17 at #17 Georgia's Sanford Stadium in Athens, GA, Clemson prevailed W (7-6) in a nail-biter. On Sept 24 at Georgia Tech's Grant Field in Atlanta, GA, Clemson won handily W (31-14) What a difference a good coach makes. Charlie Pell was a great coach. On Oct 1, at Virginia Tech's Lane Stadium in Blacksburg, VA, the Tigers defeated the Hokies W (31–13).

Virginia came to play Clemson at home on Oct 8 and the Wahoos were shut out by Charley Pell's Tigers W (31-0) before 49,830. On October 15 at Duke's Wallace Wade Stadium in Durham, NC, Clemson was victorious W 17–11. On Oct 22, NC State's Wolfpack played the Tigers at home in the Textile Bowl W (7-3).

On Oct 29, Wake Forest was beaten by #16 ranked Clemson at home W (26–0). On Nov 5, at North Carolina's Kenan Memorial Stadium in Chapel Hill, NC, the #13 Tigers tied the Tar Heels T 13–13 before 50,400 fans. On Nov12, #5 ranked Notre Dame, coached by Dan Devine, came to #15 ranked Clemson at Memorial Stadium on the campus.

The Fighting Irish barely squeaked out a win against a tough Clemson squad L (17-21). Notre Dame won the National Championship in 1977. Charley Pell's Clemson's almost pulled off the big one.

On November 19 at South Carolina, the still ranked #15 Tigers beat South Carolina at Williams-Brice Stadium in Columbia, SC in what was known as the Battle of the Palmetto State W (31–27).

Clemson 31, South Carolina 27 was good enough for Clemson fans. On Nov. 19, 1977 at Columbia, SC, Clemson jumped out ahead 24-0, but South Carolina came back and scored, and scored and scored. How could Clemson stop them? They were like determined rats trying to get off the ship. They had a 27-24 lead with less than three minutes left.

The Tigers took over for one last drive and Steve Fuller came into the Clemson huddle after we got possession and he told the team, "boys we are going down the field and scoring a touchdown to win this game," His first two passes weren't very good and it looked like CU was not going anywhere.

But Fuller finally completed a pass to Rick Weddington to keep the drive alive. He got hit after that. He then clicked with Dwight Clark with a pass on a key play. Then the culmination of the drive was a 20-yard touchdown pass to Jerry Butler, something Clemson has begun to refer to as "The Catch". Butler made a diving backwards catch with just 49 seconds left in the game, giving the Tigers a 31-27 victory.

There might have been an extra motivation for Clemson on that last drive. That year, Coach Charley Pell would give cigars to the team after every Clemson victory. He started it after the team beat Georgia in Athens by stopping the bus at a convenience store on the way back.

Clemson hadn't won in Athens since 1914, so it was a special occasion. That year, someone at South Carolina printed up t-shirts that said, "No Cigars Tonight". A lot of the South Carolina players wore them under their uniform. When they scored to go up 27-24, a lot of them raised up their jerseys and showed the Clemson players and the television audience those t-shirts. I am sure Coach (Jim) Carlen wanted to wring their necks...especially after Butler made that catch.

The Clemson Tigers had a great year. It was the first 8-or better win season since 1959. The Pell Squad was invited to the Gator Bowl played in Gator Bowl Stadium in Jacksonville FL before a crowd of 72,289, against the #10 ranked Pittsburgh Panthers. The Tigers had a few misfires in the Gator Bowl game and lost L (3-34) by a much larger margin than the pundits and scribes expected.

Charley Pell was sure a great coach and the Tigers were an equally great team.

1978 Clemson Tigers Football Coach Charley Pell

The 1978 Clemson Tigers football team represented Clemson University during the 1978 college football season as a member of the Atlantic Coast Conference (ACC). Charley Pell was the head football coach for his second of two seasons. The Tigers completed their eighty-third season overall and their twenty-sixth in the Atlantic Coast Conference with a record of 11-1-0; 6-0-0 in the ACC. The Tigers came in first in the ACC out of 7 active ACC teams. They were also ranked # 6 nationally. Steve Fuller, and Randy Scott were the 1978 team captains.

Player Highlights Steve Fuller QB (1975-78)

Steve Fuller was third-team All-American in 1978 coupled with being on the Academic All-American team for two years. He was smart and he was a great athlete.

FULLER & BUTLER

He was ACC Player-of-the-Year in 1977,78 in 1978, Fuller led Clemson to the ACC title and then to a Gator Bowl win. The team was 11-1 and ranked sixth in the final poll. Fuller chimed in with 4,359 yards passing and third in total offense with 6,096 yards in his career.

He was second in Tiger history in career touchdown responsibility (44). He was second-best pass interception avoidance percentage (3.33) in NCAA history at the time of his graduation. This tribute he shared with Frank Howard's Award along with with Jerry Butler for the 1978-79 academic year,

Fuller won it outright in 1977-78. He is the only two-time recipient of that award. The pros could not stay away from biffing on grabbing him for their team. He was a first-round draft pick (23rd overall) of the Chiefs in 1979. He played for the Super Bowl Champion Bears in 1985.

Retrospect honors came quickly. For example, he was named to the state of South Carolina Hall of Fame in 1991; the Clemson Athletic Hall of Fame in 1985, and he was one of three original inductees to the Ring of Honor in 1994. He was designated as the quarterback on Clemson's Centennial Team in 1996. Plussing all of that, he was declared Clemson's #5 gridder of all-time by the esteemed panel of historians in 1999). On top of all those accolades, Steve Fuller was the ACC 50-Year Anniversary player nominated in 2002.

Charley Pell coached Steve Fuller for two of his four years. In those years, under Coach Charlie Pell he started 27 consecutive games for him. He was an All-ACC selection in Pell's years -- '77 and '78 and was honored as the ACC Player of the Year both years. He is the only Clemson Tiger to do it twice.

Pell stepped down before the 1978 Bowl game. Nonetheless, that year, Steve Fuller quarterbacked the Tigers to their '78 Gator Bowl victory over Ohio State (the Woody Hayes game) and delivered Danny Ford his first win as a "interim" head coach.

In his 1978 senior campaign, he finished sixth in Heisman voting accounting for 2,164 yards (1,515 passing and 649 rushing) in a "three yards and a cloud of dust" style offense. The stark difference in playing style makes it near impossible to compare to modern day greats like Whitehurst and Boyd, the latter of which doubled his yardage totals in most seasons.

Fuller was drafted 23rd overall by the Kansas City Chiefs after that season. He also earned a 3.93 GPA and made the Academic All-ACC team three times. His name hangs in Memorial Stadium. He is one of the Clemson greats!

Player Highlights Jerry Butler SE 1976-1978

Jerry Butler is not the same person as the man who sang" When A Man Loves a Woman," but he could have sung "When A Man Scores a Touchdown," but the music of the touchdown was enough! Butler was "First-team AP All-American." He had a record 2,223 receiving yards and at least one catch in 35 straight games. He was a Senior Bowl participant and co-winner of the prestigious Frank Howard Award along with Steve Fuller for their prowess in the 1978-79 academic year.

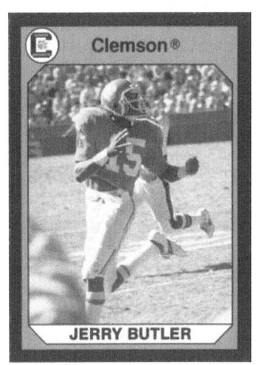

Clemson®

JERRY BUTLER

Butler will always be remembered for his game-winning catch at South Carolina in 1977 in the outstanding 31-27 Tiger win. He did his job well and reports stats such as being 10th in the nation in receiving with 4.9 catches per game in 1978.

Butler was a first-round draft pick of the Buffalo Bills, He was the fifth pick of the whole draft. His greatness did not end in Death Valley. He was Rookie-of-the-Year in 1979 by UPI and The Sporting News. He was thrilled to play in the 1980 Pro Bowl. He handled pain and stress well and so he was able to play with the Bills for nine years as a great pro. (1979-87).

In time, he was named to the Clemson Hall of Fame in 1986. He was so good that he was also named to Clemson's Centennial team in 1996. South Carolina inducted him into the State of South Carolina Hall of Fame in 1997. Butler is not a fluke. He was the real deal. He is ranked as Clemson's #4 gridder of all-time by a panel of historians in 1999. He was inducted into the Clemson Ring of Honor in 1999 and named to the ACC 50-Year Anniversary team in 2002. Jerry

Butler knew football and loved football and was a great football player.

Player Highlights Joe Bostic (1975-78)

After some sluggish years, a rebirth of Clemson football took place in 1977. The Tigers had not gone to a bowl game in 18 years prior to that season. But, a group of veteran players who had suffered through a 2-9 1975 season as freshmen, picked up the Clemson program by the bootstraps.

One of the leaders of that class and the resurgence was offensive tackle Joe Bostic. Charley Pell and Danny Ford used the running game as the staple of the offense and many of the big first downs and long runs of 1977 and 1978 were plays that started with a strong block from Bostic.

Like his quarterback Steve Fuller, Bostic helped return Clemson to national prominence in the late 1970s. Behind Bostic, Fuller and running back Lester Brown, Clemson had a dominant run game during the 11-1 season of 1978.

The ACC and Gator Bowl champions, Clemson set school records that for total rushing yards (3,469), rushing yards per game (289.1), total carries (741) and carries per game (61.8). Not even Chad Morris' up-tempo offense topped Clemson's 78.8 plays per game in 1978. Bostic was an All-America selection in 1977 and '78.

A four-year starter, Bostic became a two-year All-American and recipient of the state of South Carolina's Jacob Blocking Trophy in 1977 and 1978. He won the same award for the ACC in 1977. He was a five-time honoree as the ACC Offensive Lineman of the Week over his career.

While the accomplishments of the 1977 team were significant, the 1978 team, Bostic's senior year, reached an even higher level. Bostic along with younger brother Jeff, also a member of Clemson's great players list, led the Tigers to an 11-1 record, a number-six final Associated Press ranking and ACC Championship. The season, and Bostic's Clemson career, culminated with a 17-15 win over Ohio State in the Gator Bowl.

After appearances in various college All-Star Games, Bostic was chosen in the third round of the NFL draft by the St. Louis Cardinals. He was chosen to the 1979 NFL All-Rookie team and played 10 seasons overall with the Cardinals organization.

A very strong Clemson team, molded by a great coach -- Charley Pell -- began the season in its opener at home on Sept 16. The Clemson Fighting Tigers blew out The Citadel at Memorial Stadium on the campus of Clemson University in Clemson, SC, W (58–3). One might wonder if the first game were not so easy if Clemson would have gone undefeated.

There are pluses and minuses to having your way in the first game of a season. Clemson, ranked #8 at the beginning of the season, after a stunning blowout, lost in game 2 to an unranked Georgia team on Sept 23, at Sanford Stadium in • Athens, GA L 0–12. There would be no more Clemson losses this year. Charley Pell knew how to build a team, and then work the team to success.

On Sept 30, Clemson shut out Villanova in their first visit to
Clemson, W (31-0) On Oct 7, at home again, VA Tech took a
pounding from Clemson on the way to a W (38-7) shellacking. On
Oct 14, at Virginia's Scott Stadium in Charlottesville, VA, Clemson
worked hard for a nice win W (30–14). At home, again on Oct 21
against an always competitive Duke team. The Clemson Tigers
defeated the Duke Blue Devils W (28-8).

On Oct 28, at NC State's Carter–Finley Stadium in Raleigh, NC in
the annual Textile Bowl, # 20 Clemson dominated W (33–10). On
Nov 4, # 16 nationally ranked Clemson had a major offensive surge
against Wake Forest at Groves Stadium in Winston-Salem, NC W
(51–6). On Nov 11, North Carolina played #15 Clemson at home
and were beaten in a very close game W (13–9). On Nov 18   at a
tough #11 Maryland, # 12 Clemson played the Terrapins at Byrd
Stadium • College Park, MD and on the game W (28–24).

Game Highlights Clemson 28, Maryland 24

Nov. 18, 1978 at College Park, MD

This was a big game -- for the ACC Championship and both teams
were ranked in the top 12 in the nation.

It was a truly incredible game of big plays with many long plays.
Maryland had a star runner named Steve Atkins who had a 98-yard
run in this game. It is still an ACC record. Dwight Clark caught a 62-
yard touchdown pass from Steve Fuller and Jerry Butler caught an
87-yard touchdown pass, the longest of his career.

Maryland kicked a field goal to make it 28-24 in the fourth quarter
and then got the ball back. They drove into Clemson territory, but
couldn't get any closer and the Tigers survived the assault. And won.

When we the team got back to the Greenville Airport there were
7,000 people waiting and cheering. Cars were lined up all the way to
I-85. People were out of the cars and all over the place ready to
welcome the team. It was a great happy scene. This victory over
Maryland gave the Tigers a noteworthy 9-1 record and moved
Clemson into the top 10 in the polls for the first time since the 1950s,
so it was quite a big win. Of course, it was big enough for the

Clemson Fighting Tigers to clinch the ACC Championship. Nobody forgot that.

In the last game of the season. On Nov 25, at home. Clemson beat South Carolina in the Battle of the Palmetto State W (41–23)) It was the best season ever.

The #7 nationally ranked Tigers were invited to play #20 Ohio State in the Gator Bowl on Dec 29 at Gator Bowl Stadium in Jacksonville, FL. The Clemson Tigers played tough and won the game square W (17–15) before 72,011 fans.

Clemson's 1978 Gator Bowl Champions

Game Highlight Clemson 17, Ohio State 15

Dec. 30, 1978 at Jacksonville, FL (Gator Bowl)

Ohio State always had tough teams and they still do. In 1978, they had a freshman quarterback named Art Schlichter who was a terrific player as both a runner and passer. He completed 16-20 passes in the Gator Bowl.

Of course, the thing everyone remembers is Woody Hayes hitting Charlie Bauman after Bauman made an interception in the final minute.

Charlie Bauman was not even supposed to be in that passing lane on that play. He got knocked backwards, enabling him to make the interception. That was the only interception of his career. He was run out of bounds in the middle of the Ohio State bench, right in front of Woody Hayes and Hayes struck him in a moment of frustration to beat all such moments. Many at the game could not see it for one reason or another.

By the time, the team had exited the field after the game and got in the locker room, everyone was talking about it. Coach Ford felt bad for Coach Hayes and told the players not to comment, just talk about the game.

Bob Bradley, the Clemson Sports Information Director recounts telling Coach Ford before the game that Clemson needed to have a press conference the morning following the game, because the game was scheduled for 9:00 PM. Coach Ford's press conference was scheduled for 10:00 AM. At 9:40 AM the Associated Press reporter came into our press conference to tell us that Hayes had already been fired.

Charlie felt badly about the whole situation because he had grown up an Ohio State fan and thought a lot of Coach Hayes. For years he refused to do interviews about the incident because he didn't want to rekindle the incident and hurt Coach Hayes' legacy. Coach Hayes called him to apologize after it happened. Charlie, who was a sophomore when the play happened, invited him to come down to spring practice, but he never came.

More on the Woody Hayes Gator Bowl Incident

Charley Pell was the Clemson coach until the end of the 1978 season, when Danny Ford took over and coached the Tigers just one game -- the 1978 Gator Bowl. Many remember that game for one thing. -- the incident involving the late Ohio State Coach Woody Hayes. He was fired after an impeccable career for one stupid mistake. He punched Tigers linebacker Charlie Bauman late in a 17-15 victory over the Buckeyes. I wonder sometimes if a higher power will question how we dispose of our immortals for just one flaw. They say "One Ah crap replaces thousands of attaboys." Woody Hayes had thousands of attaboys and at least this one very public "Ah Crap!"

Clemson was particularly generous in its forgiveness of the incident right after the game. Too bad Ohio State could not have done a little better.

Some joke a bit that there were no hard feelings for "The Punch Heard Round the World" - at least not from the Clemson faction. Clemson raises gentlemen off the field. Clemson's graciousness wowed again seven months after the 1978 Gator Bowl, which was a great victory for Danny White's Tigers after Charley Pell brought them to the game that has become infamous.

To recount, Ohio State coach Woody Hayes in a burst of frustration, did the unspeakable, he slugged Clemson nose guard Charlie Bauman on the OSU sideline after Bauman made a great game-sealing interception. Having been fired for the incident, Hayes accepted a speaking engagement at the annual S.C. high school coaches' association clinic in Columbia, SC. The five-time national champion coach was welcomed by a packed hotel ballroom. It was a nice experience overall.

"The biggest crowd they'd ever had of coaches," Hayes' Gator Bowl counterpart, Danny Ford, recalled. "The coaches came out with beards and moustaches, and he chewed every one of them out." At the same time, Ford felt badly that Hayes had to be fired for his transgression.

"He was a good man," Ford said that week. "Sorry it happened against us, and all of that."

Funny thing is, Ford never even realized what happened until the wee hours that night. It was inconsequential to the elation experienced by Clemson for winning such a great Bowl Game.

"I was amazed at Charlie Bauman's composure. I don't remember him saying anything about the opponent, because we were celebrating the win," Ford said. "That was the most impressive thing about that."

Later on, as you will see in the next chapter, the nasty, corrupt, NCAA raised its ugly head again and did its best to destroy Danny Ford's career. Ironically, Ford would have been the first one to take back Woody Hayes' firing.

Charley Pell

Coach Pell moved on from Clemson after the 1978 regular season to become head coach at Florida. As you already know, Danny Ford took over the duties of head coach for the Gator Bowl.

Pell was born February 17, 1941 and he died too early at 60 years of age on May 29, 2001). He played football and he was a great coach. An Alabama native, and an alumnus of the University of Alabama, where he played his college football.

He was a two-way starter and three-year letterman at the University of Alabama under legendary Coach Paul William "Bear" Bryant, Pell was a member of the Crimson Tide's 1961 National Championship team. Charley Pell learned how to win football games from the master. He not only played for Bryant, he was also an assistant under Bryant at Alabama.

Pell is most notably remembered as the head coach of the Clemson University and the University of Florida football teams. Pell created systems at both schools that were enduring. In his second season at Clemson, he had already made the name Clemson stand for success on the field. The systems he created laid the foundation for the later success of the Clemson program and then later the Florida program. Unfortunately, his coaching career was tainted by National Collegiate Athletic Association (NCAA) rules violations.

Pell arrived at Clemson as assistant head coach and defensive coordinator under Red Parker in early 1976. After the poor 3-6-2 1976 outcome, Coach Parker was ordered to fire several assistants. When he refused, Athletic Director Bill McClellan terminated him and asked Pell to take over the reins. He turned the program around,

Charley Pell never intended to be absent for the Gator Bowl. He had made a life decision and made the mistake as some might say of telling some people about it. This stirred up controversy. Clemson officials were outraged. He had accepted the head coaching position at the University of Florida, in Gainesville, on December 4, 1978. It was before the bowl game was played. His assistant, Danny Ford, a great student of Pell's, was named as his replacement almost immediately. Charley Pell's offer to stay with the team 'til the end of the season and coach the bowl game was declined.

Of course, only Charley Pell in a league now with the Lord, where there is no NCAA knows the truth. The alternate thought is that Pell originally said he would coach the Tigers in the Gator Bowl even while building his new program in Gainesville, but had a change of heart -- perhaps prompted by the yelps of outraged alumni and fans -- and announced on Dec. 10 that he was relinquishing the reins. I suspect somebody on earth may also know the truth. My own opinion is that if Clemson wanted Charley to stay, he would have been coaching the Gator Bowl. No aspersions cast on anybody.

Danny Ford, a kid at the time got the full-time job and coached for eleven years. He got Clemson its first National Championship as a kid. His teams are the focus of the next chapter.

Chapter 21 Danny Ford Era 1978-1989

Coach # 21 Danny Ford

Year	Coach	Record	Conference	Record
1978	Danny Ford	1-0	Gator Bowl	WIn
1979	Danny Ford	8-4-0	ACC	4-2-0
1980	Danny Ford	6-5-0	ACC	2-4-0
1981*	Danny Ford	12-0-0	ACC	6-0-0
1982*	Danny Ford	9-1-1	ACC	6-0-0
1983*	Danny Ford	9-1-1	ACC	7-0-0
1984	Danny Ford	7-4-0	ACC	5-2-0
1985	Danny Ford	6-6-0	ACC	4-3-0
1986*	Danny Ford	8-2-2	ACC	5-1-1
1987*	Danny Ford	10-2-0	ACC	6-1-0
1988*	Danny Ford	10-2-0	ACC	6-1-0
1989	Danny Ford	10-2-0	ACC	5-2-0

* ACC Champions

1979 Clemson Tigers Football Coach Danny Ford

The 1979 Clemson Tigers football team represented Clemson University during the 1979 college football season

Danny Ford Leads Clemson Team to National Championship

Clemson is a member of the Atlantic Coast Conference (ACC). Danny Ford was the head football coach for his second of twelve seasons. Ford's first season lasted one game as he was a replacement coach for Charley Pell in the 1978 Gator Bowl. The Tigers completed their eighty-fourth season overall and their twenty-seventh in the Atlantic Coast Conference with a record of 8-4-0; 4-2-0 in the ACC. The Tigers came in second in the ACC out of 7 active ACC teams. They were also ranked # 6 nationally. Steve Fuller, and Randy Scott were the 1978 team captains.

Clemson shut out Furman W (21) in the home opener on Sept 8 at Memorial Stadium, on the campus of Clemson University, Clemson SC before a crowd of 55,000. A tough Maryland Terrapin squad played Clemson at home on Sept 15 and beat the Tigers L (0-19). On Sept 22, Georgia was the next home game. The Tigers beat the Bulldogs W (12-7) in a tight match. Clemson's 300th win came on this day, September 22 against Georgia. On Oct 6, at home, Clemson beat Virginia W 17-17. Then, on Oct 13, at Virginia Tech's Lane Stadium in Blacksburg, VA, Clemson won W 21–0. On October 20, at Duke in Wallace Wade Stadium • Durham, NC, the Tigers defeated the Blue Devils W 28–10.

On Oct 27 at home in the Textile Bowl, Clemson was defeated by NC State L (13-16). On Nov 3 at home, #14 Wake Forest was beaten by Clemson W (31–0). Then on Nov 10 at North Carolina's Kenan Memorial Stadium in Chapel Hill, NC, the then nationally ranked # 18 Tigers beat the Tar Heels W (19–10)   On Nov 17 at Notre Dame Stadium in Notre Dame, the Tigers defeated the Fighting Irish in a close match W 16–10.

Game Highlight Clemson 16, Notre Dame 10

Nov. 17, 1979 at South Bend, IN

anytime any team goes to Notre Dame and beats them it is an accomplishment. Notre Dame had beaten Clemson two years before and then went on to win the National Championship.
They weren't quite as good in 1979, but they still had a good ball club. Notre Dame held a 10-0 lead in the first half and looked like they had taken control of the game. Then, there was a big break for

Clemson. An ND player, Tyree Dickerson fumbled a punt that the Tigers recovered. It changed the momentum for the rest of the game.

Tim Bourret who became the Sports Communications Department Director told me later that after Dickerson fumbled the punt, he left the sideline, went to the locker room, got dressed and went back to his dorm. He had quit the team in the middle of the game. He watched the rest of the game on TV in his dorm room and never played football again.

It was Billy Lott who led the Clemson comeback in the second half. He had a 26-yard run that put the Tigers up and then Obed Ariri kicked three field goals and Clemson walked away from Notre Dame Stadium with a nice win W (16-10).

That was quite a first 11 games as head coach for Danny Ford. He was a fine coach. He beat Woody Hayes, Vince Dooley and Dan Devine all within that time. As many know, all three are in the College Football Hall of Fame.

On Nov 24 at #19 South Carolina in Williams-Brice Stadium, Columbia, SC, in the Battle of the Palmetto State, #13 Clemson lost the battle L (9–13)

In the Peach Bowl on Dec 31 v #19 Baylor at Fulton County Stadium in Atlanta, GA, the Clemson Fighting Tigers, the #18 Clemson Fighting Tigers lost the match L (18–24)

Player Highlights Bubba Brown, LB 1976-79

Marlon "Bubba" Brown is the all-time leading tackler in Clemson history. When you review the legendary list of linebackers who have played for Clemson, that is quite a statement. Bubba was finally inducted into the Clemson Hall of Fame.
It has taken a while for Brown to get his due simply because of the great teammates Brown had in his era (1976-79). Of the four players now in the Clemson Ring of Honor, three played on Clemson's 1978 team. But, a look at the statistics tells us that Brown was the team's top tackler, a ferocious hitter and enthusiastic player.

Two games stand out in his career. In 1978 Clemson traveled to Raleigh for an ACC showdown with NC State. NC State was promoting their Brown, running back Ted, for the Heisman Trophy. He had riddled Clemson for four touchdowns and 227 yards rushing three seasons earlier.

Clemson

BUBBA BROWN

Although the national media did not portray the game as a "Battle of the Browns" (Clemson also had running back Lester Brown), Bubba took the confrontation as a personal challenge. By the end of the game, Bubba had 17 tackles and had held Ted Brown under 100 yards rushing, and out of the endzone. When Sports Illustrated was released the next week, it was Bubba who caught the national headlines with his selection as National Defensive Player of the Week.

Clemson finished the 1978 season with a 10-1 record and was chosen to play Ohio State in the Gator Bowl on national television. Clemson won the historic game ,17-15. Again, the pregame headlines were all about Danny Ford's first game as head coach and his meeting with future Hall of Fame mentor Woody Hayes. Brown personally stymied the Ohio State rushing game with 22 tackles, still the second highest single game total in Clemson history.

1980 Clemson Tigers Football Coach Danny Ford

The 1980 Clemson Tigers football team represented Clemson University during the 1980 college football season as a member of the Atlantic Coast Conference (ACC). Danny Ford was the head football coach for his third of twelve seasons. The Tigers completed their eighty-fifth season overall and their twenty-eighth in the Atlantic Coast Conference with a record of 6-5-0; 2-4-0 in the ACC. The Tigers came in 4th in the ACC out of 7 active ACC teams. Lee Nanney, and Willie Underwood were the 1978 team captains.

On Sept 13 in the season opener at Memorial Stadium on the main campus of Clemson University in Clemson, SC, the Tigers defeated the Rice Owls W (19–3) to kick off the season. 60,361 were in attendance. On Sept 20 at #10 ranked Georgia's Sanford Stadium in Athens, GA, the Tigers succumbed to the Bulldogs. L (16–20). On Sept 27 at home, the Tigers beat the Western Carolina Catamounts W (17–10). On Oct 4, at home Clemson beat Virginia Tech W (13–10). On Oct 11 at Virginia's Scott Stadium in Charlottesville, VA, the Tigers defeated the Wahoos in a very close game. W (27–24).

On Oct 18 at home against Duke, the Tigers lost to the Blue Devils L 17–34 before 59,873. On Oct 25 at NC State's Carter–Finley Stadium in Raleigh, NC in the Textile Bowl, the Tigers were defeated by the Wolfpack L (20–24) On Nov 1, Clemson won its 100th ACC game against Wake Forest at Groves Stadium in Winston-Salem, NC W (35–33)   On Nov 8, #14 North Carolina beat Clemson at home L (19–24). Then, on Nov 15, in the second-last game of the season, Maryland beat Clemson at Byrd Stadium in College Park, MD L (7–34). In the Battle of the Palmetto State, the Tigers prevailed over South Carolina at home W (27-6)

1981 Clemson Tigers Football Coach Danny Ford

The 1981 Clemson Tigers football team represented Clemson University during the 1981 college football season as a member of the Atlantic Coast Conference (ACC). Danny Ford was the head football coach for his fourth of twelve seasons. The Tigers completed their eighty-sixth season overall and their twenty-ninth in the Atlantic Coast Conference with a record of 12-0-0; 6-0-0 in the ACC. The Tigers came in 1st in the ACC out of 7 active ACC teams. Nelson Stokely was the offensive coordinator. Jeff Davis was the team captain. This year a dream came true. The Clemson Tigers won the National Championship. It was a consensus of the coaches and AP polls.

On Sept 5 in the home opener, Clemson defeated Wofford W (45-10) at Memorial Stadium on Sept 12, at Tulane in the Louisiana Superdome, New Orleans, LA, Clemson won W (13–5). Then on Sept 19 at home, #4 Georgia lost to Clemson W (13-3.

Game Highlight Clemson 13, Georgia 3

Sept. 19, 1981 at Clemson, SC

Georgia came to Clemson as the defending national champion. It was a season highlight for sure for Clemson to compete well in this game. To win the game was simply remarkable. There is no question that this was Clemson's kcy regular season win on the way to winning the coveted national championship.

No one had Clemson on their scopes in their preseason top 20. As you all know, the Tigers were just coming off a frustrating 6-5 season. On top of that, Clemson vs. Georgia is a special rivalry and this is one of the games that made it that way. Herschel Walker, a name everybody knows had led Georgia to the National Championship the year before and he was ready to destroy Clemson if given the opportunity. He was a marked man by the Clemson defensive unit this day and it was quite effective.

The Clemson defense was ready as it forced nine turnovers against the Bulldogs. It was the most turnovers forced in a game in history. Clemson took a 10-0 early lead in the first half on an eight-yard touchdown pass from Homer Jordan to Perry Tuttle and a 39-yard field goal by Donald Igwebuike. Thigs were looking good.

Clemson and Georgia traded field goals in the second half and Coach Danny Ford let the defense take control to shut down the Bulldogs offensive threat. Jeff Davis was outstanding and followed Walker everywhere he went. Herschel Walker ended the day with 111 yards rushing on 28 carries, but the Tiger defense made sure that he never got into the Clemson endzone.

Georgia entered this game ranked fourth in the nation. It is still the highest ranked win in Clemson history in Death Valley. Go Tigers!

On Oct 3 at Kentucky's Commonwealth Stadium in Lexington, KY, the #14 Clemson Tigers beat the Wildcats W (21–3). On Oct 10 at home, #9 Clemson shut out Virginia W (27–0) before 63,064. Then, on Oct 17 at Duke's Wallace Wade Stadium in Durham, NC, #6 Clemson beat the Blue Devils W (38–10)

Clemson's Jeff Davis celebrates after a victory in the magical 1981 season
Photo courtesy of Clemson Tigers

In the Textile Bowl at home on Oct 24, the #4 Tigers beat the Wolfpack of NC State W (17-7). On Oct 31 in another home game, the #3 ranked Tigers routed the Demon Deacons of Wake Forest before 60,383. Then, on Nov 7 at # 9 North Carolina's Kenan Stadium in Chapel Hill, NC, the #2 Tigers got by the Tar Heels by a thread W 10–8, keeping their unbeaten season streak intact.

Game Highlights Clemson 10, North Carolina 8

Nov. 7, 1981 at Chapel Hill, NC

The thing I remember about this game was the play that Jeff Bryant made in the closing moments. We had a 10-8 lead in the closing minutes and Dale Hatcher punted the ball out of bounds at the North Carolina two.

They hadn't driven for a touchdown against us all day, so it looked good for the Tigers.

But, Scott Stankavage started to lead North Carolina up field. With 57 seconds left they had the ball on their 40 and Stankavage threw a swing pass to the right flat. It was incomplete and every player relaxed...except for Bryant. He chased after the ball and pounced on it.

Sure enough, the referees said it was a lateral and it was Clemson ball. We ran out the clock and kept our perfect record.
That one play might have helped him become a first-round draft choice because it showed his alert play. That play was shown on the Saturday night news all over the country because it was the big game of the day in college football. We were ranked second in the nation and North Carolina was eighth, the first time in history two top 10 ACC teams faced each other.

The headline in the Greenville News the next day was Tigers read "10-8cious". Since I did not get it at first either, think how *tenacious* the Tigers play had to be.

This is such a memorable game against such a major foe and it was so critical to the 1981 national Championship, that I have "borrowed a great piece of Tiger News from ClemsonTigers.com witten on September 23, 2014 by Sam Blackman. It is a great account of the game. http://www.clemsontigers.com/ViewArticle.dbml?ATCLID=209671838

Clemson is "10-8cious"

By: ClemsonTigers.com
Release: Tuesday 09/23/2014

by Sam Blackman

Clemson's road to the National Championship in 1981 included a classic game with North Carolina in Chapel Hill, N.C. on November 7th. It's considered to be one of the greatest games ever played in Atlantic Coast Conference history.

It was eighth-ranked North Carolina against second-ranked Clemson, the first meeting of top-10 ACC teams in league history.

"The North Carolina game did more for us winning the national championship than any other game," said senior linebacker and captain Jeff Davis. "It was the ultimate test for us. We expected to win in Death Valley and we expected teams to already be behind when the whistle blew to start the game. But, to go into the backyard of a top-10 football team with everything at stake, and win, that did it for us.

"Remember, North Carolina had everything to play for. It's right there for them. You can think there were people wondering 'Can Clemson stay focused?' And we beat them in a fight. It was an all-out brawl. May the best man win! It was man-on-man."

With an ACC Championship and a major bowl bid at stake, it was dubbed the biggest game to ever be played in the state of North Carolina.

"North Carolina came to play," defensive tackle and All-American Jeff Bryant said. "They were at home and they were a top-10 team. We both were striving for that goal which was to win the ACC and take it further from there.

"It was a very physical game. I can remember being sore for a couple of days after that."

It was also Homecoming Weekend in Chapel Hill, NC and it was the last game at Kenan Stadium for UNC's seniors – a class that had helped the Tar Heels win an ACC Championship the year before and beat traditional powers such as Texas and Oklahoma along the way.

To top things off, there were bowl representatives from eight bowl games in attendance, more than at any other game that afternoon across the country. Sports Illustrated had been at Clemson all week to chronicle the Tigers' magical run and was in Chapel Hill on that afternoon. ABC was broadcasting it as part of their regional coverage and carried the game throughout most of the country.

All of America's eyes seem to be placed on this small school from the foothills of South Carolina, and then Clemson Head Coch Danny Ford knew he had to do something to turn his team's focus to what was really important – beating the Tar Heels.

"Were we excited about the hype? Yes! We wanted the stakes high," said Davis. "It didn't get any better than this. This was another opportunity for us to do something in Clemson football history that had never been done.

"We took all of that into consideration. We would not have approached that game any other way because there was the crown jewel of college football standing right in front of us. We could almost touch it.

"The world was watching. We had a great opportunity. It was everything that a young man and a young student-athlete could want."

"North Carolina, for me, was a big game," Davis said. "I'm from Greensboro, North Carolina, and I wanted to beat them more than anyone else we played. This was my last opportunity to make a statement in North Carolina that I made the right decision in coming to Clemson."

"Both teams knew it was going to be a hard-fought, physical game. They had some very good athletes and they were a very good football team. We were going into their backyard. It was going to be tough."

Ford knew it was going to be tough too.

"I was concerned about how we can play physically with this team," he said. "We were out-muscled in 1980, which did not happen too often with our football teams. Their game plan in 1980 was to out-muscle Clemson, and I think they did it.

"We knew that's what they were going to try and do again."

The game started as a defensive struggle and lived up to its billing. The score was 0-0 at the end of the first quarter.

McCall had a game-high 84 yards before he left the game injured and scored the game's lone touchdown – a seven-yard run with 6:54 to play in the second quarter.   Clemson led 7-5 at the half.

North Carolina ranked second in the country running the football coming in, but Clemson held the Tar Heels to 84 yards on 42 carries. Stopping the run had been the Tigers ammo all season. With new defensive coordinator Tom Harper at the helm, Clemson led the ACC in rushing defense and ranked second in the country.

"We would put a goose egg on our (defensive) board before every game," Davis said. "We didn't do it as a mark or just to put something up there. No, we actually believed it. It was symbolic to us. You were not going to score on us. Even if you get in our territory, you might have a chance to get a field goal, but you can forget about scoring a touchdown on us.

"We took pride in that. You were not supposed to score on us. We even took pride in goal line situations in practice. I don't care how close you put the ball you were not going to score on our defense. We believed that. That was not some tough guy talk or something to motivate people. We believed it."

North Carolina running back and three-time All-ACC selection, Kelvin Bryant believed it. In his first game back after arthroscopic knee surgery earlier, he gained just 31 yards on 13 carries as did fellow running back Tyrone Anthony on eight carries.

"When I see Kelvin, he likes to joke that he gets a headache right when he sees me because we were hitting him so hard that day," Davis smiled.

Clemson's defense was stifling.

No team that season learned that any better than the Tar Heels. Twice, North Carolina had first-and-goal inside the Clemson 10, and both times it was held to short field goals by Brooks Barwick.

Early in the second quarter, North Carolina appeared to have a possible touchdown on a third-down swing pass in the flats to Tyrone Anthony, but Clemson All-American safety Terry Kinard came out of nowhcrc to drag him down at the five. The Tar Heels settled for a 22-yard Barwick field goal and led 3-0.

Now Trailing 10-5, following a Donald Igwebuike 39-yard field goal, North Carolina took its second drive of the third quarter and marched down to the Clemson four thanks to a 21-yard halfback pass from Anthony to Griffin. But, Davis and Kinard stuffed Kelvin Bryant for a five-yard loss on the next play and then Stankavage threw incomplete on second and third down, forcing the Tar Heels to settle for a 26-yard Barwick field goal.

The Tigers led 10-8 heading into the fourth period.

In the fourth quarter, North Carolina again had an opportunity to take the lead following a muffed punt by Billy Davis at the Clemson 37. After gaining just four yards on first and second down, the Tar Heels hopes for taking the lead were dashed when freshman nose guard William Perry broke through and sacked quarterback Scott Stankavage for a 10-yard loss.

"With the kind of defense we had, we never panicked," defensive tackle, Jeff Bryant said. "We are going to make the big play. It was always role call to the ball."

Following a Clemson punt, UNC again moved into Tiger territory to the 39, but again the defensive stiffened, with a tackle for a loss and two incomplete passes.

Unable to move the ball, Clemson punter Dale Hatcher then pinned the Heels deep in their own territory at the two-yard line following a 47-yard punt with 2:19 to play, setting up the final dramatics in one of the biggest victories in Clemson history.

After moving the ball out from the shadow of their own goal post , the Tar Heels found themselves with a first down at their own 40 thanks to a 12-yard scramble by Stankavage on third-and-10 from the two, then a nine-yard pass to wide receiver Ron Richardson and a 14-yard pass to Anthony.

With just over a minute to play and one timeout left, the Tar Heels called a screen pass to fullback Alex Burrus. Stankavage threw the ball behind the line of scrimmage and when Burrus went to make the catch, defensive end Bill Smith met him, knocking the ball to the ground.

The ball rolled 15 yards backwards towards the Clemson sideline, and that is where defensive tackle Jeff Bryant jumped on the football at the UNC 25-yard line.

Smith is sort of the unsung hero. The play everyone remembers is Bryant having the presence of mind to jump on what appeared to be an incomplete pass with 57 seconds to play.

The pass was ruled a lateral, and by jumping on the loose football Bryant secured Clemson's 10-8 victory in front of a then record crowd at Kenan Stadium of 53,611. But, what people don't recall is who actually caused the fumble.

That would be Bill Smith, a current member of the Clemson University Board of Trustees.

"They were moving the ball down the field, and all they needed was a field goal to win," Smith said. "That was just a timely play that happened."

Timely indeed, it was perhaps the calling-card of the 1981 defense. In 1981, Clemson ranked seventh in the nation in turnover margin and led the ACC in forced turnovers with what is still a school-record 41.

Jeff Bryant, who played 12 seasons in the NFL, had a stellar career at Clemson, but it wasn't until Tom Harper became the defensive coordinator in the spring of 1981 when he finally realized what kind of player he could be.

Harper did wonders for Bryant's play. He not only helped him become sound fundamentally, he helped him with his technique. He helped him become a better football player, and a better person.

"Tom Harper was very instrumental in my development," Bryant said. "He was a great guy. I wish I had Tom Harper all four years. I'm thankful I had him when I did, though, because he really made a difference with me."

Bryant credited Harper's instruction as one of the reasons he stayed alert and recognized the lateral on North Carolina's final drive.

"I was coming up field pretty hard because I figured they were going to pass the ball. I had a good rush on and I was about as deep as the quarterback," he said. "I noticed him throwing the ball, and I saw the hit, but I noticed he threw the ball behind him.

"Bill made a great hit, and I saw the ball coming out, so my thinking was to rush over there and get on it because no one else thought it was a lateral. I thought it was one because of the angle I was at because I was right there behind the quarterback as he threw the ball."

Smith, who admits he did not know it was a lateral at the time, sometimes wonders about the "what ifs" had Bryant not jumped on the loose ball.

"Who knows what would have happened had we lost that game, but thank goodness we can say 'what if' all we want because we didn't lose it," he said. "We won it and we did all we could do to win it. That was the mentality of that team all year."

After Jordan fell to the ground three times to run out the final 57 seconds, a mass celebration broke out on the Clemson sideline. As Tar Heel fans made their way to the exit, the Clemson players and the 10,000 or so Tiger fans that traveled up to Chapel Hill, stayed and enjoyed what they had accomplished, a 10-8 victory over North Carolina.

The next day, "The Greenville News" had in its headlines, in bold print, a very clever headline, "Clemson is 10-8cious."

"We knew that anything was possible at that point," Bryant said.

With a victory over the eighth-ranked Tar Heels behind them, Clemson for the first time, admitted the possibility of going undefeated and playing for a national championship was on its mind.

"It was important because we started thinking a little bit now about being undefeated," Davis said. "Until that point, we were not trying to touch it. There might have been a few rumblings here and there, but we were all about one game at a time.

"At that point, and where we were at, you were going to have to do something phenomenal to beat us."

The Tigers were simply 10-8cious that day and that season.

-- End of article reprint--

On Nov 14, at home the #2 Clemson Fighting Tigers beat Maryland W (21-. On Nov 21, at South Carolina's Williams-Brice Stadium in Columbia, SC, in the Battle of the Palmetto State, the #1 Tigers beat the Gamecocks W (29–13), finishing the season undefeated and in first place.

The #1 Clemson Tigers played in the Orange Bowl Game on January 1, 1982 at 8:00 p.m. against # 4 Nebraska in the Miami Orange Bowl, Miami, FL, and the Tigers came away with the victory and the National Championship

Game Highlights Clemson 22, Nebraska 15

Jan. 1, 1982 at Miami, FL (Orange Bowl)

This game was definitely for the national championship. Nebraska had future Heisman Trophy Mike Rozier, Dave Rimington, the Outland Trophy Winner and many other talented players. But Clemson had some pretty good players in our own right with Jeff Davis, Perry Tuttle, William "Refrigerator" Perry, and many others.

Nebraska scored and cut the lead to seven points, 22-15 when they converted a two-point play from the eight-yard line in the fourth quarter.

But, Clemson held the ball about the last five minutes. Homer Jordan was the key to running out the clock and not giving Nebraska another chance. He made a great run with about two minutes left that gave the Tigers a first down. What a run that was, he made so many cut backs. We held the ball to the final seconds. Nebraska had one last play with six seconds left, but Andy Headen knocked down a long pass attempt.

Homer made it to the dressing room, but he passed out once he got there from dehydration. It was a tough game. All the press wanted to talk to Homer after the ballgame, but he was in there for a long time getting IVs. By the time he got out of the training room it was past deadline for the writers. That is why all the accounts of that game don't have any quotes from Homer. He didn't do any interviews until the next day. That was certainly a magic night in Miami. Clemson was happy with the win and so what about the interviews.

Clemson's Fighting Tigers finished the 1981 season undefeated and untied (12-0) and were voted #1 in the AP and UPI polls. When they won the Orange Bowl over Nebraska, the Tigers were selected as Consensus National Champions by the AP, UPI, Football Writers Association of America (FWAA), and National Football Foundation (NFF). In the 1980-s with Danny Ford as the head coach for most of the run, Clemson was the fifth winningest Division I college football team of the decade, with a record of 86-25-4 (.765).

Danny Ford was awarded the 1981 Coach of the Year Award by the American Football Coaches Association (AFCA) and the FWAA. At the time, Coach Ford was the youngest ever to receive the award, and the youngest (33 yrs. old) to have won a National Championship.

In the 1982 Orange Bowl, Clemson QB Homer Jordan received Offensive Most Valuable Player honors. Homer earned first-team All-ACC honors in 1981, his junior season, and finished first in the ACC in passing efficiency and 12th in the nation. Jordan was an honorable mention All-American selection in 1981. He was runner-up for ACC MVP behind teammate Jeff Davis, but the team voted him MVP in 1981.

Even though Jordan was injured for much of his senior season, he helped lead the 1982 team to a 9-1-1 record and number-eight national ranking. He also earned honorable mention All-American honors as a senior. He ranked as Clemson's 18th greatest player of the century. Jordan was inducted into the Clemson Hall of Fame in 1993.

Player Highlights Jeff Bryant T 1978-1981

Clemson®

JEFF BRYANT

Jeff Bryant was a great tackle who could start on any team. Though he is a Clemson great, his name now gets lost in the shuffle with the bigger stars such as "The Fridge" and Jeff Davis.

Bryant, a 6'5" 270lb DT/DE from the Atlanta area amassed 63 sacks in his 12 year NFL career along with 11 fumble recoveries and an interception. He was a key contributor to Clemson's win over Georgia, causing two of the nine, yes you read that right, nine fumbles in the game.

Bryant was second-team All-American on the Tigers' National Championship team of 1981. He still has the 10th-best single-season tackles-for-loss mark (19) in 1981. He led the National Championship team in sacks and tackles for loss

He was First-Team All-ACC that year and he still ranks in the top 10 in Clemson history in career sacks and tackles for loss. He will always be remembered for his fumble recovery at North Carolina in 1981 late in the game of the 10-8 win that kept the national title hopes alive.

Despite newcomers doing well in recent Clemson teams, Jeff Bryant was not only a mainstay on the defensive line for the Tigers, but he went on to lead a very successful NFL career. Bryant was drafted with the 6th pick of the very first round in the 1982 draft by the Seattle Seahawks. He played with the Seahawks from 1982-1993 and he is second in Seahawk history in career sacks.

Bryant was inducted into Clemson Hall of Fame in 1996. He was also named to Clemson's Centennial team in 1996 and he was inducted into state of South Carolina Hall of Fame (2004).

Player Highlights Perry Tuttle (1978-81)

Another of the great Clemson football player of the century is still a fixture at Clemson football home games. Perry Tuttle has been hovering around the Tiger program for over 20 years as a player, supporter and now as a broadcaster on the Tiger Tailgate Show.

Perry Tuttle was one of many good receivers to come through Clemson, and was widely remembered for catching the winning touchdown pass to make the Tigers 1981 national champions.

A member of Clemson's Centennial Team, as well as its Hall of Fame, there is no question that Tuttle is one of the best Clemson receivers of all time. He is one of the most decorated receivers in Clemson history, being in the top 10 all time at Clemson for touchdown receptions, receiving yards, and receptions.

His accomplishments on the field as an All-American receiver in 1981 were electrifying. He averaged 17 yards a reception on 52 catches during that National Championship season and he score eight touchdowns. He ranked in the top 30 in the nation in receiving that year, quite an accomplishment in Danny Ford's run-oriented offense.

He saved one of his greatest moments for his last game at Clemson. He caught five passes for 56 yards in the 22-15 victory over Nebraska in the Orange Bowl, including a 13-yard scoring pass from Homer Jordan (another Clemson great player). His celebration was captured on the cover of Sports Illustrated and he remains the only current Clemson athlete in history to be featured on the cover of the world's most famous sports publication.

Tuttle finished his career with 150 receptions for over 2500 yards, still second in school history in both areas. He was the #19 selection of the NFL draft by the Buffalo Bills in the spring of 1982 and he played many years in the NFL and the CFL. In fact, a year after he was named to Clemson's Centennial Team, he was inducted into the Winnipeg Blue Bombers Hall of Fame. How's that for a great International Clemson football great?

Player Highlights Jeff Davis, LB, 1978-81

Jeff Davis made his mark at Clemson and in making that mark, he was one of several outstanding defensive players from the title-winning 1981 team. Captain Davis played a major role in clinching Clemson's only national title by earning Orange Bowl Defensive MVP honors in the 22-15 win over No. 4 Nebraska to clinch the championship.

JEFF DAVIS

Davis led Clemson in tackles that season with a then-school record 175, earning ACC Player of the Year honors and consensus All-America honors. More than a sure tackler, Davis had a penchant for forcing opponents to cough up the ball. He claimed 10 forced fumbles and eight recovered fumbles in his career. Both are school records.

Many see that Jeff Davis is ranked as Clemson's second greatest player, the school's greatest defensive player. He also could be called the school's greatest team leader, and for years, he continued that leadership, serving Clemson University as the Director of the "Call me Mister" program.

Davis was a common denominator on two of Clemson's greatest teams--the sixth-ranked 1978 squad and the 1981 National Championship team. He was Captain of the defense in 1981, and in this role, he led a Tiger point prevention unit with 175 tackles. He was named the Defensive Player of the Game in Clemson's 22-15 victory over Nebraska that gave the Tigers the National Championship.

He was the 1995 Clemson Ring of Honor Inductee as a model of consistency. He had at least 10 tackles in 22 of his last 23 games and had 30 double figure games in his 40-game career. He led the Clemson team in tackles 25 times.

In 1981, Davis set a standard for defensive players by being named ACC Player of the Year, just the second defensive player in league history to win the award. He was a first-team All-American that season by UPI, the Football Coaches, Football Writers, Football News and the Walter Camp Foundation.
Upon the completion of his Clemson career, Davis played six years with distinction with the Tampa Bay Bucs. He played 83 games in the NFL and started 72 between 1982-87, and led the Bucs in tackles three of those six seasons.

1982 Clemson Tigers Football Coach Danny Ford

The 1982 Clemson Tigers football team represented Clemson University during the 1982 college football season as a member of the Atlantic Coast Conference (ACC). Danny Ford was the head football coach for his fifth of twelve seasons. The Tigers completed their eighty-seventh season overall and their thirtieth in the Atlantic Coast Conference with a record of 9-1-1; 6-0-0 in the ACC. The Tigers came in 1st in the ACC out of 7 active ACC teams. Nelson Stokely was the offensive coordinator. Homer Jordan and Terry Kinard were the team captains. This year, with a great coach after a Championship Season, the Clemson Tigers played great football

If I am out of line, on the NCAA, please skip this part. Somehow whenever smaller, less important teams do something well like win a national Championship the NCAA seems to like to step in a ruin the party. Clemson was placed on probation near the end of this season for recruiting violations, and was ineligible for a bowl bid. Some think it was because Clemson won the National Championship and not a team the corrupt NCAA was supporting. Who knows? In this book about Clemson, I give my support to the Tigers and not to the faux Tigers in the NCAA.

"I was a senior on the 1982 team, and we voted as seniors to accept the unprecedented extra year of probation which the ACC handed down on top of two year NCAA sanctions. We were offered the invitation to play SMU in the Cotton Bowl, and turned it down so that the future teams at Clemson could accept a bowl invitation in 1985." (Carl Martin). Why is it that when adults mete out punishment, it is student athletes who get hurt? I really would like to feel differently but please note this is the fifth Great Moments book I have written. Nobody escapes the scourge of the corrupt NCAA with all of their rich and famous officials. Unless...

The home opener was not the first game this year. Instead, on Sept 6 at #7 ranked Georgia's Sanford Stadium in Athens, GA, this famous rival Bulldogs beat the former champion Clemson Tigers by no more than a hair. L (7–13). More and more fans were able to squeeze into larger and larger stadiums as in the 1980's there was a lot of building going on. On Sept 18, for the first time in a while, the always-tough Boston College Eagles played the #16 Clemson Fighting Tigers at home to a tie in the home opener at Memorial Stadium on the campus of Clemson University in Clemson, SC T (17-17).

On Sept 25 at home, Clemson beat Western Carolina W (21–10) before 61,369. On Oct 2 at home the Tigers beat the Kentucky Wildcats W (24–6). On Oct 9 at Virginia in Scott Stadium, Charlottesville, VA, Clemson pummeled the Wahoos W (48–0). Then, on Oct 16 at home, the #20 Tigers beat the Duke Blue Devils W (49–14). On Oct 23 in the Textile Bowl at NC State's Carter–Finley Stadium in Raleigh, NC, the #18 Tigers beat the Wolfpack W (38–29).

On Nov 6 at home playing #18 North Carolina, the #13 Clemson Tigers managed to beat the Tar Heels W (16–13). On Nov 13, the eternally tough #18 ranked Maryland Terrapins took on the #11 Tigers at Byrd Stadium in College Park, MD and lost W (24–22). On Nov 20, at home in the regular season finale, the big in-state rival South Carolina in the Battle of the Palmetto State lost in a nice match W (24-6 before a great crowd of 66,210.

#10 Clemson had a good year and got to go to Japan's National Olympic Stadium in Tokyo, Japan to play an always-tough Wake Forest team in the Mirage Bowl. As tough a game as it was, it was a treat for the players and the Clemson Tigers emerged victorious W (21–17) before 80,000 spectators.

Player Highlights Terry Kinard, S, 1978-82

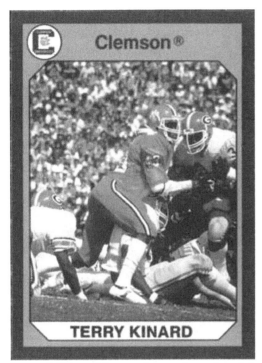

Terry Kinard was a dominant defensive back during his tenure at Clemson. He was Clemson's first of four unanimous All-America selections and the only one until 2006.

In the position of safety, hailing from Sumter, S.C., he remains the Tigers' only two-time consensus All-American. As Clemson went 12-0 and won the national title for coach Danny Ford in 1981, Kinard led the Tigers with six interceptions and added 95 tackles. He returned for his senior season in 1982 to record 89 tackles and another six picks. He is Clemson's career leader in interceptions with 17 and leads all Clemson defensive backs with 294 career stops.

Kinard is recognized as one of the best Tiger defensive backs in history. He was yet another great piece for Clemson's national championship defense alongside Jeff Davis

Player Highlights Homer Jordan (1979-82).

Jordan has the distinction of being Danny Ford's QB in the championship season. This national championship quarterback deserves his due. He played in an era of great defense and hard-nosed rushing attacks, yet was a critical piece to some of the best Clemson football teams. He was the Clemson offensive MVP in the 1981

Clemson®

HOMER JORDAN

Orange Bowl that gave the Tigers their program's National Championship.

He left it all out on the field that night. After winning the game, he passed out from heat exhaustion. In 1981, he had the second most passing TDs and the highest passing efficiency in the ACC. His stats don't tell the whole tory though. His combined record as a junior and senior at Clemson was 21-1-1. He was a top Clemson QB. He was a great one for sure.

1983 Clemson Tigers Football Coach Danny Ford

The 1983 Clemson Tigers football team represented Clemson University during the 1983 college football season as a member of the Atlantic Coast Conference (ACC). Danny Ford was the head football coach for his sixth of twelve seasons. The Tigers completed their eighty-eighth season overall and their thirty-first in the Atlantic Coast Conference with a record of 9-1-1; 7-0-0 in the ACC. The Tigers came in 1st in the ACC out of 8 active ACC teams. Nelson Stokely was the offensive coordinator. James Farr and James Robinson were the team captains. This year, with a great coach again, the Clemson Tigers played great football. Clemson was on probation for recruiting violations, and was ineligible for the ACC championship or a bowl bid.

On Sept 3, to begin the home season at Memorial Stadium on the campus of Clemson University, Clemson, SC, the Tigers overwhelmed the Catamounts of Western Carolina W (44–10) before an opening day crowd of 69,962. On Sept 10, Clemson picked up its only loss of the year at Boston College's Alumni Stadium, Chestnut Hill, MA L (16–31). On Sept 17, at home the Tigers settled for their only other mar on their record with a tie (16-16) against the Georgia Bulldogs. On Sept 24, the other Georgia team came to Clemson and the Tigers defeated the Georgia Tech Yellow Jackets W (41-14). On Oct 8 for the third home game in a row, the Tigers defeated the Virginia Wahoos W (42-21.

Duke was next on Oct 15 at Wallace Wade Stadium • Durham, NC, W (38–31). On Oct 22, at home, the Tigers beat NC State's Wolfpack in the Textile Bowl W (27-17). At home again on Oct 29, Wake Forest played tough football and came close to upsetting Clemson W (24-17). On Nov 5, Clemson defeated #10 North Carolina at Kenan Memorial Stadium in Chapel Hill, NC W (16–3). The following week on Nov 12 at home, the Tigers defeated the Maryland Terrapins W (52-27). In the season finale, with no ACC championship though no losses in the ACC, and no Bowl games to be played, the Battle of the Palmetto State was the next and final item on the season's agenda. The Tigers won this game W (22-13) for a great season record of 9-1-1 and an ACC record of 7-0-0. That's great Clemson football.

Player Highlights Rod McSwain CB 1980-1983

The role of the cornerback has changed a lot over the years from the 1980's to today. Cornerbacks, in the early 80's were expected to cover wide receivers but they were basically linebackers who were lined outside of the eight-man box.

The reason was that most teams did not throw the ball regularly. The wish-bone, the single wing, the flex bone, and the I-Formation dominated the early part of the 80's so cornerbacks had to play more run support than they had to play the pass. They were not interested in getting burned by a pass in their area but they were not tested as often as today.

In picture on next page, Rod is blocking a punt!

Rod McSwain not only excelled in the double duty, he mastered it.

McSwain was called a a lock down cornerback from Caroleen, NC. He had the size to play linebacker, but he was fast enough to play corner. He really helped the Clemson teams, including the championship 1981 team put together by Coach Danny Ford.

McSwain was taken in the 3rd round of the 1984 draft by the Atlanta Falcons, who then traded him to New England. He enjoyed a 6-year career with the Patriots where he had 6 career interceptions and a multitude of pass break ups and tackles.

It's hard to find highlight film on McSwain, because the majority of his career was played under a television ban, due to probations in effect.

1984 Clemson Tigers Football Coach Danny Ford

The 1984 Clemson Tigers football team represented Clemson University during the 1984 college football season as a member of the Atlantic Coast Conference (ACC). Danny Ford was the head football coach for his seventh of twelve seasons. The Tigers completed their eighty-eighth season overall and their thirty-first in the Atlantic Coast Conference with a record of 7-4-0; 5-2-0 in the ACC. The Tigers came in 2nd in the ACC out of 8 active ACC teams. Nelson Stokely was the offensive coordinator. Mike Eppley, and William Perry were the team captains. This year, with a great coach again, the Clemson Tigers played great football. Clemson was on probation for recruiting violations, and was ineligible for the ACC championship or post season play.

On Sept 1 in the home opener at Memorial Stadium on the campus of Clemson University in Clemson, SC, the Clemson Tigers began the season with a nice victor W (40-& over the Appalachian State Mountaineers. On Sept 8, at Virginia's Scott Stadium in Charlottesville, VA, Clemson's Tigers shut-out the Wahoos, W (55–0). After a week break, on Sept 22, at #20 Georgia, the #2 ranked Clemson Tigers met with its first defeat of the season in a nail-biter L (23-26). On Sept 29, at #20 Georgia Tech 's Grant Field in Atlanta, GA, #13 Clemson found its second close loss in a row. L (21–28). On Oct 6 at home, The Tigers defeated the North Carolina Tar Heels W (20-12).

On Oct 20, at home, the Tigers beat the Duke Blue Devils W (54-21). Next on Oct 27, at North Carolina State in Carter–Finley Stadium, Raleigh, NC in the Textile Bowl, Clemson prevailed W (35–24). On Nov 3 at home the Tigers beat the Wake Forest Demon Deacons W (37-14). On Nov 10, at home, Clemson defeated Virginia Tech W (17-10). The third loss of the Clemson season came on Nov 17 at Maryland in Memorial Stadium, Baltimore, MD L (23–4). In the season finale on Nov 24, in the Battle of the Palmetto State the Tigers lost the battle to the Gamecocks in a close one L (21-22).

Player Highlights Mike Eppley QB (1980-84)

Eppley took over in 1983 following the departure of Clemson's national champion QB, Homer Jordan. The Tigers had been whacked by probation prior to the start of 1983 and was therefore unable to officially win the ACC. Clemson was robbed by officialdom of another great record.

Nevertheless, Eppley led Clemson to a perfect ACC

record in a year in which they finished 9-1-1 and beat a top 10 UNC in Chapel Hill. UNC (along with UVA) had pushed for the additional penalties, making the win all the sweeter and inspiring a fan to make a sign reading "King of the Heel."

In that '83 season, Eppley had the best passing efficiency and the second-best completion percentage in the ACC. Over his career he passed for more TDs and fewer INTs than Jordan, but Clemson's dominance faded in 1984 as the probation began to show on the field and they only finished 7-4. Even then, Eppley led the ACC in passing TDs and total TDs.

DONALD IGWEBUIKE

Player Highlights
Donald Igwebuike K
1980-84

Igwebuike made the third-team AP All-American team simply because he booted the longest field goal in the ACC in each of his last three seasons. Donald led the nation and the ACC in field goal percentage with a .941 senior season mark.

His story is like that of other kicking sport greats who took a shot at football. Igwebuike came to Clemson to play soccer, and he did play in two NCAA tournaments in 1980 and 1981but he went for football for his own reasons. He tied for 13th in the nation as a senior in kick-scoring with an 8.1 average...a perfect 43-43 on PATs in his career and made 32-43 field goals

He is the only Tiger to boot at least one 50-yard field goal in four straight seasons. He kicked five career field goals of 50 or more yards to set Clemson records. In his last three seasons, he was phenomenal at 107-180 on non-returnable kickoffs.

Coach Danny Ford built a National Championship team on defense, and the leg of Donald Igwebuike. In 1981 the Tigers won by scores of 10-8, 13-3, 13-5 respectively.

Igwebuike kicked three field goals (41, 41, 36yds) in the Orange Bowl game against Nebraska. A field position, and distance kicking specialist, Igwebuike definitely is an all-star on anybody's list.

When he was out of Clemson, he was a 10th-round pick of the Tampa Bay Bucs after the 1984 season. He played from 1985 to 1989. He was no slouch with his foot as he is the fourth-place all-time scorer for the Buccaneers with 416 overall points.

He would often kick barefoot. Igwebuike also played for the 1990 Minnesota Vikings and he put time in the Canadian Football League with the Baltimore Stallions in 1994 and the Memphis Mad Dogs in 1995.

Igwebuike lasted 6 years in the NFL before kicking in the CFL with three different teams.

Player Highlights #7 William Perry (1981-84)

As a freshman at Clemson, Perry helped the Tigers to the 1981 national title. That season, Perry came off the bench to 48 tackles and four sacks, including two in a key win over North Carolina.

That was only the start for the 300-pound lineman, who earned his nickname as a senior at Clemson after earning consensus All-America honors as a junior. In his final season in 1984, Perry led the nation with 27 tackles for a loss and had 100 tackles – as a nose guard – to earn ACC Player of the Year honors.

Only three ACC defensive players and two players from Clemson since then have earned such honors.

"The Refrigerator" made a great debut at Clemson. They say he had a knack for the "big" debut, even before he helped the Chicago Bears' dominant defense to the Super Bowl as a rookie in 1985.

The

Fridge Starring on the Bob Hope Show

The job of William, "The Refrigerator" Perry was to patrol the middle of the Clemson defense from 1981-84. The Refrigerator was perhaps the most feared defensive player in the South. Opposing defensive coordinators had to make special plans, sometimes triple teaming assignments for Clemson's 320-pound anchor of the line.

Perry, who came to Clemson as a then unheard of 310-pound freshman, held legendary status at Clemson through his career and still. All the stories you heard about "The Fridge" are true. From the time that he once blocked the opposing team's punt by shoving the upback into the punter, to Perry Tuttle taking him to lunch at a McDonald's and spending $22, Perry was a superhuman almost fictional character. He was also a sportswriter's dream. "Even when I was little I was big," said Perry, perhaps the Yogi Berra of Clemson football from an interview standpoint.

On the field, he was a three-time All-American, joining Anthony Simmons as the only Tigers who could make that claim. In 1984, he led the nation in tackles for loss with 27 and he tied the Clemson single season sack record with 10. He was a finalist for the Lombardi Award that season and was the ACC Player of the Year in 1984, the second defensive player in league history to win the honor.

In 1985, Perry was a first-round draft pick of the Chicago Bears. As a freshman at Clemson he started on the Tigers National Championship team. As a rookie in the NFL he started on the Bears Super Bowl Championship team, the first of his nine great NFL seasons.

1985 Clemson Tigers Football Coach Danny Ford

The 1985 Clemson Tigers football team represented Clemson University during the 1985 college football season as a member of the Atlantic Coast Conference (ACC). Danny Ford was the head football coach for his eighth of twelve seasons. The Tigers completed their eighty-ninth season overall and their thirty-second in the Atlantic Coast Conference with a record of 6-6-0; 4-3-0 in the ACC. The Tigers came in 4th in the ACC out of 8 active ACC teams. Nelson Stokely was the offensive coordinator. Steve Berlin and Steve Reese were the team captains.

On Sept 14 @ Virginia Tech in Lane Stadium, Blacksburg, VA the Tigers beat the Hokies W (20–17). On September 21 in the home opener at Memorial Field on the campus of Clemson University in Clemson SC, the Tigers lost to the Georgia Bulldogs, L (13–20) before 80,473. On Sept 28, at home, Clemson lost to Georgia Tech L (3–14). On Oct 5 at Kentucky's Commonwealth Stadium in Lexington, KY, the Tigers beat the Wildcats L (7–26). On Oct 12, at home, Clemson beat Virginia W (27-24)

Clemson traveled to Duke on October 19 at Duke's Wallace Wade Stadium in Durham, NC, and beat the Blue Devils W (21–9). On Oct 26, the next week at home, the Tigers defeated NC State in the Textile Bowl W (39–10). Then on Nov 2, at home Clemson defeated Wake Forest W (26-10). On Nov 9 at North Carolina's Kenan Memorial Stadium in Chapel Hill, NC, the Tigers were overcome by one point L (20–21). Then, on Nov 16 at home, Clemson was defeated by Maryland l (31-34). The next week in the season finale, aka the Battle of the Palmetto State, the Tigers managed to beat the Gamecocks by a touchdown W (24-17).

Clemson qualified for a Bowl game and played on December 21st against Minnesota in the Independence Bowl in Independence Stadium, Shreveport, LA and lost by a touchdown. L (13–20) before 42,800 fans.

1986 Clemson Tigers Football Coach Danny Ford

The 1986 Clemson Tigers football team represented Clemson University during the 1986 college football season as a member of the Atlantic Coast Conference (ACC). Danny Ford was the head football coach for his ninth of twelve seasons. The Tigers completed their ninetieth season overall and their thirty-third in the Atlantic Coast Conference with a record of 8-2-2; 5-1-1 in the ACC. The Tigers came in 1st in the ACC out of 8 active ACC teams. Terrence Flagler and Terence Mack were the team captains.

Clemson began the season on Sept 13 losing one of just two games that it would lose in the entire season. This game was the home opener in Memorial Stadium on the campus of Clemson University, Clemson, SC. The Hokies of Virginia Tech defeated the Clemson Fighting Tigers L (14-20) before 75,930. On Sept 20, at #14 Georgia's in Sanford Stadium, Athens, GA, Clemson prevailed W (31–28). Then on Sept 27 at Georgia Tech's Grant Field in Atlanta, GA, Clemson won W (27–3). On Oct 4, at home, the Tigers shut out The Citadel W (24–0). On Oct11 at Virginia's Scott Stadium in Charlottesville, VA, Clemson won another W (31–17).

On Oct 18 at home against Duke, the #17 ranked Tigers walloped the Blue Devils W (35–3). On Oct 25 at #20 NC State's Carter–Finley Stadium in Raleigh, NC, playing in the annual Textile Bowl, Clemson bowed to the Wolfpack L (3–27). On Nov 1 at Wake Forest's Groves Stadium in Winston-Salem, NC, the Tigers squeaked by the Demon Deacons W (28–20). On Nov 8 at home the Clemson Fighting Tigers defeated the North Carolina Tar Heels W (38-10). On Nov 15, at Maryland at Memorial Stadium, Baltimore, MD, the teams played to a tie T (17–17). On Nov 22, at home, South Carolina tied the Tigers in the Battle of the Palmetto State T (21–21).

The #21 Tigers were invited to the Gator Bowl on Dec 27, 1986 to play #20 Stanford in Gator Bowl Stadium in Jacksonville Florida before 80,104. The Tigers defeated the Cardinal in a well-played close game W (27-21).

Player Highlights Terrence Flagler TB 1984-1986

Flagler was a first-team All-American pick by the Football Writers Association and runner-up in the ACC Player-of-the-Year voting in 1986. He finished 13th in the nation in rushing, but he was also superb coming in third in yards-per-carry among players with at least 800 yards.

He was the third Clemson player to score four touchdowns in a single game. When this was written he still held the Clemson single game record for all-purpose running with 274 yards at Wake Forest in 1986. He also held the Clemson rushing record for yards gained in a three-game, five-game, six-game and seven-game series. Flagler set Clemson regular season record for yards per game with 106.9 figure in 1986...

After Clemson, he was drafted by the San Francisco 49ers in the first round (25th pick) in 1987 draft. He earned two Super Bowl Championship rings with the 49ers. He played in the spring of 2000 for Jacksonville in the Arena Football League.

He was very resilient as he played for five different professional Football teams from 1987 to 2003. That is a lot of football.

1987 Clemson Tigers Football Coach Danny Ford

The 1987 Clemson Tigers football team represented Clemson University during the 1987 college football season as a member of the Atlantic Coast Conference (ACC). Danny Ford was the head football coach for his tenth of twelve seasons. The Tigers completed their ninety-first season overall and their thirty-fourth in the Atlantic Coast Conference with a record of 10-2-0; 6-1-0 in the ACC. The Tigers came in 1st in the ACC out of 8 active ACC teams. Michael Dean Perry and John Phillips were the team captains.

On Sept 5 in the home opener played on the campus of Clemson University at Memorial Field in Clemson, SC, Coach Danny Ford's Clemson Fighting Tigers shut out Western Carolina to get the season rolling W (43-0). On Sept 12, at Virginia Tech's Lane Stadium in Blacksburg, VA, the #10 Tigers won again W (22–10). Back home, on Sept 19, the #18 Georgia Bulldogs were defeated by Clemson's Tigers W (21-20).

Game Highlights Clemson 21, Georgia 20

Sept. 19, 1987 at Clemson, SC

Clemson was down 20-16 with about five minutes left in this game when Rusty Seyle hit a punt that was downed by Chinedu Ohan on the half-yard line. A couple of plays later, the Clemson Tigers defense swarmed on Georgia quarterback John Jackson and tackled him for a safety and the two points that come with it.

The Tigers took the "safety kickoff," which was a punt with about five minutes left and drove the ball down the field, one successful play after another behind the running of Terry Allen and Wesley McFadden.

Clemson was behind by two at this point and successfully drove the ball to the three yard-line. Clemson brought out kicker David Treadwell to make the winning kick. It was just like an extra point. Thigs got confused near the end of the game and it was a little hairy because the Clemson team was all out of timeouts. Nonetheless Coach Ford got the Clemson squad / the field goal team on the field and Treadwell got the kick through the uprights with just two seconds left.

Treadwell a great kicker and this was not the first time he had amazed the crowd. He had a number of game winning kicks. He had done the same thing the year before at Georgia, kicking a 46-yard field goal to win 31-28 in Athens. I wonder if Treadwell had his own horseshoe.

In addition to the success so far in the season, Clemson also won four more home games in the following five home encounters. The first was when #9 ranked Clemson went against Georgia Tech on Oct 3 W (22-12). The second was when the #8 Tigers went against the Virginia Wahoos on Oct 10 W (33–12). And then the third was when #7 Clemson played Duke's Blue Devils on Oct 17 for the win W (17-10). At this point, at 6-0 for the season, The Tigers suffered a tough home loss to NC State in the Textile Bowl on Oct 24 L (28-30). The fourth win of the last five home games came on Oct 31, when the #14 Tigers defeated the Wake Forest Demon Deacons W (31-17).

On Nov 7, at North Carolina's Kenan Memorial Stadium, Chapel Hill, NC, the Tigers beat the Tar Heels in a close game W (13–10) Next on Nov 14 at home, the Tigers back to #9 nationally, handily beat Maryland W 45–16. Now, looking for a nice top ten finish and a great Bowl Game, the #8 Clemson Tigers were disappointed in the Battle of the Palmetto State as #12 South Carolina pulled out all the stops and defeated CU at South Carolina's Williams-Brice Stadium • in Columbia, SC L (7-20 Clemson was ranked #14 after the game and were invited to the Citrus Bowl.

Citrus Bowl

On Jan 1, 1988, the #14 Clemson Tigers squared off in the Florida Citrus Bowl Game against the #20 Penn State Nittany Lions in the Citrus Bowl Stadium, Orlando, FL (Florida Citrus Bowl). Clemson beat up Penn State in the game W (35–10) and finished #11 in the AP poll and #12 in the Coach's Poll for the year. The Tigers had previously won the ACC Championship.

Player Highlights John Phillips OG 1984-1987

PHILLIPS & PERRY

John Phillips was named first-team All-American as a junior and became a second-team All-American as a senior. He made the All-ACC team two consecutive years and captured the Jacobs Blocking Trophy for South Carolina two years in a row.

Phillips had the single-season record of 103 knockdown blocks as a junior, he concluded his career with 245 knockdown blocks, which at the time was third in Clemson history. He is still the only Tiger with a pair of 100-knockdown block seasons, he had 100 in 1986 and 103 in 1987.

Phillips started 32 games and played in 47 for his career. He was co-captain of Clemson's 1987 team with Michael Dean Perry. He was a graduate assistant coach at Clemson for 1990 and 1991. Phillips was inducted into Clemson's Hall of Fame in Fall in 1999.

Player Highlights Michael Dean Perry, 1984-87

Some knew him as the Refrigerator's brother. But, he was more than just a familiar name along the Clemson defensive line. Michael Dean Perry picked up right where his brother left off and he exceeded him in some areas. Like his brother, he was one of a handful of defensive players to win ACC Defensive Player of the Year (1987). Michael also broke William's ACC records for career tackles for a loss (61) and career sacks (28).

He remains Clemson's sole record holder for career tackles for a loss and was tied for career sacks by Gaines Adams in 2006. Perry's best season came in 1987 when he recorded 24 tackles for a loss and 10 sacks as Clemson went 10-2 with an ACC title.

1988 Clemson Tigers Football Coach Danny Ford

The 1988 Clemson Tigers football team represented Clemson University during the 1988 college football season as a member of the Atlantic Coast Conference (ACC). Danny Ford was the head football coach for his eleventh of twelve seasons. The Tigers completed their ninety-second season overall and their thirty-fifth in the Atlantic Coast Conference with a record of 10-2-0; 6-1-0 in the ACC. The Tigers came in 1st in the ACC out of 8 active ACC teams. Rodney Williams, and Donnell Woolford were the team captains.

The Tigers began the season with three home games in a row. On Sept 3 in the home opener played on the campus of Clemson University at Memorial Field in Clemson, SC, Coach Danny Ford's Clemson Fighting Tigers defeated Virginia Tech W (40-7) to get the season rolling. On Sept 10, #3 ranked Clemson beat Furman W 23–3 before   80,620. Then, on Sept 17, the Tigers suffered their first loss at home against #10 Florida State in a nail biter L (21-24).

On Sept 24, at Georgia Tech's Bobby Dodd Stadium in Atlanta, GA, the #12 Tigers defeated the unranked Bulldogs W (30-13). Then, at Virginia's Scott Stadium in Charlottesville, VA, Clemson got the best of the Wahoos W 10–7. On Oct 15 at home, the #11 Tigers beat the #22 Duke Blue Devils W (49–17) before a packed house of 83,356. Then, on Oct 22 at #24 ranked NC State's Carter–Finley Stadium in Raleigh, NC in the Textile Bowl, the Wolfpack got the best of the Tigers L (3–10).

On Oct 29 at Wake Forest's Groves Stadium in Winston-Salem, NC, the Tigers defeated the Demon Deacons W 37–14. On Nov 5, at home North Carolina was defeated by Clemson W (37–14). On Nov 12, at Maryland's Byrd Stadium in College Park, MD, the Tigers defeated the Terrapins W (49–25). Then, in the season finale v South Carolina—the Battle of the Palmetto State, the Tigers beat the Gamecocks W 29–10. Of the second year in a row, Clemson accepted an invitation to play in the Citrus Bowl.

Citrus Bowl

On Jan 1, 1989, in the Florida Citrus Bowl post-season game, Coach Danny Ford's #9 Clemson Fighting Tigers defeated Coach Barry Switzer's #10 ranked Oklahoma Sooners in the game played at the Citrus Bowl Stadium in Orlando, FL. The Tigers won W (13-6) The game was seen on ABC TV and by the 53,571 in the stadium.

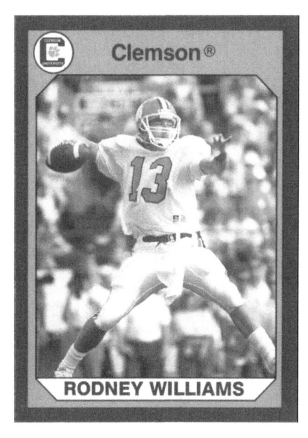

RODNEY WILLIAMS

Player Highlights Rodney Williams QB (1985-88)

Though it was not in the 1981 championship season, Williams was coached by Ring of Honor inductee, Danny Ford. Rodney Williams is without a doubt among the great QBs in a continual team of great Clemson quarterbacks.

He held the record for the most games won by a quarterback (was tied with Boyd at 32), most consecutive passes without interception (122), consecutive games completing a pass (46), most games started by a quarterback (44), and won three straight ACC Championships.

With DeShaun Watson and the impressive cadre before him, all of these records no longer stand but at the time, Rodney Williams was the best and he brought home a lot of fine Clemson victories.

Player Highlights Donnell Woolford (1985-88)

Clemson under coach Danny Ford, was the fifth winningest team in college football in the 1980s and one of the reasons was the play of two-time All-American Donnell Woolford, one of the great Tiger gridders of the century. Woolford was the mainstay of a Clemson defense that helped the Tigers to a 28-6-2 record from 1986-88, an era in which Clemson won the ACC Championship every year.

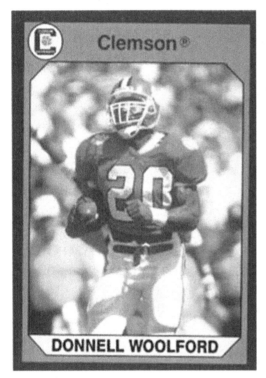

DONNELL WOOLFORD

Woolford was a defensive back who might be regarded as the best modern-day cover corner in school history. In 1987, Woolford, he chalked up five interceptions with no interception return yards. Why no yards? All his interceptions were diving grabs while he was blanketing the opposition.

His interception total dropped to one during his senior year because rarely did the opposition throw in his direction. No receiver that he was assigned to cover caught more than two passes in any game during the 1988 season.

In addition to his job of effectively patrolling the secondary, Woolford was one of the top punt returners in the country. He averaged 15 yards a return in 1987, third best in the nation. He had a pair of opponent back breaking punt returns for touchdowns that year, one against Georgia Tech and one against Wake Forest.

Woolford may best be remembered for his performance in the final game of his career. Playing against Oklahoma's famed Wishbone Offense, Woolford was moved to a rover back position by Clemson defensive coordinator Bill Oliver. It was his job to disrupt the attack, which he did. Oklahoma failed to score a touchdown in a game for just the second time in the decade of the 1980s.

A first-round draft choice of the Chicago Bears, Woolford started for the Bears from 1989-96 and for the Pittsburgh Steelers in 1997. He earned a berth in the Pro Bowl in 1993.He is clearly a Clemson great!

1989 Clemson Tigers Football Coach Danny Ford

The 1989 Clemson Tigers football team represented Clemson University during the 1989 college football season as a member of the Atlantic Coast Conference (ACC). Danny Ford was the head football coach for his twelfth and last of twelve seasons. The Tigers completed their ninety-third season overall and their thirty-sixth in the Atlantic Coast Conference with a record of 10-2-0; 5-2 in the ACC. The Tigers came in 3rd in the ACC out of 8 active ACC teams.

The Tigers began the season with a home game. On Sept 2 in the home opener played on the campus of Clemson University at Memorial Field in Clemson, SC, Coach Danny Ford's #12 Clemson Fighting Tigers shut-out Furman W (30-0) to get the season off to a fine start before 80,508 fans. On Sept 9 at No. 16 Florida State in Doak Campbell Stadium, Tallahassee, FL, the Tigers beat the Seminoles W (34–23).

Game Highlight Clemson 34, Florida State 23
Sept. 9, 1989 at Tallahassee, FL

This might have been the best performance ever for Clemson. The Tigers were ahead 21-0 in the first quarter after two 73-yard plays. Wayne Simmons had a 73-yard interception return and Terry Allen had a 73-yard run for a touchdown. Allen's run was simply amazing because it took place right before half-time. Clemson was simply trying to run out the clock on a sweep and it went all the way.

The Tigers controlled this game the entire night. Clemson held a nice 34-17 lead with six seconds left before Florida State scored a very late touchdown. This was not a fluke against a poor FSU team. No! This Florida State team ended the season at #2 in the nation in the final

Coach's poll. When you talk to Clemson fans who attend lots of Tiger games, this might have been the most fun they have ever had at a road game. This was the year after the "puntrooskie Game" so Clemson Fans were pretty fired up.

To help with that memory, in the prior year's Florida State against Clemson-- in the famous 1988 "Puntrooskie Game;" Dayne took the snap from center on the play, put the ball between the legs of the upback, Leroy Butler, who then raced down the sideline for 78-yards to the three-yard line. Bobby Bowden's squad orchestrated the play to perfection and it had its intended result—a Clemson loss after the field goal L (21-24).

On Sept 16 at Virginia Tech's Lane Stadium in Blacksburg, VA, the Tigers defeated the Hokies W (27–7). The next week at home, #7 Clemson defeated Maryland W (31-7). On Sept 30, at Duke's Wallace Wade Stadium in Durham, NC, the #7 Tigers fell by a score of L (17–21).

On Oct 7 at home, the #15 Tigers defeated the Wahoos of Virginia W (34-2). On Oct 14 at home, Clemson was defeated by Georgia Tech L 14-30) before 81,550. On Oct 21 in the Textile Bowl at home the Tigers prevailed over NC State's Wolfpack W (30-10). On Oct 28 at home Clemson beat the Wake Forest Demon Deacons W (44-1). Next up v #17 Clemson was North Carolina's Tar Heels at Kenan Memorial Stadium in Chapel Hill, NC W (35-3). Then came the regular season finale against arch rival South Carolina in the Battle of the Palmetto State at Williams-Brice Stadium in Columbia, SC. The Tigers shut out the Gamecocks W (45–0). Clemson was invited to the Gator Bowl

Gator Bowl

On Jan 1, 1989, in the Gator Bowl post-season game, Coach Danny Ford's #14 Clemson Fighting Tigers defeated Coach Don Nehlen's #17 ranked West Virginia Mountaineers in the game played at the Gator Bowl Stadium in Jacksonville, FL. The Tigers won W (27-7) The game was seen on ESPN and by the 82,911 in the stadium.

Player Highlights Terry Allen, RB 1987-89

Terry Allen was noted for his toughness, perhaps the most resilient runner in Clemson history. The native of Georgia was Clemson's top rusher in 1987 and 1988, and only a knee injury prohibited him from leading the team in 1989.

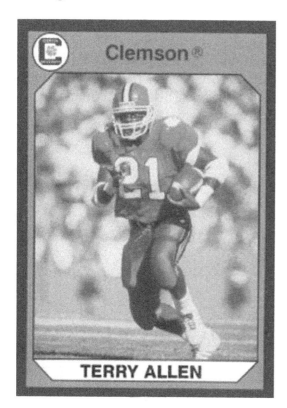

TERRY ALLEN

As is the case with many of the players on this 25-man list, Allen was not a highly recruited player out of high school. In fact, the overriding reason he decided to come to Clemson was Danny Ford's willingness to give him a shot at tailback. Every other school wanted him to be a defensive back because they had measured his speed at less than blazing.

But, those other coaches failed to measure Allen's heart. After red-shirting the 1986 season, Allen burst on the scene in 1987, leading the ACC in rushing and setting a Clemson freshman record. A key victory for the Tigers that year took place against Georgia, a 21-20 verdict. His straight ahead, run over the opposition approach, was pivotal on Clemson's winning touchdown drive. In 1988 as a sophomore, he again led the team in rushing, and the year was climaxed with his selection as the offensive MVP of the Citrus Bowl victory over Oklahoma.

Allen's junior year was a constant battle against injury. He geared up for one last stand against South Carolina, and he responded with 89 yards in the first half, leading Clemson to a convincing lead. But, on his final carry of the first half, he was struck square in the knee, the area that had been giving him trouble. He never carried the ball again for the Tigers.

After that season, Allen decided to turn pro, a decision that was met with criticism due to his injuries. He felt if a team could draft him, they would be responsible for him and realize his work ethic. An injury during a senior year at Clemson would effectively end his career.

The gamble paid off. He was drafted in the 10th round by the Minnesota Vikings. He was injured during 1990, but the Vikings stayed with him. In seven healthy seasons, he has had four 1000-yard seasons and is the only running back in NFL history to come back from torn ACL injuries on both knees.

Chapter 22 Ken Hatfield Era 1990 - 1993

Coach # 22 Ken Hatfield

Year	Coach Record	Record		Conference	
1990	Ken Hatfield	10-2-0	ACC		5–2-0
1991	Ken Hatfield	9-2-1	ACC		6-0-1
1992	Ken Hatfield	5-6-0	ACC		3-5-0
1993	Ken Hatfield	9-3-0	ACC		5-3-01
1993	Tommy West	Bowl Game WIn		Score	20-0

1990 Clemson Tigers Football Coach Ken Hatfield

The 1990 Clemson Tigers football team represented Clemson University during the 1990 college football season as a member of the Atlantic Coast Conference (ACC). Ken Hatfield was the head football coach for his first of four seasons. The Tigers completed their ninety-fourth season overall and their thirty-seventh in the Atlantic Coast Conference with a record of 10-2-0; 5-2-0. They were tied for second in the ACC. out of 8 active ACC teams. Stacy Fields and Vance Hammond were team captains.

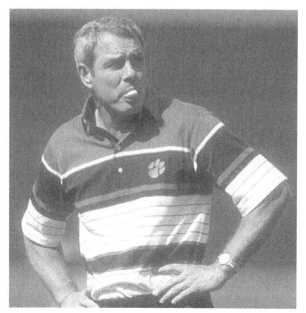

<<< Coach Ken Hatfield

The Tigers began the season with a home game. On Sept 1 in the home opener played on the campus of Clemson University at Memorial Field in Clemson, SC, Coach Ken Hatfield's #10 Clemson Fighting Tigers shut-out Long Beach State W (59-0 to get the season off to a great start before 74,250 fans. On Sept 8, at #14 Virginia's Scott

Stadium in Charlottesville, VA, the Tigers lost to the Wahoos L (7–20) On September 15 at Maryland's Memorial Stadium, the Tigers barely won against the Terrapins in a tough battle W (18-17). On Sept 22 at home Clemson beat Appalachian State W (48–0) before 77,716. On Sept 29, at home the Tigers defeated the Duke Blue Devils W 26–7.

On Oct 6, at home the Tigers defeated Georgia W (34-3). Next, on Oct 13 at #18 Georgia Tech, the #15 Clemson Tigers lost to the Yellow Jackets by two points at Bobby Dodd Stadium in Atlanta, GA L (19–21). On Oct 20 at NC State's Carter–Finley Stadium in Raleigh, NC, in the annual Textile Bowl, the Tigers beat the Wolfpack W (24–17). On Oct 27, at Wake Forest's Groves Stadium in Winston-Salem, NC, the Tigers whipped the Demon Deacons W (24–6) before 25,317 fans. On Nov 3, at home, the #18 Tigers beat North Carolina W (20-3). On Nov 17 at home, in the Battle of the Palmetto State, Clemson defeated South Carolina W (24-15) before a sellout plus of 83,823. For a nice year and a #14 finish, Clemson earned an invitation to the Gator Bowl

Hall of Fame Bowl

On January 1, 1991, the #14 ranked Clemson Fighting Tigers took on the # 16 ranked Illinois Fighting Illini in Tampa Stadium • Tampa, FL in the Hall of Fame Bowl. It was viewed on NBC. The Fighting Tigers shut out the Fighting Illini W (20-0) before 82,911 spectators.

Player Highlights Stacy Long OT 1987-1990

Long was a consensus first-team All-American as a senior and he was First-Team Sporting News All-American as a junior.

He was an Outland Trophy finalist in 1990, the second Tiger so honored. He made First-Team All-ACC twice. Additionally, he had 141 career knockdown blocks, a record for an offensive tackle. He was also two-time ACC Player-of-the-Week in 1990 and a six-time choice in his career. This is more than any other Tiger. Clemson won 40 games from 1987-90, fourth-most in the nation.

Long finished his tenure with Clemson as an 11th-round draft pick for the Bears. He was named to Clemson's Centennial team in 1996 and was inducted into Clemson Hall of Fame in 2004.

Player Highlights Chris Gardocki K/P 1988-1990

Chris Gardocki was a master of both kicking and punting, Gardocki pulled double duty during his time at Clemson, and excelled at both, enjoying a decent career with the Pittsburgh Steelers. If Tiger fans can remember one kicker or punter, it's Chris Gardocki. After all, he did do both.

His achievements as a punter and placekicker are unprecedented in Clemson and college football history. He was even ranked top kicker in college football for the 1990s.

Only one player in NCAA history has ranked in the top 10 in the nation in punting and field goals per game in two different seasons and Chris Gardocki is that player. His abilities in both aspects of the game gave Clemson one of the top special teams in the nation from 1988-90.

In 1989, as a sophomore, Gardocki ranked sixth in the nation in field goals and was 10th in punting with a 42.7 average. As a junior, he was fourth in both areas, averaging 1.73 field goals per game to go with a 44.34 punting average.

He is a native of Stone Mountain, GA. Gardocki tied an ACC record for the longest field goal with a 57-yarder against Appalachian State in 1990, and hc saved his longest punt for his final punt in Death Valley, a 78-yarder in the 1990 South Carolina game.

He concluded his career with 63 field goals and had a record 72 consecutive PATs. As a punter, he averaged 43.48 yards boot for his career, including a 39.1 net average. A one-step punter, Gardocki had just one punt blocked his entire career at Clemson and has never had a punt blocked in the NFL. The Tigers were 30-6 in Gardocki's career.

Gardocki was an All-America punter all three years he played in Tigertown. Gardocki became the starting punter for the Cleveland Browns of the NFL. He was an All-Pro selection in 1996 when he led the NFL in net punting.

Gardocki was second-team All-American as a junior and a third-team choice as a sophomore place-kicker. He was an honorable mention choice at punter as well by UPI as a freshman, sophomore, and junior. He ranked fourth in punting and tied for fourth in placekicking in the nation as a junior.

Ironically, Gardocki was a two-time All-America placekicker at Clemson, but has been a punter in the National Football League. He was an honorable mention. He was a third-round draft pick of the Chicago Bears in 1991, he left Clemson after his junior year. He was an All-Pro choice with Colts in 1996. Then he went with the Cleveland Browns.

He was named to Clemson's Centennial team in April 1996. He is ranked as Clemson's #19 gridder of all-time by a panel of historians in 1999. He was inducted into the Clemson Hall of Fame in 2001. He could sure kick

1991 Clemson Tigers Football Coach Ken Hatfield

The 1991 Clemson Tigers football team represented Clemson University during the 1991 college football season as a member of the Atlantic Coast Conference (ACC). Ken Hatfield was the head football coach for his second of four seasons. The Tigers completed their ninety-fifth season overall and their thirty-eighth in the Atlantic Coast Conference with a record of 9-2-1; 6-0-1. They took first place in the ACC. out of 8 active ACC teams. Rob Bodine, DeChane Cameron, and Levon Kirkland were team captains.

The Clemson Fighting Tigers began the season with a home game. On Sept 7 in the home opener played on the campus of Clemson University at Memorial Field in Clemson, SC, Coach Ken Hatfield's #8 Clemson Fighting Tigers shut-out Appalachian State W (34-0) to get the season rolling quickly in a positive direction. On Sept 21, Temple played # 8 Clemson at home in Memorial Stadium. The Tigers beat the Owls W (37-7) before 74,575. On Sept 28, at home Clemson barely got by a tough Georgia Tech Team W (9-7) On Oct 5, at Sanford Stadium in Athens, #6 Clemson lost to the Yellow Jackets L (12–27) before 85,434 fans. Then on Oct 12 at home against Virginia, Clemson tied the Wahoos T (20-20).

On Oct 26 at home against # 12 NC State, the Tigers beat the Wolfpack W (29-19) before 79,832. On Nov 2 at home, the Tigers beat the Demon Deacons W 28–10. Then a week later on Nov 9 at North Carolina at Kenan Memorial Stadium in Chapel Hill, the Tigers won W (21–6). On Nov 16, at home, the Fighting Tigers defeated the Terrapins W (40-7) before 71, 881.

On Nov 23, in the Battle of the Palmetto State at South Carolina's Williams-Brice Stadium, Columbia, SC, #12 Clemson beat the Gamecocks W (41-24). On Dec 1, in the season finale, the Tigers defeated the Blue Devils of Duke in the Tokyo Dome Japan in the Coca Cola Classic W (33-21) before 50,000. For a great season, Clemson accepted a bid to the Citrus Bowl.

Citrus Bowl

On Jan 1, 1992, the #13 ranked Tigers of Clemson lost to #14 California in the Florida Citrus Bowl played at Citrus Bowl Stadium in Orlando, Florida before 64,192. The score was L 13-27).

Player Highlights Ed McDaniel LB 1988-1991

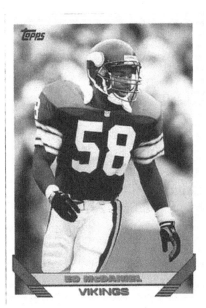

McDaniel was a first-team All-American by College and Pro Football Weekly and an honorable mention choice by Football News. He was listed as a third-team AP All-American and a first-team All-ACC choice by AP/ACSWA.

Ed was the number-one tackler on the defense that led the nation in rushing defense in 1991. His 114 tackles were tops for Clemson. He led the Tigers in tackles three of the four years he played, including 1990 when Clemson won the national title in total defense, 1991 when Clemson won the national rushing defense crown and 1988 when the Tigers also ranked in the top five nationally in total defense

Ed McDaniel ranks fourth in Clemson history in total tackles with 389. In a given season, he went over the century mark in tackles three times. He was one of four semifinalists for the 1991 Butkus Award. When he closed out his Clemson career, he was a fifth-round draft pick of the Vikings in 1992. He started at LB with the Vikings from 1994-2001. Ed was proud to be named a Pro-Bowler in 1998.

Player Highlights Jeb Flesch OG 1988-1991

Flesch was a first-team All-American by AP, UPI, Football News, and Walter Camp, and he was a first-team All-ACC choice. He was also the leader of the offensive line that led the Tigers to the ACC title in total offense in 1991.

Flesch was team leader in knockdown blocks during the 1991 regular season with 72. He led the team in that category in six different games with 262 knockdown blocks for his career. This was just 10 shy of tying the Clemson record.

He was a guy the team could count on. In terms of offensive action, he was involved in 2,630 plays for his career. He started 45 straight games, Flesch ended his career ranked second in Clemson history in career starts by an offensive lineman and second in starts by any player regardless of position.

He signed as a free-agent with the Seahawks in 1992.

Player Highlights Rob Bodine MG 1988-1991

Rob Bodine was the guy Clemson counted on to stop the run. He was the first defender a running back ever saw. He was first-team All-American in 1991 by the Football Writers, a second-team selection by AP, Sporting News, and College & Pro Football Weekly.

Bodine was an honorable mention All-American by UPI and Football News. He was First-Team All-ACC by AP/ACSWA in 1991 for the second straight year. He also led the nation in tackles for loss (27) as a senior, tying the school record.

He ranked fourth in school history for career tackles for loss with 48. He also ranked 20th in Tiger history in tackles. As noted, he anchored the defensive line on the unit that led the nation in rushing defense in 1991.Bodine accomplished all of this in just three years of Clemson playing time, He had played at North Dakota as a freshman. He was the only walk-on non-kicker in Tiger history to be a first-team All-American. He was a great Clemson player.

Player Highlights Levon Kirkland (1988-91)

Having been victimized by NCAA sanctions several times in its history, it was always a great sign to see the light at the end of the sanctions tunnel. Clemson re-emerged from NCAA sanctions and a recruiting scandal in the late 1980s with defense once again at the forefront.

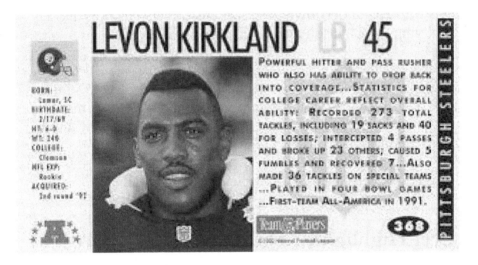

After recording 71 tackles as a freshman, Levon Kirkland enjoyed a breakout game at the end of his sophomore season in the Gator Bowl. With nine tackles and a sack, Kirkland was the Gator Bowl MVP as the Tigers' defense held Heisman finalist Major Harris to 119 passing yards in a 27-7 win over West Virginia.

Kirkland was a second-team All-American as a junior and a consensus first-team All-American as a senior, leaving school with 273 career tackles and 19 career sacks.

Many would on the spot declare Levon Kirkland to be the most popular Clemson football player in recent history. He was a three-time All-ACC first team selection and two-time All-American, Kirkland was a mainstay of four straight seasons in which Clemson lost just two games. The Tigers were 39-8-1 in his four years, with Coach Danny Ford and Ken Hatfield. He teamed with classmate and linebacker Ed McDaniel to make Clemson one of the most feared defenses in the NCAA.

In many ways, he was like the great Anthony Simmons, in that he was an impact player from his freshman year. When Clemson clinched the ACC Championship in 1988 at Maryland, Kirkland had one of the finest games of his career, collecting a career high 13 tackles, including three for loss, a sack and to top that off, he also caused a fumble. In 1989 as a sophomore, he was the MVP of the Gator Bowl victory over West Virginia as he chased Heisman Trophy Candidate Major Harris all over the Jacksonville facility.

In 1990, Kirkland was a defensive demon of the only Clemson unit in history to lead the nation in total defense. Kirkland, a virtually unrecruited player out of high school, was a finalist for the Butkus Award, the only underclassman on the list. The 1991 defense, again with Kirkland leading the way, led the nation in rushing defense. Kirkland was a semifinalist for the Lombardi Award that year.

Kirkland concluded his career as one of just three Clemson players in history to be named first-team All-ACC. Like Michael Dean Perry, Kirkland was a second-round NFL draft choice who has gone on to a celebrated career. His career included being a first-team All-Pro selection who started in the Pro Bowl. He also led the Steelers in tackles in the 1996 Super Bowl.

By 1996, he was recognized as one of the top inside linebackers in the league, and had a stellar performance in Super Bowl XXX against the Dallas Cowboys at the end of the season. In that game, the Steelers defense held the Cowboys to just 15 first downs and Emmitt Smith and the Cowboys powerful running attack to just 56 yards, despite losing 27-17 in large part due to two key interceptions thrown by Steelers quarterback Neil O'Donnell. Kirkland had 10 tackles and a key sack of Dallas quarterback Troy Aikman.

Kirkland was All-Pro in 1996,97. He was so good that he had the distinction of being the highest paid linebacker in the NFL in 1999. He played with the Eagles in 2002.He was named to Clemson's Centennial team in 1996. He was one of the best. Ranked as Clemson's #8 gridder of all-time by a panel of historians in 1999. He was inducted into Clemson Hall of Fame in 2001.

Player Highlights Chester McGlockton DT 1988-91

<< C. McGlockton

Chester McGlockton was a man amongst boys when he arrived on Clemson's campus. Standing 6'4" and tipping the scale at just over 300 lbs., McGlockton madc an immediate impact on the Clemson defensive line.

Fleet footed, nimble, and mean as a rattle snake, opponents feared McGlockton. McGlockton was a High School All-American as a Tight End/Defensive Lineman at Whiteville High School in Whiteville, NC. During his senior year he led the Whiteville Wolfpack to a 15-0 record, a State Championship, and a USA Today National Ranking.

He played great college football at Clemson University under both Danny Ford and Ken Hatfield. He scored a touchdown as a freshman in the 1989 Gator Bowl vs. the West Virginia Mountaineers.

He had a stellar career at Clemson, beginning with Coach Danny Ford and ending with Ken Hatfield, McGlockton was drafted with the 16th pick of the 1st round in the 1992 draft by the Oakland Raiders. This was a match made in heaven.

McGlockton was a no nonsense, physical, street fighter style of defensive tackle and Al Davis couldn't get him to Oakland fast enough.

He played six seasons with the Raiders, earning all four of his Pro Bowl appearances with them. McGlockton also played for the Kansas City Chiefs, the Denver Broncos, and ended his career by playing one season with the New York Jets. McGlockton finished his 12-year NFL career with 51 sacks including a career season high of 9.5 in 1994.

He collected over 500 tackles, 51 sacks and even grabbed four interceptions. Chester McGlockton passed away on November 30th, 2011 at the age of 42, due to an enlarged heart. His memory will live on in Tiger fans hearts forever.

1992 Clemson Tigers Football Coach Ken Hatfield

The 1992 Clemson Tigers football team represented Clemson University during the 1992 college football season as a member of the Atlantic Coast Conference (ACC). Ken Hatfield was the head football coach for his third of four seasons. The Tigers completed their ninety-seventh season overall and their fortieth in the Atlantic Coast Conference with a record of 5-6-0; 3-5-0 in ACC. They finished in seventh place in the ACC. out of 9 active ACC teams. It was a poor year for Clemson by recent standards. Robert O'Neal, Daniel Telley, and Wayne Simmons were team captains.

The Clemson Fighting Tigers began the season with a home game. On Sept 5. This and all home openers are played on the campus of Clemson University at Memorial Field in Clemson, SC, Coach Ken Hatfield's #8 Clemson Fighting Tigers defeated Ball State W (24-10) to get the season off to a good start. On Sept 12, at home the Tigers lost to the #5 ranked Florida State Seminoles L 20–24 before 83,170. Florida State had just become a member of the ACC, which was ready to swell as interest in the conference was booming. s

After a two-week break, on Sept 26 at Georgia Tech in Bobby Dodd Stadium • Atlanta, GA, the Tigers suffered another loss L (16–20). Now, at 1-2 for the season, on Oct 3 at home, Clemson faced

Chattanooga and won the game in a blowout W (54-3) before 71, 486. On Oct 10, the barely ranked #25 Tigers squeezed out a one-point win against #10 Virginia at Scott Stadium, Charlottesville, VA W (29–28).

Game Highlights Clemson 29, Virginia 28

Oct. 10, 1992 at Charlottesville, VA

This game is known as "The greatest comeback in Clemson Football History." Some may take issue with that but none can argue how great a comeback this game actually was. Virginia was up on Clemson 28-0 with 32 minutes left in the game.

Right before the half Louis Solomon made a 64-yard touchdown run to give the Tigers some momentum going into halftime. Coach Hatfield made some second half defensive adjustments which were more than enough to shut Virginia out.

Clemson made this comeback simply by running the ball effectively. The squad clocked off over 400 yards rushing for the day, a highly unusual way to make a major comeback. Rudy Harris had a big day and Rodney Blunt scored a key late touchdown. In the second half, Virginia just couldn't stop Clemson.

The Tigers got the ball back in the final minutes, down by two-points, 28-26. Using the running game, Clemson drove the ball up the field, very effectively on the ground. The crowd was still as the snap came for the field goal. Nelson Welch made the 32-yard field goal look easy to win the game. It was phenomenal comeback because Clemson did it on the road against a top 10 team. It is still the greatest comeback by an ACC team against another ACC team. I bet you cannot prove me wrong on that one.

Then, on Oct 17 at home, Clemson defeated the Duke Blue Devils W (21-6) before 77.532. On Oct 24, at #23 NC State at playing in Carter–Finley Stadium in Raleigh, NC in the annual Textile Bowl, the Tigers succumbed to the Wolfpacks L (6–20). On Oct 31 at Wake Forest's Groves Stadium in Winston-Salem, NC, the Tigers could not hold on to the win and lost L (15–18) before an attendance of 21,839.

On Nov 7 at home, the Tigers beat the Tar Heels of North Carolina W (40–7). On Nov 14 at Maryland's Byrd Stadium, College Park, MD, the Tigers lost to the Terrapins L 23–53. It was not a typical Clemson season in the recent years as losses were now being recorded more frequently than wins. On Nov 21, at home, South Carolina was the next loss in the Battle of the Palmetto State L (13–24). The game was played before another huge crowd for this annual classic -- 83,312. With a losing season, there would be no post-season opportunities for the Tigers in 1993.

1993 Clemson Tigers Football Coach Ken Hatfield

The 1993 Clemson Tigers football team represented Clemson University during the 1993 college football season as a member of the Atlantic Coast Conference (ACC). Ken Hatfield was the head football coach for his fourth and last of four fine seasons. Because Ken Hatfield moved on from Clemson after the regular season, Tommy West took over for the bowl game in his first year as head coach for 1994. The Tigers completed their ninety-eighth season overall and their forty-first in the Atlantic Coast Conference with a record of 9-3-0; 5-3-0 in the ACC. They finished in third place in the ACC. out of 9 active ACC teams. It was another fine year for Clemson. Richard Monreef was the team captain.

As is usually the case, The Clemson Fighting Tigers began the season with a home game. On Sept 4. As with all home games, this home opener was played on the campus of Clemson University in Memorial Field in Clemson, SC, Coach Ken Hatfield's #22 ranked Clemson Fighting Tigers defeated UNLV W (24-14) starting the season undefeated at 1-0. #1 ranked Florida State was in the beginning of a National Championship Season and they played like the champs in Clemson's second game of the season. Nobody likes to admit getting whooped and shut-out by Florida State in the same game but the #22 Tigers sure did at Doak Campbell Stadium in Tallahassee, L 0–57. Though Florida State won the Championship, it was not undisputed.

Florida State's Seminoles were the unanimous choice for #1 beginning with the October 19 poll and the three polls after that, receiving all 62 votes. Then, Notre Dame's defeated FSU 31-24 on November 13, and the Fighting Irish got all 62 first place votes in the next poll. But polls change as teams win and lose. Take a look at what happened below:

WEEKS	#1	#2	Event	Date
PRE to 7	FSU	Al	Tenn 17; Alabama 17	Oct 16
8 - 11	FSU	ND	ND 31; FSU 34	Nov 13
12	ND	FSU	BC 41; ND 39	Nov 20
13-15	FSU	Neb	FSU 18; Neb 16	Jan 1

FSU was declared National Champions; ND came in 2nd place

There was controversy because ND had beaten FSU in head to head.

We show this in this book because FSU had a great team and it was unusual for Clemson to take such a beating in any game—especially a game v a rival such as FSU. Bobby Bowden was a great coach but no team wanted to lose when playing FSU.

On Sept 25 at home, Clemson was about to begin to win again. They beat Georgia Tech W (16-13 before 72,511. On Oct 2, at home, Clemson beat NC State W (20-14). On Oct 9, at Duke's Wallace Wade Stadium in Durham, NC, the Tigers beat the Blue Devils W (13–10). On Oct 16, at home Clemson's Tigers were defeated by the Wake Forest Demon Deacons in a very close match L (16-20). On Oct 23, at home, the Tigers shut out East Tennessee State W (27-0). On Oct 30, at home. The Tigers defeated the Maryland Terrapins W (29–0) before 66,147

On Nov 6 at 7:30 p.m.at # 16 North Carolina in Kenan Memorial Stadium Chapel Hill, NC, the Tigers lost to the Tar Heels in a shut-out l (0–24). Then on Nov 13 at home, the Tigers beat # 18 Virginia W (23–14). Now ranked #24, Clemson looked forward to the season finale v South Carolina in the big rivalry game. It was a good season but one in which the team could take nothing for granted. Against South Carolina, the Clemson Fighting Tigers got enough to win by three over a tough Gamecocks squad in the annual South Carolina Supremacy battle called the Battle of the Palmetto State. This year's encounter was on Nov 20 at Williams-Brice Stadium in Columbia,

SC where the Tigers charted the win W (16–13). The Tigers accepted the Peach Bowl bid.

Peach Bowl

Tommy West took over for coach Hatfield in the Peach Bowl as this Bowl game was his first game as head coach for the Clemson Tigers and for 1994. On Dec 31 @ 6:00 p.m. New Year's Eve, Kentucky squared off against # 23 ranked Clemson at the Georgia Dome in Atlanta, GA for the (Peach Bowl. It was a thrilling game and the Tigers got it all together to win in the end, W (14–13) before 63,416 fans.

Emery Smith Starred in Coach Tommy West's 1993 Peach Bowl Win!

Player Highlights Stacy Seegars OG 1991-1993

<< Stacy Seegars

Offensive Guards typically are on the short end of the stick when plaudits are given out. Not true of Stacy Seegars. In fact, Seegars is one of the most decorated linemen in Tiger history, he was a first-team All-America choice by AP, Walter Camp, Scripps-Howard, and Football News in 1993 and was a second-team choice of AP and UPI in 1992.

A smart Guard, He was also selected to the 1993 Academic All-ACC football squad. He was the fourth Tiger to reach 200 knockdown blocks in his career; he had 213. Seegars averaged five knockdowns per game for his career. In addition to being All-American. He was also a two-time All-ACC Guard. He tied the Tiger single-season record for knockdown blocks (103) in 1992.

Chapter 23 Tommy West Era 1993 to 1998

Coach # 23 Tommy West

Year	Coach	Record	Conference	Record
1993	Tommy West	Bowl Game Win	Score 20-0	
1994	Tommy West	5–6	ACC	4-4-0
1995	Tommy West	8-4	ACC	6-2
1996	Tommy West	7-5	ACC	6-2
1997	Tommy West	7–5	ACC	4–4
1998	Tommy West	3-8	ACC	1-7

1994 Clemson Tigers Football Coach Tommy West

The 1994 Clemson Tigers football team represented Clemson University during the 1994 college football season as a member of the Atlantic Coast Conference (ACC). Tommy West was the head football coach for his second of six seasons.

Clemson Coach Tommy West

Because Ken Hatfield moved on from Clemson after the 1993 regular season, Tommy West was asked to take over for the bowl game in his first year as head coach (one Bowl game) in the 1993 post-season.

The Tigers completed their ninety-ninth season overall and their forty-second in the Atlantic Coast Conference with a record of 5-6-0; 4-4-0 in the ACC. They finished in sixth place in the ACC, out of 9 active ACC teams. It was at best a mediocre year for Clemson. Tim Jones and Louis Solomon were the team captains.

As is usually the case, The Clemson Fighting Tigers began the season with a home game. On Sept 3. As with all home games, this home opener was played on the campus of Clemson University in Memorial Field in Clemson, SC, Coach Tommy West's #24 ranked Clemson Fighting Tigers defeated Furman W (27-16) for a fine start of the season. On Sept 10 at home, Clemson lost the Textile Bowl to NC State L (12-29) before a light crowd of 67, 127. On Sept 17 at Virginia's Scott Stadium in Charlottesville, VA, the Tigers lost for the second time in two games against the Wahoos L (6-9).

On Oct 1, at home, Clemson defeated Maryland W (13-0). On Oct 8, at Georgia's Sanford Stadium in Athens, GA, the Tigers lost their third match of the year L (14–40). On Oct 15, at #15 Duke's Wallace Wade Stadium in Durham, NC, the Tigers lost to the Blue Devils. Carrying four losses as the season's baggage so far, the Tigers traveled to #7 Florida State's Doak Campbell Stadium in Tallahassee, FL and lost their fifth game of the season L (0-17). On Oct 29, the Tigers made a comeback at home against Wake Forest W (24–8).

Then, on Nov 5 at No. 19 North Carolina's Kenan Memorial Stadium in Chapel Hill, NC, the Tigers beat the Tar Heels W (28–17) before 50,000. On Nov 12 at home, Clemson defeated Georgia Tech W (20-10). The last game of the season, hoping to get over 500 and stay there, the Tigers lost the battle to South Carolina at home in the Battle of the Palmetto State L (7–33) before a max crowd of 85,872.

1995 Clemson Tigers Football Coach Tommy West

The 1995 Clemson Tigers football team represented Clemson University during the 1995 college football season as a member of the

Atlantic Coast Conference (ACC). Tommy West was the head football coach for his third of six seasons. The Tigers completed their one hundredth season overall and their forty-third in the Atlantic Coast Conference with a record of 8-4-0; 6-2-0 in the ACC. They finished in third place in the ACC, out of 9 active ACC teams. It was a fine year for Clemson. Louis Solomon was the team captain.

The Clemson Fighting Tigers home opener resulted in a big win on Sept 2 on the campus of Clemson University in Memorial Field in Clemson, SC, Coach Tommy West's unranked squad shellacked Western Carolina W (55-9) for an excellent start to the season. On Sept 9, at home, #1 ranked Florida State powered by Clemson L 26-45). Florida State would eventually lose two games and one in the ACC tying Virginia for ACC Champions and coming in fifth nationally. The Clemson Tigers had a tough time each year with the Seminoles. Things would change over time.

On Sept 16 at Wake Forest's Groves Stadium, Winston-Salem, NC, the Tigers beat the Demon Deacons W 29–14. On Sept 23, #11, ACC Champ this year, played the Tigers at home. The Wahoos were a fine team this year and they beat the Tigers L (3-22). On Sept 30, at NC State's Carter–Finley Stadium in Raleigh, NC in the Textile Bowl, the Tigers got the best of the Wolfpack W (43-22). On Oct 7, at home, the Tigers lost by bust two points to Georgi L (17-19).

On Oct 21, at Maryland's Byrd Stadium, College Park, the Tigers shut out the Terrapins W (17-0). Then, on Oct 28, at Georgia Tech's Bobby Dodd Stadium in Atlanta, GA, the Tigers beat the Yellow Jackets W (24-3). On Nov 11 at home the #24 Tigers defeated the Duke Blue Devils W (34-17). Then, in the Battle of the Palmetto State the following week on Nov 18, at South Carolina's Williams-Brice Stadium, Columbia, the #24 Tigers beat the Gamecocks W (38-17). The Tigers were invited to the Gator Bowl to be played Jan 1, 1996.

Gator Bowl

Typically, great performers in Bowl Games, the # 23 Clemson Tigers were unexpectedly shut out in the Gator Bowl on January 1, 1996 by the Syracuse Orangemen at Jacksonville Memorial Stadium in Jacksonville FL L (0-41) before 45,202 and an NBC TV national audience.

Player Highlights Brian Dawkins, (1992-95)

Like many pretty good football players, Dawkins didn't fully blossom until his professional career, which ended in his retirement after the 2011 season. Before his Pro Football Hall of Fame career for 16 years in the NFL, Dawkins was a productive safety for two coaches (Ken Hatfield and Tommy West) at Clemson.

A three-year starter, Dawkins was a second-team All-ACC selection as a sophomore and junior before emerging as a second-team AP All-America selection as a senior in 1995. He finished his career with 11 career interceptions and 251 tackles. Dawkins showed a glimpse of what was to come in his pro career when he intercepted three passes against Duke in his final home game with the Tigers.

Brian Dawkins has it all: the coverage skills, the tackling, the aggressiveness. All that you want in a safety, Dawkins has it.

Able to play both positions, Dawkins made his name as one of the best all-time safeties at Clemson and one of the more notable ones in the NFL, and could probably be the first and only Clemson player enshrined in the NFL Hall of Fame. But, not yet!

1996 Clemson Tigers Football Coach Tommy West

The 1996 Clemson Tigers football team represented Clemson University during the 1996 college football season as a member of the Atlantic Coast Conference (ACC). Tommy West was the head football coach for his fourth of six seasons. The Tigers completed their one hundred-first season overall and their forty-fourth in the Atlantic Coast Conference with a record of 7-5-0; 6-2-0 in the ACC. They finished in third place in the ACC, out of 9 active ACC teams. It was a fine year for Clemson. Louis Solomon was the team captain.

Due to a "rules change" during the postseason of 1995, college football games played from 1996 on cannot end in a tie. At the beginning of this season, the NCAA Football Rules Committee added an overtime procedure to end the chance of a tied game. Though Clemson had no ties in 1996, it would have had a tie in 1997 if it were not for this new rule. Every now and then, the NCAA does something because it is the right thing. Don't count on many more NCAA decisions that take fans or entities other than the NCAA insiders into consideration.

The Clemson Fighting Tigers season opener resulted in a big loss on Aug 31 at Memorial Stadium in Chapel Hill NC. Coach Tommy West's unranked squad was shut-out by North Carolina L (0-45). The Clemson Fighting Tigers followed this loss up with a win in their home opener on Sept 7. All Clemson home games are played on the campus of Clemson University in Memorial Field in Clemson, SC, Coach Tommy West's team defeated Furman W (19-3) for their first home victory. On Sept 21 at Missouri's Faurot Field in Columbia, MO, the Tigers were defeated L (24–38). Then a week later on Sept 28 at home, the Tigers beat the Wake Forest Demon Deacons W 21–10 before 63,263.

Then, on Oct 2, another iteration of a tough Florida State program invited the Tigers to play at Doak Campbell Stadium in Tallahassee, FL. The Seminoles got the best of the Tigers L (3–34) before 76,360. On Oct 12, at Duke in Wallace Wade Stadium, Durham, NC, Clemson beat the Blue Devils W (13–6) before a crowd of 23,586. On Oct 19, at home, the unranked Clemson Tigers defeated the # 22 Georgia Tech Yellow Jackets in a close match W (28-25). Then, on Nov 2, at home again, the Tigers beat the Terrapins of Maryland in a blowout W (35-3).

On Nov 9, at # 15 Virginia in Scott Stadium, Charlottesville, VA, the Tigers commanded the victory over the Wahoos W 24–16. On Nov16, at NC State's Memorial Stadium •in the Textile Bowl, the Clemson Tigers whooped the Wolfpack W (40–17) before 63,796. On Nov 23, at home, in the SC rivalry game of the year, the Battle of the Palmetto State, #22 Clemson played its best but lost to the Gamecocks L (31-34 before 82, 929. After this game, the Tigers found they were eligible for a Bowl Game and they chose to play in the Peach Bowl.

The Peach Bowl

On Dec 28, 1996, at 8:00 PM, the Fighting Tigers of Clemson University engaged the #17 Louisiana State Tigers at the Georgia Dome in Atlanta, GA for the Peach Bowl, seen by 63,622 at the stadium and millions of others on ESPN. The Tigers played a tough game but were beaten L (7–10) by the other Tigers from Louisiana.

1997 Clemson Tigers Football Coach Tommy West

The 1997 Clemson Tigers football team represented Clemson University during the 1997 college football season as a member of the Atlantic Coast Conference (ACC). Tommy West was the head football coach for his fifth of six seasons. The Tigers completed their one hundred-second season overall and their forty-fifth in the Atlantic Coast Conference with a record of 7-5-0; 4-4-0 in the ACC. They finished in fifth in the ACC, out of 9 active ACC teams. It was an OK year for Clemson. Raymond Priester and Raymond White were the team captains.

The Clemson Fighting Tigers season opener resulted in a nice home win on Sept 6 at Memorial Stadium in Clemson, SC, Coach Tommy West's team defeated Furman W (23=12) for their first home victory before 62,405 for the 1997 season. On Sept 13 at NC State, the $19 ranked Tigers traveled to Carter–Finley Stadium, Raleigh, NC for the annual Textile Bowl and they won by two points over the Wolfpack W 19–17 before 50,000. On Sept 20, at home, the games against Florida State were getting closer as the #5 Seminoles gained a one touchdown advantage over the #16 Tigers and won the game L (28–35) before 80,939 fans. Then, on Sept 27 at Georgia Tech, the Yellow Jackets beat the # 17 Tigers at Bobby Dodd Stadium in Atlanta, GA L (20-23) Then, on Oct 4, at home, which is also my wedding Anniversary that I am not permitted to forget ever, no matter what the reason, the Tigers got out of the funk and beat the visiting UTEP Miners from Texas, W (30-7)

On Oct 11, at home, as Virginia was playing tougher and tougher football, they were not even close to pushovers and this year, they beat the Tigers L 7–21 before 74,987. On Oct 25 at Maryland's Byrd Stadium in College Park, MD, the Tigers had winning in the blood and beat the Terrapins W 20–9, before 27,270. On Nov 1, at Wake Forest's Groves Stadium in Winston-Salem, NC, the Tigers defeated the Demon Deacons W (33–16) before 23,411 fans.

Then on Nov 8, at home Clemson defeated Duke in overtime since there were no more ties in College football W (29-20.) So, how can such a score occur in OT. Here's how: Clemson and Duke met in the first overtime game between two ACC teams in 1997. The Tigers won the contest by the unusual score of 29-20. David Richardson kicked a field goal on Clemson's possession, then Rahim Abdullah intercepted a pass and ran 63 yards for a score, giving Clemson the nine-point win.

On Nov 15, at home, North Carolina beat Clemson plain and simple in a one – touchdown game L (10–17) before 71,514. Then, On Nov 22, at 6:00 p.m. at South Carolina's Williams-Brice Stadium in Columbia, SC in a rendition of the Battle of the Palmetto State, the Tigers were forced to flex some muscle to defeat the Gamecocks W

47–21 before 83,700. For a great year, the unranked Clemson Tigers, were invited to the Peach Bowl

January 2, 1998 Peach Bowl

On January 2, 1998 at 3:00 p.m., the Clemson Tigers squared off against the Auburn Tigers in the first game between the two in many years. This was a post-season game called *The Peach Bowl* played at the Georgia Dome in Atlanta, GA (Peach Bowl) L (17–21) before 71,212 fans.

Player Highlights Anthony Simmons (1995-97)

Compared to some other notable great Clemson football players, Simmons did not play during the best years of Clemson football. The Tigers had a respectable record of 22-14 during his three seasons starting with the Tigers, but Simmons was a dominant force anyway.

He started all but one game in his three seasons at Clemson, racking up 486 career tackles. In 1996, Simmons set a school record with 178 stops, topped only by Keith Adams' 186, three years later. Simmons earned consensus All-America honors the following seasons.

And so, Simmons goes down in Clemson Football History as one of the all-time great Clemson players of the 20th century. He made an impact on the team from day one of his freshman year. It took about 10 days of preseason practice for Anthony Simmons to move into the starting lineup. By season's end he was a third-team

AP All-American and UPI National Freshman of the Year. He was the first defensive player in history to win that national award.

Simmons was a precocious linebacker who combined speed and power with a keen knowledge of the game. It is safe to say he had the finest (true, not red-shirt) freshman season in school history, regardless of position. Possibly regardless of sport. He posted 150 tackles that year to lead the team.

The rest of his career was just as stellar. He accumulated 178 tackles in 1996 as a sophomore, again an All-America season for the native of Spartanburg, SC. He was a model of consistency throughout his career. He was Clemson's leading tackler in 28 of the 36 games he played and had a streak of 17 straight games with at least one tackle for loss, another Clemson record. He concluded his career with 486 tackles, second in Clemson history. He went pro after his junior year or would have shattered Bubba Brown's record had he returned.

Just the second ACC player in history to be named an AP All-American in three different seasons, Simmons was a first-round draft choice of the Seattle Seahawks in 1998 and played seven seasons of outstanding professional football.

1998 Clemson Tigers Football Coach Tommy West

The 1998 Clemson Tigers football team represented Clemson University during the 1998 college football season as a member of the Atlantic Coast Conference (ACC). Tommy West was the head football coach for his sixth and last of six seasons. The Tigers completed their one hundred-third season overall and their forty-sixth in the Atlantic Coast Conference with a record of 3-8; 1-7 in the ACC. They finished in eighth in the ACC, out of 9 active ACC teams. It was a terrible year for Clemson. Donald Broomfield and Holland Postell were the team captains.

The Clemson Fighting Tigers season opener resulted in a nice home win on Sept 5 at Memorial Stadium in Clemson, SC, Coach Tommy West's team shut out Furman W (33=0) for their first home victory before 70,855 for the 1998 season. Though this was a fine start, Clemson would find the winning column just two more times this season. Sept 12 was not one of those two as Virginia Tech followed Furman to the home field a week later and shut out the Tigers L (0-37). On Sept 19, in a very close loss at Virginia's Scott Stadium in • Charlottesville, VA, the Tigers were defeated by the Wahoos L 18-20.

The next loss was at home against Wake Forest on Sept 26 L (19-29). This was followed by another loss on Oct to North Carolina at Kenan Memorial Stadium in Chapel Hill, NC L 14–21. On Oct 10, Clemson found a way to win at home against Maryland W (23-0). On Oct 17, Clemson took a bad beating and a big shutout loss from #6 Florida State at Doak Campbell Stadium in Tallahassee, FL L (0–48) before 80,310. On Oct 24, the losses continued at Duke's Wallace Wade Stadium in Durham, NC, L 23–28 before 30,630.

On Oct 31 at home in the Textile Bowl, Clemson lost to NC State L (39–46). Then, the losses kept mounting on Nov 12 at home against #22 Georgia Tech L 21–24. Then came the big Battle of the Palmetto state before 84,423 at home. Clemson found enough stamina and determination to defeat the Gamecocks in a nice game W (28-19)

Player Highlights Antwan Edwards DB 1996-98

Edwards was first-team All-American by Football Digest for his last season with Clemson – 1998. He was third-team choice by Football News and Associated Press. He was also first-team All-ACC at cornerback. He was called as a first-round draft pick (25th overall) of the Packers in 1999. He was ranked 10th in the nation in kickoff returns with 26.9 average in 1998.

Edwards was a semi-finalist for the Thorpe Award, which

is given to the top defensive back in the nation. He finished his college career ranked third in Clemson history in career passes broken up with 35. He had 14 "break-ups" in his senior year to lead the club and rank second in the ACC.

Antwan Edwards was the first player in Clemson history to have two 80-yard plays in the same game. He had a 93-yard fumble return for a touchdown and an 85-yard kickoff return at Virginia.

He became Clemson's career leader in return yards on takeaways. He had 10 takeaways in his career for 299 yards. An exceptional player, he was chosen to play in the 1999 Senior Bowl and the 1999 East-West game. He was second-team All-ACC in 1997. His career also included two interceptions, including one he returned 42 yards for a score at South Carolina in 1997.

Selected in the first round of the 1999 NFL Draft by the Green Bay Packers, the first of three consecutive defensive backs the Packers would take in that draft; the others being Fred Vinson and Mike McKenzie.

Edwards would play all sixteen games of his rookie season, starting one of them. During the course of the year, he made a total of thirty tackles (twenty-six solo), had four interceptions, and was named to the College & Pro Football Weekly All-Rookie team.

After five years with the Packers, he played with three other teams to finish a robust eight-year NFL pro career.

Chapter 24 Tommy Bowden Era 1999-2008

Coach # 24 Tommy Bowden

Year	Coach	Record	Conference	Record
1999	Tommy Bowden	6-6	ACC	5-3
2000	Tommy Bowden	9–3	ACC	6-2
2001	Tommy Bowden	7-5	ACC	4-4
2002	Tommy Bowden	7-6	ACC	4-4
2003	Tommy Bowden	9–4	ACC	5-3
2004	Tommy Bowden	7-5	ACC	4-4
2005	Tommy Bowden	8-4	ACC	4-4
2006	Tommy Bowden	8-5	ACC	5-3
2007	Tommy Bowden	9-4	ACC	5-3
2008	Tommy Bowden	7-6	ACC	4-4
2008	Dabo Swinney	4-3	interim coach last 7 games	

1999 Clemson Tigers Football Coach Tommy Bowden

The 1999 Clemson Tigers football team represented Clemson University during the 1999 college football season as a member of the Atlantic Coast Conference (ACC). Tommy Bowden was the head football coach for his first of ten seasons.

Coach Tommy Bowden Prepares to lead his Clemson Tigers onto the Field

The Tigers completed their one hundred-fourth season overall and their forty-seventh in the Atlantic Coast Conference with a record of 6-6; 5-3 in the ACC. They finished in fourth in the ACC, out of 9 active ACC teams. It was a terrible year for Clemson. Donald Broomfield and Holland Postell were the team captains.

The Clemson Fighting Tigers season opener resulted in a close loss on Sept 4 at Memorial Stadium on the campus of Clemson University in Clemson, SC. New Coach Tommy Bowden's team battled it out with Marshall and lost L (10-13) for their first home loss of the 1999 season before an attendance of 79,181. On Sept 11 at home, the Tigers defeated #22 Virginia W (33-14). On Sept 23, at Virginia Tech's Lane Stadium in Blacksburg, the #19 ranked Tigers were defeated L (11–31). On Ocr 2 at home, Clemson beat North Carolina W (31-20). Then, on Oct 9 at NC State's Carter-Finley Stadium in • Raleigh, NC, the Tigers lost the Textile Bowl L (31–35)

On Oct 16 at Maryland's Byrd Stadium in College Park, MD, the Tigers came out of their three losses and learne how to win again W (42–30). On October 23 against #1 Florida State, in the battle of the Bowdens at home, (The Bowden Bowl) Clemson almost brought down the vaunted Bobby Bowden Florida State Seminoles L (14–17) before a over-packed packed house of 86,092. On Oct 30 at Wake Forest's Groves Stadium in Winston-Salem, the Tigers won in a low-scoring game W (12–3) before 21,105.

On Nov 6 at home, the Tigers were learning how to score big and they defeated the Duke Blue Devils in a rout W (58-7). On Nov 13, against #13 Ga Tech at Bobby Dodd Stadium in Atlanta, GA, the Tigers almost won in a shootout L (42–45) . Then, on Nov 20, at South Carolina's Williams-Brice Stadium in Columbia, SC in the Battle of the Palmetto State, the Tigers beat the Gamecocks W (31-21) At 6-6, the Tigers barely qualified for the Bowl Season.

On Dec 30 at 7:30 PM vs. Mississippi State in the Peach Bowl postseason battle, the Tigers played at the Georgia Dome in Atlanta, GA, and lost to the Bulldogs L (7-17) in a tough played match before 73,315

2000 Clemson Tigers Football Coach Tommy Bowden

The 2000 Clemson Tigers football team represented Clemson University during the 2000 college football season as a member of the Atlantic Coast Conference (ACC). Tommy Bowden was the head football coach for his first of ten seasons. The Tigers completed their one hundred-fifth season overall and their forty-eighth in the Atlantic Coast Conference with a record of 9-3; 6-2 in the ACC. They finished in third in the ACC, out of 9 active ACC teams. Chad Carson, Rod Gardner, and Chad Speck were the team captains.

The Clemson Fighting Tigers season opener resulted in a shut-out win on Sept 2 at Memorial Stadium on the campus of Clemson University in Clemson, SC. Coach Tommy Bowden's #17 ranked team shellacked and shut out The Citadel W (38-0) for their first home win of the 2000 season before an attendance of 75,086. In the second of three home games in a row, on Sept 9, the #17 Clemson Tigers walloped and shut-out the Missouri Tigers W (62-0). The next home game on Sept 16 was a nice win against Wake Forest W (55-7). The #11 Tigers made it four in a row against Virginia at Scott Stadium in Charlottesville, VA W 31–10.

On Sept 30, at Duke's Wallace Wade Stadium in Durham, NC, the Tigers defeated the Blue Devils W (52–22) On Oct 7, at home, the #5 Tigers won their sixth in a row against NC State in the annual Textile Bowl W (34-27) On Oct 14, the Tigers were undefeated after six games, and ranked #5. They beat Maryland W (35–14) before 83,752 for #7. Keeping the win streak alive, the Tigers got #8 in a row on Oct 21 at North Carolina's Kenan Memorial Stadium in Chapel Hill, NC, W (38–24)

The Tigers would lose the next two out of three regular season games. The first loss was at home on Oct 28 v Georgia Tech L (28–31). The second loss in the Bowden Bowl was a thumping to #4 Florida State at Doak Campbell Stadium L (7–54). Clemson came back to win the Battle of the Palmetto State at home against # 25 South Carolina W (16–14) before 85,187.

2000 Gator Bowl.

On January 1, 2001 at 12:30 PM, the #16 Tigers took on #6 Virginia Tech at Alltel Stadium in Jacksonville, FL in the Gator Bowl. The Tigers could not get a full head of steam rolling and lost to the Hokies L (20–41). 68,741 were in attendance

Player Highlights Rod Gardner WR 1998-2000

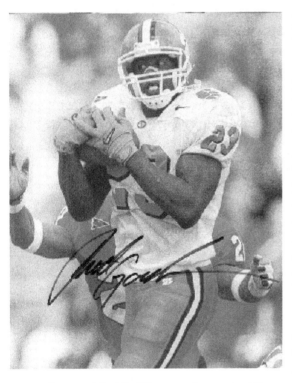

Rod Gardner was a first-team All-American by Gannett News Service and College & Pro Football Weekly. He was one of 10 semifinalists for the Biletnikoff Award in 2000. He left Clemson as the school's all-time leader in total receptions with 166, He set the record with seven for 94 yards against Virginia Tech in the 2001 Gator Bowl.

Gardner ranked third in career reception yardage with 2,498 and fifth in total touchdown receptions with 13. He was the only Clemson receiver in history with a 1000-yard receiving season, he actually had two. He set Clemson's record with 80 catches for 1,084 yards in 1999...He had at least two catches in his last 28 games, at least one in his last 30 games. He had nine 100-yard receiving games in his career to set a school record.

Gardner also tied Clemson's single-game record with 11 catches against Marshall in 1999. He also tied Clemson's single game record for touchdown receptions with three against North Carolina in 2000

He ranked 23rd in the nation in reception yards per game in 2000 and led the ACC in total receptions in 1999. He made second-team All-ACC as a junior and a senior. Along the way, he set nine records at Clemson. He will always be remembered for his 50-yard reception with 10 seconds left that set up the game-winning field goal against South Carolina in his final home game. That's not all. He also had the game deciding touchdown catch at South Carolina in 1999. He was named the IPTAY Athlete-of-the-Year for 2000-01.

Gardner was sought after by the pros. He was a first-round draft choice of the Washington Redskins in 2001, the 15th selection of the entire draft. He moved on to be the wide receiver for the Washington Redskins from 2001-04. Gardner could throw a ball and was one time a QB. This experience would prompt the Redskins to utilize him on trick plays during games.

For example, during the 2003 NFL season he was 2-for-3 for 46 yards and two passing touchdowns (to Chad Morton and Trung Candide). He had a seven year NFL career finishing up with three different teams including the Carolina Panthers.

Player Highlights Keith Adams, LB 1998-2000

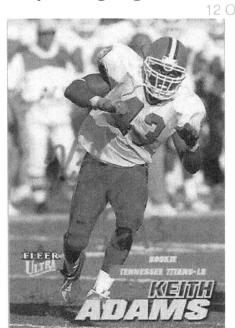

Keith Adams was always an effective, hard-nosed, downhill blitzer at the linebacker position. His ability to shoot the gap is something that Clemson would love to always have and surely would love to squeeze from its current group of talented linebackers. Adams was effective in this regard, giving Clemson a great pass rushing threat in addition to the monster of a defensive line it already possessed.

He was a two-time All-American in both 1999 and 2000. He was

ACC Defensive Player of the Year (1999. @00 was a great year for Adams as he was selected as a Finalist for the Butkus Award and the Bednarik Award (2000, and he was declared National Defensive Player of the Year Finalist by Football News (2000).

In his career, he set Clemson's single season record for tackles (186) and sacks (16) in 1999. He set Clemson single game tackle record with 27 vs. South Carolina in 1999. His totals are outstanding as he had 379 career tackles, ninth in Clemson history even though he played just three years.

When he came out to the pros, they were ready and he played seven years in the NFL with Dallas, Philadelphia, Miami and Cleveland

2001 Clemson Tigers Football Coach Tommy Bowden

The 2001 Clemson Tigers football team represented Clemson University during the 2001 college football season as a member of the Atlantic Coast Conference (ACC). Tommy Bowden was the head football coach for his third of ten seasons. The Tigers completed their one hundred-sixth season overall and their forty-ninth in the Atlantic Coast Conference with a record of 7-5; 4-4 in the ACC. They finished in fourth in the ACC, out of 9 active ACC teams. Brad Scott served as the offensive coordinator, and Reggie Herring served as the defensive coordinator.

The Clemson Fighting Tigers season opener resulted in a win on Sept 1 at Memorial Stadium on the campus of Clemson University in Clemson, SC. Coach Tommy Bowden's #19 ranked team squeaked by UCF W (21-13) for their first home win of the 2001 season before an attendance of 81,482. On Sept 8 at home, #20 Clemson defeated Wofford W (38-14). On Sept 22, at home, Virginia barely beat the Tigers L (24-26). On Sept 29, The Tigers put it in gear and had enough left to finish off the Georgia tech Yellow Jackets W (47-44).

Game highlights Clemson 47 v GA Tech 44 (OT)
Sept 29, 2001 in Atlanta Georgia.

This game was another overtime thriller. It was also another victory on the road for Clemson against a top-10 team.

In 2001, Clemson had high hopes to capture the ACC title. Standing in its way was rival Georgia Tech, a team going into this game ranked #9 in the nation.

It was quarterback Woody Dantzler who made play after play, guiding the Tigers to a thrilling overtime victory by being personally responsible for 418 of the team's 502 total yards.

In overtime, on a 3rd-and-6 play from the Tech 11-yard line, Dantzler ran a draw untouched into the end zone to win the game.

On Oct 13, at NC State's Carter-Finley Stadium • Raleigh, the Tigers won the Textile Bowl over the Wolfpack W (45–37).

On Oct 20 at home, the North Carolina Tar Heels beat the Clemson Tigers L (3-38) before 84,869. On Oct 27, at Wake Forest's Groves Stadium, Winston-Salem, NC, the Tigers defeated the Deamon Deacons W (21–14) before 21,290. On Nov 3, at home, Florida State beat Clemson again in the Bowden Bowl L (27-41) before 85,036. On November 10 , at #13 Maryland in Byrd Stadium, College Park, MD the Terrapins prevailed over the Tigers L (20–37). On Nov 17, at South Carolina's Williams-Brice Stadium in Columbia, SC in the annual Battle of the Palmetto State, the Gamecocks beat the Tigers L (15-20). On Dec 1, at home the Duke Blue Devils were soundly defeated by the Clemson Tigers W (59–31) before 72,577 in the regular season finaale.

2001 Humanitarian Bowl

Thirty days after the close of the regular season, the Clemson Fighting Tigers were ready to face another opponent in the Humaniatarian Bowl The opponent was Louisiana Tech and the venue was Bronco Stadium in Boise, Idaho. The Tigers prevailed against Tech W (49-24) before 23,472 and a national TV audience provided by ESPN.

Player Highlights Kyle Young C 1998-2000

Kyle Young is among the most decorated players in Clemson history in any sport. He was an All-American on the field and off in both 2000 and 2001. He joined the PGA Tour professional Jonathan Byrd as the only athletes in Clemson history to be named All-American on the field and in the classroom in the same year in two different seasons.

Young was a third-team All-American in 2001 by The Sporting News and Football News...a first-team Academic All-American for the third year in a row. He became just the second offensive lineman in college football history to do that and just the second ACC player. The only other offensive lineman to do it was Jim Hansen at Colorado (1990-92) and the only other ACC player was Mike Dominick at Duke (1986-88)

Kyle was also the winner of the National Football Foundation Scholarship. He was the first Tiger to achieve that since 1978 (Steve Fuller). He was honored in New York as one of just 18 Division I players.

He was also the winner of the Jim Tatum Award as outstanding scholar athlete football player in the ACC and the winner of a Weaver-James-Corrigan Scholarship from the Atlantic Coast Conference for excellence on and off the field.

He had a Clemson record 168 knockdown blocks in 2001, he broke his own Clemson record for knockdown blocks in a season. His total included 18 in the bowl win over Louisiana Tech when he helped the Tigers to 49 points and 548 yards of total offense.

He was named to Sports Illustrated's All-Bowl team for 2001. He was a smart player and a smart student with an average grade of 90.5 percent for the season, best on the team.

He was one of the top 24 candidates for the Outland Trophy at mid-season. He was also a finalist for the Dave Rimington Award, one of five for that honor. The prime reason for that was that Clemson averaged 432 yards a game of total offense—second best average in Clemson history.

Young started every game at center his final three years and 40 in a row over four years. He tied Clemson's record for starts by a center in a career with 36. He also started four at guard as a freshman.

He is a big reason why Woodrow Dantzler broke 53 Clemson records in his career. He was three-time first-team All-ACC by Football News He was rugged and resilient and he played over 3,000 snaps in his Clemson career.

He had a record-tying 21 knockdown blocks against N.C. State in his 100 plays of participation with just six missed assignments in 845 plays by coach's grading system. This was the fewest among all starters on the Clemson team.

Young was the big reason why Clemson averaged a school record 446 yards per game and set school records for touchdowns and total points scored in 2000.

Kyle Young earned his degree from Clemson in secondary education with a minor in economics in May of 2001, he was a graduate student during the 2001 season...He had a 3.98 GPA in his undergraduate career, having received just one B and the rest of his courses were A. He is now an Administrative Assistant on the Clemson Athletic Department staff.

Player Highlights Woody Dantzler QB (1998-01)

At the turn of the millennium, Woodrow Dantzler was one of the most electrifying running quarterbacks in the nation. It was part way through his sophomore season in 1999 that he took over as starting quarterback for Tommy Bowden's then 1-2 football team and he led them to a Peach Bowl.

In his junior year, the Tigers finished with 9 wins, but it was his senior season that was his most amazing. He tallied 2,360 passing yards and 17 passing touchdowns along with another 1,004 yards and 10 touchdowns on the ground. With that, he became the first player in NCAA history to pass for 2,000 yards and rush for 1,000 yards. He set 53 Clemson records and is in the Clemson football Hall of Fame.

2002 Clemson Tigers Football Coach Tommy Bowden

The 2002 Clemson Tigers football team represented Clemson University during the 2002 college football season as a member of the Atlantic Coast Conference (ACC). Tommy Bowden was the head football coach for his fourth of ten seasons. The Tigers completed their one hundred-seventh season overall and their fiftieth in the Atlantic Coast Conference with a record of 7-6; 4-4 in the ACC. They finished in fifth, out of 9 active ACC teams. Nick Eason, Bryant McNeal, and Jackie Robinson were the captains for 2002.

The Clemson Fighting Tigers season opener resulted in a loss on Aug 31 at Georgia's Sanford Stadium • Athens, GA-- L (28-31) In the Clemson Tigers Home Opener at Memorial Stadium on the campus of Clemson University in Clemson, SC. Coach Tommy Bowden's unranked Tigers Beat Louisiana Tech W (33-13) for the Tigers' first home win of the 2002 season before an attendance of 72, 616. On Sept 14 at home, Clemson beat Georgia Tech's Yellow Jackets W (24-19). Then on Sept 21 at home, the Tigers defeated Ball State W (30-7) before 73,945. Waiting to win a Bowden Bowl was continued another year at #11 Florida State's Doak Campbell Stadium, Tallahassee, FL resulted in a one-year postponement of the inevitable L (31-48) (Bowden Bowl), ESPN, L (31–48) before 78,841

On Oct 12, at Virginia's Scott Stadium in Charlottesville, VA, the Tigers could not overcome the Wahoos and went down L (17–22) before 54,114 fans. On Oct 19 at home, Clemson beat Wake Forest W (31-23). On Oct 24, at home, # 12 NC State beat the Tigers in the Textile Bowl L (6–38) before 78,904. On Nov 2 at Duke's Wallace Wade Stadium, Durham, the Tigers beat the Blue Devils W (34–31). On Nov 9 at North Carolina's Kenan Memorial Stadium in Chapel Hill, NC, the Tigers beat the Tar Heels W (42–12) before 42,000/

On Nov 16at home against # 19 Maryland, the Terrapins got the better of the Tigers L (12–30) before 74,707. On Nov 23, at home against South Carolina's Gamecocks, the Tigers won in a close matchup for the Battle of the Palmetto State, W (27–20) before 83,909

Tangerine Bowl

The Tigers won enough to be scheduled in a non-January Bowl game. On December 23at 5:30 p.m. vs. Texas Tech in the Citrus Bowl Stadium in Orlando, FL, playing in the Tangerine Bowl. Texas Tech whooped the Tigers Texas-style in the fashion of Florida State's whoopings. The Tigers were making a great reappearance on the national stage but every great showing needs a little time.

2003 Clemson Tigers Football Coach Tommy Bowden

The 2003 Clemson Tigers football team represented Clemson University during the 2003 college football season as a member of the Atlantic Coast Conference (ACC). Tommy Bowden, son of Florida State's famous Coach Bobby Bowden was the head football coach for his fifth of ten seasons. The Tigers completed their one hundred-eighth season overall and their fifty-first in the Atlantic Coast Conference with a record of 9-4; 5-3 in the ACC. They finished in third, out of 9 active ACC teams. Tony Elliott, DeJuan Polk, and Gregory Walker were the team captains for 2003.

The Clemson Fighting Tigers season opener resulted in a shutout loss on Aug 30 at home against the Georgia Bulldogs L (0-30). On Sept 6, in the Clemson Tigers Home Opener at Memorial Stadium on the campus of Clemson University in Clemson, SC. Coach Tommy Bowden's unranked Tigers Beat Furman W (28-17) for the Tigers' first home win of the 2003 season before an attendance of 71,477. On Sept 13 at home, Clemson defeated Middle Tennessee State W (37–14). On Sept 20, at Georgia Tech's Bobby Dodd Stadium, Atlanta, GA, the Tigers dominated the Yellow Jackets the whole game W (39–3) Then, on Oct 4 at Maryland's Byrd Stadium, College Park, MD, the Terrapins defeated the Tigers L (7–21) before 51,545 fans. On Oct 11, at home, #25 Virginia put up the fight of a lifetime seeking a Win but failed by a hair, W (30–27) in Overtime.

Then on Oct 16, a week later at NC State's Carter–Finley Stadium, Raleigh, NC in the Textile Bowl, the Tar Heels beat the Tigers by just two points L (15–17). On Oct 25, at home, North Carolina did not have enough juice and were defeated by Clemson W (36–28) before 77,512 fans. The next week on Nov 1 at Wake Forest's Groves Stadium, Winston-Salem, NC, the Tigers were overwhelmed by the Demon Deacons L (17–45) before 35,643.

Then on Nov 8, history was made in the Bowden Bowl at 7:45 p.m. as #3 Florida State went in to Clemson Memorial Stadium expecting another blowout but instead faced strong opposition. The younger Tommy Bowden's team defeated his dad Bobby Bowden's team for the first time. History was made with the Clemson win W 26–10

Game highlights Clemson 26, Florida State 10
Nov 8, 2003 in Death Valley

No single win from the past decade tasted sweeter than on a clear November night. The son finally bested the father.

After 11-consecutive losses against Florida State, Clemson finally got the monkey off its back and got Tommy Bowden his first ever win against his dad.

The Tigers thoroughly dominated the game, especially considering FSU didn't get its first (and only) touchdown until 2:14 left in the fourth quarter.

The Seminoles came into the game ranked third in the nation, making them the highest ranked opponent Clemson knocked off the entire decade.

Clemson out-rushed the Noles 152 to 11, and had a 13-minute advantage in time of possession.

This win was monumental in that it really helped turn things around for Tommy Bowden. Just a week before, Clemson had been humiliated by Wake Forest 45-17, a loss that had many fans calling for Bowden's job.

He would finish the season on a four-game winning streak, including this win, a win over Duke, the 63-17 thrashing of South Carolina, and knocking off Tennessee in the Peach Bowl.

Bowden's job may not have been cast in cement but it was on firm footing after this great win.

On Nov 15 at home, a scrappy Duke team as defeated by Clemson in a one-sided match W 40–7. On Nov 22 at 7:00 p.m. at South Carolina's Williams-Brice Stadium in Columbia, SC in the major Battle of the Palmetto State, the Tigers walloped the Gamecocks W (63–17) before 83,987.

Game highlights Clemson 63, S. Carolina 17
Nov 22, 2003 in South Carolina.

It's always great to beat your rival. It's really nice to beat your rival in its own building. Better still? Beating the team by 46 points when Lou Holtz is its coach.

In what was a key victory in saving Tommy Bowden's job in 2003, quarterback Charlie Whitehurst tossed four touchdowns to give the Tigers their largest-ever point production against their in-state rivals.

After a great season, the Tigers were invited to the Peach Bowl.

The 2003/2004 Peach Bowl

On the day after New Year's Day on Sunday January 2, 2004 at 4:30 in the afternoon, # 6 Tennessee and unranked Clemson paired off to play a tough Peach Bowl Game in the Georgia Dome, Atlanta, GA, shown on TV by ESPN and watched by 75, 125 at the Dome. The Clemson Fighting Tigers played the best that day and beat Tennessee W (27–14).

Game highlights Clemson 27, Tennessee 14
Jan 2, 2004 in Peach Bowl Game Atlanta GA.

For at least one evening, Clemson laid claim to this truth: The ACC can outplay the SEC.

The Vols, ranked No. 6 in the nation, were run all over by the Tigers, namely Chad Jasmin who rushed for a career high 106 yards and a touchdown in the Peach Bowl win.
The win capped off what could be defined as the best season Clemson had under Tommy Bowden. But even this postseason bowl win wasn't the best Tiger W of the decade.

2004 Clemson Tigers Football Coach Tommy Bowden

The 2004 Clemson Tigers football team represented Clemson University during the 2004 college football season as a member of the Atlantic Coast Conference (ACC). Tommy Bowden, son of Florida

State's famous Coach Bobby Bowden was the head football coach for his sixth of ten seasons. The Tigers completed their one hundred-ninth season overall and their fifty-second in the Atlantic Coast Conference with a record of 6-5; 4-4 in the ACC. They finished in seventh, out of 11 active ACC teams. Eric Coleman, Airese Currie, and Leroy Hill were the team captains for 2004.

The Clemson Fighting Tigers season opener resulted in a tough win on Sept 4 at home against Wake Forest W (37-30) This home opener was played as always at Memorial Stadium on the campus of Clemson University in Clemson, SC before 78,624. On Sept 11, at home, the Tigers lost to the Yellow Jackets of Georgia Tech L (24–28) before 81,427. In another tough loss, Clemson teed off on Sept 18 at Texas A&M's Kyle Field at College Station, TX L (6–27). Then on Sept 25 at 3:30 p.m. against #8 Florida State in their home park of Doak Campbell Stadium, Tallahassee, FL in the now infamous Bowden Bowl, the Seminoles did not forgive anything about being beaten the prior year and proved their dominance again against the younger Bowden L 22–41 before 83,538.

On Oct 7, at #10 Virginia, Scott Stadium • Charlottesville, VA, the Tigers could not muster up an offense and lost L (10–30). Then, on Oct 16, at home, Clemson got the best of Utah State W (35–6). On Oct 23, at home the Tigers squeaked by the Maryland Terrapins W (10–7) before 76,603. On Oct 30 at home, NC State lost to Clemson in the annual Textile Bowl W (26–20). On Nov 6 at #11 Miami (FL) in a game played in the Miami Orange Bowl in Miami, FL, the Clemson Tigers were on-key and ready to play. They came up with the victory over the Hurricanes in OT W 24–17 before 55,225.

Game Highlights Clemson 24, Miami 17
Nov 6, 2004 in Miami Orange Bowl.

Miami and Clemson have a record together that shows they just can't finish games in four quarters.

In fact, every game between the two teams in this particular decade has been decided in overtime. This one was completely unexpected. Clemson wasn't having its best of seasons—having been crushed by

Florida State, Texas A&M, and Virginia earlier in the season. Miami was ranked first in the ACC and #10 nationally.

Reggie Merriweather had 114 yards rushing and three touchdowns to spark the Tigers. It was the Clemson defense, however, that got the job done in overtime, forcing three straight Miami incompletions to seal the deal.

To commemorate the win Clemson celebrated over a tombstone – a ceremony they put on for every road win against a top-25 team.

On Nov 13 at Duke's Wallace Wade Stadium, Durham, NC, the Blue Devils got the best of the Tigers by three points L (13–16) before 24,714 fans. On Nov 20, at home. The Tigers defeated the South Carolina Gamecocks in the Battle of the Palmetto State W (29–7) before 82,372 screaming fans. This was Clemson's 600th team win. The game was notable for a brawl between the two teams. Due to the brawl, the Tigers declined a bowl bid in part because of the unsportsmanlike nature of the fight.

And so, this year, there is no reporting of another fine Clemson Bowl win. But, next year we'll see?

Player Highlights Justin Miller KR 2001-2004

Justin Miller set the NCAA single-game record for kickoff return yards with 282 at Florida State in 2004. He also had two kickoff returns for scores in that game to set a Clemson record and tie an NCAA record. In addition to being a kick returner, Miller was a three-year starter at cornerback. But his forte is being one of the greatest kick returners in Clemson history. He was among the final 12 for the Thorpe Award in 2004.

He was also a great cornerback. He finished his career ranked third in Clemson history in interceptions (13,) trailing only College Football Hall of Fame inductee Terry Kinard, who had 17 between 1978-82, and Fred Knoebel, who had 15 (1950-52).

Miller topped off his career with a 30.7-yard kickoff return average, the best in ACC history and fourth best in NCAA history. He had 50 kickoff returns for 1,534 yards. The 30.7 average is the best in NCAA history given a minimum of 50 returns.

He was ranked #14 in ACC history in total kickoff return yards (1,534; second in Clemson history in that category behind former teammate Derrick Hamilton. Miller was just 18 yards short of Hamilton's total. He led the nation in kickoff returns in 2004 with 33.1-yard average on 20 returns and had a 13.0-yard average in punt returns to rank in the top 25 in the nation.

He also had a punt return for a score in the season opener against Wake Forest; that gave him a Clemson record three kick returns for touchdowns in the same season and a career standard of five (three kickoffs and two punts). He is one of only two players in Clemson history to return both a kickoff and punt for a touchdown (Bobby Gage is the other).

He had seven tackles in the 2003 win over #3 Florida State, seven tackles and three pass breakups against #6 Tennessee in a Peach Bowl win, and 148 return yards in an overtime win over #10 Miami (FL) in 2004. He was named to Sports Illustrated's All-Bowl team for his performance against Tennessee in the 2004 Peach Bowl...He was a second-round draft choice of the New York Jets. He played four years with the Jets and finished his career with a season stint in Oakland.

2005 Clemson Tigers Football Coach Tommy Bowden

The 2005 Clemson Tigers football team represented Clemson University during the 2005 college football season as a member of the Atlantic Coast Conference (ACC). Tommy Bowden, son of Florida State's famous Coach Bobby Bowden was the head football coach for his seventh of ten seasons. The Tigers completed their one hundred-tenth season overall and their fifty-third in the Atlantic Coast Conference with a record of 8-4; 4-4 in the ACC. They finished in third out of 6 ACC Atlantic Division teams. The Offensive Coordinator was Rob Spence and the Defensive Coordinator was Vic Koenning.

The Clemson Fighting Tigers season opener resulted in a tough win on Sept 3 at home against #17 Texas A &M W (25-24) This home

opener was played as always at Memorial Stadium on the campus of
Clemson University in Clemson, SC before 79,917.

Game highlights Clemson 25 v Texas A&M 24
Sept. 3, 2005 at Death Valley.

1 OF 10

Many recall the ugly loss to the Aggies in 2004. This year, Clemson
kicked off the 2005 season with a rematch against A&M, this time it
was in Death Valley with the Aggies ranked No. 17 in the nation.

It took WR Chansi Stuckey returning a punt 47 yards for a
touchdown and Jad Dean kicking a Tiger-record six field goals,
including the game winner with six seconds remaining, to send the
Tigers to their victory party.

After this close win over a ranked Texas A&M team, the Tigers then
beat Maryland in another close game on Sept 10 at Byrd Stadium
College Park MD W (28-24).

However, Clemson then lost the following three games at home v
#13 Miami on Sept 17 L (30-36); Boston College at home on Sept 24
L (13-16), and at Wake Forest on Oct 1 L (27-31) The losses to
Miami and Boston College came in overtime. Clemson then
rebounded to win the next two games at NC State on Oct 13 W (31-
10) and Temple on Oct 22 W (37-7).

The next week, on Oct 29, Clemson lost a close game to Georgia
Tech L (9-10) and then closed out the regular season with three
straight wins over Duke on Nov 5 W (49-20), ACC rival Florida
State in a big win in the Bowden Bowl W (35-14), and at instate rival
South Carolina in the Battle of the Palmetto State W (13-9)

Champs Sports Bowl

In the post-season, Clemson received an invitation to play in the 2005 Champs Sports Bowl at the Citrus Bowl Stadium in Orlando FL. The game was played on Dec 27 against Colorado. Clemson won the game, W (19–10), to finish the full season at 8–4.

Clemson had a great year by all accounts. It could have been a little better with some better luck. The Tigers finished the season ranked in the top 25 (21st in both the AP and the Coaches' Poll) for the second time in three years. Clemson also recorded wins against three AP top 20 teams in the 2005 season for just the fourth time in school history. Clemson lost its four games by a combined 14 points. The two words *if only* come to mind but nobody was complaining.

Player Highlights C. Whitehurst QB (2002-'05)

Charlie Whitehurst had the height, the arm, and the leadership to be the quarterback on any great team. Those are some of the many qualities that made Charlie Whitehurst a Clemson great. Clemson fans missed those attributes deeply when he departed. The former Tiger quarterback broke the Clemson passing record books, becoming the school's leader in many of its passing categories, and including breaking the all-time leading passer record.

To top it all off, and a point well taken by all Tigers' Fans is that Charlie is still the only Clemson quarterback besides DeShaun Watson to go undefeated against South Carolina.

Having his fame attached to beating South Carolina four times, Charlie Whitehurst took over after QB Woody Dantzler. As a sophomore, he threw for 3,561 yards with 21 TDs.

That season was his high point as the Clemson Tigers won nine games including great and memorable wins over FSU (the start of their decline), South Carolina (63-17), and Tennessee (who was ranked #4 entering the Peach Bowl. Whitehurst owned the Clemson record for completions (817) and pass attempts (1,368) until Tajh Boyd passed him on both marks with 901 completions in 1,402 attempts. Then of course we have DeShaun Watson in the last few years.

A few items barely keep him out of the top five. He won just 7, 6, and 8 games in his freshman, junior, and senior seasons, respectively. His career TD-INT ratio is only 49-46. (His junior season is largely to blame for that as he posted a poor 7-17 TD-INT Ratio). Although beating South Carolina is always fun, we also have the fond memory of just how awful those Gamecock teams really were during that period with just one bowl appearance and zero bowl wins in those four seasons.

Whitehurst was a fine QB regardless of the circumstances.

2006 Clemson Tigers Football Coach Tommy Bowden

The 2006 Clemson Tigers football team represented Clemson University during the 2006 college football season as a member of the Atlantic Coast Conference (ACC). Tommy Bowden, son of Florida

State's famous Coach Bobby Bowden was the head football coach for his eighth of ten seasons. The Tigers completed their one hundred-eleventh season overall and their fifty-fourth in the Atlantic Coast Conference with a record of 8-5; 5-3 in the ACC. They finished in fourth out of 6 ACC Atlantic Division teams. The Offensive Coordinator was Rob Spence and the Defensive Coordinator was Vic Koenning.

Entering the season, the Tigers had high expectations, hoping to compete for a spot in the ACC Championship Game. After a heartbreaking loss at Boston College in the second game of the season, Clemson rolled off six straight victories, during which they averaged nearly 42 points a game. But things soon fell apart, with Clemson losing four out of their last five, including a loss to Kentucky in the Music City Bowl, and a 31–28 loss to arch rival South Carolina. The team finished the season with a disappointing 8–5 record.

The #18 ranked Clemson Fighting Tigers season opener resulted in a blowout / shutout win on Sept 2 at home against Florida Atlantic W (54-6). This home opener was played as always at Memorial Stadium on the campus of Clemson University in Clemson, SC before 78,693. After this blowout win, the #18 Tigers played a tough Boston College Team in Alumni Stadium, Chestnut Hill, MA on Sept 9. The Eagles got the win after two overtimes L (33-34) before 44,500 happy Eagles' Fans.

In the most important bowl game for Coach Tommy Bowden, the Bowden Bowl, the younger Bowden got to clock in his third win against his dad. Surely the Thanksgiving dinners were sweeter for Tommy but then there was this guy named Joe Paterno fighting his dad for most wins. So, on the 16th of the month, playing for all the Bowden marbles plus who gets the most stuffing at the big family T-day dinner, at 7:45 p.m. on this fine Saturday night in September, # 10 Florida State at Doak Campbell Stadium in Tallahassee, FL, could not keep up with the kid coach and so Clemson's Tommy Bowden got himself another win, his third v Dad W (27-20). It was a home game before 83,510. Nobody, especially a Bowden ever took a CU v FSU game less than seriously. The taste of the Turkey rode on it. Go Tommy!

In another home game on Sept 23, before 81,886 Clemson Fans and a big TV audience of Clemson fans, North Carolina played # 23 Clemson at home W (52-7) before 81,886. On Sept 30, the #18 Tigers shut-out Louisiana Tech at home W (51–0) before 81,564. On Oct 7 at Wake Forest's Groves Stadium, Winston-Salem, NC, Clemson won the game W (27–17) before 35,920.

Then on Oct 12, v Temple's Owls, the #12 Tigers got a big win at Bank of America Stadium in Charlotte, NC W (63–9) before 30,246. On Oct 21, at home the Tigers defeated the Yellow Jackets of # 13 Georgia Tech W (31-7).

Game highlights Clemson 31 v GA Tech 7
Oct 21, 2006 at Death Valley.

ESPN's College Gameday show made its first-ever appearance in Clemson for the game between the Tigers and the Georgia Tech Yellow Jackets on October 21. Kirk Herbstreit mentioned both during and after the show, that he felt that Clemson hosted one of the best Gameday audiences he'd ever seen. The Gameday audience at Clemson also set a new noise record when measured in the latter-half of the show.

The Tigers were ranked 12th nationally, while the Yellow Jackets came in No. 13 in the nation. The game was the most hyped game the ACC had seen in years.

And yes, Clemson rocked with all purple uniforms.

James Davis ran for 216 yards and two touchdowns while CJ Spiller had some mind-numbing touchdown plays of his own to lead Clemson to the easy victory. GT star wide receiver Calvin Johnson was held without a catch.

This was perhaps the most dominating performance Clemson had all decade against a top 25 team.

On Oct 26, at Virginia Tech, the #11 Tigers engaged the Hokies at Lane Stadium in Blacksburg, VA, but could not keep up with their offense, L (24–7) before an attendance of 66,233. On Nov 4, at home Maryland beat the #19 Clemson Tigers L (12-13) in a very close match—but no cigar. On Nov 11, at home, NC State lost in the big rival Textile Bowl to Clemson W (20-14). before 81,785.

On Nov 25, at home, against   South Carolina, in the annual battle for the supremacy of South Carolina – the Battle for the Palmetto State, Clemson's Tigers barely lost to the South Carolina Gamecocks L 31–28 before 83,428.

Music City Bowl

On Dec 29 at 1:00 p.m. vs a tough Kentucky squad, at LP Field in Nashville, TN, the Wildcats defeated the Tigers in the Music City Bowl, shown on ESPN and 68,024 fans at the stadium L (28–20)

Player Highlights Gaines Adams DE (2002-2006)
9 OF 20

Gaines Adams was a great speed rusher off the edge who could keep quarterbacks in the pocket where they belong and he could then wreak even more havoc for the good of the defense.

The late Gaines Adams, who died an untimely death, along with the Perry brothers, are near the top of the all-time sacks list, so it makes sense to pick a guy like Adams for aby all-start Clemson team. Imagine teaming him up with the Perry Brothers. Can you imagine the frustration of any offensive line trying to deal with these three all-time Clemson pass rushers? Gaines Adams was enough by himself.

Adams began to attend Clemson in 2002 and after being redshirted, in 2002, he played through 2006. As a redshirt freshman in 2003, he did not see much action as the second-team defensive end, only totaling 15 tackles and a sack. In 2004, he had 35 tackles with 8 sacks, and two blocked punts playing on special teams. For his hard work on special teams, Adams was awarded the 12th Man Award for Clemson's defense. Adams considered coming out for the NFL Draft after his sophomore year, but after the underclassman panel gave him a conservatively low ranking he decided to stay for his junior year.

Adams' 2005 junior season was a breakout year for him. He totaled 56 tackles, 9.5 sacks, and forced three fumbles while starting at boundary defensive end. Before his senior year in 2006, he was slated to be among the best defensive ends in the college football. Adams lived up to his reputation by starting all 12 games, recording 12.5 sacks, causing 2 fumbles and recovering 3.

By the end of the 2006 season, Adams recorded a total of 28 career sacks, tying the school record set by Michael Dean Perry (1984–1987). In addition, Adams was named to all five All-America teams acknowledged by the NCAA in 2006, and was recognized as one of seven unanimous first-team All-Americans that year.

Gaines Adams was off to a great career but his life ended suddenly. He was drafted in the first round of the 2007 NFL Draft, and played professionally for the Tampa Bay Buccaneers and Chicago Bears of the NFL. Adams died unexpectedly in 2010 from a previously undetected heart condition.

2007 Clemson Tigers Football Coach Tommy Bowden

The 2007 Clemson Tigers football team represented Clemson University during the 2007 college football season as a member of the Atlantic Coast Conference (ACC). Tommy Bowden, son of Florida State's famous Coach Bobby Bowden was the head football coach for his ninth of ten seasons. The Tigers completed their one hundred-twelfth season overall and their fifty-fifth in the Atlantic Coast Conference with a record of 9-4; 5-3 in the ACC. They finished in second of 6 ACC Atlantic Division teams. The Offensive Coordinator was Rob Spence and the Defensive Coordinator was Vic Koenning.

Clemson started 4-0, including a victory in the season and conference opener over the Florida State Seminoles in the ninth "Bowden Bowl", which pits father Bobby Bowden, coaching the Seminoles, against his son, Tommy. Following their 4-0 start, Clemson gave up two losses to Georgia Tech and Virginia Tech respectively. Following the two-game losing streak, the Tigers went on to another four-game winning streak. The team then finished the season with its toughest loss of the season (losing in the final seconds to Boston College, 20-17) and greatest triumph (defeating rival South Carolina 23-21 with a last-second field goal). With a record of 9-3, the Tigers received a bid to play in the 2007 Chick-fil-A Bowl.

Clemson played host to the Florida State Seminoles on Labor Day, Monday, September 3, 2007 in both teams' season opener. The game was played before a primetime national audience on ESPN as the only college football game in that time slot. It was only Clemson's second regular season Monday night game, the last being in 1982 against the University of Georgia.

The unranked Clemson Fighting Tigers season opener resulted in a great win on Sept 2 at home against Florida State W (24-18) in the annual Bowden Bowl. This home opener was played at Memorial Stadium on the campus of Clemson University in Clemson, SC before 81993.

Game highlights Clemson 24 v Florida State 18
Sept. 3, 2005 at Death Valley.

In this Labor Day night classic, Clemson knocked off the No. 19 Seminoles 24-18 behind James Davis' solid performance running the ball (18 carries, 102 yards, one TD) and Will Proctor's efficiency (14-24, 160 yards, 2 TDs).

The Tigers jumped out to a 21-0 lead, but FSU would storm back to be down by only six in the fourth quarter. Clemson's defense held off the Seminoles on three-straight drives to end the game.

He may not have known it, but Tommy Bowden would coach his last game ever against his father that night.

After this win, on Sept 8, the #25 Tigers played at home again against Louisiana Monroe and won W (49-26). During this September 8th game against UL-Monroe, Clemson quarterback Cullen Harper threw five touchdown passes, setting a new school record for most touchdown passes thrown in a single game

On Sept 15, at home again, this time against Furman, the #20 ranked Tigers won again for three in a row W (38-10). On Sept 22 at NC State's Carter–Finley Stadium in Raleigh, NC in the annual Textile Bowl, the Tigers won again – four in a row W (42–20). The following week on Sept 29, Georgia Tech spoiled the win streak at Bobby Dodd Stadium, Atlanta, GA, and beat Clemson L (3-13) before 54,635

On Oct 6 at home, #14 Virginia Tech made it two losses in a row as they beat the Tigers L (23-41). At home again on Oct 20, Clemson walloped Central Michigan W (70-14) making it 5-2 for the season. Then, on Oct 27 at Maryland's Byrd Stadium in College Park, MD, the Tigers defeated the Terrapins W (30–17) before 50,948.

On Nov 3, at Duke's #24 Wallace Wade Stadium in Durham, NC, Clemson got a big win W (47-10 before 20,457. On Nov 10, at home, the Tigers defeated the Wake Forest Demon Deacons W (44-10) before 82, 422. On Nov 17 at home, #18 Boston College beat #16 Clemson in a close match L (17-20) before 83,472. Wrapping up the regular season on Nov 24, #22 Clemson won the Battle of the Palmetto State over South Carolina at Williams-Brice Stadium in Columbia, SC. The margin was just two points W (23-21).

On December 2, 2007, it was announced that Clemson had accepted a bid to play in the 2007 Chick-fil-A Bowl opposite the Southeastern Conference's Auburn Tigers. The game will be played December 31 in front of a national audience on ESPN. It would be Clemson's 7th appearance in the bowl, tying NC State for most appearances in the game.

Chick-Fil-A Bowl

Ranked at #16, Clemson's Tigers took on the #21 Auburn Tigers in the 2008 Chick-Fil-A Bowl game, played at the Georgia Dome in Atlanta GA on New Year's Eve. The Clemson Tigers entered the post-season ranked 15th nationally, while Auburn came in 22nd. The game was particularly notable as it was Walter Riggs (Clemson's first football coach) who came to coach at Clemson from Auburn and who brought with him many traditions, including the Tiger Mascot Auburn barely beat the Tigers L (20-23) but got the win nonetheless. 74,413 were in attendance plus the ESPN audience.

2008 Clemson Tigers Football Coach Tommy Bowden

Following a 9–4 season in 2007, in which Clemson finished second in the ACC Atlantic Division and played in the Chick-Fil-A Bowl, and with several players returning in the skill positions, many expected Clemson to be a strong candidate to win the ACC and a dark horse in the national championship picture. The Tigers' main areas of concern heading into the 2008 season was on the offensive line and linebackers. The offensive line would be very young and inexperienced heading into the season, while the linebacker corps was thinned by graduation and off-field issues. Despite these areas of concern, Clemson was tabbed as preseason favorites to win the ACC and was ranked 9th in both the AP and ESPN/USA Today preseason polls. In addition, QB Cullen Harper was tabbed as the preseason favorite for the ACC's Player of the Year. The best laid plans of mice and men gang oft aglay.

The 2008 Clemson Tigers football team represented Clemson University during the 2008 college football season as a member of the Atlantic Coast Conference (ACC). Tommy Bowden, son of Florida State's famous Coach Bobby Bowden was the head football coach for his tenth (last) of ten seasons. The Tigers completed their one hundred-thirteenth season overall and their fifty-sixth in the Atlantic Coast Conference with a record of 7-6; 4-4 in the ACC. They finished in fifth of 6 ACC Atlantic Division teams. The Offensive Coordinator was Rob Spence and the Defensive Coordinator was Vic Koenning.

Head coach Tommy Bowden stepped down after the first six games of his tenth and last season. He was replaced by coach Dabo Swinney in the interim. Swinney was retained and of course in 2016, his Tigers brought in the School's second National Championship. Rob Spence left after Six games and was replaced by Billy Napier in the interim.

The #9 ranked Clemson Fighting Tigers season opener was played at the Georgia Dome in Atlanta GA in the Chick-fil-A Kickoff Classic held on August 30. It was a tough loss against #24 Alabama L (10-34). Some believed that coach Nick Saban's Crimson Tide's youth and inexperience would prove a serious disadvantage against an experienced team like Clemson. However, Alabama quickly took control in what would eventually be a lopsided victory. By the end of the first quarter, Bama led 13–0, and they extended their lead to 23–3 by halftime.

The only scare came when C. J. Spiller returned the second half kickoff 96 yards for a touchdown. However, the Tigers failed to score again. James Davis and C. J. Spiller combined for only 20 yards on the ground, while the team's rushing total was 0. Clemson's redshirt senior quarterback, Cullen Harper, completed 20 of 34 passes but had no touchdowns and one interception. Alabama's John Parker Wilson completed 22 of 30 passes with no interceptions. He threw two touchdowns to Nick Walker and Julio Jones, and rushed for one himself. The Crimson Tide went on to win by a score of 34–10.

The home opener was played as always at Memorial Stadium on the campus of Clemson University in Clemson, SC against the Citadel on Sept 6 before 76,794. After this win, on Sept 13 the #23 Tigers played again at home again against NC State in the Textile Bowl/Hall of Fame Day and won W (27-9. Let's look at this in more detail

As we have reported for the duration, there are many every-year things at Clemson and one of those is the Textile Bowl between the Tigers and the NC State Wolfpack. The annual renewal of the "Textile Bowl" between the Clemson Tigers and N.C. State Wolfpack unexpectedly got off to a rocky start for the Tigers this year.

On the first play of the game, Nate Irving intercepted a Cullen
Harper pass and returned it 33 yards for a touchdown, putting the
Wolfpack up 6–0. The Tigers responded by blocking the PAT. In the
next offensive series, the Tigers started on their own 24 and drove the
length of the field, capping the drive with a 16-yard touchdown pass
from Harper to Jacoby Ford. A 30-yard run by Ford on a reverse also
highlighted the drive. The Mark Buchholz PAT put Clemson up 7–6.
The next three drives saw the Tigers and Wolfpack trade punts. With
13:51 left in the 2nd quarter, Clemson began its next scoring drive
from its own 33. A 28-yard reception by Jacoby Ford highlighted the
drive, with rushes by James Davis, C. J. Spiller, and Cullen Harper
helping to aid the drive. With 4th and 2 on the N.C. State 5-yard line,
Buchholz came on for a 22-yard field goal to put the Tigers up 10–6.

After the next N.C. State drive stalled, Clemson got the ball back on
their own 41-yard line. Clemson scored after two passes from Cullen
Harper – the first a 31-yard strike to Aaron Kelly, and the second a
28-yard touchdown pass to C. J. Spiller. The PAT put Clemson
ahead 17–6.

The Wolfpack got back on the board late in the fourth quarter with a
25-yard field goal by Josh Czajkowski to close the gap to 17–9. The
Tigers started the next drive on the N.C. State 47 and drove it down
to the 13, but the drive stalled after an apparent touchdown run by
Spiller was negated by a holding penalty. Buchholz kicked a 31-yard
field goal to increase the lead to 20–9.

N.C. State's next drive resulted in their first turnover of the game,
when Crezdon Butler intercepted a pass at the Clemson 4-yard line.
The Tigers then sealed the game with a 13-play drive that consumed
7:01 of the clock, capping the drive with a 12-yard touchdown run by
Spiller. That would be the final score of the game, as the Tigers
prevailed 27–9 and extended their current win streak in the series to
five. The last efforts by the Wolfpack to close the gap were snuffed
out by an interception by Chris Chancellor.

In the stats column, the Tigers gained 426 yards of total offense.
Cullen Harper was 20–28 for 262 yards and 2 touchdowns and 1
interception. C. J. Spiller had a great day as a dual threat, finishing
with 61 rushing yards, 35 receiving yards, and 2 touchdowns. Jacoby
Ford lead all receivers with 106 receiving yards and a touchdown, in

addition to 48 rushing yards. The Tigers defense held the Wolfpack to 288 yards on offense, no offensive touchdowns, and recorded two interceptions.

The third home game in a row was on Sept 20 as #21 Clemson shutout and in fact, shellacked SC State W (54-0).

The first ever meeting between the Clemson Tigers and S.C. State Bulldogs turned into a lopsided contest, as the Tigers defeated their second FCS team on the season to improve to 3–1. Clemson's Tigers received the opening kickoff and struck first on a 68-yard drive capped off by a 1-yard touchdown run by James Davis. S.C. State was unable to respond on any of its two possessions in the first quarter, as they ended in a punt and missed field goal. Clemson, meanwhile, had its next two drives end in interceptions from Cullen Harper.

The Tigers broke the game open in the second quarter. Chris Chancellor intercepted an S.C. State pass early in the quarter. On the next possession, Davis and C. J. Spiller spearheaded the offensive attack, which ended in Davis' second touchdown of the day. The Tigers defense would cut the Bulldogs' next drive short with an interception by Crezdon Butler. Davis would score his third touchdown of the day on the next drive. A safety and a 1-yard touchdown plunge by Cullen Harper would give the Tigers a 30–0 halftime lead.

S.C. State received the ball to start the third quarter, but it would be the Tigers who opened scoring as Chris Clemons would pick off a Bulldog pass and return it for a touchdown. The next three drives saw two Bulldog drives and a Tigers drive stall.

Clemson would get back on the scoreboard with a Mark Buchholz field goal. Clemson would begin placing reserves in on offense late in the third quarter. Early in the fourth, the Tigers scored their fifth rushing touchdown of the day on a one-yard run by backup quarterback Willy Korn. Korn would later throw the Tigers' first passing touchdown of the day on a five-yard passes to tight end Michael Palmer. The defense recorded its fourth turnover of the day when Brandon Thompson recovered an S.C. State fumble. The Tigers would then run out the clock, giving the Tigers a 52–0 victory.

Cullen Harper completed 14 of 23 passes for 152 yards with no touchdowns and two interceptions. Willy Korn went 7–7 for 73 yards and a touchdown. James Davis lead the Tigers rushing attack with 93 yards and 3 touchdowns. Tyler Grisham lead the receiving corps with 41 reception yards on 3 receptions.

C. J. Spiller had 105 all-purpose yards on the day (66 rushing, 39 punt return). Overall, the Tigers offense compiled 432 yards of total offense (225 passing, 207 rushing) and 31 first downs. The defense held the Bulldogs to only 149 yards of total offense and eight first downs, while compiling four turnovers on the day.

In the fourth home game in a row, on Sept 27, Clemson lost to Maryland L (17-20). Against the Terrapins, Clemson firmly held the momentum of the game for the first half, with their running backs able to exploit holes in the Terps' defensive line. Clemson racked up two touchdowns and a field goal. Despite gaining excellent field position through recovering a fumbled punt on the Clemson 19-yard line and a recovered fumble on the Clemson 30-yard line, Maryland was able to produce just two field goals from those turnovers. The Terrapins drives were also blunted through penalties for two false starts and a holding call.

In the second half, the Terrapins began with a series that fizzled out after a run attempt for a loss, an additional false start, and two incomplete passes. However, the Terrapins defense took the field and stopped a Clemson drive, allowing the Maryland offense another chance. On the first play of their second series, wide receiver Darrius Heyward-Bey executed a reverse, gaining 76 yards before being run down at the Clemson 4-yard line. This set up a short Chris Turner touchdown pass to receiver Torrey Smith, and irreversibly shifted the game's momentum in favor of the Terps.

In the fourth quarter, three completions to Danny Oquendo set the stage for a one-yard rush into the end zone by Da'rel Scott. The Maryland defense remained stalwart, allowing Clemson just 31 rushing yards and no points in the second half, compared with 204 yards on the ground and 17 points in the first.

The upset marked the fourth consecutive Maryland win against a ranked opponent (the others: #23 Cal, and, in the 2007 season, #8 Boston College and #10 Rutgers). It is also the fourth consecutive time that the visiting team has won the Maryland-Clemson series.

On Oct 9, at #21 Wake Forest, an unranked Clemson lost to the Demon Deacons L (7–12) before 33,988. Riley Skinner's 7-yard touchdown pass to DJ Boldin with 5:28 to go gave the Deacons a 12–7 win against Clemson. In a defensive battle, the Deacons' defense managed to hold Clemson to less than one yard per carry. Wake Forest dominated the game statistically but were unable to capitalize on several scoring chances.

The sole turnover in the game was a Cullen Harper pass intercepted by Alphonso Smith, who tied a school record with his 17th career interception. Riley Skinner also threw for 186 yards and a touchdown on 22-of-34 passing, and also added 73 yards on the ground.

Clemson had been expected to win the ACC Conference and at the season midpoint, Tommy Bowden found the team hurting at 3-3, having not achieved the expected. So, he resigned. Dabo Swinney was named interim coach.

On Oct 18, at home, with Dabo Swinney as the new interim head coach, Georgia Tech defeated Clemson in a close match L (17-21). Nobody could deny that on Oct 13, Clemson had a shocker as head coach Tommy Bowden resigned and was replaced by receivers' coach Dabo Swinney.

Fife days later Swinney is playing John Heisman's old team, Georgia Tech and they have always been a tough squad to control. Tech's defense controlled the ebb and flow of the game against the Tigers forcing six turnovers, which included four interceptions and two fumble recoveries.

Safety Dominique Reese returned an intercepted pass from wide receiver Tyler Grisham for Tech's first touchdown. Morgan Burnett added two additional interceptions, the final in the last second of the game.

Offensively, Tech continued to produce with its ground game against the Tigers racking up 207 yards rushing. Josh Nesbitt ran untouched for 5 yards for Tech's second score and passed 24 yards to Demaryius Thomas for Tech's go ahead and eventual game winning score. Tech was 6–1 for the first time since 1999. Overall, Swinney did fine in a reserve role but he is the type of coach who likes to do his best to win.

On Nov 1, at Boston College's Alumni Stadium in Chestnut Hill, MA, playing for the O'Rourke–McFadden Trophy, Clemson got the win and the Trophy W (27–21) before 41,863.

On October 27, it was announced that the Boston College Gridiron Club will be sponsoring the O'Rourke-McFadden Trophy and it would be awarded to the winner of the Boston College-Clemson game on November 1. The trophy is named after Charlie O'Rourke and Banks McFadden, who were the respective quarterbacks for Boston College and Clemson during the 1940 Cotton Bowl (the 1st meeting between the Eagles and Tigers).

Clemson captured the O'Rourke-McFadden Trophy and its first victory over the Eagles since 1958 (and first win since Boston College joined the ACC) with a 27–21 victory. After the Eagles received the opening kickoff, both teams traded possessions. After Steve Aponavicius missed a 31-yard field goal, the Tigers took over on their own 20-yard line. C. J. Spiller broke a 56-yard run that drove the Tigers into BC territory, and James Davis capped the drive with a 24-yard touchdown run to put the Tigers up 7–0.

Later in the 1st quarter, Brandon Maye recovered a fumble to give the Tigers the ball back on their own 30-yard line. Cullen Harper connected with a 23-yard reception to Tyler Grisham and a 45-yard reception to C. J. Spiller to get to the Eagles 2-yard line. Harper then capped the drive with a 2-yard run to increase the lead to 14–0. After trading possessions again for the remainder of the 1st quarter and part of the second, Clemson started their next scoring drive with 8:12 left in the 2nd quarter. Driving from their own 20, the Tigers made their way to the Eagles 10-yard line before having to settle for a Mark Buchholz field goal to increase the lead to 17–0.

Boston College mounted a comeback in the second half, sparked by a McLaughlin interception of Harper to set up the Eagles at the Tigers 7-yard line. Josh Haden would punch the ball in from 1 yard out to make the score 17–7.

Early in the 4th quarter, the Eagles would block a Jimmy Maners punt, which was returned by Roderick Rollins 20 yards for a touchdown to close the margin to 17–14. After Davis intercepted another Harper pass to give the Eagles great field position, the Eagles would score on a 16-yard pass from Chris Crane to Brandon Robinson to take 21–17 lead. However, Spiller would take ensuing kickoff 64 yards to set up the Tigers on the Eagles 15-yard line.

The Tigers would capitalize on the drive, completing the drive with a 4-yard touchdown pass from Harper to Aaron Kelly to take a 24–17 lead. On the next drive, DeAndre McDaniel forced a fumble that was recovered by Daquan Bowers. The Tigers would put away the game for good with a Buchholz field goal on the next possession. The victory would give interim head coach Dabo Swinney his first win.

Offensively for the Tigers, Harper finished the game completing 21 of 33 passes for 252 yards, 1 touchdown, and 3 interceptions. C. J. Spiller lead the Tigers in rushing (55 yards) and receiving (105 yards), while compiling 242 all-purpose yards for the entire game. James Davis scored the 42nd rushing touchdown of his career, breaking the Tigers' all-time rushing touchdown record. Aaron Kelly recorded his 19th career touchdown reception in the game, which gave him Clemson's record for career touchdown receptions. Defensively, the Tigers held the Eagles to 236 yards and forced three fumbles (2 of which the Tigers recovered).

On Nov 8, at #24 Florida State's Doak Campbell Stadium in Tallahassee, FL, Clemson lost in what would have been the tenth Bowden Bowl but Swinney was the coach L (27-41).

On Nov 15, the Homecoming game was won by Clemson against the Duke Blue Devils W (31-7). The Tigers came into their homecoming game against the Duke Blue Devils in need of winning the last three games for bowl eligibility. Clemson received the opening kickoff, but both teams ended up trading punts in the first four possessions of the game. Duke's second possession of the game saw starting quarterback

Thaddeus Lewis suffer a sprained ankle while trying to elude a Clemson defender, which knocked him out of the game and hampered the Blue Devils' offense for the remainder of the game.

On the Tigers' third offensive possession, James Davis had three consecutive rushes for 18 yards. After a loss of three yards, Clemson faced 3rd and 10 on the Duke 48-yard line. Cullen Harper completed a pass to Tyler Grisham, who turned it into a 19-yard gain. On the following play, C. J. Spiller ran the ball 24 yards for the game's first touchdown.

After trading possession, which saw Duke having to punt twice and a Clemson drive stall on a missed 53-yard field goal, the Tigers took over again with 9:23 left in the second quarter. In this possession, Clemson added to the lead with a 39-yard field goal by Mark Buchholz.

After the Tigers' defense forced the Blue Devil offense to go three and out, Clemson got the ball back around midfield. After Cullen Harper completed several completions to Spiller, Jacoby Ford, and Aaron Kelly, the Tigers had the ball on the Duke 1-yard line. James Davis then punched it in to give the Tigers a 17–0 halftime lead.

Duke received the opening second-half kickoff, but the drive ended up stalling around midfield, forcing another punt. Clemson's next drive proved to be very short on terms of time off the clock, as Harper connected on a screen pass to Spiller, who raced 83 yards for his second touchdown of the day.

Michael Hamlin then intercepted Duke's back-up quarterback Zach Asack on the next possession on the game's first turnover. After a 15-yard reception to Ford and a 26-yard reception to Davis, the Tigers had worked themselves to the Blue Devil three-yard line. Davis then scored his second touchdown of the day to give the Tigers a 31–0 lead. Duke would finally score late in the fourth quarter on a 28-yard pass from Asack to Eron Riley to close the final gap to 31–7. A late drive by Duke was cut short deep in Clemson territory by an interception by Coty Sensabaugh.

Offensively, it was the Tigers all the way with 466 yards for the game (326 passing and 140 rushing), 25 first downs, and converted 6 of 16 third downs. Cullen Harper completed 20 of 26 passes for 292 yards, 1 touchdown, and no interceptions. C. J. Spiller lead the Tigers in rushing and receiving for the second time in three games, rushing for 71 yards and a touchdown, and 108 receiving yards and a touchdown.

James Davis had 43 rushing yards, 26 receiving yards, and two rushing touchdowns. Aaron Kelly had 96 receiving yards on the day and broke the ACC reception record held by Desmond Clark with two back-to-back receptions late in the 4th quarter. Defensively, the Tigers held the Blue Devils to 168 total yards (85 passing and 83 rushing), 2 of 14 on third down conversions, and forced two turnovers. Clemson held the time of possession advantage, controlling the ball for 35:36 compared to Duke's 24:24 of possession.

On Nov 22 at the Virginia Wahoo's Scott Stadium in Charlottesville, Clemson won W (13-3) before 51,979. The Tigers kept their bowl hopes alive with a close 13–3 victory over the Virginia Cavaliers in Charlottesville. With the victory, Clemson captured their first victory in Charlottesville since 2000 and improved the series record against the Cavaliers to 36–8–1.

Neither offense was able to generate much production, as the Tigers barely outgained the Cavaliers 192–190. Cullen Harper completed 18 of 28 passes for 121 yards, no touchdowns, and no interceptions. C. J. Spiller only had 57 all-purpose yards, but completed his 1st career touchdown pass in the first quarter, completing a 15-yard pass to Tyler Grisham for the game's only touchdown. James Davis lead the Tigers with 65 rushing yards, while Jacoby Ford lead the receiving corps with six catches for 42 yards.

Mark Buchholz was 2–3 on field goals (good from 32 and 23 yards; missed from 58 yards) and connected on the game's only PAT attempt. Clemson's defense forced four turnovers against the Cavaliers. Michael Hamlin lead the defense with 8 total tackles, an interception, and a pass break up. Crezdon Butler and DeAndre McDaniel also recorded interceptions, while Byron Maxwell forced a fumble that was recovered by Jock McKissick late in the first quarter.

On Nov 29 at home, in the Battle for the Palmetto Stake aka the Solid Orange Game, the Tigers defeated the Gamecocks W (31-14) before 82, 456.

Clemson won its second straight game over South Carolina and extended the overall series lead against the Gamecocks to 65–37–4. After the Tigers lost a fumble on the opening drive, the Gamecocks had the chance to score first. However, Chris Chancellor intercepted a Chris Smelley pass.

On the next drive, Clemson scored the game's first touchdown after an 85-yard drive highlighted by a 39-yard run by C. J. Spiller and capped by a 1-yard touchdown by James Davis. Clemson then blocked a Gamecock punt on the next possession and followed it up with a 22-yard field goal by Mark Buchholz to take a 10–0 lead. In the second quarter, the Tigers again intercepted a Chris Smelley pass (this time by Chris Clemons) to get the ball back around midfield.

Two plays later, Cullen Harper threw downfield to Jacoby Ford as he was being tackled by a Gamecock defender. Ford turned the pass into a 50-yard touchdown reception to give the Tigers a 17–0 lead. The Tigers started their next drive at the South Carolina 41-yard line following an interception by Michael Hamlin. Davis capped the drive with a 20-yard touchdown run to give the Tigers a 24–0 lead.

The Gamecocks would score late in the second quarter after the defense recovered a fumble by Harper. Starting at the Clemson 33-yard line, the Gamecocks capped the drive with a 16-yard touchdown pass from Smelley to Patrick DiMarco to cut the Tigers' lead to 24–7.

The Gamecocks opened the third quarter with a 69-yard scoring drive, capped by a 23-yard touchdown pass from Smelley to Wesley Saunders to cut the margin to 24–14.

However, Clemson would counter that several drives later with a 44-yard touchdown drive, capped by Davis' third touchdown run of the day, to push the lead to 31–14. In the fourth quarter, Chris Chancellor recorded his second interception of the day (and the defense's fourth against Gamecock quarterback Chris Smelley) to cut short a potential Gamecock scoring drive and leave the final margin at 31–14 in favor of the Tigers.

With the victory, the Tigers secured bowl eligibility and gave interim head coach Dabo Swinney his fourth win since taking over at midseason following Tommy Bowden's resignation. Offensively, the Tigers finished the day with 383 yards of total offense. Cullen Harper completed 12 of 17 passes for 199 yards, 1 touchdown, and no interceptions. James Davis led Clemson's rushing attack with 91 yards and 3 touchdowns in his final game in Death Valley.

Aaron Kelly led the Tigers' receivers with four catches for 76 yards. C. J. Spiller had 199 all-purpose yards (88 rushing, 35 receiving, and 76 kick/punt return yards). Defensively, the Tigers held the Gamecocks' offense to 304 yards. Clemson led in time of possession 32:47–27:13 and forced four turnovers compared to two by the Gamecocks.

For their efforts, Clemson was invited to the Gator Bowl.

2009 Gator Bowl

On January 1, 2009 at 1:00 p.m. Nebraska squared off against Clemson at Jacksonville Municipal Stadium in Jacksonville, FL for the Gator Bowl. It was a close loss but a loss nonetheless L (21-26) for the Tigers before a crowd of 67,282 plus a TV audience.

The Nebraska win was a come-from-behind 26–21 finish to the 2009 Gator Bowl. The game remained in doubt until the very end, as Clemson marched from their own 23 to the Nebraska 10. With 1st and goal to go and about two minutes remaining on the clock, Cullen Harper came up short, resulting in a 16-yard sack and three Clemson incompletions to seal the outcome of the game. The game was played only days after Nebraska's Head Coach Bo Pelini and Defensive Coordinator Carl Pelini returned from their father's funeral in Ohio.

The best way to describe Tommy Bowden's departure from Clemson after a reasonably good tenure is to turn the writing floor over to Mark Schlabach an ESPN Senior writer who wrote this piece right when it happened in mid-season, 2008. He tells it as he saw it right after it happened.

Schlabach titled his piece:

"Bowden out at Clemson; coach 'deserved' fate, QB says.

It was written on Oct 14, 2008. Here it is:

Mark Schlabach ESPN Senior Writer

"Clemson ousted football coach Tommy Bowden on Monday, four days after the Tigers -- who were the favorites to win the ACC championship -- lost to Wake Forest and fell to 3-3.

Bowden informed his assistant coaches of his ouster Monday morning. Assistant head coach/wide receivers coach Dabo Swinney has been named interim coach for the final six regular-season games and potential bowl game. Clemson offensive coordinator Rob Spence also has been ousted, a source close to the situation said.

Athletic director Terry Don Phillips said his intent Monday morning was to have a candid heart-to-heart with Bowden about the football team. But Phillips said he was surprised when Bowden offered to resign.

"There wasn't a gun to his head," Phillips said.

"He put it on the table for the sake of the program," Phillips said. "I agreed."

Bowden will be paid through the end of the season, then get $3.5 million as a buyout negotiated in the contract extension the two sides agreed to in December 2007.

Bowden sat next to Phillips in McFadden Auditorium, where he has held meetings and news conferences the past 10 seasons. He thanked the school, its administrators and his latest group of players.

"I wish them nothing but success, and I will be their biggest fan on Saturday" against Georgia Tech, Bowden said.
With that, Bowden left the stage without taking questions, walked into his office and shut the door as Phillips detailed the day's dramatic events.

In an earlier statement, Bowden said: "Terry Don Phillips approached me this morning and we agreed that this is the best solution for the direction of the program. Clemson has been very good to me and my family. Both of our children are Clemson graduates.

"I appreciate the opportunity Clemson University gave me and the support of the administration while I was here. I also want to thank all the players and coaches who worked so hard for this program the last 10 years. I wish Clemson University nothing but the best in the future."
Clemson's season started with a big thud, a 24-point loss to then-No. 24 Alabama that senior quarterback Cullen Harper said "really hurt our confidence."

Harper, who was benched after the Tigers' loss to Wake Forest and replaced by highly regarded sophomore Willy Korn, said the program needed to cut ties with Bowden.

"It's what he deserved," Harper said. "Dabo Swinney is a fine man and will do an excellent job."

Later Monday, Harper expanded on his comments, explaining that Bowden "tried to motivate us, but guys were off the bandwagon. There were things I disagreed with and that my teammates disagreed with. I didn't appreciate it when he would say some off-the-wall things about me to the media. I guess one thing I can say is he gave me an opportunity to come to Clemson and play."

Harper struggled playing behind an inexperienced offensive line this season. His father, Jeff Harper, an offensive lineman on Georgia's 1980 national championship team, said Bowden's dismissal was justified.

"I'd call it karma," he said. "I thought it needed to be done. I think anytime a head coach or someone in a leadership position starts to place blame on his coaches and players, it weakens their respect on the team. His past experiences have shown he's done that."

In the wake of Bowden's ouster, two highly touted recruits have dropped Clemson from their lists, according to JC Shurburtt, who covers Southeast recruiting for ESPN.com. Safeties Craig Loston from Aldine, Texas, and Devonte Hollomon from Rock Hill, S.C., have said they are looking elsewhere. Loston is the No. 1 safety on the ESPN150 list of safeties and is No. 8 overall; Hollomon is No. 3 on the safeties list and No. 20 overall.

The Tigers were ranked No. 9 in the preseason Associated Press Top 25 poll and were favored to win their first ACC championship in Bowden's 10th season as coach. But now-No. 2 Alabama blasted the Tigers 34-10 in the Aug. 30 opener in Atlanta's Georgia Dome, and Clemson then lost to Maryland at home and again to Wake Forest, falling to 1-2 in ACC play.

Bowden received a lucrative contract extension from Clemson after the 2007 season and after considering a potential coaching position at Arkansas. A son of Florida State coach Bobby Bowden, Tommy Bowden was 72-45 with eight bowl appearances at Clemson.

Bobby Bowden said in a statement Monday that his son "felt like it was fixin' to happen; he felt like it was inevitable."

Clemson's 10th season under Tommy Bowden unraveled quickly. The Tigers were expected to contend for the ACC

"He's thankful for the experience he got there at Clemson," Bobby Bowden said. "He has no hard feelings towards them. This is just the nature of this game right now. He's disappointed but he's got his priorities in order in his life, so he'll move on and won't lose a minute of sleep over it. At least I don't have to worry about him beating me again."

Clemson center Thomas Austin said he was "caught off guard" by Bowden's departure.

"You hear rumors, but I've heard that before, so I'm definitely surprised," Austin said. "We were definitely struggling. I think that this could hopefully unify our team in the long run. We've got six games left and definitely have the ability to turn things around."

Clemson running back C.J. Spiller had mixed emotions in seeing the program move away from Bowden.

"I'm shocked. We are 3-3 because we didn't make enough big offensive plays," Spiller said. "I'm shocked by our record, and now I'm shocked that our coach is gone.

"I enjoyed playing for coach Bowden and I liked him, but in the end, he was yelling at us to be leaders and it wasn't working. He did all he could to motivate us, but guys weren't buying into what he was saying. And he said a lot of the same things over and over again.

"He let the offensive coordinator [Spence] run the show, and we got away from me and James [Davis]. I think part of the problem was when he benched Cullen. Some people wanted the offensive coordinator fired; [Bowden benched] the quarterback and then he got fired."

Phillips praised Bowden for his success and the generally upstanding program he ran. But Phillips was no different from most Clemson fans in expecting that this year's team had a prime opportunity to win the ACC.

"We both understood the conference championship was critically important," Phillips said.

Mark Schlabach covers college football for ESPN.com. ACC blogger Heather Dinich, SEC blogger Chris Low, ESPN reporter Joe Schad and The Associated Press contributed to Mark Schlabach's report.

Player Highlights C.J. Spiller, RB 2006-09

The consensus is that Spiller is Clemson's most dynamic offensive playmaker of the Athlon era (since 1967). He was quite a runner for sure with top-level football skills.

If you were forming the players who would be part of the all-time Clemson dream team, to add a little spice and a game-changer at running back, you would assure CJ Spiller was on the squad.

Spiller was a threat to score from anywhere on the field. He proved he could be the feature back of an offense when he returned for his senior season, and was one of the most explosive players of 2009, scoring at least one touchdown in every single game.

With his ability to catch out of the backfield and his blazing speed next to tall, strong-armed, very capable QB, any offense with Spiller would be one to watch.

C.J. Spiller came to Clemson from Lake Butler, Fla. He was an elite all-purpose recruit. He was not just a great RB. He delivered in all areas, earning ACC Player of the Year honors in 2009.

He was the first Clemson player to receive the award since Michael Dean Perry in 1987 and the first offensive player from Clemson to earn the award since quarterback Steve Fuller in 1978. Spiller had only one 1,000-yard season in his career (with 1,212 yards as a senior), but his 7.27 career yards per carry was the second-best average in Clemson history and the best since 1950.

Though listed as a running back, Spiller was a threat as a runner, receiver and return man, Spiller shattered the Clemson record for all-purpose yards with 7,588 in his career, an ACC record and the third-most in NCAA history. His 51 total touchdowns (31 rushing, 12 receiving, seven on kickoff returns, one on a punt return) is a school record.

Chapter 25 Dabo Swinney Era 2008-2017+

Coach # 25 Dabo Swinney

Year	Coach	Record	Conference	Record
2009	Dabo Swinney	9-5	ACC	6-2
2010	Dabo Swinney	6-7	ACC	4-2
2011	Dabo Swinney	10-4	ACC	6-2
2012*	Dabo Swinney	11-2	ACC	7-1
2013	Dabo Swinney	11-2	ACC	7-1
2014	Dabo Swinney	10-3	ACC	6-2
2015*	Dabo Swinney	14-1	ACC	8-0
2016*	Dabo Swinney	14-1	ACC	7-1
2017	Dabo Swinney		ACC	

* ACC Championship; 2016 National Championship

2009 Clemson Tigers Football Coach Dabo Swinney

The 2009 Clemson Tigers football team represented Clemson
University during the 2009college football season as a member of the
Atlantic Coast Conference (ACC). Dabo Swinney was the head
football coach for his second of many seasons.

This was Swinney's first full season after completing seven games of Coach Tommy Bowden's final year in 2008. The Tigers completed their one hundred-fourteenth season overall and their fifty-seventh in the Atlantic Coast Conference with a record of 9-5; 6-2 in the ACC. They finished in first place of 6 ACC Atlantic Division teams. The Offensive Coordinator was Bill Napier and the Defensive Coordinator was Kevin Steele.

The Tigers had an overall good year and won the ACC Atlantic Division, but after securing the title lost to in–state rival South Carolina in the Palmetto Bowl 34–17, before losing for the second time in the season to Georgia Tech in the ACC Championship Game. Clemson closed the season with a win over Kentucky in the Music City Bowl.

The unranked Clemson Fighting Tigers home season opener resulted in a win on Sept 5 at home against Middle Tennessee W (37-14). This home opener was played as always at Memorial Stadium on the campus of Clemson University in Clemson, SC before 78371. After this home win, on Sept 10, the unranked Tigers played at No. 13 Georgia Tech's Bobby Dodd Stadium in Atlanta, GA where they were defeated by the Yellow Jackets L (27–30) before 52,029. On Sept 19, at home, Boston College took it on the chin big time W (25-7).

On Sept 26, at home, Clemson lost to #14 TCU L (10-14). Then, on Oct 3, at Maryland's Byrd Stadium in College Park, MD, Clemson lost again L (21-24) before 46,243. Two weeks later on Oct 17 at home, the Tigers defeated the Wake Forest Demon Deacons W (38-3). On Oct 24, unranked Clemson played the #10 Hurricanes of Miami University at Land Shark Stadium in Miami Gardens, FL., The game was nip and tuck and finally the Tigers beat the Hurricanes W (40-37) in OT before 43, 778.

Game highlights Clemson 40 v Miami 37 (OT)
Oct 24, 2009 in Miami Gardens FL.

This was a huge game for Clemson's 2009 season.

The Tigers were coming off two tough losses to Maryland and TCU. Clemson had hammered Wake Forest the week before. Heading to

Miami, Clemson was considered a huge underdog against the #8 Hurricanes.

There were more back-and-forth blows in this game than a heavyweight fight. Nonetheless, Clemson managed to outlast the Canes in overtime 40-37. CJ Spiller had 300-plus all-purpose yards while Kyle Parker threw for 326 yards and three touchdowns, including a 26-yard pass in overtime to cap off an instant classic.

On Oct 31, as Dabo Swinney's team was beginning to know how great they were, Coastal Carolina's Chanticleers came to Clemson's campus for the Clemson Homecoming game. It was a great homecoming as the Tigers got the best of the visitors in a walloping game W (49-3). In the non-Bowden Bowl of 2009, it was Bobby Bowden's last year coaching Florida State. The game was Nov 7 and it was at home in a celebration called Solid Orange Day. The Tigers hit the Seminoles with all they had and the Seminoles fought back but lost the game W (40-24), giving Dabo Swinney a great win and putting a mar in Bobby Bowden's last season (7-6) at FSU with Jimbo Fisher as his offensive coordinator.

On Nov 14 at NC State's Carter-Finley Stadium in Raleigh, NC, the Tigers outplayed the Wolfpack in the Textile Bowl W (43–23) before 57,583. Then, on Nov 21 at home, #19 Clemson beat Virginia's Wahoos W (34-21) before 77,568. Finishing up a better season than was ever delivered by a fine coach Tommy Bowden, on Nov 28, at South Carolina's Williams-Brice Stadium in Columbia, SC, the #16 Tigers lost the game to the unranked Gamecocks L (17–34)). But, there was still one or two games left in the postseason.

At the end of the season, Head Coach Dabo Swinney announced that they would retire the #28 jersey worn by C. J. Spiller at a ceremony when the Tigers play Maryland at home on Oct. 16, 2010.

2009 Post Season – Championships and Music City Bowl

On December 5 at 8:00 p.m. vs. #12 Georgia Tech, at Raymond James Stadium in Tampa, FL, Clemson lost the ACC Championship L (34–39).

The Tigers got a bowl bid anyway. On Dec 27at 7:30 p.m. vs. Kentucky at LP Field in Nashville, TN, the Clemson Tigers with Dabo Swinney found enough muster to defeat Kentucky in the Music City Bowl W (21–13) before 57,280.

Game highlights Clemson 21 v Kentucky 13
Dec 27, 2009 in Nashville TN.

Not only was it Dabo Swinney's first bowl win as Clemson's head coach, it was also CJ Spiller's last game as a Clemson Tiger.

Spiller gained 172 all-purpose yards and scored a touchdown in his 14th consecutive game.

Kentucky came out and scored quickly on its first drive. Clemson's defense then snapped from its slumber and held UK to just a couple of field goals the rest of the game. This was just Clemson's fourth bowl win of the decade despite being bowl eligible every single season.

2010 Clemson Tigers Football Coach Dabo Swinney

The 2010 Clemson Tigers football team represented Clemson University during the 2010college football season as a member of the Atlantic Coast Conference (ACC). Dabo Swinney was the head football coach for his third of many seasons. The Tigers completed their one hundred-fifteenth season overall and their fifty-eighth in the Atlantic Coast Conference with a record of 6-7; 4-4 in the ACC. They finished fifth of 6 ACC Atlantic Division teams. The Offensive Coordinator was Bill Napier and the Defensive Coordinator was Kevin Steele.

The unranked Clemson Fighting Tigers home season opener resulted in a win on Sept 4 at home against North Texas W (35-10). This home opener was played as always at Memorial Stadium on the campus of Clemson University in Clemson, SC before 74,356. After this home win, on Sept 11, the unranked Tigers played at home against Presbyterian for the first time in many years. The Tigers won the game in a big way but Presbyterian played tough on both sides of the ball W (58-21).

On Sept 18, The Clemson Tigers were playing the #15 Auburn Tigers again. This encounter was at Auburn's Jordan–Hare Stadium in Auburn, AL. The Auburn Tigers won the game L (24–27) in Overtime before 87,451. On Oct 2, at home, #16 Miami was the homecoming guest team but homecoming did not go well as the Tigers went down L (21-30 at the hands of the Hurricanes.

On Oct 9, at North Carolina's Kenan Memorial Stadium in Chapel Hill, NC, the Tar Heels beat the Tigers L (16–21) before 60,000. Then, on Oct 16, at home v Maryland, the Tigers beat the Terrapins W (31-7) In the next home game on Oct 23, Georgia Tech was forced to give it up for the Tigers of Clemson W (27-13).

Finding it just as tough as for Notre Dame v Boston College, this game on Oct 30, at the diminutive Alumni Stadium in Chestnut Hill, MA, found the Tigers on the bottom side of the score against the Eagles L (10–16) before 37,137. On Nov 6, at home, # 25 NC State decided to win the Textile Bowl, but played just a notch short as Clemson won the game by one point W (14–13) before 75,906.

On Nov 13 at Florida State's Doak Campbell Stadium in Tallahassee, FL, an annoying rivalry, Clemson lost L (13–16) before 72,228. Then, on Nov 20 at Wake Forest's BB&T Field, Winston-Salem, NC, the Tigers put a good grip on the Demon Deacons and beat them W (30–10) before 31,783. On Nov 27 at home in the Battle of the Palmetto State, Clemson Tigers played # 17 South Carolina and the Gamecocks defeated the Tigers L (7–29) before 81,355. In an off-year bowl game, Clemson accepted to play in the Meineke Car Care Bowl Game.

Meineke Car Care Bowl Game

On Dec 31 at Noon, against South Florida at Bank of America Stadium in Charlotte, NC, after playing the entire Meineke Car Care Bowl, South Florida had beaten Clemson L (26–31) before 41,122.

Player Highlights DeAndre McDaniel S 2007-2010

The safety who was closest to Dawkins' level during their time with Clemson was DeAndre McDaniel. He had the coverage skills and ability to make the secondary thrive. The Tigers sorely missed McDaniel in 2011 as a deep safety.

As a freshman in 2007, McDaniel made first-team All-ACC freshman selection by Sporting News after recording 33 tackles and two interceptions. As a sophomore in 2008 the Tigers moved him to linebacker. He finished the season with 77 tackles and an interception. He was a fine player.

In June 2008, McDaniel had a tough personal year after an argument with his girlfriend which resulted in some "serious bodily injury".

In 2009, McDaniel was back and he was also moved back to safety, where he recorded eight interceptions, with one returned for a touchdown. After a bowl victory over Kentucky, McDaniel decided to return to Clemson for the 2010 season. His eight interceptions tied a Clemson school record.

In 2010, McDaniel finished with 4 interceptions and 75 total tackles, including 12 in the Meineke Car Care Bowl. Despite his strong collegiate career and physical talent, he was not selected in the NFL Draft, perhaps because of his personal conflicts.

McDaniel was not drafted in 2011. On July 25, when the NFL lockout ended, McDaniel announced that he was signed by the New Orleans Saints. After practicing he hit some hard luck and was waived on August 30. McDaniel was signed to the practice squad of the Indianapolis Colts on September 7, 2011. He was released on September 12.

Player Highlights Daquan Bowers DE 2008-2010

10 OF 20

Bowers was not the best player in Clemson History but there is no question he could play football. Some might argue that he was not all-star category but perhaps they never played against him. His raw ability as a pass rusher at Clemson cannot go unnoticed.

It did take a little longer for to develop but when his light came on, Bowers proved he had the motor, the moxie, and the ability to give quarterbacks plenty of headache and concern.

He graduated early to enroll at Clemson University in January 2008, where he was a member of the Clemson Tigers football team from 2008 to 2010. He went through the 2008 spring drills and was impressive with a game-high seven tackles in the 2008 Spring Game. As a true freshman in 2008, Bowers started six of 13 games, finishing the season with 37 tackles including 8 for loss.

When he was a sophomore, he recorded 46 tackles, 10.5 for loss and three sacks, in spite of an injury that forced him to miss three games. Then, as a junior in 2010, Bowers snagged 67 tackles, 26 tackles for loss and 15.5 sacks. Bowers led the nation in sacks and was tied for the most tackles for loss.

Following the season, he was a first-team All-ACC selection, and was recognized as a unanimous first-team All-American. He was also honored as the ACC Defensive Player of the Year, and was the recipient of the Bronko Nagurski Trophy.

Bowers was selected in the 2nd round (51st overall) of the 2011 NFL Draft by the Tampa Bay Buccaneers. He had torn his Achilles tendon on the practice field on May 10, 2012, during the Bucs off-season program. Bowers was activated on Oct 25, 2012. He played his first game of the 2012 season that same night against the Minnesota Vikings.

His tenure with Tampa Bay came to an end following the 2014 season after yet an unproductive season. Da'Quan Bowers re-signed on July 27, 2015 for the upcoming training camp in order to grab a spot-on Tampa Bay's roster. After not making their 53-man final roster, on September 4, 2015, Bowers was cut from the Bucs. On December 15, 2015 Bowers re-signed with the Buccaneers to finish the season after the Bucs were plagued by injuries. He is currently and unsigned free agent.

2011 Clemson Tigers Football Coach Dabo Swinney

The 2011 Clemson Tigers football team represented Clemson University during the 2011college football season as a member of the Atlantic Coast Conference (ACC). Dabo Swinney was the head football coach for his fourth of many seasons. The Tigers completed their one hundred-sixteenth season overall and their fifty-ninth as a member of the Atlantic Division of the Atlantic Coast Conference. Their overall record was 10-4; 6-2 in the ACC. They finished first of 6 ACC Atlantic Division teams. The Offensive Coordinator was Chad Morris and the Defensive Coordinator was Kevin Steele.

Clemson finished the previous season 6–7, losing in the Meineke Car Care Bowl to South Florida. They began the 2011 season unranked, but after a three-game winning streak against ranked opponents in late September, rose to #8 in the AP and Coaches Poll. However, the Tigers lost three of their final four regular-season contests (with two of the losses to unranked opponents). And, so, they fell back to #21 in the polls.

However, their early start was enough to clinch a spot in the 2011 ACC Championship Game. They won that game with a dominant performance over Virginia Tech, 38–10. In the process, they won their first ACC title since 1991, and with it, they received an automatic berth in the 2012 Orange Bowl.

It was the Tigers' first-ever Bowl Championship Series berth, as well as their first major-bowl appearance since the 1982 Orange Bowl. They lost the game to West Virginia and made history at the same. The game's score of 70–33, set a bowl record for points conceded in a game.

The Games of the 2011 Season

The unranked Clemson Fighting Tigers home season opener resulted in a win on Sept 3 against Troy W (43–19). The Clemson home opener was played as always at Memorial Stadium (also known as Death Valley) on the campus of Clemson University in Clemson, SC before 73,458. In the game, The Tigers offense had a shaky first half adapting to offensive coordinator Chad Morris's faster new spread set. They had a tough time getting it going and were 0-for-8 on third down conversions and had only four first downs. Sophomore quarterback Tajh Boyd had several bad throws and near interceptions as the team was actually booed off the field at half time.

Clemson was down 16–13 with 6:56 left in the third quarter, but Swinney's squad finally converted their first third down as tight end

Dwayne Allen grabbed a 54-yard touchdown pass from Boyd to put the Tigers ahead. On the next drive, Boyd completed all of his passes including a seven-yard touchdown pass to Jaron Brown. The scoring run continued in the fourth quarter, ending in a 43–19 rout.

Boyd finished the game 20-for-30 for 364 yards and three touchdowns in his debut as Clemson's starting quarterback. Sammy Watkins had seven catches for 81 yards while Andre Ellington rushed 18 times for 89 yards. Freshmen accounted for 266 of Clemson's 468 yards. They promised good things to come.

After this home win, on Sept 10, the unranked Tigers played again at home this time against Wofford. The Tigers won the close match W (35-27). In wcek two, the inexperienced Tigers defense struggled to contain Wofford's triple-option offense throughout thc game. The Terriers led 21–13 with 4:03 remaining in the second quarter, but Tajh Boyd led a six-play, 72-yard drive and a two-point conversion to tie the game before half time.

Wofford's last lead in the game came in the opening series of the second half with a field goal. Clemson scored a touchdown each in the third and fourth quarters before stopping Wofford on fourth-and-2 with 3:30 remaining in the game to hold on for a 35–27 victory. Boyd was 18-for-29 for 261 yards and three touchdowns. Andre Ellington had 22 carries for 165 yards. His 74-yard touchdown run was the longest of his career.

On Sept 17, at home again against the #21 Auburn Tigers, the Clemson Tigers prevailed W (38–24) before 81,514. Defending national champions #21 Auburn took a 14–0 lead in the first quarter before Tajh Boyd began finding his passing rhythm. Boyd completed 30 of 42 passes for 386 yards and four touchdowns. The game was tied 21–21 at half time, but Clemson's defense restricted Auburn to a field goal in the second half while Boyd threw two touchdown passes to earn a 38–24 win, ending a 17-game winning streak for Auburn.

Clemson's offense totaled 624 yards, its record against an SEC opponent. Fans swarmed the field at the end of the game. Coach Dabo Swinney remarked, "I couldn't think of a better place to end the streak than Death Valley, South Carolina, baby."

On Sept 24, at home against #11 Florida State, the #21 ranked Tigers beat the Seminoles W (35-30). After Auburn, Clemson entered week four ranked #21. They faced Atlantic Division champions Florida State in their fourth straight home game. FSU was without injured starting quarterback E. J. Manuel. Clemson opened up a 21–10 lead by halftime, and were in control for the rest of the game. Tajh Boyd was 23-for-37 for 344 yards and three touchdowns and had a rushing touchdown. Freshman receiver Sammy Watkins had eight catches for 141 yards and two touchdowns while Andre Ellington rushed for 72 yards.

On Oct 1, at # 11 Virginia Tech's Lane Stadium in Blacksburg, VA, Clemson's Tigers defeated the Hokies W (23–3) before 66,233. For Clemson's first road game, The Tigers' defense turned in its best effort of the season in a 23–3 victory against the #11 Hokies. The Clemson defense led by Andre Branch held the Hokies to 258 yards and no touchdowns. Branch had three sacks and was involved in 11 tackles. Tajh Boyd threw one touchdown to Dwayne Allen and one interception while Andre Ellington and Mike Bellamy both recorded a rushing touchdown apiece. This win marked the first time any ACC team had ever beaten three top 25 AP opponents in a row. It was also the second time Virginia Tech had not scored a touchdown in Lane Stadium under Frank Beamer and was the first time since 1995.

On Oct 8, at home, the #8 Tigers beat the Boston College Eagles on Homecoming W (36-14) and the Tigers picked up the O'Roarke-McFadden Trophy. Clemson controlled the Eagles for the majority of the game. Boyd scored 2 touchdowns (1 passing, 1 rushing) before being replaced by Cole Stoudt after suffering a hip injury. Andre Ellington (rushing) and Jaron Brown (receiving) each scored a touchdown, Sammy Watkins recorded 152 receiving yards, while Chandler Catanzaro hit a career-high 5 field goals (38, 42, 28, 20, and 47 yards). This win marked Clemson's best start since 2000.

On Oct 15 at Maryland's Byrd Stadium in College Park, MD, the #8 Tigers beat the Terrapins in a shootout W (56–45). Tajh Boyd threw four touchdown passes, Andre Ellington rushed for a career-high 212 yards and two touchdowns for the Tigers, and freshman Sammy Watkins scored three TDs (two passing, one kick-off return) as No. 8

Clemson rallied from an 18-point deficit against Maryland to remain unbeaten with a 56–45 victory.

The defense, however, yielded 468 yards and had no answer for sophomore quarterback C.J. Brown, who ran for 162 yards and a touchdown and threw three scoring passes in his first college start. The 18-point deficit was the second largest in Clemson University history. Sammy Watkins also broke the school record for most all-purpose yards in a game (345 yards) held previously by Clemson great C.J. Spiller (312 yards).

On Oct 22 at home, the #8 Tigers beat the North Carolina Tar Heels in another shootout W (59-38) Clemson was scoring big while giving up a large # of points. A 35-point third quarter explosion highlighted Clemson's home win over the Tar Heels, including a 5-touchdown performance by quarterback Tajh Boyd. Defensive end Kourtney Brown scored two defensive touchdowns, once on an interception and another on a fumble return. Boyd threw for 367 yards and rushed for one touchdown. Wide receiver DeAndre Hopkins had 157 yards receiving and a touchdown. Clemson's defense held UNC running back Giovani Bernard to 44 yards rushing, ending his five-game streak of 100 yards or more.

On Oct 29. At, 8-0 things looked very promising. Then came arch rival Georgia Tech. On Oct 29 at Georgia Tech's Bobby Dodd Stadium in Atlanta, GA, the #6 Tigers lost its first game of the season against the Yellow Jackets L (17–31) before 55,646. Georgia Tech's triple option attack was seemingly unstoppable for the Clemson defense as Yellow Jacket quarterback Tevin Washington scampered for 176 yards on 27 carries and a touchdown.

Clemson's high-powered offense never left the gates in the first half, although the Tigers made a play for a comeback in the second half with a 48-yard touchdown catch by Sammy Watkins. Following a Rashard Hall interception to the Georgia Tech 9, the Tigers looked to have a chance to rally back, but Tajh Boyd threw an interception in the end zone to Jemea Thomas on the next play. Clemson's four turnovers in the game would ultimately prove to be costly for the Tigers.

On Nov 12, at home, Wake Forest's Demon deacons came in tough and almost beat the Tigers in a close match W (31-28) but Clemson won the game in the end. Clemson clinched its second ACC Atlantic Division title in a nail-biter game against the Demon Deacons in Death Valley. The Tigers' 14–7 third quarter lead quickly deteriorated following a 50-yard Mike Campanaro punt return for Wake Forest. Demon Deacon running back Brandon Pendergrass added two more scores to put Wake Forest up 28–14.

Clemson also lost Sammy Watkins for the second half following an injury on a third-quarter kick return. The Tigers, however, rallied back with two touchdown tosses from quarterback Tajh Boyd. Following a missed 47-yard field goal try by Demon Deacon kicker Jimmy Newman, the Tigers orchestrated a drive to set up a 43-yard game-winning kick by Chandler Catanzaro as time expired. With the win, Clemson secured its trip to Charlotte for the ACC Championship Game and finished undefeated at home for the first time since 1990.

On Nov 19, the #7 ranked Tigers lost to the NC State Wolfpack at Carter–Finley Stadium in Raleigh, NC in the annual Textile Bowl L (13-37). NC State shocked a heavily favored Clemson team in Raleigh, including a dominant 27-point second quarter performance.

Wolfpack quarterback Mike Glennon threw for 253 yards and three touchdowns while Clemson quarterback Tajh Boyd, despite throwing 238 yards, threw two interceptions, no touchdowns, and was replaced in the 4th quarter by Cole Stoudt. NC State's aggressive pass rush hindered Boyd and Clemson's big play ability throughout the game, and the Tigers' four turnovers to NC State's none proved costly. The Wolfpack stymied Clemson's running game with running back Andre Ellington the team leader at only 28 yards

Then, on Nov 26 at #12 South Carolina's Williams-Brice Stadium in Columbia, SC, the Gamecocks beat #18 Clemson and won the big Battle of the Palmetto State L (13–34) before 83,422. Still reeling from the loss to NC State, the Tigers entered hostile territory in Columbia against the 12th-ranked Gamecocks. Clemson's offense again felt the heat from South Carolina's stingy defense, which held the Tigers to 153 total yards.

Clemson's defense struggled as well against the Gamecocks' balanced attack and quarterback Connor Shaw, who threw for 210 yards and three touchdowns as well as rushing for 107 yards and a touchdown. The Tigers' tone for the game was set early when wide receiver Sammy Watkins dropped a sure touchdown pass early in the game. Although Clemson was able to keep the turnovers down this game, the tough Gamecock defense proved too relentless for the Tigers to open up any options on offense. The loss marked Clemson's third straight to its archrival.

2011 Post Season Games

#21 Clemson won their division championship in the ACC and got to play #5 Virginia Tech for the full ACC Championship on December 3 at 8:00 p.m. at Bank of America Stadium in Charlotte, NC. The Clemson Tigers won the game and grabbed the championship W (38–10) before 73,675 football fans. Clemson was invited to the Orange Bowl game for winning the championship.

Devastating losses to NC State and South Carolina had Clemson's future looking bleak for the rematch against Virginia Tech in the ACC Championship. Nonetheless, the Tigers regained their form from earlier in the season to secure their first ACC Championship game win and their first ACC title in 20 years.

Quarterback Tajh Boyd threw for 240 yards and three touchdowns, including a 53-yard strike to Sammy Watkins during the Tigers' 21-point third quarter rally. Clemson defense forced three touchdowns and kept the Hokies scoreless in the second half. The defense also held running back David Wilson, the ACC's player of the year, to only 32 yards rushing. Clemson running back Andre Ellington ran for 125 yards and one touchdown on 20 carries. With the win, Clemson solidified its first 10-win season since 1990, a spot in the Orange Bowl and its first BCS bowl bid in school history

On January 4, 2012 at 8::30 p.m., the #14 Clemson Tigers took on the #23 West Virginia Mountaineers at Sun Life Stadium in Miami Gardens, FL. The Tigers were beaten in a shootout L (33–70) before 67,563. Not everything goes as planned. Clemson's best season in 20 years came to a crashing halt with arguably the worst bowl loss in school history. What at first appeared to have the makings of a high-scoring shootout between the Tigers and West Virginia turned into a shellacking on par with a video game score in the second quarter.

Following Andre Ellington's fumble at the goal line and the 99-yard touchdown return by Mountaineer safety Darwin Cook, the floodgates opened for the Tigers. West Virginia quarterback Geno Smith was electrifying, and Clemson's defense did not have an answer for him as he rattled off 407 yards passing and 6 touchdowns. Although Clemson coughed the ball up four times on offense, the real story lay in the defense's inability to stop Smith and the Mountaineer offense. The result was a record in points in a bowl game for West Virginia.

2012 Clemson Tigers Football Coach Dabo Swinney

The 2012 Clemson Tigers football team represented Clemson University during the 2012college football season as a member of the Atlantic Coast Conference (ACC). Dabo Swinney was the head football coach for his fifth of many seasons. The Tigers completed their one hundred-seventeenth season overall and their sixtieth as a member of the Atlantic Division of the Atlantic Coast Conference. Their overall record was 11-2; 7-1 in the ACC. They finished tied for first with Florida State of 6 ACC Atlantic Division teams. Since FSU beat the Tigers in head to head, they got to compete for the ACC title. The Offensive Coordinator was Chad Morris and the Defensive Coordinator was Brent Venables. They were invited to the Chick-fil-A Bowl where they defeated LSU. The Tigers had their first 11-win season since 1981.

The unranked Clemson Fighting Tigers season opener resulted in a win on Sept 1 in the Chick-fil-A Kickoff Game against Georgia at the Georgia Dome in Atlanta GA. W (26-19). The Clemson home opener was played at Memorial Stadium (also known as Death Valley) on the campus of Clemson University in Clemson, SC before 79,557. In this game on Sept 8, the #12 Tigers defeated Ball State W (52-27). On Sept 15 at home, the Tigers defeated the Paladins of Furman, W (41-7) before 83,574.

On Sept 22 at 8:00 p.m., in Clemson's most disappointing game of the year, the #10 undefeated Tigers lost to #4 Florida State at Doak Campbell Stadium in Tallahassee, FL L (37-49). On Sept 29 at

Boston College's Alumni Stadium in Chestnut Hill, MA, the Tigers again captured the (O'Rourke–McFadden Trophy in a nice win against the Eagles W (45–31) before 40,138. On Oct 6, at home, the Clemson Tigers beat the Georgia Tech Yellow Jackets W (47-31).

On Oct 20 at home, #14 Clemson beat the Virginia Tech Hokies W (38-17). On Oct 25, at Wake Forest's BB&T Field in Winston-Salem, NC, the Tigers routed the Demon Deacons W 42–13. On Nov 3, at Duke's Wallace Wade Stadium • Durham, NC, the #10 ranked Tigers defeated the Blue Devils W (56–20) before 31,894.

On Nov 10 at home, the #10 Tigers pounded the Terrapins of Maryland W (45-10). At this game, Clemson set a school record with their 12th straight home win at Death Valley. On Nov 17, at home, the Tigers whipped NC State in a shootout W (62-48). On Nov 24, at home #12 Clemson was defeated by #13 South Carolina in the Battle of the Palmetto State L (17-27). Clemson was invited to participate in the Chick-fil-A Bowl game.

On Dec 31 at 7:30 p.m. the #15 Clemson Tigers faced the #9 LSU Tigers at the Georgia Dome in Atlanta, GA in the Chick-fil-A Bowl game and Clemson won the match by one point W (25–24) before 68,027.

2013 Clemson Tigers Football Coach Dabo Swinney

The 2013 Clemson Tigers football team represented Clemson University during the 2013college football season as a member of the Atlantic Coast Conference (ACC). Dabo Swinney was the head football coach for his sixth of many seasons. The Tigers completed their one hundred-eighteenth season overall and their sixty-first as a member of the Atlantic Division of the Atlantic Coast Conference. Their overall record was 11-2; 7-1 in the ACC. They finished second of 6 ACC Atlantic Division teams. The Offensive Coordinator was Chad Morris and the Defensive Coordinator was Brent Venables. They were invited to the Orange Bowl where they defeated Ohio State.

The unranked Clemson Fighting Tigers season opener resulted in a win at home on August 31against Georgia W (38-35). This Clemson home opener was played at Memorial Stadium (also known as Death

Valley) on the campus of Clemson University in Clemson, SC before 63830. In the next home game on Sept 7, the #4 Tigers defeated South Carolina State W (52-13). On Sept 19 at NC State's Carter–Finley Stadium in Raleigh, NC in the Textile Bowl, Clemson defeated the Wolfpack W (26–14) before 57,583.

On Sept 28 at home, the Tigers whooped Wake Forest's Demon Deacons W (56-7). Then on Oct 5, at Syracuse in the Carrier Dome in Syracuse, NY, the Tigers defeated the Orangemen W (49–14). Then, on Oct 12, at home, the Tigers defeated the Eagles W (24-14) and they took away the O'Rourke–McFadden Trophy before 77,506.

On Oct 19, at home, #5 Florida State shellacked the #3 Tigers L (14-51). The week after this thumping, on Oct 26 at Maryland's Byrd Stadium in College Park, MD, the Tigers regrouped and beat the Terrapins W (40-27). On Nov 2at Virginia's Scott Stadium in Charlottesville, VA, the Tigers routed the Wahoos W (59-0) before 46,959. Then at home on Nov 14, in a shootout, the #8 Tigers defeated Georgia Tech W (55–31) before 75,324.

Then on Nov 23 at home, Clemson beat the Citadel W (52-6). The following week on Nov 30, at No. 10 South Carolina, the #6 Tigers lost to the Gamecocks L (17-31) in Williams-Brice Stadium • Columbia, SC in the defining Battle of the Palmetto State before 84,174 fans.

Player Highlights Tajh Boyd, QB, (2010-13)

Boyd holds the Clemson records for career completions, passing yards, and passing touchdowns. Tajh Boyd also holds the ACC record for total touchdowns and passing touchdowns (breaking Philip Rivers' passing TD record with one less season as the starter). He compiled a 32-8 record, tying him for the most wins by a QB in school history. Additionally, he is one of four Clemson QBs to ever win the Orange Bowl, the others being Billy Hair in the '50 season, Homer Jordan in the '81 season, and Deshaun Watson in the '15 season.

The few negatives on Boyd include a reputation, deserved or underserved, for his occasional poor play on a big stage. This was evident in his first two starts against South Carolina and his last matchup with FSU. Still, nobody wins them all. in his career Boyd, beat Virginia Tech, Auburn, LSU, UGA, and Ohio State, hardly pushovers.

With that, he led Clemson to an ACC Championship (after a two-decade drought) and two Orange Bowl appearances. After the first of those appearances ended in a blowout to WVU, he led Clemson to a 22-4 record in his RS junior and RS senior seasons.

Like Steve Fuller, Boyd revitalized Clemson's program. When the Tigers finally reached the mountain top winning the title three seasons after Boyd left Clemson, LB Ben Boulware stood on the stage and said past players who got the program to that point are part of the championship. He called out Tajh Boyd specifically - a recognition Boyd surely deserves.

Before DeShaun Watson, Tajh Boyd was the all-everything all-time best QB in Clemson History. Boyd did in fact return the Tigers to

ACC supremacy with its first league championship in two decades as just a sophomore.

He then shattered most Clemson and some ACC passing records as a junior in 2012. He owned the single-season school record for passing yards (3,896) and the ACC single-season touchdown record with 36 scoring strikes. In 2015 DeShaun Watson broke his single season record with a 4104 performance and Watson broke his own record in 2016 with 4593 season yards.

He posted back-to-back seasons of at least 4,000 total yards of offense and has a chance to finish as the ACC's most productive player in history (passing yards and total offense). Against NC State, Boyd set an ACC record by accounting for eight total touchdowns (5 pass, 3 rush) and at the time, the third best total offense game in ACC history (529). How fortunate for Clemson for DeShaun Watson to come so quickly after Tajh Boyd.

Who knows what will happen at QB in the fall, 2017, but it can only be good as there will be five quarterbacks on the roster vying to be the Clemson Tigers starter for the 2017 season. I trust Dabo Swinney to make the right choice if he has not done so already.

- **Player Highlights Sammy Watkins WR (2011-2013)**

Sammy Watkins slammed onto the national stage as one of the top wideouts in the nation in 2011. He was not as adept in 2012 as his production decreased somewhat. Though many of his numbers were nearly equal to 2011 on a per-game basis.

In the 2013 season, Sammy returned to his freshman form in and even better. He was recognized as one of the best wideouts in the nation with

240 receptions for 3,391 yards and 27 touchdowns, 339 yards on 52 carries and one touchdown, six punt returns for 23 yards, and 60 kickoff returns for 1,376 yards and one touchdown in 1,717 snaps over 36 games (29 starts) in his career.

In his day, Sammy was first in school history in receptions, first in receptions per game (6.7), first in receiving yards, first in receiving yards per game (94.2), first in 100-yard receiving games (15), tied for first in receiving touchdowns, second in all-purpose yards (5,129), and fifth in kickoff return yards ... three-time, first-team All-American, the first Tiger to be a multi-year first-team All-American since 2000,01 (Kyle Young) ... two-time First-Team All-ACC selection (media).

On May 28, 2014, Watkins signed his rookie contract, a fully guaranteed four-year deal worth $19.94 million, with a $12.8 million signing bonus. He caught his first career touchdown reception from EJ Manuel in a Week 2 29-10 victory over the Miami Dolphins. In Week 7 against the Minnesota Vikings, Watkins caught nine passes for 122 yards for two touchdowns. His second touchdown was the game winner coming with one second remaining in the game. He played three years with Buffalo

On May 2, 2017, the Buffalo Bills declined Watkins' fifth-year option, making him a free agent after the 2017 season.

Watson was deserving of all the accolades he received at Clemson and at Buffalo. He would get a place on most pundit's All-Clemson Team after his stellar and historic freshman campaign. He has been one of the best freshman receivers the Tigers have had for some time.

Watkins was known to be able to work from anywhere on the field, and he seemed to catch everything that came his way. His smooth route running and speed allowed the offense to do a myriad of things. Imagine having an offense with both Florida natives CJ Spiller and Sammy Watkins on the field at the same time. Amen!

2014 Orange Bowl

On January 3, 2014 at 7:30 p.m., the #12 Clemson Tigers defeated the #7 Ohio State Buckeyes at Sun Life Stadium in Miami Gardens, FL when playing the Orange Bowl Game. W (40–35) before 72,080

2014 Clemson Tigers Football Coach Dabo Swinney

The 2014 Clemson Tigers football team represented Clemson University during the 2014 college football season as a member of the Atlantic Coast Conference (ACC). Dabo Swinney was the head football coach for his seventh of many seasons. The Tigers completed their one hundred-nineteenth season overall and their sixty-second as a member of the Atlantic Division of the Atlantic Coast Conference. Their overall record was 10-3; 6-2 in the ACC. They finished second of 6 ACC Atlantic Division teams. The Offensive Coordinator was Chad Morris and the Defensive Coordinator was Brent Venables. The Captains were Stephone Anthony, Sam Cooper, Adam Humphries, and Grady Jarrett. Clemson was invited to the Russell Athletic Bowl where they defeated Oklahoma.

The unranked Clemson Fighting Tigers season opener resulted in a loss at #12 Georgia's Sanford Stadium Athens, GA (Rivalry) L (21–45). In the Clemson home opener, on Sept 6 played at Memorial Stadium (also known as Death Valley) on the campus of Clemson University in Clemson, SC, Clemson completely destroyed South Carolina State W (73-7) before 81,672 fans, In the next game on Sept 20, the #22 Tigers were defeated by #1 ranked Florida State at Doak Campbell Stadium, Tallahassee, FL in a major rivalry L (17–23) in one OT before 82,316.

On Sept 27 at home, Clemson defeated North Carolina W (50–35). On Oct 4, at home in the Textile Bowl V NC State, the Tigers shut out the Wolfpack W (41-0. On Oct 11 at home, Clemson beat Louisville W (23–17) before 81,500. On Oct 18 at Boston College's Alumni Stadium in Chestnut Hill, MA, the Tigers won the O'Rourke–McFadden Trophy again, W (17–13) before 42,038.

On Homecoming evening on Oct 25 at 7:00 p.m., #21 Clemson beat Syracuse in a close match, W (16–6). On Nov 6, at Wake Forest's

BB&T Field in Winston-Salem, NC, the Tigers beat the Demon Deacons W (34–20) before 28,846. On Nov 15 at # 24 Georgia Tech's Bobby Dodd Stadium in Atlanta, GA (Rivalry), the Tigers lost to the Yellow Jackets L 6–28. On Nov 22 at home, Clemson shut out Georgia State W 28-0) On Nov 19 at home in the Battle of the Palmetto State, the Tigers beat the Gamecocks W 35–17 before 82,720. Clemson was invited to the Russell Athletic Bowl.

Russell Athletic Bowl

On Dec 29 at 5:30 p.m., the Oklahoma Sooners squared off against the #18 Clemson Tigers in the Russell Athletic bowl played at the Orlando Citrus Bowl Stadium in Orlando, FL. The Tigers whooped the Sooners W (40-0) before 40,071.

Player Highlights Vic Beasley DE 2012-2014

Beasley was one of two "Two-time consensus All-Americans," in Clemson history. The also great Terry Kinard was the other. Vic Beasley was also a two-time, first-team All-ACC performer. When he departed from Clemson, he was its career leader with 33 sacks, while compiling 52.5 tackles for loss (fourth-most in school history at the time).

Beasley was First-team All-American by Athlon, Bleacher Report, CBSSports.com, SBNation.com, SI.com, Sporting News, USA

Today and Walter Camp in 2013. He was second-team All-American by AP, FWAA and Phil Steele in 2013.

Along the way to his great college career with Clemson he had 44 tackles, 23 tackles for loss, 13 sacks, 12 quarterback pressures, six pass breakups, four caused fumbles and one recovered fumble in 560 snaps over 13 games (13 starts) in 2013.

He was ACC Defensive Player of the Year in 2014, when he was first-team All-American according to AFCA, AP, College Sports Madness and Walter Camp ... second-team All-American in 2014 by Athlon, CBS Sports, FWAA, Lindy's, Phil Steele, Scout.com and USA Today.

He was a finalist for the Bednarik, Hendricks and Lombardi awards in 2014 ... posted 37 tackles, a team-high 21.5 tackles for loss, a team-high 12 sacks, nine quarterback pressures, three pass breakups, two caused fumbles, one recovered fumble and a 16-yard fumble return for a touchdown in 557 snaps over 13 games in 2014. He was selected No. 8 overall in the first round of the 2015 NFL Draft by his hometown team, the Atlanta Falcons. He has two successful years under his belt for Atlanta now and has played in every Falcon game over that period.

2015 Clemson Tigers Football Coach Dabo Swinney

The 2015 Clemson Tigers football team represented Clemson University during the 2015 college football season as a member of the Atlantic Coast Conference (ACC). Dabo Swinney was the head football coach for his eighth of many seasons. The Tigers completed their one hundred-twentieth season overall and their sixty-third as a member of the Atlantic Division of the Atlantic Coast Conference. Their overall record was 14-1; 8-0 in the ACC. They finished first of 6 ACC Atlantic Division teams and they won the ACC Championship. The Offensive Coordinators were Tony Elliott and Jeff Scott Chad Morris and the Defensive Coordinator was Brent Venables. The Captains were Travis Blanks, B.J. Goodson, Eric MacLain, Charone Peake, D.J. Reader, and Stanton Seckinger.

Clemson had a great year with just one major disappointment. The Tigers won the 2015 ACC Championship Game by defeating the

North Carolina Tar Heels, 45–37, capping their first undefeated regular season since winning the national title in 1981. Ranked No. 1 throughout the College Football Playoff (CFP) rankings, Clemson defeated the No. 4 Oklahoma Sooners, 37–17, in the 2015 Orange Bowl to advance to the College Football Playoff National Championship. On January 11, 2016, the No. 2 Alabama Crimson Tide (13–1) defeated the No. 1 Clemson Tigers (14–0) in the 2016 national championship, 45–40. Both Clemson and Alabama finished the season 14–1.

Clemson announced their 2015 football schedule on January 29, 2015. The 2015 schedule consisted of seven home and five away games in the regular season. The Tigers hosted ACC foes Boston College, Florida State, Georgia Tech, and Wake Forest, and travelled to Louisville, Miami, NC State, and Syracuse. Clemson hosted #4 seed Oklahoma in the Orange Bowl in the first round of the 2015-16 College Football Playoff. The Tigers then hosted #2 seed Alabama in the 2016 College Football Playoff National Championship in University of Phoenix Stadium.

The unranked Clemson Fighting Tigers season and home opener resulted in a rout against Wofford W (49-10) before 81,345. The game was played on Sept 5 at Memorial Stadium (also known as Death Valley) on the campus of Clemson University in Clemson, SC. On Sept 12 at home, Clemson beat Appalachia State W (41-10). In the next game on Sept 17, at Louisville's Papa John's Cardinal Stadium in Louisville, KY, the Tigers nipped the Wildcats for the win W (20-17)

On Oct 3 in a pivotal game at home, with the start at 8:00 p.m. in what most would call torrential rain at Memorial Stadium, the undefeated #12 Clemson Tigers got the best of the #6 Notre Dame Fighting Irish W (24-22). All-Everything Deshaun Watson threw for two touchdowns, ran for a third and Clemson's defense stopped DeShone Kizer on a tying two-point conversion as the 12th-ranked Tigers held on to beat No. 6 Notre Dame.

On Oct 10 at home, the #6 Tigers beat Georgia Tech W (43–24) before 80,983. On Oct 17, at home, the Tigers beat the Eagles on homecoming night W (34-17). On Oct 24, at Miami (FL) at Sun Life Stadium, Miami Gardens, FL, the Clemson Tigers shellacked the

Miami Hurricanes W 58–0 before 45,211. On Oct 31, at NC State's Carter–Finley Stadium in Raleigh, NC in the annual Textile Bowl, the Clemson Tigers defeated the NC State Wolfpack in a major shootout W (56–41) before 57,600.

In what might have been the season spoiler at home, the #3 Tigers engaged #16 Florida State and prevailed W (23-13) before 83,099. On Nov 14 at the Syracuse carrier Dome in Syracuse NY against Syracuse, the #1 ranked Tigers defeated the Orangemen W (37-27) before 36,736. On Nov 21 at home, the #1 Clemson Tigers defeated the Demon Deacons of Wake Forest W (33-13). Then, on Nov 28 at South Carolina's Williams-Brice Stadium in Columbia, SC in what is now known as the Palmetto Bowl, Clemson squeaked out its second-last win to earn an undefeated regular season W (37–32). The Tigers also won their Division Championship and would next play for the big ACC honors.

2015 Post Season Games

On Dec 5 at 8:00 p.m. v #8 ranked North Carolina, Coastal Division Champ, the #1 Clemson Tigers, Atlantic Division Champs engaged at the Bank of America Stadium in Charlotte, NC in the ACC Championship Game. In a tough game, Clemson prevailed W (45-37 before 74,514.

On Dec 31, New Year's Eve, at 4:00 p.m. vs. No. 4 Oklahoma, #1 Clemson defeated the Sooners at Sun Life Stadium in Miami Gardens, FL in the Orange Bowl Game – CFP Semifinal. Clemson won the encounter W (37-17) setting the stage for a game against Alabama for the National Championship.

On January 10, 2016, at 8:30 p.m., #1 Clemson played #2 Alabama at University of Phoenix Stadium in Glendale, AZ for the CFP National Championship. In a great game, Alabama held on for the win L (40-45) before 75,765

2016 Clemson Tigers Football Coach Dabo Swinney

The 2016 Clemson Tigers football team represented Clemson University during the 2016 college football season as a member of the Atlantic Coast Conference (ACC). Dabo Swinney was the head football coach for his ninth of many seasons. The Tigers completed their one hundred-twenty-first overall and their sixty-fourth as a member of the Atlantic Division of the Atlantic Coast Conference. Their overall record was 14-1; 7-1 in the ACC. They finished tied for first of 7 with Louisville but got to play in the championship because they had beaten Louisville in head to head earlier in the season. They also won the ACC Championship. The Offensive Coordinators were Tony Elliott and Jeff Scott Chad Morris and the Defensive Coordinator was Brent Venables.

The # 2 ranked Clemson Fighting Tigers season opener was played on Sept 3 at Auburn's Jordan-Hare Stadium, Auburn, in the long-time rivalry. Clemson won the close game W (19-13) before a packed house of 87,451. On Sept 10, game # 2 was played at home at Memorial Stadium (also known as Death Valley) on the campus of Clemson University in Clemson, SC. The Tigers had another close game against Troy but prevailed W (30-24). On Sept 17 at home against South Carolina State, Clemson shut out the Bulldogs W (59-0). On Thursday, Sept 22 at Georgia Tech's Bobby Dodd Stadium in Atlanta, GA, the Tigers won again W (26-7) before 53,932.

On Oct 1, now at 4-0 for a great season start after a #2 finish in 2015, the #5 Clemson Tigers took on #3 Louisville at home and beat the Cardinals in a close one W (42-36).

Sometimes, Top 5 matchups fail to live up to their billing. They're blowouts—decided long before the final horn. Or maybe they're slogs, where points are at a premium, and turnovers are prevalent. That wasn't the case with Clemson-Louisville. The No. 5 Clemson Tigers and No. 3 Louisville Cardinals put on a show that the 80,000-plus in attendance at Memorial Stadium will likely never forget.

At halftime, it appeared that the quarterback showdown between Clemson's Deshaun Watson and Louisville's Lamar Jackson was one-sided on Watson's behalf, with the Tigers holding a 28-10 lead. But Jackson was just getting started, leading a Cardinals rally with his arm and legs that spanned 22 minutes in the third and fourth quarters for a 26-0 run and a 36-28 Louisville edge with 7:52 left.

The Tigers and Watson struck back, with Watson leading a pair of touchdown drives, the second ending with a 31-yard Jordan Leggett catch-and-run score for a 42-36 lead with 3:14 remaining. Jackson led one final drive inside the Clemson 15, and on 4th-and-12, he found James Quick. But one yard short of the first down, Quick was forced out of bounds, and Clemson hung on for a wild 42-36 win and a huge feather in its College Football Playoff push.

Lamar Jackson and Louisville came up just short against Clemson

Then on Oct 7 at Boston College's Alumni Stadium in Chestnut Hill, MA, the Tigers snagged the O'Rourke–McFadden Trophy again in a blowout W (56–10) before   44,500. On Homecoming Day, Clemson played the Textile Bowl game against NC State and in a nail-biter overtime game, escaped with the win W (24-17). On Oct 29 in another nail-biter game—this one against #12 Florida State at Doak Campbell Stadium, Tallahassee, FL, the #4 Tigers escaped with the win W (37–34).

Bleacher report suggests that Clemson-Florida State is always meaningful in the ACC race. Lately, it has taken on importance in the College Football Playoff picture, too. When the Tigers and Seminoles met in late October, a pair of FSU losses had robbed the game of some of its significance. But that didn't stop the rivalry tilt from turning into an instant classic.

In 2016, Florida State erased an early 14-0 Clemson lead and led 28-20 after three quarters. A Wayne Gallman touchdown and a Greg Huegel field goal gave the Tigers a one-point lead with 5:25 remaining, but FSU had one final push. The Seminoles struck back with an eight-play, 80-yard touchdown drive, capped off by Dalvin Cook's eight-yard touchdown run with 3:23 left

That was too much time for Deshaun Watson and Clemson, however. He led a five-play, 75-yard drive that finished with a 34-yard touchdown to tight end Jordan Leggett, and the Tigers held on for a tense 37-34 victory.

On Nov 5, at home, the #3 Tigers shut-out the Syracuse Orangemen W (54-0) before 80, 609. Sitting at 9-0 at home with recent ACC team Pittsburgh coming to play football, Clemson could not grab the win and lost by one point L (42-43).

Clemson made a habit of edge-of-your-seat victories in 2016. Call Dabo Swinney's Tigers the Cardiac Cats; six games were decided by a touchdown or less. Play with fire that much, however, and you're bound to get burned eventually. Clemson found that out the hard way at home on Nov. 12 against Pitt. The cats had run out of luck.

The No. 2 Tigers hadn't lost to an unranked foe since November 2011, but a combination of mistakes, poor defense and untimely penalties caught up with them against the scrappy Panthers. Even with quarterback Deshaun Watson throwing for an ACC-record 580 yards, Clemson couldn't put Pitt away, with its biggest lead being eight points. Pitt closed to 42-40 on James Conner's 20-yard touchdown run with 5:17 left, and the Tigers just had to run out the clock. But the Panthers stuffed Wayne Gallman on 4th-and-1 from their 35 with 58 seconds left, giving themselves one more chance.

Pitt quickly got into field-goal position, and the aptly named Chris Blewitt nailed a 48-yard field goal on the game's final play, lifting the Panthers to a shocking 43-42 upset. Clemson still made the College

Football Playoff, but Pitt and head coach Pat Narduzzi had a win they'll never forget.

Clemson 42 Pittsburgh 43

On Nov 19, the #5 Tigers recovered and beat Wake Forest's Demon Deacons at BB&T Field, Winston-Salem, NC, W (35–13). The next scheduled game was on Nov 26 at home against South Carolina in the Palmetto Bowl. The Tigers defeated the Gamecocks in a big-time shellacking W (56-7)

The 2016 Post Season

After finishing the regular season 12-1 with a win over Coastal Division champion #23 Virginia Tech in the 2016 ACC Championship game, the #2 Tigers advanced to the 2016 College Football Playoff semifinal and went on to defeat the #3 Ohio State Buckeyes 31-0, in the 2016 Fiesta Bowl on December 31, 2016. Both top ranked Clemson and Alabama met again in college football's first rematch in National Championship game history, the 2017 CFP National Championship game in Tampa, Florida.

On January 9, 2017, the Clemson Tigers would go on to defeat the Alabama Crimson Tide in the rematch by a score of 35 to 31, winning their first consensus National Football Championship since 1981. Clemson subsequently finished with #1 rankings in both the Associated Press Poll and the AFCA Coaches' Poll for the 2016 season. Here are the stories

In the ACC Championship game on Dec 3, against #19 Virginia Tech, played at Camping World Stadium in Orlando, Clemson prevailed in a close match W (42-35) to gain the full ACC Championship before 50,628. Ranked #2, the Tigers would be playing in the Fiesta Bowl in a game known as the CFP Semifinal.

On December 31, New Year's Eve two games were played and the winner would play on January 9 for the National Championship. #2 Clemson shut out #3 Ohio State in the Fiesta Bowl at7:00 p.m.at University of Phoenix Stadium, Glendale, AZ CFP Semifinal. W (31-0). In a game earlier in the day at 3:00 PM, #1 Alabama beat the #4 Washington Huskies W (24-7) earning them a berth to play Clemson for the championship on January 9, 2017

On Monday, January 9, 2017 at 8:30 p.m., the #1 ranked Alabama Crimson Tide (14-0) were looking for a repeat National Championship against the #2 ranked Clemson Tigers (13-1) at Raymond James Stadium in Tampa, FL in the CFP National Championship game. Clemson pulled out the win in a magical fashion.

The 2017 National Championship Game

Uncommitted football fans across the world enjoyed one of the best football games of all-time on Monday evening January 9, 2007, from 8:00 PM to way past bedtime at 12:25 AM. For the committed Clemson fans, the victory was sweet after waiting a year for a rematch. For the committed Crimson Tide fans, the loss was simply heartbreaking. Clemson knew the feeling for the prior year and the victory was even that much sweeter.

In this game, the song lyrics, *what a difference a day makes* took a back seat to *what a difference a few seconds make*. Clemson did all it could to win, battling to the last second. Alabama came literally one second away from a repeat title. Clemson fans all remember that with Alabama holding a three-point lead after rolling down the field and scoring on a Jalen Hurts' 30-yard touchdown run with just 2:01 remaining, Clemson took the second-last kickoff of the game and simply refused to be stopped. It was exhilarating to watch for sure.

Deshaun Watson was the game's super-hero. However, Watson had to perform all night to get the win and he had the ball in his hands again as the game ended after a Clemson onside kick was recovered by Clemson with one second still on the clock.

It took many fans and the entire Crimson Tide by surprise as Clemson executed an onside kick with one second left in this Monday night national championship game. The Tigers, had kicked it after scoring a game-winning touchdown so as to avoid letting Alabama run the kick back, recovered it, leaving just a kneel down left for the Tigers to seal their big victory.

Just before that, without his two-yard TD pass with 1-second left after the score, the super-hero acclaim would have gone to the Alabama defense. The big guys from the Crimson Tide spent the night chasing Watson, keeping the talented QB from overcoming Alabama's early lead.

But, not this time. Not this game. Clemson would not be denied and the Tigers had both the talent and the luck, on their side. Clemson's heralded QB, and the best QB in the nation per his coach Dabo Swinney calmly led his team to victory and to him goes the credit as game super-hero.

This QB, who is also a two-time Heisman Trophy finalist, (who should have received the Heisman -- third in the Heisman voting in 2015, then second in 2016) performed flawlessly on this all-important drive down the field. Watson was the master on the field and the results have already made the history books. Clemson won by four. They are the 2017 National Champions for the 2016 season and will be so forever.

DeShaun Watson, interviewed after the game told reporters that his message to his teammates on the drive was to stay calm; don't get nervous; and they would prevail. They did.

Watson guided the Clemson Tigers 68 yards in nine plays, completing a 24-yard pass to Mike Williams to Alabama's 39-yard line and a 17-yard pass to tight end Jordan Leggett that gave Clemson a first-and-goal at the 9. The Tigers got to the 2 when Alabama cornerback Anthony Averett was flagged for pass interference in the end zone.

"Everything was calm, and nobody panicked," Watson said. "I walked up to my offensive line and my receivers, and I said, 'Let's be legendary.' God put us here for a reason."

Coach Swinney offered: "He didn't lose out on the Heisman. The Heisman lost out on him."

From the two-yard line, with about 6 seconds left, Alabama was either going to be playing in OT with a field goal if Clemson's next play did not work; or time would run out by mistake; or of course option 3 was that the play would result in a touchdown.

Much to Alabama's chagrin, option 3 was operative. When Alabama double-teamed 6' 3" Mike Williams on the left side, Clemson decided to go right against man to man coverage. They executed a perfect touchdown play that some Alabama fans still claim was illegal. But, in football, the referees have the final word.

Regardless, along with other referee miscues, the officials said it was legal. On the play, Deshaun Watson's rolled right and threw a perfect 2-yard touchdown pass to Hunter Renfrow with just 1 second remaining. Clemson can take that call to the bank.

This gave Clemson their wild 35-31 win over Alabama in the College Football Playoff national championship game. Clemson fans were ecstatic as they felt they should have won the marbles one year earlier. Alabama fans of course were generally heartsick.

Sure, Alabama could have played better. Their offense was sluggish and they depended on their defense after Bo Scarbrough was no longer on the field. Clemson did not miss an opportunity when the going got tough. There is no denying the Tigers this great win.

There were a lot of ups and downs in the game, especially at the end. Alabama quarterback Jalen Hurts had just given the Crimson Tide a 31-28 lead on his 30-yard scramble with 2:01 remaining. This had countered Wayne Gallman's 1-yard touchdown run with 4:38 remaining that had put the Tigers up 28-24. Two minutes is an awful long time and Watson engineered a drive that used it all up right to the last second before he passed for the score.

Last year Watson threw for almost 500 yards and this year, the Crimson Tide managed him better; but he still stole 420 yards on 36-of-56 passing and three touchdowns. Renfrow caught ten of his passes for 92 yards and two touchdowns and big 6'3" leaping Mike Williams adding eight receptions for 94 yards and one score.

Clemson packed in 511 total yards to 376 by Alabama and the Tigers posted a 31-16 edge in first downs. Alabama's bright side in the game was not its offensive production and because of that, its D had little time to rest.

Clemson ran 99 plays. All season long it was only Arkansas W (49-30) that had anything close to that (84 plays). Though in great shape, the D was not as well backed up as the 2016 team. Some say that this huge number of plays helped wear down the mighty Tide defense with tempo and consistent movement on offense. One thing for sure is that Clemson bested the vaunted Crimson Tide.

Alabama did not get much rest as the offense ran just 66 plays. Its defensive depth was not at the same level as the 2015 team. The wear of those extra plays on the Alabama defense was evident in the second half. Clemson visited the red zone four times and they scored four times. Alabama had typically rejected opponents on two of every three red zone attempts. On the field, fatigue surely was a factor though there are no real excuses. Nick Saban is not looking for excuses. He knows his team was beaten.

Nick Saban's Crimson Tide were clearly denied a fifth national championship in eight seasons under this highly successful coach.

The Tide managed just 131 passing yards, as Hurts had a tough night going 14-of-32.

Nick Saban saw it as it was. "They made the plays and we didn't," Saban said. "We could have done some things better, but I'm proud of the way our guys competed." Dabo Swinney has proven that he is one of the best coaches of all time at any university.

Alabama struggled in the second half but did take a 24-14 lead on a 68-yard touchdown pass from Hurts to O.J. Howard with 1:53 remaining in the third quarter. Clemson fans quickly remembered Howard as the MVP of last year's title game with 208 yards on five receptions. Alabama had faked the look of a quick screen before Howard raced behind a confused Clemson secondary for the catch. And the TD.

"Not to have him [Bo Scarborough] was probably a little bit of a disadvantage for us," Saban gave it a positive slant when he said. "I was pleased with our other backs who had an opportunity in this game, Josh Jacobs and Damien Harris, but we always miss a guy who's Bo Scarbrough 's size when we want to run the ball and take some time off the clock."

Alabama had to punt after a three-and-out on the night's opening possession. Clemson on its first drive then moved across midfield before they were stuffed by Tony Brown on a fourth down and 1 try on a pitch to Gallman. Alabama then took over on their own 41.

Bama got going on their second possession on a 20-yard scramble by Hurts down the right sideline to the Clemson 39-yard line and grabbed a 7-0 lead at the 9:23 mark of the first quarter on Bo Scarbrough's 25-yard scamper around left end.

Watson was a bit shaky at first but calmed down as the O-line settled down. He fumbled a low shotgun snap late in the first quarter. Alabama outside linebacker Ryan Anderson recovered the fumble at Clemson's 35-yard line, Mistakes stopped an Alabama advance. There was a false start on Cam Robinson and a 2-yard loss by Scarbrough and the Tide was forced to punt.

When they got the ball back, ArDarius Stewart started Alabama's second touchdown drive with a 25-yard run to Clemson's 49-yard line early in the second quarter. From here, Scarbrough broke loose moments later from 37 yards out to make it 14-0.

The Alabama fans and the Clemson fans had a feeling that Alabama was on the verge of breaking things open until Tigers receiver Deon Cain took a short Watson pass and weaved 43 yards to Alabama's 39. It was the juice Swinney's Clemson squad needed to convince them they "could." It was a major momentum shift.

Watson was energized and calm by then. He completed a third-and-10 pass for Leggett for 26 yards to the Alabama 13 and ran in for an 8-yard score to pull the Tigers within 14-7 with 6:09 before halftime. That would be the end of the first-half scoring, with the Tide held the seven-point lead at the break even though they had been outgained 203-183.

Alabama's Anderson struck again early in the second half, stripping Tigers tailback Gallman of the ball and returning the fumble to the Clemson 16. For whatever reason Alabama, just as it had done after Anderson's first fumble recovery, could not move the ball and had to settle for a 27-yard Adam Griffith field goal for a 17-7 lead.

Clemson was no longer intimidated to say the least. They reduced the lead to 17-14 with 7:10 left in the third quarter on a 24-yard touchdown pass from Watson to Renfrow. After a Tide, TD, The Tigers then pulled within 24-21 in the first minute of the fourth quarter on a 4-yard touchdown pass from Watson to Williams.

Clemson coach Dabo Swinney is one of Alabama's own. Swinney became just the second person to have won an Associated Press national championship as a player and coach. Swinney was a wide receiver on Gene Stallings' 1992 Alabama team that won the AP national championship and now he has coached Clemson to a national title over his alma mater Crimson Tide. Swinney still has a lot of love for Alabama and its supporters. He is a good guy

Coach Dabo Swinney was all emotion as he described the victory for Clemson: "This has been the most incredible team I've ever been around," Swinney said. "You saw their heart, and it's been there all year."

It was a big loss for Nick Saban. It was his first ever in a championship game. in six tries. Afterwards, speaking with ESPN's Tom Rinaldi, he was very gracious in defeat. Saban praised his team for all it accomplished in 2016, while also congratulating Dabo Swinney and Clemson on the victory.

Watch out next year folks! It will be another great Clemson football year. You can take that to the bank.

Player Highlights Deshaun Watson QB (2014-16)

Only if you have never seen him in action would there be any doubt?
Following the Tajh Boyd era, a great era, which ended with an
Orange Bowl win over Ohio State, the Clemson Tigers began the
2014 season with QB Cole Stoudt at QB due in part to DeShaun
Watson having suffered a collar bone injury prior to the season. In
the season opener in Athens v and always tough Georgia Tech
Yellow Jackets squad, Watson did take a few snaps and he secured
his first TD pass as a Tiger.

From that moment, Clemson fans knew they had another one of
those magical quarterbacks, and they knew the next few years would
be special. Watson unfortunately was plagued with injuries for most
of that 2014 season. He famously played with a torn ACL in the
Palmetto Bowl and beat South Carolina to snap their five-game
winning streak. Not ever to like seeing a loss on the scorecard,
Watson would go 3-0 in his career against the Gamecocks.

Deshaun Watson shook the injury prone label the following year in 1915 as he led the Tigers to their first undefeated regular season since 1981. He was a finalist for the Heisman. He was simply a superman but for some reason, though John Heisman coached at Clemson, Clemson is always skipped over for the Heisman Trophy.
Watson's stats were remarkable as he posted 5,209 total yards (4,104 passing, 1105 rushing) and 42 TDs (35 passing, 12 rushing). After beating UNC in a high scoring ACC Championship game and Oklahoma in the Orange Bowl, the DeShaun Watson-led Clemson Tigers played for the National Championship v Alabama, Clemson would lose that game due to defensive lapses and special team gaffes, but the contest is largely remembered for the 405 yard, 4 TD performance by a great QB, Deshaun Watson.

In his final season as a Tiger, Deshaun Watson tallied 4,593 passing yards and was once again a Heisman finalist. Again, Clemson was denied a Heisman. Lamar Jackson won the award, but after what Watson did in three postseason games that came after the vote, there was no doubt about him being the best player in the nation.
Following an 11-1 regular season, the Tigers used a five TD performance from Deshaun Watson to get past Virginia Tech, earn a second-consecutive ACC title and make another trip to the College Football Playoff.

The Tigers would win their first ever Fiesta Bowl by beating Urban Meyer's tough Ohio State team 31-0. In the title game, as noted, they got to play Alabama again.

The Tigers fell behind 0-14, but then, Coach Swinney's squad with Watson leading the offensive action outplayed the Tide for most of the night and finally took the lead with under five minutes remaining. Despite struggling to move the ball since early in the game, Alabama used a third-and-long completion, a fourth down conversion, a WR-pass, and a QB scramble to score the go-ahead touchdown with 2:07 remaining.

That's when Deshaun Watson calmly told his teammates to be "legendary," and they were. The greatest QB and greatest player in Clemson history took the field for the final drive of his illustrious career and cemented his legacy with "The Drive." Go Tigers!

2017 Clemson Tigers Football Coach Dabo Swinney

The 2017 Clemson Tigers football team represents Clemson University during the coming 2017 college football season as a member of the Atlantic Coast Conference (ACC). Dabo Swinney is the head football coach for his tenth of many seasons. The Tigers will complete their one hundred-twenty second overall and their sixty-fifth as a member of the Atlantic Division of the Atlantic Coast Conference. Their overall record should be very good overall and in the ACC as they have a fine returning team

Tigers will enter the 2017 season as defending national champions, having finished the 2016 season 14–1 with a win over Alabama in the CFP National Championship game.

Clemson announced its schedule for the 2017 season on January 24, 2017. The Tigers' schedule consists of 7 home games and 5 away games. Clemson will host conference opponents Boston College, Florida State, Georgia Tech, and Wake Forest, and travel to Louisville, NC State, Syracuse, and Virginia Tech. The Tigers will host out of conference games against Kent State, Auburn, and The Citadel, and travel to arch rival South Carolina to close out the regular season. Clemson's out of conference opponents represent the MAC, SoCon, and SEC.

The Tigers will play 10 total teams who played in the postseason in the 2016 season: 2 New Year's Six participants (Auburn and Florida State), 7 other bowl teams (Boston College, Georgia Tech, Louisville, NC State, South Carolina, Wake Forest, Virginia Tech), and 1 FCS playoff participant (Citadel).

Here is the schedule

Date	Opponent#	Site
September 2	Kent State*	Clemson
September 9	Auburn*	Clemson
September 16	Louisville	Papa John's in KY
September 23	Boston College	Clemson
September 30	Virginia Tech	Lane Stadium VA
October 7	Wake Forest	Clemson, Homecoming
October 13	Syracuse	Carrier Dome, Syr, NY
October 28	Georgia Tech	Clemson
November 4	NC State	Carter-Finley Stad. NC
November 11	Florida State	Clemson
November 18	The Citadel	Clemson
November 25	South Carolina	Williams-Brice Stad. SC

Meet Clemson Football's 2017 signees

Dan Hope, daniel.hope@independentmail.com Published 8:34 a.m. ET Feb. 1, 2017 | Updated 3:21 p.m. ET Feb. 1, 2017

http://www.greenvilleonline.com/story/sports/college/clemson/2017/02/01/clemson-football/97330202/

The Clemson football team signed a small but highly-touted recruiting class on Wednesday:

Hunter Johnson, Brownsburg HS, Brownsburg, Indiana: Johnson is an instant contender for the Tigers' QB1 role in 2017 after carrying the No. 1 QB prospect ranking for much of the last couple seasons. Johnson can hit the deep throw, as well as short and immediate routes and throw on the run. A dual-sport athlete with track, Johnson can pull the ball down and run as well. He rushed for 525 yards and three touchdowns last season, while averaging 2.5 touchdowns passes per game. As a junior, Johnson had a 98.4 QB rating with 31 touchdowns to 12 interceptions, averaging 8.1 yards per attempt. The five-star is already on campus and ready to compete with Kelly Bryant, Zerrick Cooper and Tucker Israel. He looks equipped to handle the hype, but getting down the playbook will key how much he's playing in 2017.

Matt Bockhorst, St. Xavier HS, Cincinnati, Ohio: Bockhorst was a first-team all-state offensive lineman for the state of Ohio as a junior, which earned him a spot on the Under Armour All-America Game. Bockhorst missed his entire senior season of high school football, however, after tearing his ACL at the Nike Opening camp last summer.

Bockhorst is still recovering from that injury, but he has the potential to develop into Clemson's next great guard once he gets healthy. He already looks like a college offensive lineman with his size and strength, while he demonstrates the quickness to get off the line of scrimmage and block defenders downfield.

Although he played left tackle at St. Xavier, Bockhorst is expected to play inside at Clemson. He will likely start his career at guard but could be asked to cross-train at the center position.

Amari Rodgers, Knoxville Catholic HS, Knoxville, Tennessee: From his ability to make plays with the ball in his hands to the No. 3 he wore in high school, Rodgers' film makes him look like recently graduated Clemson wide receiver Artavis Scott.

Rodgers gained 1,238 yards and scored 18 touchdowns on just 40 catches in his senior year. His lack of height could hurt him in one-on-one situations, but he can beat defenders deep with his speed. He is agile in the open field while also well-built and strong enough to fight his way through tackles.

Competition to get on the field at wide receiver will be tough in 2017, but Rodgers has enough talent to work his way into the rotation at the field receiver position or in the slot.

Clemson opened a new football center, just in time for Signing Day

Which Clemson recruits will make an impact in 2017?

Tee Higgins, Oak Ridge HS, Oak Ridge, Tennessee: For a school that has had many star wide receivers who have gone on to make their mark on the NFL in recent years, Higgins has all the physical tools to be next in line.

A two-time Mr. Football award winner in Tennessee, Higgins has height and leaping ability give him the ability to make contested catches even when he is covered. He also has the speed to run away from defensive backs, and he shows good maneuverability in space for a player with his length.

Higgins is the third five-star wide receiver recruit to sign with Clemson in Dabo Swinney's tenure as head coach, following Sammy Watkins (2011) and Deon Cain (2015).

Logan Rudolph, Northwestern HS, Rock Hill, South Carolina: Rudolph comes to Clemson from state powerhouse Northwestern, so facing high expectations is not new for him. He comes into Clemson after missing most of his senior season with a torn labrum. In just two games, he tallied 11 tackles.

During his junior year, Rudolph finished with 62 tackles, 15 sacks and nine tackles for loss. Rudolph is a high-motor player that gets out of his stance quickly, which allows him to keep offensive linemen's hands off of him. His strength is rushing the passer. While he is being recruited to play defense, Rudolph could be a candidate to move to offense to play tight end. In his junior year, he hauled in eight passes for 110 yards and a touchdown. The Tigers are very deep and talented along the defensive line, but there are questions at tight end with the departure of Jordan Leggett.

Travis Etienne, Jr., Jennings HS, Jennings, Louisiana: Coming out of a run-geared Jennings (Louisiana) scheme, the two-time 3A offensive MVP produced some eye-popping numbers over the last two seasons, topping 2,000 rushing yards twice and hitting nearly 3,000 as a junior (2,952) with 50 touchdowns.

Etienne has been timed with a 4.38-second 40-yard dash and used that speed for several home-run hits in recent seasons. At 6-foot, Etienne has a frame he can build on to add strength to the speed. A late addition to Clemson's recruiting radar, Etienne immediately adds competitive depth to the lineup, where like most young players, learning the fine points of pass protection will guide his path to early playing time.

Noah DeHond, The Peddie School, Rochester, NY: DeHond has tremendous size, which will give him a chance to contribute immediately. While many offensive linemen need a year or two in a strength program before being ready to play at the college level, DeHond already has a great build on a long frame.

While DeHond was only a three-star recruit, he drew offers from some of the top programs in the nation, including Alabama. He doesn't appear to have elite quickness, but his size will be a big asset if he can quickly pick up offensive line coach Robbie Caldwell's techniques.

Although Clemson has a strong young trio of Mitch Hyatt, Sean Pollard and Tremayne Anchrum at offensive tackle, he could still have a chance to earn playing time, as the Tigers have regularly included freshmen in their offensive line rotation in recent years.
Jordan Williams, Frank W. Cox HS, Virginia Beach,
Virginia: Williams has the combination of strength and explosiveness off the line of scrimmage that can enable a defensive end to develop into a great pass-rusher.

After dominating mostly on physical gifts in high school, Williams' strength and skill will be put to the test at Clemson, but the U.S. Army All-American appears to have the upside to continue Clemson's recent tradition of star defensive linemen who have gone on to the NFL.

Clemson has a strong group of returning talent at the defensive end position, so Williams could be a candidate to redshirt in 2017.

Justin Foster, Crest HS, Shelby, North Carolina: The Shelby native comes to Clemson after playing outside linebacker for the Chargers. Foster led the team with 83 tackles, 14 tackles for loss, six sacks and an interception and helped Crest to the second round of the playoffs.

Foster is referred to as a "tweener," and could play either linebacker or defensive end in college. Recruiting analysts believe he will likely end up on the defensive line. While he is able to cover the pass, Foster is most comfortable charging the line of scrimmage and rushing the passer. Clemson has been on a trend of bigger linebackers, though, with recent recruits like Tre Lamar, Shaq Smith, Chad Smith and Jamie Skalski.

Foster will likely play defensive line where the two-deep returns all but one player from last season.

Baylon Spector, Calhoun HS, Calhoun, Georgia: The Northwest Georgia native comes to Clemson after helping the Yellow Jackets reach the third round of the Class AAA playoffs. Spector projects best as a free safety and has a good mix of size and length. Along with bringing a ball-hawk mentality to the secondary, Spector is also a big hitter who can fill a void in the middle of the defense. Depending on how he develops, some scouting services project Spector will eventually grow into a linebacker.

Spector also spent time at wide receiver in high school, showing good long speed and the ability to high-point the ball on fade routes. Blake Vinson, North Marion HS, Ocala, FL: With former top-100 prospect Jake Fruhmorgen's transfer, Vinson and fellow 3-star prospect Noah DeHond enter the mix in a position of need this recruiting calendar.

Vinson earned an invite to Nike's The Opening last summer, but had to sit out due to labrum surgery. His high school film shows the makings of a physical run blocker and he has a frame that's ideal for offensive tackles.

Vinson will be working his way back from injury, but he enrolled early this January for a head-start. Vinson fielded impressive offers from around the nation, including Alabama, Florida and LSU. Chase Brice, Grayson HS, Grayson, Georgia: Brice continues a line of players coming to Tiger Town from powerhouse Grayson, nestled between Atlanta and Athens. He brings good size and an above-average arm that puts nice touch on his passes. While he is not a pure dual-threat quarterback, Brice has enough mobility to move around the pocket and pick up yards when needed.

Brice enters a crowded field with a starting spot up for grabs. Along with having to compete against current quarterbacks Zerrick Cooper and Kelly Bryant, Brice must also go against fellow freshman Hunter Johnson, ranked by many recruiting services as the nation's No. 2 quarterback.

At a bare minimum, Brice provides quality depth and will add to the quarterback competition.

LeAnthony Williams, Roswell HS, Roswell, Georgia: Williams stacked another all-region campaign to his resume after committing to Clemson last February, totaling 42 tackles with five interceptions in Roswell's run to the state title game in his senior year.

Following the footsteps of former teammate Tre Lamar to Tiger Town, Williams gets off blocks well to make plays behind the line of scrimmage, as well as using that speed and strength to track down balls downfield.

He enters at a talented position for Clemson, but not without its fair share of opportunity with Cordrea Tankersley moving on to the next level. Williams has the skills to step in and contribute at least on special teams from day one.

A.J. Terrell, Westlake HS, Atlanta: Terrell earned MVP honors for region 2-AAAAAAA in Georgia after leading Westlake to the semifinals, where fellow Clemson signee LeAnthony Williams Jr. and Roswell came out on top.
Terrell's playmaking abilities are impressive as is, showing skills as a ballhawk and delivering big hits, but standing 6-foot-2, Terrell's potential is big-time in matching up with bigger receivers on the boundary.

Opportunity is there at corner with Cordrea Tankersley moving on, but there will be fierce competition at both cornerback spots and nickel.

Will Swinney, Daniel HS, Central: The son of Clemson coach Dabo Swinney signed his Letter of Intent to Clemson as a preferred walk-on.

The 5-foot-9, 175-pound wide receiver led Daniel with 48 catches for 603 yards and six touchdowns as a senior.

He is unlikely to see immediate playing time in a deep group of Clemson wide receivers, but he is a candidate to be the team's new holder, where the Tigers are replacing Seth Ryan.

Check back to GreenvilleOnline.com and IndependentMail.com for more updates.

That's All Folks!

**We hope to bring out another version in about five years that
focuses on Tiger football and offers a commentary on what's new
Thank you for choosing this book among the many that are in your
options list. I sincerely appreciate it! We plan to offer two new CU
titles over the next six months highlighting great players and great
coaches of the Tigers over the years.**

The best to you all – Go Tigers!

LETS GO PUBLISH! Books by Brian Kelly
(Sold at www.bookhawkers.com; Amazon.com, and Kindle.).

PATERNO: The Dark Days After Win # 409. Sky began to fall within days of win # 409 .

JoePa 409 Victories: Say No More!: Winningest Division I-A football coach ever

American College Football: The Beginning From before day one football was played.

Great Coaches in Alabama Football Challenging the coaches of every other program!

Great Coaches in Penn State Football the Best Coaches in PSU's football program

Great Players in Penn State Football The best players in PSU's football program

Great Players in Notre Dame Football The best players in ND's football program

Great Coaches in Notre Dame Football The best coaches in any football program

President Donald J. Trump, Master Builder: Solving the Student Debt Crisis!

President Donald J. Trump, Master Builder: It's Time for Seniors to Get a Break!

President Donald J. Trump, Master Builder: Healthcare & Welfare Accountability

President Donald J. Trump, Master Builder: "Make America Great Again"

President Donald J. Trump, Master Builder: The Annual Guest Plan

Great Players in Alabama Football from Quarterbacks to offensive Linemen Greats!

Great Moments in Alabama Football AU Football from the start. This is the book.

Great Moments in Penn State Football PSU Football, start--games, coaches, players,

Great Moments in Notre Dame Football ND Football, start, games, coaches, players

Four Dollars & Sixty-Two Cents—A Christmas Story That Will Warm Your Heart!

My Red Hat Keeps Me on The Ground. Darraggh's Red Hat is magical

Seniors, Social Security & the Minimum Wage. Things seniors need to know.

How to Write Your First Book and Publish It with CreateSpace

The US Immigration Fix--It's all in here. Finally, an answer.

I had a Dream IBM Could be #1 Again _The title is self-explanatory

WineDiets.Com Presents The Wine Diet Learn how to lose weight while having fun.

Wilkes-Barre, PA; Return to Glory Wilkes-Barre City's return to glory

Geoffrey Parsons' Epoch... The Land of Fair Play Better than the original.

The Bill of Rights 4 Dummmies! This is the best book to learn about your rights.

Sol Bloom's Epoch ...Story of the Constitution The best book to learn the Constitution

America 4 Dummmies! All Americans should read to learn about this great country.

The Electoral College 4 Dummmies! How does it really work?

The All-Everything Machine Story about IBM's finest computer server.

Brian has written 119 books. Others can be found at amazon.com/author/brianwkelly

81784059R00251

Made in the USA
Columbia, SC
26 November 2017